ANCIENT ROME

This book provides a comprehensive political and military history of ancient Rome from the origins of the city in the Italian Iron Age to the deposition of the last emperor in A.D. 476. The reasons for Rome's conquest and absorption of Italy, and how this gave the Romans a manpower reserve that allowed it to conquer the Mediterranean in a half a century, are vividly described. The military responsibilities attendant upon these conquests undermined the political institutions of the Republic, with the Emperor Augustus managing to set up surreptitiously a monarchical form of government, which effectively secured two centuries of peace. New military pressures then caused a significant change in the structure of the Imperial government, which eventually succumbed to invasion in the western portions of the Empire. The influence on the adoption of Christianity as the state religion by the Imperial government is also discussed.

Christopher Mackay is Associate Professor at the University of Alberta. He has published numerous articles on all periods of Roman history. An associate editor of the American Journal of Ancient History, he is the auther of a new translation and critical edition of the Malleus Maleficarum, a fifteenth-century handbook on witch-hunting.

ANCIENT ROME

A MILITARY AND POLITICAL HISTORY

CHRISTOPHER S. MACKAY

University of Alberta

CAMBRIDGE
UNIVERSITY PRESS

CAMBRIDGE UNIVERSITY PRESS
Cambridge, New York, Melbourne, Madrid, Cape Town, Singapore, São Paulo, Delhi

Cambridge University Press
32 Avenue of the Americas, New York, NY 10013-2473, USA

www.cambridge.org
Information on this title: www.cambridge.org/9780521809184

First published 2004
6th printing 2007
First paperback edition 2007
Reprinted 2007

Printed in the United States of America

A catalog record for this publication is available from the British Library.

Library of Congress Cataloging in Publication Data

Mackay, Christopher S., 1962–
Ancient Rome : a military and political history / Christopher S. Mackay.
p. cm.
Includes bibliographical references and index.
ISBN 0-521-80918-5
1. Rome – History – Kings, 753–510 B.C.   2. Rome – History – Republic,
510–30 B.C.   3. Rome – History – Empire, 30 B.C.–284 A.D.   I. Title
DG231.M33 2004
937 – dc22   2004040682

ISBN 978-0-521-80918-4 hardback
ISBN 978-0-521-71149-4 paperback

To Kelly
who helped so much

CONTENTS

ILLUSTRATIONS

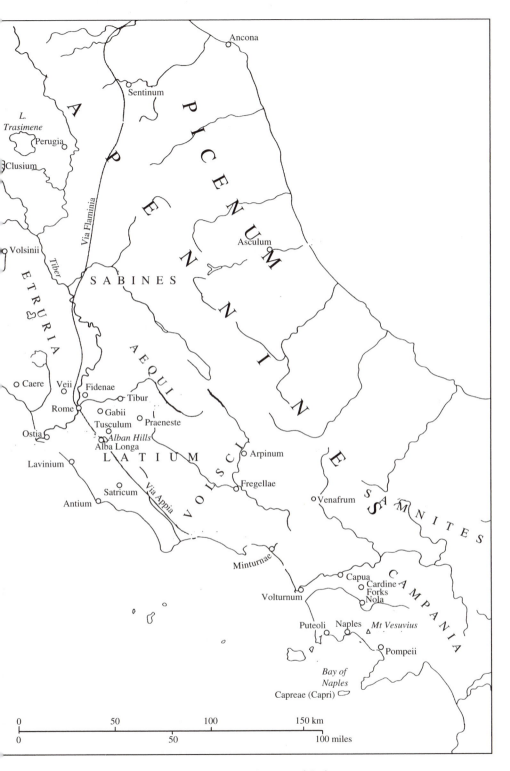

Map 1. Locations in central Italy

Map 2. Locations in Italy

Map 3. Locations in western Europe and North Africa

Map 4 Locations in Greece and the Near East

CASPIAN SEA

PERSIAN GULF

PARTHIA/PERSIA

MESOPOTAMIA

Ctesiphon
Seleucia
Babylon

CAUCASUS MTNS

ARMENIA

Tigris

Hatra

N. MESO-POTAMIA

Tigranocerta

Euphrates

ARABIA

500 km
400
300 miles
300
200
200
100
100
0

Edessa
Carrhae
OSROENE
Samosata

Palmyra

Antioch
SYRIA
Orontes
Emesa
Damascus

PHOENICIA

BLACK SEA

PONTUS
Cabira
Zela

CAPPADOCIA

CILICIA

Tyre
Nazareth
Caesarea
JUDAEA
Jerusalem

CRIMEA

Heraclea

BITHYNIA and PONTUS
Chalcedon
Nicaea Nicomedia
Byzantium (Constantinople)
Adrianople

GALATIA
Ancyra

ASIA MINOR

PHRYGIA

CYPRUS

Abrittus

THRACE

Hebrus

Lysimacheia
Dardanus
Pergamum
Magnesia
Ephesus
Lesbos
ASIA
Maeander
LYCIA
Rhodes
RHODES

MEDITERRANEAN SEA

Alexandria

DACIA

Danube

Naissus

BALKANS

Mursa

Philippi

MACEDONIA
Pydna
Dyrrachium

EPIRUS
Phoenice
Nicopolis
Actium
AETOLIA
THESSALY
Cynoscephalae
Pharsalus
Thermopylae
Orchomenus
Delphi
BOEOTIA
Chalcis
EUBOEA
ACHAEA
Corinth
Athens
PELOPON.
NESUS
Sparta

Delos

CRETE

CYRENAICA

Cyrene

ITALY
Brundisium
Tarentum

ADRIATIC SEA

ILLYRICUM

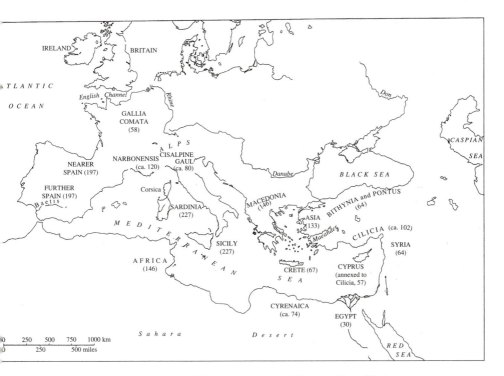

Map 5. Expansion of the Roman Republic outside of Italy

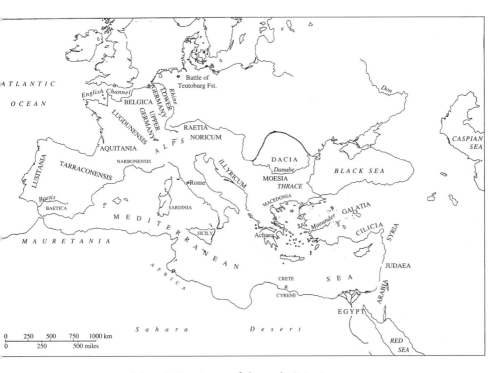

Map 6. Provinces of the early Principate

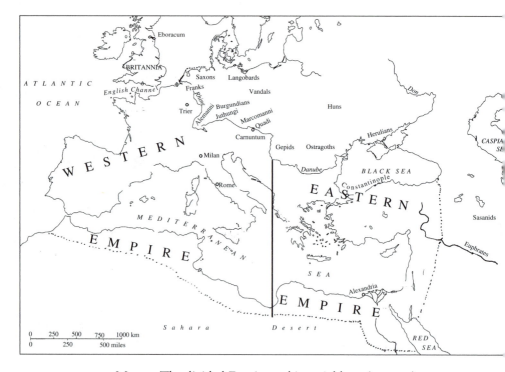

Map 7. The divided Empire and its neighbors (A.D. 395)

INTRODUCTION

This book is intended to provide a general introduction to the public affairs of the Roman People for a reader with no prior knowledge of the subject. As an introduction to public affairs, the work concentrates on political institutions and activities and thus could be considered to reflect a "traditional" view of history. Much modern scholarship, on the other hand, has turned to new perspectives on the past, for example social history that examines the lives and experiences of the lower-class population, women and slaves, segments of the population that are generally ignored by the ancient sources; cultural history that investigates the interaction between the Romans and the foreign peoples with whom they came into contact during their conquest of Italy and then the Mediterranean; and economic history that studies the economic patterns and institutions that played a large role in determining the political structure of the Republic and Empire. These and other topics not treated here would undoubtedly deepen the analysis but at the cost of inordinately expanding the length of the work and of obscuring the purpose that it is intended to serve. It is my view that the new historical disciplines complement rather than supplant traditional history. My aim, then, is to provide a readable and up-to-date general history on the basis of the numerous refinements in our understanding of traditional political history that have been made in recent years.

The desire to make this work both concise and readable has led to two decisions that the reader must always bear in mind. The first has to do with the nature of the source material available for ancient history. In studying modern (and even much of medieval) history, it is generally possible to take the overall course of events for granted, and the task becomes one of deciding how to interpret the evidence. This is seldom the case with ancient history. The surviving literary sources are often written many years (even centuries) after the facts they record on the basis of unknown intermediate sources.

Contemporary documentary sources in the form of inscriptions, papyri, and the legends of coins are extant for some periods, but the extent to which such sources can supplement the literary evidence is limited. The upshot is that very frequently there are discrepancies in the sources, and a large part of the job of historians of antiquity is to attempt to use various forms of source criticism to evaluate the divergent information available in order to recreate the reality of the historical events narrated in the ancient sources. Hence, there is virtually no declarative statement in this work that could not be qualified with expressions like "most likely" and "apparently." No doubt a full-scale discussion of Roman history would entail constant reference to the (often uncertain) evidence that lies behind the analysis, but such an elaborate (and confusing) procedure would obviate the very limited goal of the present work. I have therefore restricted myself to a short discussion of the sources of information available at the start of each of the five parts into which the book is divided and provide in the corresponding section of the bibliography a concise listing of the main sources. No one is more aware than I am of the extent to which our understanding of antiquity is dependent upon the subjective interpretation of the evidence.

The result of this uncertainty inherent to the ancient evidence is that there is much scholarly dispute not simply about the interpretation of events but often about the mere course of events. This, in turn, means that alternative scholarly views are available for practically every statement I make. To go into detailed discussion of those alternatives and to argue at length for my own position would defeat the purpose of this book. My aim is to give the novice student of Roman history a general overview of the developments of more than a millennium of history, and my hope is that this book will stimulate the reader to delve into the literature on specific points and see both what the available evidence is and why various scholars interpret it as they do. If this work achieves this modest goal, I will be content.

Because Roman personal names appear so frequently in the text, an appendix provides a discussion of the Roman system of nomenclature, which differs significantly from our own.

PART ONE

OBSCURE BEGINNINGS,
TO 264 B.C.

How do we know anything about ancient Rome? Surviving written texts represent the main source of information, which may be supplemented with physical remains revealed by archaeology. Writing was introduced into Italy in the eighth century B.C. from Greek settlements in the south. Written sources can be divided into two categories. The first consists of official documents inscribed on materials that have been preserved to the present day (mainly inscribed on rock or metal, but in the later period some documents written with ink on papyri are preserved). Little documentary evidence survives from before the third century B.C. This is also the period when literary evidence, the second category of written evidence, begins to be preserved. In the later third century B.C., the Romans began to write literature (that is, texts composed with a self-conscious artistic aim in mind) under the influence of Greek literature. Included in this literary activity was the writing of history. Romans began to write histories of their own affairs, and as Rome grew to be the dominant power of the Mediterranean, Greeks began to write about them too. In order to assess the validity of the information about the earliest period of Roman history preserved in this literary tradition, it is necessary to consider both the information that would have been available to the writers in this tradition and the methods they used in conveying this information.

The ancient historians had access to documentary evidence that has since been lost. They occasionally refer to old inscriptions, but surviving examples show that the archaic language used in such documents would have been hard to understand, and for the most part we are not in a position to assess the accuracy of the interpretations put on them by the ancients. In any case, though some significant documents of unknown authenticity are preserved in the literary tradition, ancient historians tended not to engage in historical research involving primary documents and instead reworked the material provided by their predecessors. The question really is, what information was available to those who began the literary tradition about early Rome? In addition to any stray documents that were known, there were presumably oral traditions about the past that were current when the literary tradition was first drawn up. Stray pieces of information do suggest that there were other traditions extant that differed from the one preserved in the literary tradition, but we are in no position to assess the accuracy of any of them. There was, however, one sort of chronicle surviving from the pre-literary period that had a major influence on early Roman historians: the *annales maximi*.

The term *annales* comes from the Latin adjective meaning "annual" and refers to a year-by-year account. The *annales maximi* were a register of annual events kept by the *pontifex maximus* (head of the Roman board of priests called *pontifices*). These accounts are not preserved for us, though ancient references give us some notion about them.

Every year the *pontifex maximus* kept a whitewashed board on public display near his official residence. This board had the name of the eponymous magistrates at the top and apparently listed the other magistrates. The board served as a form of official register; whenever something happened that was considered worth recording, it was listed under the date on which it occurred. The kinds of events that it contained included eclipses, famines, the beginning and end of wars, and triumphs (official victory celebrations). It apparently did not list the passage of laws or decrees of the senate.

When this record began to be kept is unknown; it ceased to be kept around 130 B.C. Apparently, the information on the yearly boards had been preserved permanently (presumably copied down in a more manageable format). At some point, the information contained in this way was published in eighty books, and this record purported to preserve events going back to the very foundation of the city (seemingly the Republic began around book eleven).[1] Since the record could not have been begun at the foundation of the city, at some point the events for the period before the record began to be kept must have been fabricated on an unknown basis. Another source of information was the list of magistrates going back to the foundation of the early Republic, the *fasti*, whose accuracy will be discussed in Chapter 2 (see pp. 25–26).

The literary tradition that began in the late third century B.C. was eventually superseded by the Augustan historian Livy, whose work was based on that of his predecessors and so surpassed them (in literary quality at least) that the earlier works are lost, apart from a few quotations preserved in other authors. The annalistic tradition is preserved not only in Livy but also in the Greek

---

1 That is, what the ancients considered a "book," which was a papyrus roll that contained about as much information as fifty printed pages. Thus, a work that we could consider a "book" actually often consisted of many books.

authors Dionysius of Halicarnassus and Diodorus Siculus, who also wrote in the time of Augustus.

The earliest authors of these Latin annals were mostly magistrates and seem to have anachronistically transferred into the history of the earliest period the concerns of their own day (e.g., agrarian legislation). Often these additions are obvious, but not always. In the first century, the annalistic tradition continued but took a turn for the worse in terms of content. The later annalists were not senators familiar with the workings of the Roman state but "armchair historians" who belonged to the landowning class and whose main aim in writing was entertainment. For patriotic purposes, they exaggerated Roman success, and in addition to fabricating false documents, they generally twisted their narrative for dramatic reasons. Unfortunately, Livy often used these sources, and it is at times difficult to distinguish fact from fiction in his narrative.

A general trend perceptible throughout the development of the literary tradition is the expansion of the history of the early Republic. The earliest accounts have been compared to an hourglass: the earliest history (the Kingdom) and recent history were treated at length and the early Republic rather less fully. Over time, it was felt that this imbalance had to be rectified, and since little additional information was available, only fiction of one kind or another could provide the necessary material.

According to the Greek conception, history concentrated on great public events, especially wars, and tended to interpret events through the actions of the highest political leaders. Thus, the ancient histories are quite limited in their perspective. Furthermore, ancient historians were expected not simply to "tell the truth" but to shape their material according to some moral or educational purpose. This is always a problem in assessing ancient historical writings, but the problem is particularly acute in the case of the earliest history, when much of what was written must have been conjectural. Fundamentally, one must always ask, when faced with ancient literary evidence about early Rome, how would anyone have known that?

Finally, one additional source of literary information is worth mentioning. In the first century B.C., a certain number of educated Romans engaged in what we would call "antiquarian" research, that is, the attempt to explain primitive practices and ceremonies that dated back to the early days of Rome. (Being a conservative people, the Romans preserved a number of such institutions whose significance was no longer clear.) While these antiquarians preserve a fair amount of detail about such survivals, the interpretation of the information, which pretty much by definition has been removed from its original historical context, is often controversial.

In short, the literary tradition for the period down to the third century B.C. is subject to grave doubts. While the general chronological framework for the period from the foundation of the Republic is reliable, the period for the Kingdom is much more dubious, and the reliability of the details about even the early Republic, especially those involving internal politics, is also uncertain. For the earliest period, archaeology provides useful indications of the overall physical development of the city and gives important clues about the nature of society, but this sort of evidence is difficult to assess in terms of political history.

I

FOUNDATIONS AND KINGDOM,

TO CA. 507 B.C.

R ome began, in the first half of the first millennium B.C., as a small
settlement on the northernmost reaches of Latium, the area occupied
by the Latins (for details about the Latins' ethnic identity, see Chapter 2).
There are two main sources of information for the history of Rome before the foundation of the Republic at the end of the sixth century B.C.:
the evidence uncovered by archaeological excavation and the ancient literary
tradition that was written down many centuries after the Republic's foundation. When archaeological evidence first began to be discovered in the
nineteenth century, the natural procedure was to attempt to explain it in
light of the ancient tradition. As more physical remains were recovered and
as the defects of the literary tradition became better understood, it came
to be realized that these two sources of information are in many ways incompatible. Such theoretical issues cannot be addressed in detail within the
compass of this treatment. Instead, we will look at the picture of early Rome
that emerges from the archaeological evidence and then examine the written
tradition.

Place names in Italy indicate that the peninsula was at some point occupied
by people who did not speak an Indo-European language. The speakers of the
Indo-European languages (including Latin) that are called "Italic" must have
arrived from elsewhere (probably the Balkans or central Europe), but the date
or direction of their migration cannot be discerned from the archaeological
record. During the Bronze Age (the period when bronze was the main metal
used for making weapons and other instruments and the use of iron was
unknown), which stretches from the early 2000s to the late 1000s B.C., Italy
was sparsely populated, and the physical remains are characterized by a cultural
uniformity that is in strong contrast to the diversity of the succeeding Iron
Age. In the northwest of Italy during the early Iron Age, there was a general
tendency to cremate the dead and bury the ashes, and this culture is known as

Villanovan. Cremation was introduced to Italy in the last stage of the Bronze Age, which is known as the Proto-Villanovan period (ca. 1200–900 B.C.). Cremation was at that time a widespread practice in central Europe, and it is not clear whether the adoption of cremation represents merely the borrowing of a cultural practice by the indigenous population of Italy or the migration into Italy of new populations from central Europe. If the former process is the case, the Italic speakers were already present in Italy during the Bronze Age; in the latter situation, the Proto-Villanovan period saw their arrival. In any case, it would seem that the regional cultural groupings perceptible in the archaeological remains for the Iron Age correspond to the linguistic groups that inscriptions and literary evidence show to have existed from 500 B.C. on.

In the early twentieth century, the Iron Age was divided into four phases (subperiods) referred to by capital Roman numbers. Phases II and IV have been divided into two with the addition of the capital letters A and B. Within Villanovan culture, the area of Latium can be distinguished by the fact that the urns used for burying ashes often took the form of small pottery models of huts, and this culture is called Latial. The approximate dates for these subperiods are as follows:

PHASE	DATES B.C.	CULTURAL DEFINITION	HISTORICAL DEFINITION
I	1000–875	Final Bronze Age (Proto-Villanovan)	Pre-urban
IIA	875–800	Early Iron Age (Villanovan)	Pre-urban
IIB	800–750	Early Iron Age (Villanovan)	Proto-urban
III	750–700	Early Iron Age (Villanovan)	Proto-urban
IV	700–580	Orientalizing	Urban

Much in this dating is quite arbitrary. Datable imported Greek pottery provides the only firm chronology framework, but unfortunately no Greek ware appears until Phase IV, though imitations are detected in Phase III. Since Latial I is thought to begin late in the Proto-Villanovan period (1200–900 B.C.), its start is placed in 1000 B.C. The lengths assigned to Phases IIA and IIB are little more than guesses.

The characteristics of these phases as they appear in Latium can be summarized as follows:

Latial I (1000–875 B.C.) There is little attestation for this period (the last of the Bronze Age). A few urn burials have been found in the area of the Roman Forum. No Latial I sites of habitation have been found.

Latial II (875–750 B.C.) The division of this period into two is a result of the situation in Rome, where two major areas of burial were found in the nineteenth century. The goods found at the two sites are generally similar, but there are a few noticeable differences. It used to be thought on the basis of the literary tradition that this situation represented two separate population groups, but one site is probably later in date.

Our knowledge of life during this period has been greatly enhanced as a result of excavations at the site of ancient Gabii, a settlement about eleven miles east of Rome. Here two cemeteries were found, and these apparently represent two separate family groups with similar but distinguishable customs. The level of economic development is rather low, and there was little wealth in this subsistence economy, each family apparently making its own pottery and wool. The village is estimated to have contained about 100 people. Burials indicate distinctions on the basis of age, sex, and function in the group, but no social stratification or economically distinct classes. In effect, there were two extended family groups living in close proximity to each other, but depending on their own (meager) resources and "managed" by some male head of the household.

Latial III (750–700 B.C.) Settlements increase in size, and there was a trend towards economic advancement and specialization. Olive and wine production was introduced, along with use of the potter's wheel. Pottery making was now an independent craft, and while no imported pottery is known, domestic patterns appear to be influenced by Greek pottery styles. There is clear distinction among tombs on the basis of wealth.

Latial IV (700–580 B.C.) Goods from the east, especially Greece, began to be imported, and hence this is called the "Orientalizing" period, by analogy with the period of about the same time when Greece was influenced by imports from the Near East. This period also witnessed a great increase in both the wealth exhibited in the burials of certain individuals and in the scale of building, both public and private.

In Latial IV, tombs exhibit

1. an increase in disposable wealth available for ostentation in burial;
2. a celebration of the military prowess and feasting of wealthy members of the community; and
3. a perpetuation of the family line over generations.

Though it is impossible to know the exact nature of political authority, this evidence suggests that certain "leaders" had established for themselves control of a disproportionate share of the agricultural surplus and had also led the military force of the community through their ability to acquire expensive iron armor and weapons. It has been hypothesized that these men were the leaders of the clans (*gentes*) that were dominant at the time of the Kingdom's downfall, but this is pure speculation. The fact that military equipment was sometimes buried with women suggests that political authority (represented by the tools of warfare) was an abstract notion divorced from actual military leadership and that it was hereditary, devolving upon women in the absence of a male heir.

The wealth of this new class (presumably landowners) is also reflected in the large increase in the size of buildings. Down to 650 B.C., there is little evidence for anything but mud-and-daub houses (walls made of interlaced branches smeared with a mud covering), but after that date, large stone houses began to be built (one found near Siena and dating to ca. 575 B.C. had a roof of 3,000 square meters). These new stone houses were a marked development in the growth of real cities (urbanization). Another step was represented by planned necropolises. These were special areas for the dead with carefully arranged tombs above ground. Urbanization is also reflected in the development of public spaces. In about 650 B.C., huts were demolished on the site of the present Roman Forum and a beaten earth floor installed. About 625 B.C., the forum area was expanded: a number of large public buildings were built there, and at around the same time, private houses of stone and tiled roofs were erected nearby. Evidence for an impressive temple dating to ca. 600–550 B.C. has also been found. Thus, by 600 B.C., not only had certain individuals managed to take control of the agricultural surplus developed over the preceding two centuries, but the resources had in some way been tapped to erect large buildings for public use.

Clearly some sort of major development went on in the political structure of the community between Latial II and Latial IV. Presumably the increase in wealth that started in Latial III made the process of urbanization possible, but the archaeological evidence does not give any indication of the political organization of the new cities. By the Latial IV period, large-scale communal constructions were possible, which indicates the existence of some sort of centralized authority that could take a portion of the agricultural surplus to organize and fund such activities. The "familial" activities of the earlier period indicate the absence of such communal structures. One might presume that the earlier society fit into the category known as "tribal," in which society is organized by leaders of kinship groups ("chieftains"). One might hypothesize that such "chieftains" became the heads of the *gentes* that are dominant in the

Early Republic, though there is no direct attestation of this. Anthropological interpretations of the development of the primitive ("proto") state tend to view this as a straightforward process by which a centralized authority assumes abstract power at the expense of social groupings based on kinship. The pattern in archaic Greece and the existence of evidence for the (continuing?) importance of the *gentes* into the Early Republic in Rome suggest that the process by which the "public" institutions (at first the kingship) came to exercise power was a prolonged and gradual development in which the kinship groups continued to hold large amounts of authority despite the presence of a primitive "state." It has been suggested that the model of the Greek colonies that were planted in the south of Italy starting ca. 750 B.C. served as the model for the development of urbanization, but there is no real evidence to support this hypothesis, and the impetus to urbanization may have been purely domestic.

Now it is time to turn to the literary evidence for the origins of Rome. The foundation of the city was universally attributed by the Roman tradition to a man called Romulus. On the other hand, a tradition arose that the Trojan hero Aeneas of the Greek epic tradition was the founder of the Roman people. These two traditions do not cohere easily in chronology, and at some point, certain obviously false additions were made to the story of Aeneas in order to bring the two elements into agreement. The Aeneas tradition was clearly concocted to fit the origin of the Romans into Greek chronological conceptions, and it can be discounted as a historical account.

The name *Roma* is a noun of the feminine gender and means nothing (it is said to be Etruscan). The names Romulus and Remus are both derived from it. Romulus is a masculine diminutive ("Little Rome"), and the different vowel of Remus represents a variation common in Indo-European languages. Hence, they are named after the city, not the other way around, a frequent practice in mythological stories about foundations. This makes their historical reality rather dubious.

The uncertainty of the literary tradition might even be taken to bring the very existence of an early kingdom into question. There is, however, much evidence to show that there was a regal period in early Rome.

1. Under the Republic, there was a priest called the *rex sacrorum* ("king of sacrifices"). This office was specially instituted at the foundation of the Republic to carry out the sacrifices that the king had performed during the Regal period. Exactly the same phenomenon is recorded at Athens, where, even under the democracy, there was a magistrate called the "king" to perform the old royal rites.
2. The Forum had a religious building called the *Regia* ("Royal [house]"), which presumably is a holdover from the old palace.

3. An archaic inscription found in the Roman Forum mentions a *rex*. (Strictly speaking, this could refer to the *rex sacrorum,* but there is no good reason not to take the word in its prima facie sense as referring to a real king.)

4. Apart from Romulus, the kings have traditional, two-part Roman names, but their *praenomina* are unusual, and their *nomina* do not reflect names of powerful clans from the Early or Middle Republic as one would expect if their names had been fabricated at a later date.[1] The very peculiarity of the details suggests that the names are authentic.

This evidence does not, however, demonstrate the accuracy of the details in the Roman literary tradition about the kings.

Though one readily grants that there were kings and that the names of all but Romulus may well be accurate, the tradition of the length of the reigns of the kings is dubious. There are said to be seven kings, giving a total of 244 years of rule for an average reign of thirty-five years. This seems impossible. In Great Britain, there were eleven monarchs in the 244 years from 1066 to 1310, but whereas dynastic principles allowed youthful successions there, the Roman kings all supposedly assumed power as adults. For instance, by the traditional dating, the last king took power 82 years after his father's accession and died 121 years after that date. Furthermore, since the method used to establish the date for the city's foundation (eventually fixed at 753 B.C.) was apparently to proceed back from the foundation of the Republic on the basis of the reigns of the known kings, the literary date for the foundation means nothing.

One possible solution is to accept the seven kings and reject the length of their reigns. On what basis these lengths were established is unknown, but the uniformity of the tradition about them suggests that they go back to a single source. Hence, if one assumes that that source was simply making them up without a sound tradition, then they can be ignored. Furthermore, it can be argued that the kingdom is to be equated with the final "crystallization" of Rome as an urban community around 625 B.C. or somewhat later. In this view, the earlier kings are credited with the establishment of the civic institutions that are associated with urban life. There is some appeal to this theory through its internal logic, but it should be stated that the Greek historical record leads to exactly the opposite conception. There, kings arose in the pre-urban "Dark Ages" and were overthrown by the landowning aristocracy around the time of urbanization. The "date lowering" theory assumes that the kings arose with urbanization, but the record attributing the establishment of various institutions to the kings is hardly certain, and if the lengths of their reigns are fabricated, then the traditions about the kings may well also be fictitious.

---

1 For the Roman system of nomenclature, see the Appendix.

Fundamentally, all one can say is that the names of the six kings attested after Romulus have some air of authenticity about them, but there is no way of knowing when in fact they reigned and whether there were earlier kings not preserved by the tradition. It cannot be known how or when the kingship was established in Rome.

The tradition about the earliest kings is suspiciously schematized. Romulus, the first king, is described as the originator of many characteristic institutions like the senate, but this is simply a reflex of the fact that he was "first." Numa Pompilius, the second king, is then said to have established the full panoply of Roman religious rites. The third king, Tullus Hostilius, is portrayed as a martial figure, in direct contrast with the "peaceful" Numa. This characterization is generated by Hostilius' name, which is clearly related to the Latin *hostilis,* the adjective of the word meaning "foreigner, (military) enemy." Thus, the tradition seems to ascribe institutions to the early kings on the basis of abstract theorizing and not because of a sound historical record.

We have to ask ourselves how the Roman historians who began to write about early Roman history in the later third and the second centuries B.C. knew anything about the Kingdom, which had been abolished three centuries before. There is no evidence of any previous written tradition, and the core must have been based on some sort of oral tradition. Though none of the earliest literary histories survives intact, their scope can be determined from later citations, and it is clear that these histories discussed the Kingdom at disproportionate length compared to the period of the early Republic. This arrangement is understandable in that the Romans had a strong tendency to ascribe many Republican institutions to the Kingdom, but that alone makes the tradition suspect. It is equally clear that as the literary tradition was continued down towards the late Republic, more and more detail was concocted to fill in the story. The final state of the tradition is preserved for us in the first book of the historian Livy (begun in the late 30s B.C.), and the vast majority of the details preserved there about the kingship are fabrications.

The literary tradition preserves indirect evidence for Regal Rome. Some of this is "mythological" and can be "interpreted" by comparative means. For instance, the story of Romulus and Remus has them suckled as babies by a wolf, leading a band of "brigands" during their youth, and then founding a community of young men that lacked women and acquired them through theft from their neighbors. It is a common phenomenon among Indo-European (and other) societies organized on a tribal basis that men in young adulthood would separate from their communities and form bands that would live an "anti-social" life of stealing before settling down. Such groups are often associated in name and attire with wolves, and occasionally they are attested as seizing control of settlements. Could the story of the brigand leaders with their wolf mother indicate that Rome was either founded or taken over by such a group of young men? Such interpretations can be interesting, but it is impossible to assess how accurate they are.

A different sort of "indirect" evidence consists of archaic festivals that seem to date to a very early period. For instance, various priesthoods would parade around the outskirts of differing groups of hills in Rome, and if it is assumed that the expansion of the area encompassed in these rites records the expansion of the city in the past, it would seem that the inhabited area began with a settlement on the Palatine and gradually expanded from there. One has to wonder, however, why these ceremonies should have become fossilized at divergent dates and to what extent they really do reflect the boundaries of the community. Such theories are again interesting but hardly compelling.

As for direct statements about the political situation of early Rome, according to the literary tradition, the Kingdom was not hereditary. The kings were elected by an assembly, which apparently had some sort of legislative power. Numa is said to have been a foreigner, Hostilius the offspring of a famous Roman warrior, and Marcius the grandson of Numa by a daughter. Not much of a pattern here. The Roman tradition ascribed to Romulus the creation of three hereditary tribes (with Etruscan names). Though most historians accept the reality of these tribes, it is clear that they were a figment of the rationalizing antiquarians of the Late Republic who interpreted the obscure names of certain units in the centuriate assembly on the basis of false etymology and false analogy with the hereditary tribes of primitive Athens. There was also apparently some sort of assembly based on *curiae*. The word *curia* may mean a "gathering of men," and the *curia* appears to have been a political division of the populace based on descent (i.e., specific *gentes* belonged to specific *curiae*) though the names of some seem to be geographical. In any case, the *curiae* met in an assembly called the *comitia curiata*. This assembly survives in a vestigial form into the Republic (it was typical of the Romans to maintain the outer form of an institution long after it had lost any real substance). Since the tradition is uniform in saying that (with one exception) each king had a law concerning his *imperium* passed by the *comitia curiata*, it seems that this was the normal assembly of the early Kingdom.

A major influence on Rome in the later Regal period came from Etruscans to the north. The salient characteristic of the Etruscans is that they spoke a unique non-Indo-European language. There is an ancient tradition that the Etruscans emigrated from Asia Minor to Italy, but modern archaeologists prefer to emphasize the continuity of physical remains in Etruria and to discount the notion of their arrival from abroad. Overall, however, it seems best, given the overlap of the Villanovan area with the later extent of Etruscan inhabitation in the historical period, to imagine that the appearance of Proto-Villanovan culture does mark the arrival of the Etruscans, though the circumstances of their arrival are unknown.

The cities of Etruria appear to have been at the forefront of the great development in urban life that took place in the Orientalizing Period (seventh and sixth centuries), and it seems that in the fifth and sixth centuries the city-states saw a change of government. The kings were overthrown by the land-owning aristocracy, and a government of annual magistrates was introduced, though the details are poorly known.

There appears to have been a fair amount of interaction between the early Romans and the Etruscans. In Veii (the closest Etruscan city north of Rome), we have an inscription mentioning in Etruscan a Titus Latinus, clearly a Roman name, while in Rome a votive gift with an Etruscan inscription was found in a sanctuary of the Orientalizing Period. The Romans themselves attributed a number of the symbols of their magistrates to the trappings of Etruscan kings, and Roman political and religious practices were strongly influenced by the Etruscans, as were early Roman art and religion. The Romans also developed their writing system from the Etruscans (who borrowed it from the Greeks). These borrowings took place during a time of Etruscan political expansion.

In the seventh century, the Etruscans began to expand outside of their original homeland, though the details are poorly attested. For our purposes, the important direction of expansion was to the south. Around 650 B.C., they established themselves in Campania (the area south of Latium), creating a major settlement at Capua. It seems that at the same time they established some sort of hegemony in Latium in general and Rome in particular. Rome was strategically important because it was situated on a ford of the Tiber, the southern boundary of Etruria, and thus gave (or hindered) access to the south. In 524 B.C., the Etruscans attacked Cumae, the major Greek city of Campania, and were defeated. This marked a decline in Etruscan power, which presumably explains (at least in part) the expulsion of the last (Etruscan) king of Rome in ca. 507 B.C.

Given that many of the trappings of the chief magistrates in Rome are of Etruscan origin and that the literary tradition about the last kings indicates that the fifth and seventh were Etruscans, it has been assumed that there was a period of Etruscan domination in Rome at the end of the Kingdom. This hypothesis was expanded when archaeological evidence indicated large amounts of building occurring at Rome in the late Orientalizing Period: since the Etruscans were thought to be the leaders in the process of urbanization in the seventh century, it seemed natural to associate the building in Rome with Etruscan influence. Certainly, the Romans themselves strongly associated with the Etruscans the building of the great temple of Jupiter Optimus Maximus on the Capitoline Hill. Though there is much dispute about the exact extent of the Etruscan "hegemony," the various strands of evidence do indicate some sort of strong Etruscan influence in the decades immediately preceding the establishment of the Roman Republic.

The literary tradition has it that the fifth king, L. Tarquinius Priscus, immigrated to Rome from Tarquinii, an Etruscan city (given his name, this origin seems fictional). Becoming an important councilor to Ancius Marcius, he managed to get himself elected king despite the fact that the old king had sons (who eventually secured his assassination). The tradition about what exactly he did as king seems to have been a bit lacking in substance, since actions attributed to his "son," the last king of Rome, are also attributed to him.

The sixth king, Servius Tullius, is a rather mysterious figure. The *praenomen* Servius was normal if uncommon in the later Republic and is clearly a derivate of the Latin word for "slave" (*servus*). Hence, the ancient tradition that Servius Tullius was originally a slave is suspect. In any case, Servius Tullius became a close associate of Tarquinius Priscus and married his daughter, Tanaquil. When Priscus died, news was suppressed so that matters could be arranged to ensure the election of Servius as king, which duly happened. Oddly, the tradition directly states that he did not have his *imperium* ("royal power") confirmed by passage of the *lex curiata,* which suggests that his accession was some sort of seizure of power (this point is important in terms of a variant tradition about him).

The Roman tradition looked upon him as the founder of many of the characteristic elements of the Republic (for instance, the old walls of the city, though archaeological evidence shows that the walls ascribed to him were actually built in the early fourth century). Rather peculiarly, the main political divisions of the population under the Republic were ascribed to him (this arrangement being known as the "Servian Constitution").

Servius is said to have established both the census with its fivefold division of the populace and the political assembly based on those divisions. In the census, people were assigned to one of five "classes" on the basis of wealth. These divisions were used to assign military duty, and the members of the various classes were supposed to provide different kinds of armor for themselves. Various procedural practices from the later Republic show that the centuriate assembly was originally the army drawn up to make political decisions, but the system attested for the Republic was divorced from its military origin. (The wealthiest class has the largest number of centuries, but in a real military organization, the less wealthy must have provided larger numbers of units.) Hence, Servius Tullius could not have founded the centuriate assembly in the form ascribed to it in the sources.

Once it is recognized that the form of the assembly attested in the historical period cannot go back to the Kingdom, one is free to hypothesize about the original organization. One theory is based on the later strength of the Roman legion and suggests that there were originally only sixty centuries, but this is groundless conjecture. A better hypothesis is based on etymology. The word *populus* is used under the Republic to signify the totality of the Roman People: everyone with Roman citizenship belongs to the *populus*. Etymologically the word signifies "army" (the Latin verb *populari* means "to plunder" and is clearly derived from the noun[2]). It would seem, then, that at some point, presumably under Servius Tullius, the army (*populus*) came to vote on political matters. This role became formalized, and the centuriate assembly became the highest-ranking assembly of the Republic and the old word for "army" came to designate the body politic. Down to the end of the Republic a vestigial form of the curiate assembly had to confirm the real election of magistrates that was carried out in the centuriate assembly, and this indicates that the voting in the centuriate assembly was originally a usurpation of the powers of the curiate assembly, which was compelled to ratify the actions of the army. Presumably, then, the curiate assembly was the normal assembly of the early Kingdom, and its powers were taken over by the army, which voted in the centuriate assembly on the basis of its military units (centuries). Could this new centuriate organization be connected with the fact that Servius Tullius had had no *lex curiata* passed to confirm his own *imperium*? Was he nominated, then, by the army and forced upon the civilian curiate assembly by the army? As so often in the Regal period, the questions are easier to pose than to answer.

The details are a little jumbled in the sources, but it would seem that Servius Tullius was also credited with the creation of the geographically based tribes that were fundamental to the political organization of the Republic. The word "tribe" here has nothing to do with primitive ethnic groups, as the English derivative suggests.[3] Rather, the word signifies "district," and at the end of the Kingdom, Roman territory was divided into four urban tribes to cover those who lived in the city, while the countryside had twenty. (Later, as the Romans expanded, the number of tribes was gradually increased to a final figure of thirty-five.) Every citizen was enrolled in a tribe during the census, and these tribes were later used as the voting units in the tribal assembly.

The names of the earliest twenty rural tribes were derived from the names of *gentes*. This differs from the later practice, when the new tribes were given geographical names. Presumably, the *gentes* after whom the tribes were named were dominant in the area of their tribe. Some of the *gentes* that gave their

---

2 Similarly, in Old English the verb *herrigean* ("to plunder") is derived from the noun *here* ("army").

3 This sense of the word derives from *tribus* being used as the Latin translation for the "Twelve Tribes" of Israel in the Old Testament, a meaning conveyed to English via French.

names to tribes were important in the political history of the Republic, but some were not. The literary tradition preserves a single story that seems to attest such a *gens* acting in an independent "public" capacity,[4] and presumably this is a holdover from a much more extensive and independent activity on the part of the *gentes* during the Kingdom, activity that was forgotten by the time the historical tradition was created. That the tribes were sometimes named after clans that played little or no role in the history of the early Republic suggests that the names predate the Republic, some clans having declined in importance before its foundation. This does not, however, prove that Servius Tullius created these tribes.

We have a tantalizing glimpse into an Etruscan story about Rome that has no reflection in the Roman tradition. The emperor Claudius (A.D. 41–54) had been an amateur historian in his youth and wrote a now lost work on Etruscan affairs. In a speech preserved in an inscription, Claudius cites an Etruscan version of the story of Servius Tullius. According to the emperor, an Etruscan called Mastarna was a follower of a military leader called Caelius Vibenna, and after various adventures and a final disaster, betook himself with the remaining troops to Rome, changed his name, and became king. This is at complete variance with the Roman literary tradition that Servius Tullius was born in lowly circumstances in Rome. Instead of being a companion of the preceding king, Mastarna/Tullius seems to have arrived as an adult with a military following. Claudius does not explain how Mastarna/Tullius came to the throne or what the change in name signifies. Other Roman sources allude to two brothers, Caeles and Aulus Vibenna, ascribing the name of the Caelian hill to the former. These two brothers appear to have been celebrated in Etruria; at any rate several works of art portray them (though without making it clear what they had done).

The most puzzling evidence comes from paintings in the famous François tomb (named after its discoverer) found at the site of the Etruscan city of Vulci. On one wall are painted scenes portraying the incident in the *Iliad* in which Achilles has the Trojan captives slaughtered. On the other wall are vignettes from Etruscan history that presumably parallel the scenes from the *Iliad*. Here (Etruscan) names are written alongside the figures. Apparently, Macstarna (=Mastarna) is being held captive with Aulus Vibenna and makes good his escape, freeing Vibenna in the process. Presumably, this event is part of the earlier adventures of Vibenna that Mastarna shared. Yet, the tomb scene also shows a Marce Camiltnas (=a Roman called Marcus Camillus?) killing a Cneve Tarchunies (=Gnaeus Tarquinius?) of Rome. Who is this

4 About thirty years after the foundation of the Republic, the Fabii, who were prominent leaders of the early Republic and gave their name to a tribe, by themselves mounted a campaign against the Etruscan town of Veii (see p. 44).

Tarquinius? The two kings are known as Lucius according to the literary tradition, but since there seems to be little attestation for the father, perhaps he was really named Gnaeus.[5] In any case, how does this relate to Claudius' story that Mastarna seized Rome and became king after the death of Vibenna? Can we even be sure that Claudius was justified in associating this Mastarna with Servius Tullius? Conceivably, this association was a stopgap measure intended to assimilate the Etruscan story to an entirely different and unrelated Roman account. The answers to these questions are unknowable, but we have tantalizing evidence that there were alternative versions of the history of the Kingdom that differed significantly from the story told in the Roman literary tradition.

Known as L. Tarquinius Superbus ("the Arrogant"), the seventh and last king is described in the literary sources in terms borrowed directly from Greek sources to portray the typical tyrant of the Greek world, since according to Roman tradition, it was his (and his family's) wickedness that led to the abolition of the Kingdom. While the king was off on campaign, the misbehavior of his son led relatives, L. Tarquinius Collatinus and L. Junius Brutus, to raise a revolt against the king. They founded the Republic, and when the king returned, they shut the gates against him. The king then enlisted the help of Veii and Tarquinii, nearby Etruscan towns, and Brutus defeated them in battle but was killed. The king now got help from Lars Porsenna, king of distant Clusium. According to the main Roman tradition, the king was impressed by examples of virtue on the part of various Romans and then used their assistance in a campaign against the Latins, though some Roman sources say that Porsenna did, in fact, take Rome. When attacked, the Latins called upon Aristodemus, the tyrant of Cumae who had defeated the Etruscans in Campania in 524 B.C. The Greeks and Latins then defeated the Etruscan army, which withdrew from Latium. Tarquinius enlisted against Rome the help of the Latins, who were defeated about ten years after the foundation of the Republic.

The story is very confused. The role of Porsenna is by no means clear, nor is the position of the Romans compared to the Latins. Was Porsenna really trying to restore Tarquinius? If he took Rome, why did he not restore the king? What does his campaign against the Latins have to do with Rome? Were the Romans actually fighting for Porsenna? What role did the Greek intervention have in these events? One gets the impression that the fall of the monarchy was in some way involved in resistance to an Etruscan attempt to maintain or establish control of Latium. The Latins called in Greek help from Campania, and perhaps the story about Porsenna reflects Etruscan control of Rome. In

---

5 Conceivably the *praenomen* Lucius reflects a later attempt to assimilate the Etruscan title *lucumo* ("king") to a Roman name.

any case, what does all this have to do with the abolition of the monarchy? Once again, there seems to be more going on here than the tradition tells.

Thus, we have two basic sources of information, archaeological evidence and the literary tradition. Scholars have proposed numerous theoretical reconstructions of early Rome on the basis of one or the other of these two major strands of evidence or on a combination of them, but none is very convincing. Fundamentally, the evidence does not allow a full reconstruction of Rome in its earliest stages. Archaeological data is reasonably securely datable, and while physical remains do give implicit evidence for the state of society, this evidence can go only so far. It can show, for instance, increasing levels of economic disparities through variation in the wealth in tombs, but it does not explain how such a society is "governed." The literary evidence may well preserve some authentic information, but it is clearly unreliable and at the same time is greatly elaborated with fiction.

As a minimalist picture of the earliest history of Rome, one may accept the following. In the earliest period of the Iron Age, Rome, like the rest of Latium, was sparsely inhabited by economically self-sufficient families that practiced rudimentary agriculture. The seventh century saw the culmination of a gradual process of economic development. Certain members of the community took control of a substantial agricultural surplus and used this to construct impressive houses and tombs for themselves. At the same time, concentrated areas of habitation with economic specialization among the inhabitants coalesced into small "towns." It would seem that by the end of the Iron Age, at least supreme political power was in the hands of a king, a prominent role in this society was played by clans whose exact powers are not clear, and some sort of political assembly also exercised influence. By the late sixth century at least, the Etruscans were a major influence in Rome, probably as part of their expansion to the south, and at least one if not several Etruscans established themselves as king. The last Etruscan king was driven from Rome by a conspiracy of Roman nobles that may have been connected with a general decline of Etruscan power at the hands of the Latins and Greeks to the south.

2

DOMESTIC HISTORY OF THE EARLY

REPUBLIC, CA. 507 B.C.–CA. 287 B.C.

With the expulsion of the last king, the Roman aristocrats set up an elective form of government known as the Republic. The history of the first 250 years of the Republic is beset with difficulties. The literary tradition is filled with a detailed account, much of which is clearly fictional. There is, however, much institutional continuity with the later Republic, though at times it is hard to determine how much of later practice can be attributed to the establishment of the Republic. In addition, there was a list of the chief magistrates going back to the first year of the Republic. This list provides an overall chronology in which to set the facts that can be recovered from the literary tradition.

The Romans did not have a system of numbering years. Instead, each year was named after the two chief magistrates (consuls) who held office during that year, and the list of consuls is called the *fasti* (a Latin word for "calendar"). The early Roman and Greek historians attempted to correlate the list of magistrates with various Greek chronological systems. The modern practice is to take these correspondences and attempt to assign absolute dates B.C. to them. Down to 300 B.C., there is no real dispute. For the period before that date, there is much confusion. The standard set of dates given for the foundation of the city and establishment of the Republic (753 and 509 B.C.) belong to a chronological scheme thought up in the Late Republic and are manifestly incorrect. One might expect that one could simply equate the *fasti* with Greek chronology at the Late Republic when there was no dispute as to the correspondence, and then calculate back according to the Roman list. In the first place, while there was agreement on most of the magistrates in the list, there were a few (minor) uncertainties. Furthermore, a certain amount of artificial manipulation of the *fasti* was required to make them correspond with preconceived notions of the overall chronology.

The most important element in establishing the ancient chronology for the early Roman Republic was a single fixed correspondence ("synchronism") between the Greek and Roman systems: the sack of Rome by the Gauls in the early fourth century. Why this synchronism took on such importance is unknown. This event was equated with a year in the Greek chronology (=387/6 B.C.[1]), and then the foundation of the city was established on the basis of a Roman document that stated that the year before the sack was the 119th year since the establishment of the Republic. The accuracy of this dating is completely unknown, but it set the establishment in 508/7 B.C.

This equation of the sack of Rome with the Greek equivalent to 387/6 B.C. was clearly not made on the basis of the Roman *fasti*. Between the consular year traditionally reckoned as equivalent to 301 B.C. and the sack, there are only eighty-one eponymous years, leaving a shortfall of five "missing" years. One year was picked up on the assumption that there was a year without magistrates during the troubles of the Sextian-Licinian tribunate (see p. 37). This left four more years to be made up. Two solutions were concocted to fill the gap: one was to increase the period without magistrates to five years, the other was to make up four years in late fourth century B.C. in which dictators took the place of the consuls. These stopgap measures would cause trouble when the early chronology was standardized in the late first century B.C.

This standard is called "Varronian" after one of its creators. It became the official reckoning system used under the Roman Empire and is generally followed today to give the dates of Roman history. For dates after 300 B.C. the Varronian system is accurate, but for the earlier fourth century, it is manifestly off by four years, since it adopted both the extra four years without magistrates and the four "dictator" years, which pushed the date of the sack back to 390 B.C. This system puts the establishment of the Republic 119 years before the sack in 509 B.C. Apparently the *fasti* used to reach this date lacked two years compared to the scheme used in Greek sources that saw the sack as the 120th year of the Republic.

Two considerations are fundamental for evaluating the chronology created in the later Republic for the establishment of the Republic:

1. Is the synchronism of the sack accurate? We have no idea why it was made, but the evidence of the *fasti* suggests that the sack took place four to five years after the date implied by the synchronism with the Greek year corresponding to 387/6 B.C.

---

1 This is the correct dating; one Greek source erroneously set the corresponding events in Greek history one year earlier, which threw his dating of Roman chronology off by one year!

2. Was the private document correct in setting the 119th year of the Republic two years before the sack? While the dating given by the document seems to agree (within one year) with the later *fasti*, the document is not likely to be contemporary and may well have been made up in the later Republic on the basis of the already established chronology.

Judged purely on the basis of the *fasti*, the chronology adopted in antiquity for the fourth century is at least four if not five years too long, and the synchronism of the sack with the Greek year equivalent to 387/6 B.C. erroneous. This would pull the date of the establishment of the Republic down to 505–502 B.C. In the absence of any method to assess the reliability of the evidence used in antiquity to establish the Republic's foundation, it is impossible to be more specific than to say that the Republic was founded in the last decade of the sixth century.[2]

Given the paucity of reliable information for the early Republic in the literary tradition, modern accounts must examine in detail the list of consuls called the *fasti*. This list is preserved in a number of authors, who give basically the same list, though in a few instances there is uncertainty about the names for specific years, and there is some disagreement about the stopgap years added to make the *fasti* fit various preconceived notions. The fundamental question is whether the lists are reliable for the first two centuries of the Republic.

There are various a priori objections to the *fasti* as we have them (e.g., some consider the establishment of the consulship in one fell swoop at the end of the monarchy to be too precipitous, and they prefer a gradual process of stripping the king of power such as can be attested at Athens), but these are too speculative to be persuasive. There are also internal objections to the *fasti*, the most serious concerning the presence in the first half century of the Republic of the names of plebeian *gentes* despite the fact that the literary tradition is unanimous that in the beginning only patricians were allowed to be consuls. As will be shown, in fact the fault here lies with the literary tradition, which ascribes to the foundation of the Republic the patrician monopoly that only arose over the succeeding decades (see pp. 32–33).

An argument in favor of the *fasti*'s overall accuracy is provided by the very names in them. If the *fasti* were fabrications drawn up at some later date, one would expect them to contain lists of *gentes* prominent at the time of fabrication. The early *fasti* do list such *gentes*, like the Fabii, Cornelii, and Claudii. But they also list *gentes* that either reached the consulship again only

---

2 There is some external confirmation of this in the story of Aristodemus' assistance to the Latins against Lars Porsenna (see p. 21), although the uncertainty of the story's accuracy and of the exact relationship of Porsenna to the expulsion of Tarquin weakens this confirmation.

in the Late Republic, long after the *fasti* were established (e.g., the Tullii), or were never prominent in later politics at all (e.g., the Larcii). Among the last group, one subset is particularly important: *gentes* which gave their names to Servian rural tribes (e.g., Horatii, Lemonii, Menenii, and Romilii). This strongly suggests that these *gentes* were prominent in the late Regal period (see pp. 19–20). Therefore, there is every reason to believe that these families should have had some prominence in the Early Republic, and while the connection between the names of the *gentes* and those of the tribes of the Republic is obvious enough, the Roman literary tradition seems not to have made this connection, and hence there is no reason to think that the consuls' names were fabricated on the basis of those of the tribes. Some tribal names (e.g., the Scaptia) have no correspondence in the *fasti*, and presumably the *gentes* from which these tribes derived their names had already sunk into oblivion before the foundation of the Republic. Furthermore, the distribution of consuls from *gentes* giving their names to tribes is by no means even, as one might expect if the consuls were made up on the basis of tribal names. For instance, while the Menenii provide a large number of consuls, there is only one Romilius and one Lemonius. All told, the *fasti* contain names that are very hard to explain if they were later fabrications and that other evidence suggests ought to have been prominent in the Early Republic. If this is so, then despite the few inevitable disagreements over various points of detail, the *fasti* should be taken as giving an accurate list of the magistrates going back to the establishment of the Republic.

Now that the chronology for the Early Republic has been discussed, it is time to describe its constitution. A fundamental elemental in the constitutional order is signified by the word *pomerium*. The *pomerium* was the sacred boundary of the city, the area within it being designated "home" (*domus* in Latin) and the world outside being referred to as *militia* in Latin, that is, the area of military service. This conception clearly derives from a time when the military threat began immediately outside the city. The early Roman constitution was pervaded with the distinction between the civil activities at "home" and the military sphere beyond the *pomerium*. One notable distinction during the early period is that while the chief magistrates held the power of life and death beyond the *pomerium*, this power was restricted within it. This distinction between the world within the *pomerium* and the world beyond it continued to be constitutionally important throughout the Republic, long after the conquest of Italy had robbed it of its original meaning.

The executive element in the Roman state was provided by the magistrates. Indeed, in many ways it is inappropriate to speak in the abstract of the "state" for most of the Republic. There were no abstract, permanently staffed institutions of government that would continue to exist whether or not someone was in charge of them. Instead, there were individuals to whom powers were given through elections, and if there were no magistrates to exercise those powers, they simply lapsed.

The magistrates set up at the beginning of the Republic were few in number and their functions fairly simple, but the basic principles governing their actions became fundamental for all magistracies set up later:

- Collegiality. With the exception of the dictator (not a normal magistrate), magistrates always came in boards called "colleges." All members of a college had equal powers, and in the event of conflict, the negative wish prevailed, that is, one member's opposition was sufficient to thwart another member's action.
- Popular election. Roman magistrates were always elected by the Roman People in their various assemblies.
- Annual term of office. Apart from the censors, Roman magistrates held office for only one year. While in office, they were not subject to legal prosecution, but the restriction of office to only one year meant that they were soon accountable for their actions. (By the fourth century, this restriction was found to be militarily inconvenient, and an extension of office called prorogation was instituted to allow magistrates to continue to operate outside of the *pomerium* for more than one year.)
- Prohibition of direct election from one office to another. Although this was not apparently a fixed rule at first, the Romans soon developed the idea that a magistrate should not be elected to another office while already holding one. The reason for this is obvious given the immunity of magistrates from prosecution.

The power to command that the chief magistrates of the Roman state inherited from the kings was called in Latin *imperium*. The etymological origin of the word is not clear, but the verb derived from it means "to command," which presumably reflects the understood sense of *imperium*. *Imperium* gave the magistrate the right to enforce his will through corporal and capital punishment (restricted within the *pomerium*).

The chief magistrates of the Roman Republic were the two consuls. The consuls were the eponymous magistrates at Rome, that is, the Roman year was named after the consuls holding office during that year. The literary tradition describes the establishment of the two consuls as one of the major acts in the immediate aftermath of the expulsion of the last king. The consuls had the power to raise and command armies. While their power of execution was restricted within the *pomerium*, they had (until the second century B.C.) the unlimited right to execute citizens outside the *pomerium*. Consuls had the power to summon the Roman People to assemblies, to preside over elections, and to convene the senate. The *imperium* of the consuls derived from the right to determine the will of the gods through taking the auspices. When a consul went on campaign he made a vow to Jupiter Optimus Maximus, the chief god of the state religion, and, if successful, he could enter the city in triumph, a formal religious ceremony of victory.

In 326 B.C., the Romans took a step that shows that already at that early date, the annual term of office was incompatible with the military requirements of their prolonged campaigns away from the city. In that year, a consul was waging war in southern Italy, and it was decided that it would be inopportune to replace him in command. Hence, a law was passed to extend his command. This procedure (prorogation) soon became so common and the passage of appropriate legislation was so uncontroversial that the legislation was dispensed with, and the senate acquired the right to extend the *imperium* of magistrates away from the city. Magistrates who continued to exercise *imperium* after their term in office were known as proconsuls or propraetors, and while the Romans did create additional positions with *imperium* to govern the provinces they began to create in the late third century, it was increasingly the case that there were insufficient regular magistrates with *imperium* to manage Rome's wars and administrative needs, and the extra magistrates were provided by a regular use of prorogation. Promagistrates lost their *imperium* as soon as they passed back into the city over the *pomerium*.

The term "dictator" has negative connotations in English, but in origin it was a perfectly respectable office within the Roman state. In times of crisis, one consul would appoint a dictator (thus the only magistrate not elected by the People). The normal magistrates continued in office, but the dictator had a form of *imperium* superior to that of the consuls (and one consul could be chosen as dictator by his colleague). Dictators normally held office for six months. The original title of the dictator was *magister populi* ("master of the *populus*"). Here *populus* seems to have been used in its original sense of "army," and his original function was presumably to provide a unified military command in time of crisis. At a later date, dictators were appointed to carry out necessary tasks like elections when the consuls were off on campaign far from Rome. The first dictator was appointed about ten years after the establishment of the Republic.

The holding of the census, that is, the distribution of the citizenry into the five Servian classes, was originally the responsibility of the consuls, but in the fifth century, the office of censor was established to take over this duty, the first pair elected in either 443 or 435 B.C. Two censors were elected every five years for an eighteen-month term. Eventually they took on other tasks, including letting out state contracts and reviewing the roll of senators. (The fact that they could expel men from the senate for immorality gives the word its modern sense.)

The consuls each had an assistant called a quaestor, who did not hold *imperium*. It seems that the quaestors were originally appointed by the consul but began to be elected in 447 B.C. Two more are said to have been added in 421 B.C., and the number expanded over time until there were twenty in the last century B.C. Their original power is not clear, but eventually they came to be financial magistrates. While some operated independently (two controlled the treasury in Rome), each magistrate with *imperium* was assigned a quaestor to manage his finances and serve as his trusted assistant.

Between Varronian (i.e., by the Varronian system of dating) 444 and 367 B.C., the Roman tradition asserts that the consuls were replaced by colleges of magistrates called "military tribunes with consular power." A military tribune was a junior office (each legion had six), and for some reason in the early Republic, it was often decided on an irregular basis to replace the consuls with colleges of three, four or six military tribunes invested with the power of consuls. Some ancient sources claim that the intention was to allow plebeians to hold the chief magistracy in the state while maintaining the exclusive patrician claim to the consulship. This can hardly be so, as only two plebeian names appear among these tribunes before 400 B.C. Another explanation is the need for additional independent commanders as a result of increased military activity. While it is not apparent that the larger number of tribunes was used to command an expanded number of military contingents, the increase in officials may have had something to do with the expanding role of the public administration in the later fifth century B.C. The office ceased to be used after 367 B.C., when a general reform of the Roman magistracies was implemented.

There were certain colleges of priests for public cults. These colleges were in the beginning self-selecting, and the members were normally from senatorial families. As all public activities had religious procedures associated with them, these public priests could influence the course of those activities.

The assemblies of the Roman People had theoretical control over a number of important areas of public life, and their powers suggest a strong role in the administration. The assemblies

- elected magistrates,
- passed laws (called *leges* [singular *lex*]),
- judged accusations of criminal misbehavior, and
- decided on declarations of war.

A number of peculiarities of the Roman assemblies greatly restricted popular interference in public policy:

- Lack of power of initiative. A Roman assembly could only meet when summoned by a magistrate with the right to do so.

- Lack of power of deliberation or modification. The People could vote only on a proposal put to them by a magistrate and could only vote for or against it.
- Voting by unit. While every adult male had one vote, these votes did not have equal weight because they were not counted individually. Instead, the voters were assigned to different units in the various assemblies, and the majority of votes in each unit decided that unit's vote. Each unit had a single vote, and the outcome of the election was decided by counting the units' votes.

The main assembly of the Early Republic was the centuriate assembly. It elected magistrates with *imperium,* decided whether the Roman People should go to war, and judged capital cases. It was in origin the Roman army drawn up outside the *pomerium.* It was organized by centuries, which were originally military units of 100 men, but in the form in which we first meet it in the Early Republic, it was no longer organized by any military considerations and had been considerably modified. It consisted of 193 centuries, or voting units. Of these, 170 were distributed unequally among the five Servian census classes. These classes were based on wealth, 11,000 sesterces worth of property being needed for enrollment in the fifth (lowest) class and 100,000 for the first (highest) class.[3] The soldiers had to provide their own equipment, and the census classes reflected the increasing cost of various sorts of equipment (see pp. 54–55). Of the centuries assigned to each class, half were given to those of the age of full military service (ages seventeen to forty-five) and half to older men normally assigned only to garrison duty (ages forty-six to sixty). Thus, the votes of the fewer, older voters outweighed those of the younger. All those with property rated below the minimum figure (the majority of the population) were grouped into a single century. Thus, political control of the community was given to those who could perform military service. In addition, eighteen centuries were given to men serving in the cavalry. Since owning a horse was an expensive proposition, these cavalrymen were young men who would otherwise belong to the first census class. The five remaining

3 These are the figures given in the Middle and Late Republic. It is not clear how valid they would have been for the earlier period. In the fifth century B.C., when the Romans still did not use coins, they appear to have assessed value in terms of the *as,* a fixed weight of bronze. This amount began to be minted in the form of coins only in the third century B.C., and as the value of the money decreased, the standard coin for assessing value became the larger sesterce. Presumably, the values later attested in terms of sesterces had previously been expressed in terms of *asses.* There is no way of knowing whether the numbers attested for the census qualifications in the Middle Republic are valid for the earlier period, but the ratios between the qualifications are not likely to have changed substantially.

centuries were given over to various professional services in the army. The first class originally had eighty centuries (later reduced to seventy), and thus they and the even wealthier members of the cavalry centuries had virtual control over the centuriate assembly by themselves.

The other assembly was the tribal assembly, which elected magistrates without *imperium* and voted on noncapital trials. In dividing the voters by tribes, its procedure was modeled on that of the assembly of the plebs (see p. 36).

Under the Republic, the senate never had any legal power, but eventually came to have great moral authority, and it took a powerful man to ignore its wishes. The word "senate" comes from the Latin word for "old man," and hence the senate was in origin a council of elders. Presumably it originated as the council of the kings, who appointed whomever they wished to it. Under the Early Republic, the consuls appointed men to the senate, but starting in 318 B.C. the censors drew up the list of senators, normally from the ex-magistrates. Thus, the senate was the assembly of ex-magistrates, and its decrees were, in effect, the collective opinion of the office-holding class.

The senate had some of the same restrictions as the assemblies, convening only when summoned by a magistrate and voting on the proposals set before it. Unlike the assemblies, however, it was a deliberative body: after an open debate, the magistrate set before it two alternate resolutions to the issue at hand. The alternative chosen by the majority of the senators was called a decree of the senate; these decrees were merely advisory and did not have the force of law.

The senate seems at first to have had some power to ratify decisions of the assemblies. This is called the *auctoritas patrum* ("authorization of the fathers," i.e., senators), and the very term *auctoritas* implies some sort of non-binding sanction, perhaps of the religious correctness of the procedure used in the assembly. The literary tradition holds that laws of the Middle Republic obligated the senate to give its authorization of acts of the popular assemblies in advance. This suggests that the senate had previously been able to cast the legitimacy of a law into doubt by withholding its authorization, but there is no evidence that they had an actual veto over the decisions of the assemblies.

The Roman state seems to have been rather rudimentary in the beginning. The two consuls elected every year inherited the powers of the kings and were elected by an assembly that was basically equivalent to the army and could also pass laws. Over the years, this system was elaborated by the addition of new magistrates to handle the increasing administrative load as the Roman state expanded. Another complication in the development of the constitution was the process by which the separate organs of the Roman plebs were incorporated into the state as a result of the so-called Struggle of the Orders.

The internal history of the first two centuries of the Republic is pervaded by the Struggle of the Orders ("order" meaning a grouping in society). As the ancient sources portray the matter, the political and religious offices of the state were at first monopolized by a group called patricians. The Struggle of the Orders represents the efforts of nonpatricians to gain access to political office and to redress their economic complaints.

The Roman People as a whole were known as the *populus Romanus*, and the "state" was known as the *res publica populi Romani* or "communal affairs of the Roman People." Within the Roman People, there was a fundamental distinction based on descent. Certain families were recognized as possessing patrician status; all others belonged to the plebs. Eventually, certain actions taken by the plebs were recognized as being binding on the People as a whole, but in the legal conception of the Romans, these actions were quite distinct. While the ancient sources assert that this distinction had always existed, having been instituted by Romulus himself, the evidence of the *fasti* suggests otherwise.

The origins of the patricians lay in the distant past, and the Romans themselves were unclear about the significance of many aspects of the concept. Patricians were entitled to wear special clothing, and throughout the Republic only patricians were entitled to hold certain priesthoods. (This same restriction originally applied to other priesthoods, which were opened to plebeians in the fourth century.) In some manner, the patricians had acquired in the Early Republic the sole right to hold the auspices, the religious procedure of publicly consulting the will of the gods through examining the flight of birds. Though some scholars wish to dispute this as a fundamental characteristic of the patricians, the right to hold the auspices seems to be the major bone of contention at the time of the Struggle of the Orders: the auspices were essential to being a senior magistrate, and since only the patricians were considered entitled to the auspices, it naturally followed that they alone could hold office.

The adjective "patrician" means "connected with the rank of *pater* (father)," which was a title for senators. Hence, patrician status must have had something to do with being a senator. Though the ancient sources ascribe the creation of the patrician families to the kings, the *fasti* suggests that the monopoly on office holding by certain families called patrician was a development of mid–fifth century B.C. A law was passed at that time to prohibit intermarriage between patricians and nonpatricians, but opposition soon led to its repeal.

Examination of the *fasti* reveals the presence in the first half of the fifth century B.C. of a number of consuls belonging to *gentes* that were plebeian in the Late Republic (one can determine a *gens'* status when a member of it is attested in the later period as holding a position either reserved for or forbidden to patricians). Since some *gentes* had both patrician and plebeian families, and in the Late Republic certain plebeian families began to use the *cognomina* of earlier patrician families from which they did not directly descend, it is possible that the names in the early *fasti* belong to families that were patrician at the time and survive in the later period only as plebeians. Yet, there is no particular reason to assume this procedure for the earlier period. Careful examination of the distribution of the plebeian consuls provides a better solution. Such consuls are not, in fact, spread evenly throughout the fifth century. In the period 509–483 B.C., 21 percent of the consuls were plebeian, while in 427–401 B.C. only one consul was plebeian (1 percent). This indicates that the absolute patrician monopoly of office did not date back to the foundation of the Republic but was imposed only in the mid–fifth century B.C. Whatever the criteria used then to determine patrician status, certain families that had previously held the consulship either ceased to hold it because they were excluded from the status or failed to gain the status because they had already ceased to hold the consulship. In effect, the families that held office in the first decades of the Republic managed to convert their de facto control of the political system to an entrenched, hereditary monopoly of office. Such monopolies of political power by a limited number of families on the basis of birth can be easily paralleled elsewhere.[4] Such a development is supported by the literary tradition's report for exactly these years of an abortive attempt to ban intermarriage between patricians and plebeians, presumably to maintain the purity of the newly established patrician families.

The term *plebs* (adjective: plebeian) signifies in the Middle Republic the nonpatrician members of the *populus Romanus*. The word is related to the adjective "full" in Latin and appears to have originally meant "mob" or "throng." Whatever the exact origin of the term, the plebs as a whole opposed the patrician officeholders. Naturally, in a historical development that spans two centuries, there must have been some development in the methods and goals, but the plebs seem to have had two basic aims in their disputes with the patricians.

1. Political goals. The plebs wished to end the political monopoly held by the patricians and to be allowed to hold offices granting *imperium* and the priesthoods of the state religion, which were denied them on the technical grounds that they did not have access to the auspices.
2. Economic goals. The fifth century seems to be one of economic downturn as indicated by a precipitous drop in temple building and by a major decline in the amount of foreign pottery imported. To what extent this

---

4 For example, in the aristocracies of Archaic Greece and in the "patrician" nobility of German cities in the late medieval period.

contributed to the plight of the plebs cannot be known, but the economic grievances of the plebeian "movement" can be listed under four headings.

a. Debt. Roman law on debt (as in many primitive agricultural communities first coming into contact with the use of money) was harsh. The debtor could make himself (or his dependents) personally liable to service if the debt was not cleared. Such a contract was called a *nexum* ("bond"), and the plebs wished to abolish such debt slavery. The fact that the wealthy senators were likely to be major creditors led to a combination of political and economic resentment.

b. Hunger. There are many reports of famine in the records for the fifth century B.C. These may be accurate, since famine is one of the things that the *Annales Maximi* are said to have reported. There are reports of men trying to set themselves up as tyrants on the basis of claims that they would alleviate hunger (e.g., Sp. Maelius in 439 B.C.). While the details of these stories are unreliable, the general notion of instability arising from hunger is not unreasonable.

c. Land distribution. The sources report demands for limits on private possession of public land and for its distribution among the poor. The accuracy of these reports is hard to assess. Clearly the details recall similar agitation in the last two centuries of the Republic. The concept of early agitation for land distribution is not inherently implausible, but the evidence is suspect. In any case, since the patricians were also the largest landowners, there was an easy tendency to confuse political and economic grievances.

d. Legal reform. Though this is not directly associated with the Struggle of the Orders in the literary tradition, there was dissatisfaction with the legal system dominated by the patricians. In ca. 444 B.C., a special college of ten men was elected to draw up a legal code, and after the publication of the code (known as the Twelve Tables), they attempted to retain office. This story is greatly elaborated in the literary sources but seems to reflect an unsuccessful attempt to use popular discontent about the legal system to set up a tyranny like those common in archaic Greece. In the last decade of the fourth century B.C., the plebeian associate of a prominent patrician made a political name for himself by publishing the arcane rules for proceedings in civil law that had been kept secret among the patricians. A legal matter that may or may not be tied up with the Struggle of the Orders is the right to *provocatio* or appeal to the Roman People in cases involving physical punishment. According to this right, within the *pomerium*, Roman citizens could not be flogged or executed without the direct authorization of the People. This meant that while outside the city magistrates had unlimited power over citizens, the assemblies had control over criminal law within the city since no penalty could be inflicted without their approval. The literary tradition holds that the first law to establish the right was passed in 509 B.C. by consuls named Valerius and Horatius and that this was a fundamental move in establishing the Republic. The tradition also holds that in 449 B.C. and 300 B.C. similar laws were passed by consuls who were also called Valerius and Horatius. It is often thought on the basis of the suspicious coincidence of names that only the last law is authentic, the argument being that the right reflects a regularization of "mob justice" from the Struggle of the Orders and that the Romans later erroneously ascribed to the foundation of the Republic what they took to be a major element of their constitution. It is true that in the later period it was normally tribunes of the plebs who conducted criminal accusations before the People, but the right of *provocatio* pertains to all citizens, not just plebeians, and Cicero does claim that it is attested in the Twelve Tables, which date to the mid–fifth century B.C.

The plebs attempted to secure their aims against patrician intransigence through "secession." This means "withdrawal" and signifies that the plebs would remove themselves in a body to a site outside Rome and refuse to act in their normal role unless their wish was granted. Three secessions are recorded (494, 450, and ca. 287 B.C.), but more were threatened. The plebs also tried to get their way through violence (rioting).

During the first secession, the plebs swore an oath that they would kill anyone who harmed their elected representatives, the tribunes. This marked the beginning of the corporate organization of the plebs as a kind of "state within the state." Eventually, the organs of the corporate plebs were absorbed into the state, and to some extent the state assimilated itself to the organization of the plebs. Nonetheless, throughout the Republic there was a formal (if not always substantive) distinction between the *populus*, which included all citizens, and the plebs, which excluded the patricians.

In 494 B.C., the plebs elected two leaders called tribunes. The exact derivation of the title is not clear. It clearly is derived from the geographical district known as "tribe," but on what basis is not known.[5] By mid century, the number of the tribunes of the plebs was fixed at ten. The oath of the plebs to defend their tribunes made them "sacrosanct" (untouchable through religious sanction). They acquired the right of intervention when a plebeian was being

---

5 Although the assembly of the plebs voted by tribe, the tribes are never attested as electing their own individual "tribunes." There seems to be no connection with the military tribunes who served in the legions.

harmed by a magistrate. This right was originally backed up by threat of starting a riot but was eventually accepted as a legitimate power ("intercession"). Presumably also as a result of such a threat, the tribunes were allowed to "veto" the act of any magistrate (*veto* means "I forbid" in Latin). Tribunes could not leave Rome during their term, and their rights always had to be exercised in person. Tribunes could also summon the assembly of the plebs (*concilium plebis*) and submit proposals for laws to it or lodge accusations of violations of the law before it.

If it is correct that the first tribunes were elected in 494 B.C. and that the patricians' monopoly of office dates from the middle of the fifth century, then it naturally follows that in the beginning the tribunes were not elected as a result of political opposition to that monopoly. Given the seeming etymology of plebs as "mob," it is conceivable that the tribunate began as an organized expression of simple economic discontent on the part of the less affluent, and only later took on a political dimension. In any case, eventually the men elected as tribune tended to be wealthy nonpatricians, who both championed the discontent of the poor and used it to further their own desire to run for public office.[6] In the end, when their political aspirations were satisfied, they left the poorer plebeians to look out for themselves.

At the same time as the tribunes, another group of plebeian officials was created, the aediles (who always remained two in number). Their original function is not known, but it may have started with overseeing the grain supply. The aediles later acquired other roles; in particular, they put on public games, oversaw the market place, and superintended the roads and buildings of the city.

The assembly of the plebs was formally distinct from the assemblies (*comitia*) of the *populus*, a distinction that was maintained throughout the Republic. The tradition holds that the plebs first voted by *curiae*, the old curiate assembly being the civil assembly of the Kingdom (see p. 16), but in 471 B.C., this procedure was replaced with voting by tribe. The voters voted separately in their tribes and then the tribes cast their votes for the actual candidates or about the law in question. This method of voting was then adopted by the *populus* for the tribal assembly (see p. 31).

The assembly of the plebs had the same restrictions as other Roman assemblies: it could only be called by the tribunes and could vote only on the

---

6 It is a common phenomenon, attestable both in the archaic period of ancient Greece and in medieval Germany, that when the wealthy families of a given time establish for themselves a hereditary monopoly of office holding, unacceptable disparities will arise over time. Some aristocratic families that have become poor will retain the right to office, while previously less affluent families that have in the interim become wealthy will be excluded from office and resent this.

motion put to it by the presiding tribune, its decision being called a *plebiscitum* ("resolution of the plebs"). Originally, a plebiscite applied only to the plebs. It appears that plebiscites could be made binding on the *populus* if the senate gave its *auctoritas*. The sources give different dates for when the assembly of the plebs was allowed to legislate for the *populus*, but this power was fully established in ca. 287 B.C. From then on, the Roman state tended to rely on the assembly of the plebs for the passage of laws, since the religious procedures associated with it were much less complicated than those of the centuriate assembly, and by then the tribunes of the plebs were reliable members of the ruling oligarchy.

The process by which the plebs were admitted to public office and their institutions made part of the state (*populus*) was drawn out. Whether the increasing tendency from 444 B.C. on to replace the consulship with the office of military tribune with consular power was associated with this is not clear. The literary sources indicate that the later fifth century B.C. was dominated internally by the disturbances about debt and other forms of economic distress. Military troubles in the early fourth century led to a temporary distraction from internal turmoil, but in the 370s B.C. a major crisis seems to have broken out between the patricians and plebeians, with much agitation for both political and economic reform.

In Varronian 376 B.C., two tribunes of the plebs were elected who saw the realization of the political aims of the plebs: C. Licinius Stolo and L. Sextius Lateranus. In addition to economic measures, they proposed that the consulship be restored in place of the consular tribunate and that one of the consuls should be plebeian. To this the patricians refused to consent, and the ensuing uproar resulted in a year without magistrates.[7] After a struggle of many years, in Varronian 367 B.C., their proposals (*rogationes*) were enacted into law. These were as follows:

1. legislation opening up the consulship to plebeians,
2. debt reduction, and
3. restriction of the amount of public land an individual could own.[8]

The law on the consulship apparently only stated that plebeians could hold the consulship, and in 343 B.C., a further law stated that one consul had to be plebeian. The law treated only the symptom of indebtedness, and

---

7 This is the point when the period without magistrates was expanded in some chronologies to five years to make the *fasti* agree with the synchronism of the sack of Rome (discussed earlier in the chapter), so the ten-year period assigned to the crisis in the Varronian dating should be reduced to six.

8 The size of the restriction that is preserved in the annalistic tradition was probably made up on the basis of the legal provisions of the mid–second century B.C.

numerous laws on the matter were passed later in the fourth century B.C.; none, however, had much impact on the general problem of rural debt. One major move was the abolishing of *nexum* (debt bondage) in 326 B.C.

At the same time that the disputes of the plebs were resolved through granting them the auspices, a reform of the organs of the state was carried out.

- Praetor. A junior colleague called the praetor was established as an assistant for the consuls. He held a form of *imperium* inferior to that of the consuls. The original motive for creating the position of praetor is not known, but soon the praetor was viewed as the man who ran business in Rome while the consuls were away on campaign. (In particular, the praetors presided over proceedings in civil law and would later play a major role in the development of Roman civil law.)
- Curule Aediles. On the model of the plebeian aediles, the *populus* began to elect two aediles of its own (called "curule" because they had the right to sit in the *sella curulis*, a special chair for regular magistrates). They had exactly the same duties as the plebeian aediles, the two sets alternating by year.

Once the plebeians were admitted to the consulship, they began to hold the office in gradually increasing numbers. By the end of the fourth century B.C., a new alliance of wealthy plebeian and prominent patrician families began to form. These plebeians now ceased to champion the economic claims of the plebs and fused with the older patrician. Anyone whose ancestor had held the consulship was called a "noble" (Latin *nobilis* = "one who is well known"), and these families, which would dominate office holding from that point on, are known collectively as the nobility. Anyone who gained office from outside the established nobility was called a *novus homo* ("new man"). These new political families often came from the dominant families of Italian cities incorporated into the Roman state. Thus, the nobility that would control the Middle and Late Republic consisted of wealthy families of both patrician and plebeian origin, and while patricians would always have certain additional prestige, many of the most powerful families of the later period were plebeian.

Early in their careers, plebeian members of the nobility would stand for the tribunate and plebeian aedileship. In this way, the plebeian institutions were made a part of the state system. In effect, the organs of the plebs were co-opted by the ruling class. Only in the late second century B.C. did certain (noble) tribunes advance their careers by using the powers of the assembly of the plebs against the interests of the nobility.

The literary tradition is preoccupied with the Struggle of the Orders and has little to say about the political process when the new nobility was formed. Certain patterns in office holding have been detected by modern scholars, and on the basis of these patterns various "factions" have been identified among the families of the nobility. While it is the case that certain families seemed to be associated with others in holding office, the actual implications of this are hard to identify in the absence of any reliable information about the electoral process. One thing is clear: men often held repeated consulships throughout the fourth century B.C. and down to the early first century B.C. This may well mean that family "leaders" were able to mobilize the votes of their supporters for themselves to the exclusion of other members of the family, but this is by no means certain. At any rate, during the Hannibalic War in the late third century B.C., men held repeated consulships because of their military success, and this pattern may hold true for the earlier period. In any case, voting was done orally, so that the wealthy were able to make sure of the votes of lesser men whom they thought to be beholden to them, though there is no way of knowing exactly what criteria determined how a man was obliged to vote. What is clear is that the older patrician families and the plebeian families recently allowed to run for office were able to maintain for themselves overall control of the political system.

We have no detailed knowledge of the economic and social circumstances of the Early Republic, but the general outlines are clear. Rome was a primarily agricultural community. Slavery already existed, though it was nowhere near as pervasive as it would later become after the Middle Republic's many wars of conquest. Money began to be used in the fifth century B.C., but the monetary system was primitive. The political system was controlled by the landowners who had enough wealth to equip themselves for military service. They dominated the assemblies, and the wealthiest among them were chosen as magistrates. The fact that there was only a factor of ten distinguishing the lowest from the highest census class indicates that the differential of wealth among the comparatively well-to-do was not very great; again, the wars of conquest would greatly change this. If the *gentes* had had some broad social function under the Kingdom, this was gone by the time of the Twelve Tables, in which the later form of social organization by family is already attested. The Romans had a form of patriarchy that was theoretically very strong. A Roman man controlled the economic lives of his descendants, and upon his death the male children individually inherited control over their own descendants. (In theory, the powers of the head of the family were close to absolute, but in practice they were exercised much less rigorously with adult descendants.) Apart from a few priesthoods, public affairs were the exclusive domain of adult males.

3

CONQUEST OF LATIUM AND ITALY, CA. 507 B.C.–264 B.C.

In the first two and a half centuries of its existence, the Roman Republic conquered first Latium, then all of Italy. The Romans annexed much foreign territory to their own state, but they also established a system of alliances with all other states. This gave the Romans a vast reserve of manpower that allowed them to overthrow every major power in the Mediterranean within little more than a century after the conquest of Italy.

The concept of the Italian nation is a creation of the Romans. All of modern Italy is inhabited by people speaking various derivates of the Latin language. To understand Rome's conquest of Italy, a description of the linguistic and ethnic makeup of pre-Roman Italy is necessary. Since human groups are largely divided on the basis of language, a linguistic description will also indicate which groups the Romans would encounter in their conquest of the peninsula during the course of the Republic.

With the major exception of Etruscan, the languages of Italy were all Indo-European, that is, they all derived from an ancestral language that was originally spoken around 2500 B.C. in what is now southern Russia or the Ukraine. The largest group of languages is categorized under the rubric "Italic." Speakers of these languages formed the majority of the native population during the Iron Age and presumably were present during the Bronze Age. These languages fall into two distinct groups: Latin and Oscan-Umbrian. The other major population groups in Italy that spoke Indo-European languages at the time of the Roman conquest were the Greeks and the Gauls.

1. Latin. Latin is the language spoken in Latium. Originally the various *populi* (independent cities) of Latium each had their own dialects of Latin, but early on they adopted the variety spoken in Rome. Accordingly, there is no literary and little inscriptional evidence for the non-Roman form of Latin.

2. Oscan-Umbrian. The rest of the Italic group is divided into two: Umbrian languages and Oscan ones. Umbrian-speaking groups are found to the northeast of Rome, Oscan groups to the south. The two groups are closely related, forming a unitary group distinguishable from Latin.

The speakers of Oscan-Umbrian dialects seem to have originally inhabited the central Apennines and to have expanded outwards in the late Regal and early Republican periods. On the whole, they were non-urban peoples, who were organized as separate "tribes" sharing a common language and religious practices (not to be confused with the "tribes" that serve as subdivisions of an urban community or *populus*). The traditional story is that this expansion was carried out by means of the "sacred spring." In times of overpopulation, everything born in a given spring would be dedicated to a god (often the war god Mars) and sacrificed. The human children were spared, but when they turned twenty, they had to leave the community and conquer a new territory for themselves. According to tradition, they would often follow a sacred animal, which led them to their new territory (this is a motif in the mythological traditions of many peoples). It is conceivable that the story of Romulus and Remus owes something to a similar tradition in that they were raised by a wolf and led a band of unattached males to found a new community.

a. Umbrians. The territory of the Umbrians begins only thirty-five miles to the northeast of Rome and extends up into the Apennine mountains to the east of the Tiber, being divided into a number of fairly primitive communities. To the immediate northeast of Latium were the Umbrian Sabines, who were credited with an important role in the foundation of Rome. The first half century of the Republic saw war with the Sabines, but afterwards they quickly became Latinized. Other Umbrian communities established themselves on the eastern border of Latium around the time of the foundation of the Republic and attempted to force their way into Latium. Much of the Early Republic's foreign policy involved the attempt to contain these Umbrian invasions of Latium (see pp. 43–44). On the whole, the Umbrians to the north were incapable of common action and put up little resistance to the Romans when they subdued Umbria.

b. Oscan. The homeland of the Oscans was in the southcentral Apennines. From there, they launched major advances into Campania and southern Italy in the fifth century. The people who occupied the heartland of the Oscan territory were called the Samnites. In the Late Republic, they were considered a model of pristine valor. They lived in villages and were resistant to Hellenic influence. The villages were grouped into four tribes, which formed a loose league to cooperate militarily. The Romans found the Samnites difficult opponents and suffered a number of major defeats at their hands.

The Oscans also expanded less extensively northwards in the Apennines, establishing population groups to the east of Latium that extended down to the eastern coast of the Adriatic. These peoples were attached to Rome by treaty in a single year (Varronian 304 B.C.) and then became a major element in the military establishment of the Middle Republic.

3. Greeks. In antiquity, Greek was originally spoken on the Greek mainland and the Aegean islands plus the adjoining coast of Asia Minor. Starting in the eighth century B.C., the Greeks began to send out colonies, which were independent city-states established on the coast in foreign lands. A number were set up in southern Italy and Sicily, and like their mainland relatives, the Greeks of Italy squabbled incessantly (both within each city and in wars between the various cities). In the fifth century B.C., many towns were taken over by the Oscans during their great expansion.

4. Gauls. The last major arrivals in Italy were the Gauls, who spoke a language belonging to one of the major Indo-European families, Celtic. In the same way that the Oscans of Italy were forced by overpopulation to expand outwards, the Gauls moved out from central Europe to the south and west. By the mid–first millennium B.C., the Celts had expanded into Gaul (France), the Spanish peninsula, and Britain. They crossed the Alps ca. 400 B.C. and began to occupy what is now northern Italy (the area between the River Po and the Alps), pushing aside earlier populations. Because of its now predominantly Gallic-speaking population, this area was known to the Romans of the Middle and Late Republic as Cisalpine Gaul ("Gaul this side of the Alps") in contrast to Transalpine Gaul ("Gaul the other side of the Alps"). Only at the very end of the Republic was this area considered part of Italy. Certain Celtic tribes occupied territory south of the Po in northern Italy, and they would inflict a major defeat upon the Romans in the early fourth century B.C.

With the general ethnic situation of Italy laid out, it is time to begin with Rome's conquest of it. When the Roman Republic was instituted, Roman territory did not extend far beyond the gates of the city. In the literary tradition, there is a fair amount of information about the Kingdom that seems to be copied from what was known about the Early Republic, and it is hard to see how the early annalists could have had any reliable information about this distant period. Even for the earliest period, Rome is portrayed as trying to establish its domination over the other Latins. Whatever the case for the Kingdom, this was certainly the Roman goal in the Early Republic.

Rome was the northernmost Latin city. The Latin cities were independent communities (*populi*), which spoke a common language (Latin) and worshipped common gods. The Latin communities other than Rome belonged to a loose organization known in modern terminology as the "Latin League." The literary sources portray the Latin League as a distinct entity from Rome herself and represent the Romans as making an attempt to assert leadership over the League. Why Rome in particular should have been distinct from the other Latin communities is not self-evident. Conceivably, this distinction had not always existed, and in the earliest period (the Kingdom?), Rome was simply one among a number of other communities.

The Roman term for the other Latin communities was the "Latin name" (*nomen Latinum*).[1] The designation "league" is a modern one (ancient Greek sources also used a comparable term). The Roman term indicates a description based on a sense of common cultural traits, not on a formally constituted political organization. The so-called Latin League was a group of Latin-speaking communities that cooperated militarily, usually (as far as the sources tell us) in opposition to Rome, which acted as an entity separate from the League. Apparently, a commander was appointed to lead the troops of Latin communities on some sort of ad hoc basis not known to us.

A crucial event in the relationship between the Republic and the Latins took place about a decade after the foundation of the Republic. After a Roman dictator defeated the Latins in Varronian 499 or 496 B.C. at the battle of Lake Regillus, Sp. Cassius, the consul of 493 B.C., signed a treaty with them.[2] This treaty (known in Latin as the *foedus Cassianum* or "Cassius' treaty") was apparently written up on an inscription that was extant in the mid–first century B.C. Among other provisions, both sides were to remain at peace with each other, aid each other in the case of external attack, and divide the spoils of any joint campaigns equally.

If this document is genuine, it seems to confirm Rome's position as an entity distinct from the other Latins, the division of booty indicating that Rome alone was equal in her own right to the rest of them. Whether the treaty was actually caused by the threat to Latium by Umbrian invaders is not clear, but certainly it allowed the Romans and Latins to cooperate in protecting themselves against these incursions.

In the fifth century B.C., speakers of the Umbrian dialects began to expand from the central Apennines in all directions. By the late 490s B.C., the Volsci were in control of much of southern Latium, territory to the northeast of Rome was constantly attacked by the Sabines, and eastern Latium was threatened by the Aequi. Down to the middle of the century, virtually every year involved

---

1 The expression signifies "those designated as 'Latins.'"
2 "Sp." is the abbreviation for the uncommon *praenomen* "Spurius."

a struggle with either the Volsci or Aequi. Not only did the latter constantly invade Latin territory, but sometimes they even got as far as the walls of Rome. The details of these years are suspect, however. The real decisive battle appears to have been won in 431 B.C. The Aequi and Volsci had apparently shot their bolt, and the Romans went over to the offensive. While they continued to suffer defeats, they gradually regained control of the outlying districts of Latium. By the 390s B.C., the Romans and Latins had regained control of the plains, relegating the Aequi and Volsci to the highlands to the east.

The incursions of Umbrian hills men were not the only source of conflict for the early Republic. Rome also engaged in a long conflict with the Etruscan town of Veii, about ten miles north of Rome across the Tiber. This war was a struggle not of a settled population fighting off primitive brigands but of two developed city-states fighting for control of territory. The initial conflict involved control of the town of Fidenae, which sits between the two.

The land of the Roman Fabian tribe abutted onto territory of Veii, and the Fabian clan apparently waged a private war against Veii. At any rate, tradition held that in 479 B.C., all 300 members of the clan were wiped out in battle, with one exception. While this figure is suspiciously reminiscent of the number of Spartans killed at Thermopylae, the general sense of the story seems to indicate a holdover from an earlier period when the clans acted independently, and their dominance of various locations gave the names of the rural tribes.[3] There is some corroboration of the story in that, while the Fabii held one consulship every year from 485 to 479 B.C., none appeared again until 467 B.C. In any case, in the mid-430s B.C., the Romans finally captured Fidenae. That this major victory should have been won before Rome's final defeat of the Aequi and Volsci shows the resources available to the Romans (as well as their determination).

After a ten-year struggle, the Romans finally took Veii in 396 B.C. and destroyed the town. While Rome could at least count on the passive cooperation of the Latins, no Etruscan town helped Veii (and one seems to have favored the Romans). This is a reflection of the disunity of the Etruscan communities. The Romans were led by M. Furius Camillus, but the details seem to have been overlaid with much fiction. The period of ten years sounds suspiciously similar to the length of the Trojan War, but the literary tradition associated the siege with the introduction of pay for military duty, which does suggest a protracted campaign.

---

3 The story of the futile Spartan attempt in 480 B.C. to hold back the Persians at Thermopylae would have been well known to any ancient historian from the account of it in Herodotus' history of the Persian Wars. The coincidence in the date, which may have been considered a synchronism in some chronological schemes, would have made the association all the more appealing.

The capture of the town led to a huge increase in Roman territory (*ager Romanus* or "Roman territory," not to be confused with *ager publicus* or "public land," that is, the land actually owned by the Roman state). Around 495, the *ager Romanus* is estimated to have been about 350 square miles. The capture of Veii added about 210, for a total of nearly 620 (60 having been added in the fifth century B.C.). Thus, the capture increased Roman territory by about one-third. Individual allotments of land were given to Roman citizens, and four new tribes were created, bring the total to twenty-six (two others had already been added to the twenty inherited from the Kingdom).

With the capture of Veii, the Roman state, which had already been a match for the whole Latin League, became greatly predominant in resources. Before the Romans could establish a new relationship with the Latins, however, the Gallic disaster intervened.

In about 400 B.C., a number of Gallic tribes began to overrun the Etruscan settlements of the Po Valley. They completely occupied this region, and one tribe marched south. The literary tradition has much embroidered this event, seeking to throw the blame on the military tribunes with consular power who held office in the year before the siege with the claim that they had provoked the Gauls. Whatever the truth of this, the Gauls moved against Rome, crushed the Roman army, and then captured the city, at least in part. The story is greatly embellished, and the main tradition saves Roman dignity by claiming that the Gauls never took the citadel. In any case, it seems that the Gauls withdrew after exacting a ransom payment. The sack of the city was traumatic for the Romans, and the dating of the event formed the major synchronism to attach Roman history to Greek chronology (see pp. 24–25).

One result of the war was the construction of the Republican wall (erroneously attributed to King Servius Tullius), which survives today in a few sections. The new wall was made of stone quarried near Veii, and its circuit had a circumference of more than five miles, enclosing an area of about 1,000 acres.

Obviously the Roman defeat at the hands of the Gauls was a great humiliation and did much to undermine the prestige that the Romans had acquired by defeating the Aequi and Volsci in Latium and Veii to the north. At first, the closer Latin towns remained loyal, but revolt broke out among the towns of southern Latium, where the influence of the Volsci was strong. Down to about 376 B.C., the Romans had a hard time subduing the Volsci again and putting down revolt among certain Latin towns. It appears that the old *foedus Cassianum* was allowed to lapse.

Long-term Roman intentions were indicated by the fact that in 380 B.C., the Romans annexed the major Latin community called Tusculum. Its citizens were made Roman citizens and had all the obligations of citizens (in particular military service) while retaining a large measure of internal autonomy (see p. 51). Clearly Rome was determined to absorb Latium in one way or another.

It is noteworthy that a period of comparative peace lasted from ca. 376 to 363 B.C., the time when Rome was preoccupied with the internal disputes surrounding the Sextian-Licinian rogations (see p. 37). While this external peace may have been fortuitous, the coincidence is striking. This lull strongly suggests that the wars between the Romans and Latins were largely the result of Roman aggression: if the Romans were too busy for wars, none took place.

Starting in 362 B.C., the Romans returned to a period of major warfare. In 358 B.C., the Latins were forced to renew the *foedus Cassianum,* whose terms were presumably updated to reflect the stronger position of the Romans compared to their allies. In the same year, the Romans also began to fight the Etruscan towns to their north, forcing them by the end of the decade to sign long-term peace treaties advantageous to the Romans.

The early 340s B.C. were comparatively peaceful. In 350–349 B.C., the Gauls returned, and despite tepid assistance from the Latins, the Romans defeated them with little difficulty. In 348 B.C., the Romans entered into a treaty with the Carthaginians. The details are not clear, but it apparently recognized Roman hegemony over Latium (see p. 50). Whether the Latins would have agreed about this is doubtful, but this shows Roman attitudes at the time.

In the late 340s B.C., Rome became involved in disputes between the Oscan-speaking Campanians and the Samnites. The details are disputed, but it seems that whatever the exact circumstances, the Latins eventually took the side of the Campanians, while the Romans supported the Samnites. The result was a general revolt of the Latins. The sources indicate that the Latins were tired of being treated like subordinates and wanted equality with the Romans. This may be an anachronism in that the Italian allies had exactly the same complaints in the late second and early first centuries. Whatever the specific grievances and aims of the Latins, the revolt represents a final effort at resisting complete Roman domination of the Latin communities. This resistance was a dismal failure. The revolt began in 341 B.C., and the next year, the Romans decisively defeated the Latins and their Campanian allies at the battle of Trifanum. The Campanians immediately gave in, and the Romans spent the next two years (339 and 338 B.C.) stamping out all resistance in Latium.

In 338 B.C., the Romans made a permanent disposition of the Latins. The Latin League was abolished (their common religious rites on the Alban Hill were continued, but now the Roman consuls carried them out). The closest Latin states were directly annexed, and outlying states were either given second-class Roman citizenship or subordinated to Rome by treaty (see pp. 51–53). Roman control over Latium was now permanently assured.

Having finally achieved control of Latium, the Romans went on to subdue virtually all of peninsular Italy by about 270 B.C. In the process, they unified all of the resources of Italy under their own control and developed a military and political system that would not only survive the incredible stress of the first two wars with Carthage but go on to subdue all the major powers of the Mediterranean within the half century after the end of the Second Punic War in 202 B.C. In their conquest of Italy, the Romans showed not only their military prowess and aggressiveness but also their political acumen.

The last major native opponents of the Romans in Italy were the Samnites, with whom the Romans are said to have fought three wars. The first war began in 343 B.C. but was quickly ended by the Romans in 341 B.C. when the trouble with the Latins started.

The Great (or Second) Samnite War was a major conflict that lasted about twenty years (Varronian 326–304 B.C.). The war seems again to be the result of clear Roman aggression. In the 330s B.C., after the end of the war with the Latin League, the Romans began to advance into northern Campania, coming into contact with territory controlled by the Samnites. In 328 B.C., the Romans challenged them with a provocatively placed colony and war broke out in 326 B.C. after a dispute involving control of the Greek city of Neapolis (modern Naples). After some initial victories, the Romans suffered a major defeat at the battle of the Caudine Forks in 321 B.C., where an entire Roman army was surrounded and forced to surrender. While the literary tradition holds that the Roman commanders were compelled to make a truce that was then rejected by the senate, this is likely to be a later fiction made up on the basis of the famous incident in which the senate did reject an agreement made in 137 B.C. after a defeat in Spain (see p. 91). In any case, it seems that the Romans did suspend operations against the Samnites until 316 B.C. and abandoned their colonies in northern Campania. This suggests that the Romans were abiding by some sort of agreement that allowed their army to escape in return for a withdrawal from disputed territory and a (five-year?) truce.

The Romans spent the next few years improving their position. In 318 B.C., they added two tribes – one in northern Campania and one in the territory between Campania and Latium. At the same time the Romans subdued communities in Apulia and Lucania, the areas to the east and south of the Samnites. It would seem that the Roman intention was to surround the Samnites before resuming war with them directly.

In 316 B.C., the Roman assault on the Samnites began again. After an initial setback, the Romans regained control of northern Campania and established a number of colonies there in the late 310s B.C. The construction of the road called the Appian Way from Rome to Campania in 312 B.C.

marked a clear intent on the part of the Romans to maintain their control there.

The last decade of the fourth century B.C. saw the final resistance of a number of traditional Roman opponents, who joined with the Samnites in a last ditch effort to ward off Roman domination. First the Etruscans went to war; next some of Rome's old Umbrian opponents rose against them, and the Samnites were joined by their central Italian cousins to the east of Rome. Too late did these people realize the threat of Rome. By 308 B.C., the Etruscans were brought to heel, and in the years 305 to 303 B.C., the Romans compelled the rest, including the Samnites, to come to terms.

The opponents of the Romans were not yet ready to give up. From 302 B.C. on, annual campaigns are recorded against the Etruscans. In 298 B.C., the Samnites began the Third Samnite War. They sent forces to Etruria, and the Umbrians and Gauls also joined the coalition against the Romans. Roman command arrangements for 296–295 B.C. show that they took the threat very seriously. In 295 B.C., the Romans decisively defeated their opponents at the battle of Sentinum in Umbria. The Romans appear to have had 35,000 Roman troops and at least as many allies – a huge army for the time. For the period 292–219 B.C., the complete text of Livy, our main narrative source, is not preserved, and the details of how the Romans took advantage of their victory are lost. They invaded Samnium, and by 290 B.C., the Samnites again became the allies of the Romans.

Having dealt with the Italic tribes and the Etruscans, the Romans turned their attention to the Greek communities of the far south. By the 280s B.C., they had become involved in Greek affairs, and in 282 B.C., a war broke out between them and the city of Tarentum. In the past, the Greek communities had at times called upon generals and kings in mainland Greece to help them when in trouble, and in 281 B.C. the Tarentines approached Pyrrhus, the king of Epirus (an area of northwestern Greece). Pyrrhus was related to Alexander the Great, and wishing to engage in some adventure comparable to that of his famous kinsman, he agreed to the Tarentine request, arriving in 280 B.C. with 35,000 men and twenty elephants. The Romans promptly led an army against him and were heavily defeated at Heraclea. They had never seen elephants before, and the unfamiliar were terrified by these beasts (they were easy enough for experienced troops to deal with). Though victorious, Pyrrhus lost 4,000 men, and when congratulated for his victory, he commented bitterly that another such victory would cost him the war (hence the expression "Pyrrhic victory").

After this victory, the other Greeks, Lucanians, and Samnites went over to Pyrrhus. He marched on Rome, perhaps expecting to intimidate the Romans into submission. If so, he misjudged the situation. He found, just as Hannibal would, that even if some of the outlying Italian peoples were willing to desert the Romans, they could rely on the hardcore support of the Latins and various other communities in central Italy. In the absence of large-scale defections, Pyrrhus could achieve nothing and withdrew to the south.

In 279 B.C., he again won a costly victory against the Romans, losing another 3,500 men. At this point, he offered to make peace if the Romans agreed to guarantee the independence of the Greeks of the south and the Samnites. Though some senators were receptive, the offer was rejected.

In the meanwhile, the Carthaginians were close to conquering the Greek communities of Sicily, and Pyrrhus crossed over to Sicily in 278 B.C. to aid the Greeks there. After throwing back the Carthaginians, he returned to Italy in late 276 B.C. In 275 B.C., two Roman armies guarded against his attack to the north. His surprise attack on one army failed, and he withdrew to Tarentum to avoid being encircled. At this point, he went back to Greece with most of his army, leaving the Greek communities to their fate.

Pyrrhus' Greek troops were tactically superior to the Roman army, and he was never defeated by the Romans in battle. At the same time, the Romans showed that they were quick to learn. Furthermore, their system of extending citizenship and making alliances had created an invincible military organization. Most allies remained loyal, which meant that the Romans had an inexhaustible supply of manpower, and their leaders refused to give up, even in difficult times. Under these circumstances, no other power in the Mediterranean basin could defeat the Romans in the long run.

It appears that after the Roman victory at Sentinum in 295 B.C., the Etruscans continued to resist, but by the late 270s B.C., all of Etruria was subdued. After the expulsion of Pyrrhus, the Romans spent the years around 270 B.C. consolidating their hold on southern Italy. By this point the whole of the Italian peninsula was in the hands of the Romans, and they were ready to begin wars abroad.

The Romans clearly had a flair for incorporating such communities into their political and military system, through both direct absorption and the making of treaties. At first the Romans had to deal with Latin communities, that is, people very similar to themselves. As their conquest of the Italian peninsula advanced, the Romans had to establish relations with increasingly alien peoples. The Romans then applied the lessons they learned during their conquest of Italy to the establishment of Roman-controlled territory abroad. Eventually, these techniques allowed them to rule, and in many cases Romanize, the entire Mediterranean basin, plus some adjacent regions. The Romans' ability to accommodate foreigners into their political system strongly contrasted with the political habits of the Greeks, who in the Classical period found it difficult to absorb neighboring Greek communities, much less foreign ones.

Little is known of Rome's foreign relations during the Regal period. One noteworthy event is the absorption of Gabii, a Latin town directly to the east of Rome. The independence of the town was abolished and its territory made part of the Roman state, but it was apparently left sufficient sense of identity that it did not cease to exist altogether. Its territory had the peculiarity that it was both Roman (*ager Romanus*) and foreign (*ager peregrinus*) at the same time. Roman magistrates also adopted for certain ceremonial occasions a special costume named after the town. Thus, Regal Rome seems to have been capable of absorbing a foreign community in such a way that it still retained some separate identity, and under the Republic, the Romans would eventually develop various ways to incorporate foreign communities while leaving them a certain degree of internal self-government.

In the beginning all Latin communities shared certain "communal rights":

- *Commercium.* The right of members of one community to enforce commercial transactions in other communities. (Foreigners were otherwise debarred from local legal systems.)
- *Conubium.* The right to contract a legally valid marriage with a citizen of another community.
- The right of migration. This meant that if the citizen of one Latin community moved to another, he was entitled to the citizenship of the new community.

These rights were based on a common linguistic and cultural origin. The already existing sense of "community" among the Latins would mean that the Romans found it easy to absorb the individual Latin "states" into their own polity. Roman "receptiveness" in dealing with foreigners perhaps derives from their relations with the Latin communities.

Some uncertain light is shed on the relationship between Rome and the Latins by the Greek historian Polybius (*History* book 3, chap. 22), who relates that the consuls of the first year of the Republic entered into a treaty with Carthage. Since Polybius does not indicate the source of his information and ascribes the treaty to two consuls who did not serve at the same time according to the Roman literary tradition, it is hard to assess the accuracy of what he says. He quotes the treaty in Greek, indicating that it was between the Romans and their allies on the one hand and the Carthaginians and their allies on the other. The terms he quotes refer to the *demoi* of certain specified Latin towns and of any other Latins not "subject" to the Romans. The Greek word *demos* presumably corresponds to *populus* in Latin and implies that these were fully independent communities. Yet, Polybius claims that they were called "subjects," and the fact that Rome negotiated on their behalf seems to imply some sort of subordination on their part. It is also difficult to imagine how this situation was described in Latin.

The fifth century B.C. was a time of stress for the Romans. They entered into an alliance with the Latins on an equal footing and spent most of their time waging war against the Sabines, Aequi, and Volsci. The Romans won some small accession to their territory (perhaps sixty square miles), but this merely involved the removal of land from defeated foreign states and the absorption of small communities. In effect, adjacent depopulated territory was directly added to pre-existing Roman territory and distributed to citizens. It was only with the conquest of Veii to the north that a major community came to be incorporated into the Roman state. Following their previous practice, the Romans extinguished the independent corporate existence of the town (the archaeological record indicates no wholesale destruction of its physical fabric). To some extent this might reflect the Etruscan composition of the population. At any rate, when the Romans later subdued Etruria as a whole, they were granting Roman citizenship to various Indo-European populations, but they still refrained from doing so in Etruria.

In 380 B.C., the Romans made Tusculum, a large Latin community, a part of the Roman state. Since Tusculum was already surrounded by Roman territory, the step made logical sense and represented the first time that the Romans had to deal with the incorporation of a large community. The exact details of how Tusculum was treated are not clear, but it seems that the town retained some degree of internal independence. At the time of the incorporation, office holding in Rome was still monopolized by the patricians, and thus Tusculans were at first ineligible for office. Once the plebeians were granted the right to hold office, however, the leading families of Tusculum became the first (originally) non-Romans to be elected to office in Rome.

Thus, the Roman state was now expanding into Latium through the absorption rather than the destruction of foreign communities. This process continued when the Latin League was dissolved in 338 B.C. At that time, the Romans took a number of steps that greatly changed the Roman state and had significant implications for the future:

1. Incorporation. Most of the remaining Latin communities around Rome were directly absorbed into the Roman state. Here the pattern established with the incorporation of Tusculum was followed. The towns retained their own magistrates for local purposes, but their citizens now had the full rights and duties of Roman citizens.

2. Continued Latin status. The outlying Latin communities continued to exist as theoretically independent communities, but instead of being tied to Rome through the *foedus Cassianum*, they signed individual treaties with Rome. These towns lost the communal Latin rights among themselves but retained them with Rome. This would eventually ensure that over time their commercial and social bonds with Rome would increase, while the connections with other towns would lessen. The Latin towns

provided military contingents for the Roman army at the discretion of the consuls according to a fixed formula. Although these towns were theoretically independent, they assimilated themselves to Rome and received a particularly favored position, ranking very close to the Romans and certainly far above the Italian allies. Additional Latin communities were created through the foundation of Latin colonies, and eventually in the Late Republic Latin status was entirely divorced from the physical area of Latium, being given to privileged non-Roman populations as a status close to, but still short of, Roman citizenship.

3. Non-voting citizenship. For Volscian communities in south Latium and for certain Oscan communities in north Campania, the Romans created a special kind of citizenship that did not give the right to vote. This arrangement fully subordinated the citizens of such communities to the authority of Roman officials and compelled them to serve in the Roman legions without granting them the privileges of citizenship. This status was clearly considered a form of suppression by those upon whom it was forced, and many resisted accepting it. A person with such citizenship was called a *municeps*, which means a "taker of duties" and a town of such citizens was called a *municipium*. These towns retained internal autonomy, but the powers of their magistrates were rather limited. Eventually, the urban praetors in Rome sent out officials called prefects who would administer civil law in these outlying districts. Non-voting citizenship was very much a phenomenon of the half century following the suppression of the Latin League. It was apparently given to those who were reasonably Romanized but not yet considered ready for full absorption into the Roman state. Over the next century, communities with such status were gradually given full citizenship.

The settlement of the Latin communities in 338 B.C. took place in areas with which the Romans had been in contact for a long time. It must have been easy to tell what level of incorporation was appropriate in any given case. During their conquest of Italy, the Romans came into contact with numerous populations with which they had had no previous dealings, and in the course of their many wars, they entered into alliances with all these peoples. There were two kinds of treaties:

1. Equal treaty (*foedus aequum*). This was a treaty voluntarily entered into by equals. Such treaties were generally defensive, that is, each party agreed to come to the aid of the other in case of attack. Over the course of time, as Roman power grew, the distinction between this kind of treaty and the theoretically inferior status covered next tended to disappear, all allies being subject to the interference of the Roman state.

2. Unequal treaty (*foedus iniquum*). This was a relationship forced upon a community that had been subdued by the Romans through force of arms. On the whole, the wars after the dissolution of the Latin League saw the Romans come into conflict with practically everyone with whom they had had a *foedus aequum*, and upon reconquest the old treaty was replaced with a *foedus iniquum*. In such a treaty the ally was obliged to "maintain the greatness of the Roman People." This meant in practice that the allied community lost all control of its foreign policy, maintaining the same friends and enemies as the Roman People. The ally also was obligated to provide a certain number of troops who would fight under Roman orders.

Apart from the raising of non-voting citizens to full status and the establishment of colonies, the system set up in the seventy years after the dissolution of the Latin League became solidified. In 242 B.C., the last new Roman tribes were created (bringing the number to thirty-five), and after that there was no more expansion of the Roman franchise. Yet, in the aftermath of the Second Punic War, much territory was confiscated from rebellious allied communities and taken over by the Roman state. Despite increasing Romanization among the allies (and their clear contribution to the Roman military system) no step was taken to incorporate them further into the state. Starting in the late second century B.C., this would become a major political problem.

Nonetheless, for all its eventual failings, the Roman policy led to the development of a system of incorporations and alliances that was unequaled in the ancient world. This system gave the Romans a vast supply of manpower and was generally acceptable to the allies. At any rate, it took the massive Roman defeats at the hands of Hannibal to cause any rebellions, and even these affected marginal community. The loyalty of the central Italians was unshakable. The Romans then marshaled these resources for their remarkable conquest of the Mediterranean in the second century.

Colonies played a notable role in the Roman occupation of Italy. The word *colonus* is a Latin word for "cultivator" or "farmer," and thus *colonia* literally means the "collective of farmers." Technically it refers to a new farming community established through a formal state ceremony.

The colonies that were founded before the dissolution of the Latin League were set up as fully formed members of the League. The literary sources ascribe the leadership and initiative in these foundations to the Romans, but this is a little hard to believe (surely the League must have had some say in the matter). Colonists would be a mixture of Romans and Latins, who lost their old citizenship and became citizens of the new community. Such foundations are called Latin colonies. They were normally founded at some distance from Roman territory, and thus needed to be autonomous (they could not rely on Roman authority at all times). Since the colonies owed military forces to Rome, there was no loss in Roman manpower through the foundation of such colonies. Indeed the Roman colonists are likely to have been landless to begin with, so they had not been previously eligible for military service in any case. Thus, sending out colonists actually increased available manpower, while at the same time extending Roman influence far from Roman territory. The Romans set up colonies both as a way to extend control into new regions of Italy and to retain control of newly conquered areas. Though a few Latin colonies were set up in the early second century B.C., they are mainly a phenomenon of the Roman conquest of Italy. Later, the status of being a Latin colony would be granted to overseas communities that were thought worthy of incorporation into the Roman state but were not yet considered ready for full citizenship.

While the utility of establishing independent Latin colonies in outlying areas is clear, the idea of colonies of Roman citizens is not an obvious one. A number of considerations militated against the usefulness of citizen colonies in the Early and Middle Republic:

- The colonists would find it hard to perform their duties as citizens if they lived at a distance from Roman territory.
- It would be difficult for them to deal with the distant Roman magistrates.
- If they were to have their own local government like a Roman *municipium,* they may as well have been set up as a regular Latin colony.

Before the second century B.C., the Romans used citizen colonies in a very limited way. These citizen colonies were to act as outposts to guard the shore. They were much smaller than Latin colonies and apparently not very popular. The members of these communities would in fact be cut off from the rest of the Roman citizenry and were exempted from serving in the legions. Citizen colonies would again be sent out after the Second Punic War, but under very different circumstances.

Finally, it would be useful to know something of the Roman military organization that conquered Italy, but there is little specific information for the period before the third century B.C. The Latin word *legio* is in origin a verbal abstraction and signifies "selection." Thus, it originally indicated the concept of choosing the eligible men for service in the army. Presumably, in the early period, the eligible men would be chosen after the spring sowing, go on campaign during the summer, and disband for the fall harvest. By the Middle Republic, the legion signified not the total draft, but a semi-permanent military unit of theoretically fixed size, four normally being raised every year. The soldiers were drawn from the citizens wealthy enough to equip themselves with the expensive gear necessary for service. The literary tradition indicates that the five census classes reflected varying obligations, members of the highest class serving as the most fully equipped infantry and the lowest class providing skirmishers. By the third century B.C., such distinctions had largely been done away with. The provision of giving the troops pay during the war with Veii ca. 400 B.C. shows that military service was already beginning to obstruct the economic life of the soldiers, but the demands necessitated by the conquest of Italy were comparatively restricted and were likely counterbalanced by the opportunities for plunder. This would change once Roman armies began to fight protracted wars overseas.

PART TWO

CONQUEST OF THE MEDITERRANEAN, 264 B.C.–146 B.C.

In 264 B.C., the Romans embarked on their first overseas war, and by 146 B.C. they were far and away the dominant military power in the Mediterranean. This swift rise to power was a source of amazement to the ancients and has provoked much controversy among modern scholars. The Romans themselves claimed that their wars were always "justified," being provoked by foreign aggression, and in the nineteenth century, the predominant idea was that the Romans were not interested in conquest and merely expanded their territory as one move brought them into conflict with their new neighbors. Certainly, the Romans of the Middle Republic were not driven by a drive to conquer territory for its own sake, and in this regard they did differ from the self-consciously imperialist powers of nineteenth-century Europe, which competed with each other in acquiring foreign possessions. Yet, a lack of interest in conquest is not the same thing as a lack of aggression. In 1979, W. V. Harris changed the tone of the discussion with his *War and Imperialism in Ancient Rome,* arguing that the Romans were a violent people whose leaders won prestige and political advancement on the basis of military success. Though his moralistic attitude obstructs his case, he is correct in pointing out the tendency towards warfare in various segments of Roman society in the Middle Republic. The soldiery were happy enough to go on campaign if the wars were to be of comparatively short duration and if they were likely to make a large profit in the form of booty. The magistrates of a given year were naturally inclined to wage war in order to gain both glory and money. In fact, the opportunities for making money from warfare were vast (both through direct plunder and though "gratuities" when drawing up settlements with the conquered and governing them afterward), and the families that led Romans armies during the conquest gained undreamed of wealth. Holding all the initiative in the political process in Rome, the magistrates could nearly always get their way if they desired war. Furthermore, once they had departed on campaign, there was no means of communication to keep track of their actions, and their discretion in the field was very great.

There were other perspectives, however. Generals in the field would sometimes make peace terms, but the incoming magistrates were keen to thwart peace and could use their influence in the senate to have the terms rejected. The senate itself, as the embodiment of the ruling oligarchy, had a general disinclination to acquire territory abroad. The setup of the magistracies was fundamentally ill-suited to provide for the administration of foreign lands, and various structural reasons made it disadvantageous (from the point of view of the oligarchy) to expand the number of magistrates. This meant that while the Roman political system had a propensity to fight wars, there was at the same time a strong desire to avoid permanent obligations overseas. In effect, the Roman military was used in an irresponsible way: while their successful campaigns for profit destroyed other powers, the Romans would not assume the administrative duties of those powers. In the end, strategic necessity forced the oligarchy against its will to take over the direct government of more and more foreign territory. Eventually the Republican government proved to be incapable of bearing this burden, and in the end it had to be replaced by a military autocracy.

The First Punic War begins the period for which the historical tradition was written by contemporaries. A major source is the Greek historian Polybius, who lived as a hostage in Rome in the mid–second century B.C. and wrote a history of Rome. While he was greatly concerned with accuracy, his style was not well thought of in antiquity, and for this reason his work is preserved in (often extensive) fragments that begin with the First Punic War. The annalistic history of Livy is lost for most of the earlier third century B.C. but resumes in 219 B.C. He provides us with very detailed knowledge of the politics and wars down to 167 B.C., after which the work is lost. We are much less well informed about the mid–second century B.C., but what does survive is much more reliable than the tradition for the period before the start of the historical tradition. Hence, we can now begin to form judgments about the behavior of individuals and the collective actions and decisions of the Roman oligarchy.

4

STRUGGLE WITH CARTHAGE,

264 B.C.–146 B.C.

Soon after subduing Italy, the Romans began their first overseas war, against the Carthaginians. The Carthaginians were a Semitic people. In the early first millennium B.C., the Phoenicians, who inhabited the central portion of the coast of the eastern Mediterranean, began to engage heavily in trade. In the western Mediterranean, they set up numerous way stations for their trading enterprises. Because of their concentration on trade, these Phoenicians in the west were not particularly interested in agriculture, occupation of large tracts of territory, or the establishment of extensive political organizations. Administration was provided by the major cities in Phoenicia, especially Tyre. In the early sixth century B.C., Tyre was subjected to a prolonged siege, and at this time one settlement in the west assumed leadership of the rest: Carthage. Ancient tradition holds that Carthage was founded in what is now Tunisia on the coast of North Africa in 814 B.C., and archaeology suggests that the real date was only a few decades earlier. The Phoenician settlers in the west are known as the Punics (from the Latin word for "Phoenician"), but from the sixth century B.C. on the term "Carthaginian" refers to the residents not simply of that city but to all the Punic settlements that acknowledged Carthaginian leadership. Eventually, the Romans came to have a distinct hostility towards the Carthaginians (for example, the phrase "Punic faith" in Latin signified "bad faith"). Whether this attitude was a consequence of the huge losses that the Romans would suffer during the Second Punic War or predates it cannot be readily decided, but certainly the Carthaginians would have seemed alien to the Romans (even more than the Etruscans, who were culturally very similar to their neighbors even if their language was not). The language and gods of the Carthaginians were quite different from anything the Romans were familiar with. In particular, their gods had the unpleasant habit of demanding child sacrifice (some scholars wish to deny the practice, but the literary and archaeological evidence for the practice is irrefutable).

Since they were traders and not interested in the occupation of the interior, the Carthaginians did not have a large agricultural population from which to raise native troops and found it more cost-effective to hire mercenaries (often from southern Italy) for their armies. Scholars of the nineteenth century, who were used to conscripted national armies, disparaged this practice, but it is hard to see what alternative there was, and in any case, with one major exception, the Carthaginians were well served by their mercenaries.

In the eighth century B.C., the Greeks began to settle eastern Sicily, while at the same time Punic settlements were founded on the western end of the island, and for centuries each side struggled to conquer the other's territory. The major Greek settlement was Syracuse, and as recently as 278 B.C. the Carthaginians had come close to overwhelming it. The Syracusans appealed to Pyrrhus, who in 277 B.C. decisively beat back the Carthaginians. By the time of his withdrawal from Italy the next year, the Romans had subdued Italy as far as the Straits of Messena, and their sphere of influence now abutted on Sicily, which the Carthaginians considered their own sphere. In preceding centuries, the Romans had made a few treaties with the Carthaginians, but now they would fight them for control of Sicily.

The immediate cause of the war was the town of Messana (modern Messena) on the straits separating Sicily from Italy. In the late fourth century B.C., Campanian mercenaries (Mamertines) hired by the Greeks had seized the town, and after Pyrrhus' departure, they were attacked by Hiero, tyrant of Syracuse. They asked for and received a Carthaginian garrison, but some of the Mamertines thought better of this and requested Roman assistance against the Carthaginians.

When the senate received the Mamertines' appeal for help, it was unable to reach a decision. Some argued that since Rome had recently punished a Campanian garrison for acting similarly, they could hardly blame the Carthaginians. Others said that if the Carthaginians gained control of Sicily, the next step would be an attack on Italy. After the deadlock, the senate allowed the People to decide the matter. At the prompting of the consul, they agreed to grant the Mamertines protection, which would lead to war. Some scholars maintain that the Romans were justified in feeling threatened by the Carthaginians, but it is perverse to call this a defensive war when the Romans attacked to prevent the possibility of a Carthaginian attack. There was no particular reason to think that Carthage had either the intention to attack Italy or (perhaps more importantly) the means to do so. It is noteworthy that when the Greek historian Polybius records the reasons given for provoking a war, the prospect of plunder was prominent.

After landing in Messana in 264 B.C., the Romans moved south the following year and when the Romans defeated the Carthaginians, Hiero, the tyrant of Syracuse, abandoned the Carthaginians and joined the Romans. He was to be a loyal ally for fifty years, and a number of other Greek cities in Sicily went over to the Romans. The Romans now had a solid hold of eastern Sicily.

At this point, the Romans gave evidence of the sound grasp of overall strategy and tactical flexibility that was to characterize them. For a few years, the Romans attempted to move to the west, but they soon found that taking one town after another was a difficult and time-consuming task and realized that this was unnecessary if they could gain control of the sea and cut off the Carthaginian forces in Sicily from reinforcements. Therefore, the Romans set about building a fleet from scratch. Naval battles in antiquity were normally decided by outmaneuvering and ramming the opposing force, and the Romans realized that the superior skill of the Carthaginians would give them victory in a conventional battle. In response, the Romans used a clever device called a *corvus* ("crow" in Latin). This was a raised gangplank in the bow of the ship with a large spike on the underside. The plank was dropped onto one of the more maneuverable Carthaginian ships, and the spike held it in place. The Romans could then board the ship and use their superior troops to take it. In effect, they turned naval warfare into land warfare. In 260 B.C., the Romans won a great victory over the Carthaginians in western Sicily (Mylae), but it was not decisive, and the campaigns in Sicily dragged on. The Romans restricted the Carthaginians to the west of the island but could not drive them out. The Carthaginians also made good their naval losses.

In 257 B.C., the Romans again showed their grasp of strategy, deciding that an invasion of the Carthaginian homeland in Africa was necessary to end the war. They fitted out a huge invasion force, and in 256 B.C., both consuls defeated the Carthaginian fleet in Sicily and forced their way to Africa, which they invaded late in the summer. Although they gained much plunder, they could not defeat the Carthaginians before the end of the campaigning season in the fall. The Carthaginians sued for peace, but M. Atilius Regulus, one of the consuls, asked for excessively harsh terms, which the Carthaginians rejected. The Carthaginians were to show on several occasions that when forced into a corner, they would fight back with great determination. The Romans decided that the whole force could not be supplied during the winter in enemy territory, so one consul returned to Italy with part of the troops, leaving 20,000 troops and forty ships under the command of Regulus. He proved to be an inept commander. Meanwhile, the Carthaginians hired a Spartan general to organize their defenses, and in the spring of 255 B.C., he met the Romans in battle with a force about equal in numbers to theirs. Regulus foolishly kept his troops in tight ranks, despite the fact that the Carthaginians had elephants. The elephants broke the Roman ranks, and the Roman army was completely destroyed. The majority were killed; only 3,000 managed to escape, and 500 were captured with Regulus. A Roman fleet of reinforcements defeated a Carthaginian fleet and rescued the survivors. On the way back to Italy, it was caught in a gale, and 184 of 264 ships were dashed against the rocks near Camarina in southern Sicily. Tens of thousands were drowned, and Polybius calls it the greatest naval disaster known to him.

In the winter of 255–254 B.C. the Romans showed their doggedness, building another 140 ships. The Romans also showed their virtually bottomless reserves of manpower by raising more armies. The Carthaginians could not keep up with this. In 254 B.C., the Romans captured the major Carthaginian port of Panormus in northeastern Sicily. This weakened Carthaginian prestige in the area and led to defections of five Greek towns to Rome. The Romans failed to press home their advantage the next year and went on a pointless raid of the African coast east of Carthage. On the way back, they were caught in another gale and lost 150 ships.

Around 250 B.C., the Carthaginians sent the captive ex-consul Regulus to Rome to negotiate an exchange of prisoners. Regulus gave his word of honor to return, and it was presumed that he would argue in favor of the exchange, which would include himself. In this assumption, the Carthaginians proved to be mistaken. Regulus famously spoke against the exchange in the senate, arguing that while the Romans could afford the loss of manpower represented by the captives, the Carthaginians could not, and hence it was in Rome's interest to retain the Carthaginian captives. After successfully pleading his case, Regulus kept his word and returned to Carthage, where his captors not unreasonably tortured him to death. This story about Regulus played an important role in the Roman self-identity in the later Republic. Apart from showing the strong Roman sense of honor, it also indicates their strategic sense.

In 250 B.C., the Romans decided to rebuild their fleet yet again, managing 120. Before it could leave Italy, word came of a major Carthaginian defeat. A force had tried to retake Panormus, and 20,000 of 30,000 Carthaginian mercenaries were lost in the Roman victory. The Romans were elated and decided to use their new fleet in attempting to take Lilybaeum, the most important Carthaginian base in Sicily. This town was strongly fortified, and the Roman siege dragged on. In 249 B.C., however, the Romans suffered even more losses. One fleet suffered a major defeat at Drepana in Sicily, and when the Carthaginians threatened southern Italy, they forced a Roman fleet into an exposed position, where it, too, was dashed against the rocks.

The losses from the numerous Roman naval defeats were staggering. The Roman census of 247 B.C. indicates that the male population of Rome had declined by 17 percent since the start of the war. They did not give up the war, but it was several years before the Romans could return to the attack.

One might expect the Carthaginians to take advantage of their domination of the sea. In fact, in one of the most incomprehensible decisions of antiquity, they decided to lay up their fleet and concentrate on seizing control of the North African interior to the southwest of Carthage. It was apparently decided that Carthage could not afford both a fleet and a large army and opted for the latter. This proved to be an unfortunate decision.

By the winter of 243–242 B.C., the Romans had sufficiently recovered from the debacle of 249 B.C. to build yet another fleet of 200 ships. When this arrived off Drepana in the summer of 242 B.C., there were astonishingly no Carthaginian ships there at all. The Carthaginians managed to reactivate their fleet and send a force of 170 ships, but it was out of practice, undermanned, and burdened with supplies for the garrison. The Romans had in the meanwhile decided to train their fleet in proper seamanship, so when the Carthaginians tried to force their way past the Romans into Drepana, they suffered a major defeat. Having no remaining resources, they immediately sued for peace.

The victorious consul settled initial peace terms, but these proved unacceptable in Rome, where they were made harsher. The Carthaginians were forced to abandon Sicily and pay a large fine over ten years.

The Roman victory in this monumental war can be explained on the following grounds:

- Determination. Once the Romans resolved to attack, they kept at it regardless of unbelievable losses. Polybius remarks on the huge numbers lost in this war compared to the wars of the Hellenistic kings.
- Inventiveness and adaptability. Though not by nature a maritime people, the Romans quickly realized that control of the sea was necessary and went about securing it for themselves. First they tried the *corvus* as a way to make up for their lack of a naval tradition and eventually decided that they simply had to learn to be proper sailors.
- Reserves of manpower. The Romans not only were undaunted by the vast losses of men they suffered but came back again and again with new armies and fleets. It is noteworthy that there is no sign of revolt on the part of the Roman allies despite the huge losses. The Carthaginians were simply unable to continue the war indefinitely, while the Romans apparently were.

The only time when the Carthaginian practice of relying on mercenaries to provide the bulk of their army caused trouble was in the aftermath of the First Punic War. In 241 B.C., the troops evacuated from Sicily went into revolt and began to plunder the territory outside of Carthage when it turned out that the Carthaginians lacked the money to make good on the rewards promised to the troops. Various non-Phoenician populations joined them, and the garrison in Sardinia also revolted. The war was bloody and cruel, but the Carthaginians used all their efforts to crush the mercenaries, destroying one army in 239 B.C. and the rest the following year.

During the revolt in Africa, the Romans behaved impeccably, but in 238 B.C., they completely changed their attitude. They took the rebels in Sardinia under their protection, and when the Carthaginians objected, the Romans declared war on them. Being in no position to resume war, the Carthaginians immediately sued for peace, which was granted on the condition that they surrender Sardinia and pay a heavy fine. This action on the part of the Romans was totally outrageous. Even Polybius, who is normally well disposed to the Romans, finds it completely unjustifiable. It is also odd, given the Romans' previous neutrality. In any case, the Carthaginians were completely embittered against the Romans, who were to pay dearly for their injustice.

The Romans spent the next two decades consolidating their position. In 227 B.C., they created two new praetors to govern Sicily and Sardinia. They also engaged in a number of campaigns to subdue the population between the Po and the Alps (Cisalpine Gaul) and to intervene in disputes among the quarrelsome Illyrian populations along the eastern shore of the Adriatic. While the Romans established a permanent presence north of the Po, they merely wished to set up a protectorate along the Adriatic to avoid any problems spilling over into Italy. These activities were cut short by a new war with the Carthaginians.

At the end of the First Punic War and the humiliating outrage committed by Rome in stealing Sardinia, there was much resentment against Rome among the Carthaginians. It was clear that they needed a source of manpower like that of Rome, and they began to expand into the interior and north of Spain. This expansion was begun by Hamilcar Barca, who landed in Gades (modern Cadiz) with his nine-year-old son Hannibal in 237 B.C. In 228 B.C., Hamilcar died campaigning and was succeeded in command by his son-in-law Hasdrubal, who founded a major fortified town called New Carthage (modern Cartagena) as the main Punic position in Spain. In 226 B.C., a Roman embassy came to find out what he was doing, and Hasdrubal apparently agreed not to advance north of the river "Iber" (perhaps the modern Ebro). In 221 B.C., Hasdrubal was assassinated by some unhappy locals, and Hannibal now assumed command of the Carthaginian forces in Spain.

Hannibal is undoubtedly one of the great generals of history. He ran the Romans ragged for nearly twenty years, and his eventual defeat was the result of superior Roman resources. Because of the massive damage he inflicted on them, the Romans detested him, and the details of his life are sometimes colored by fiction. One story has it that when Hasdrubal brought Hannibal to Spain, he had him swear an oath of undying enmity against the Romans. Whether true or not, the story must basically represent his feelings. Any sensible Carthaginian should have been able to recognize that Carthage's mortal enemy was Rome. Having learned the lessons of the previous war, Hannibal set out to destroy Rome by attacking their power directly in Italy.

The immediate cause of the war was Hannibal's attack on Saguntum, a Greek town on the central Mediterranean shore of Spain south of the Iber. Apparently such a town should not have been covered by Hasdrubal's treaty agreeing not to advance north of the Iber (which would have allowed him a free hand south of it). Later Roman writers were eager to make Hannibal an aggressor and claimed Saguntum was north of the Iber, but this is false. Polybius, our most reliable source, does say that in attacking the town, Hannibal violated the agreement, but he is not specific as to why, and the legal technicalities remain problematical. Regardless of the specific circumstances, Hannibal was certainly trying to provoke a war. In the spring of 219 B.C., he attacked the town (ostensibly in defense of a local tribe that had been attacked by Saguntum), and it fell after an eight-month siege. At this time, the Romans were involved in Illyria and oddly did nothing. In the spring of the following year, the Romans sent an embassy to Carthage demanding the surrender of Hannibal. When they refused to do so, war was declared.

The Romans decided to tackle the two main Carthaginian centers at once. One consul, P. Cornelius Scipio, was to take an army to Spain via southern Gaul, and the other was to take troops to Sicily and to prepare for an invasion of Africa.

To Hannibal it was obvious that so long as Rome possessed the huge manpower reserves of Italy, there was no question but that Rome would win in the end. Hence he decided to strike at the heart and take an army into Italy. In May, he left New Carthage with a large force, and after subduing the north of Spain in August, he crossed the Pyrenees with 50,000 foot, 9,000 cavalry, and thirty-seven elephants.

By September, he had reached the river Rhone. There Scipio and his army en route to Spain were within a few days' march of Hannibal, but instead of attacking him Scipio sent the army on to Spain under the command of his brother Gnaeus and hurried to Italy to meet Hannibal with some forces that were operating in the north against a local disturbance. Already, the Roman superiority in manpower was beginning to manifest itself. By late October, Hannibal reached the Alps and took two weeks moving his army (including elephants) over the mountains into Italy in the face of opposition from tribesmen. This was an astonishing feat. By the time of his arrival, he had lost about half of the force he had had when crossing the Rhone, but his army was reinforced when the local Gauls joined him.

By this time, news of his march on Italy had led to the recall of the army moving to Carthage. In late December, the Romans met Hannibal at the river Trebia in northern Italy. Hannibal's superior tactics resulted in a rout of the Romans, who lost about half of their 36,000 foot. Hannibal's losses were much fewer (though most of the surviving elephants died). After the battle, Hannibal pointedly released the non-Roman prisoners. Clearly, his intention was to undermine the allegiance of Rome's allies.

The following spring (217 B.C.), Hannibal marched south into Etruria. The main Roman army was caught by Hannibal in a trap on the shores of Lake Trasimene, and 15,000 were killed (including the consul) and 10,000 taken prisoner. Again Hannibal released the non-Romans. After the battle, Hannibal moved to the Adriatic coast and advanced south to Apulia with the intention of fomenting defection among Rome's allies in southern Italy.

In response to this second massive defeat at the hands of Hannibal, the old office of dictator was revived – it had not been used in three decades – and given to Q. Fabius Maximus. His response to Hannibal's military invincibility was to avoid battle while keeping in close contact with him to limit his mobility and prevent any other action on his part (in particular, plundering). Such a policy is called "Fabian tactics," and it earned him the not entirely laudatory nickname *Cunctator* ("delayer"). Fabius picked Hannibal up in Apulia and shadowed him as he moved into Campania. Later he was credited with saving the situation for Rome, but this policy was not immediately popular. It took one more defeat to convince the Romans of the wisdom of avoiding a direct confrontation with Hannibal.

Fabius' term as dictator expired before the new consuls for 216 B.C. took up their office in March. They were determined to bring Hannibal to battle. Polybius says that they were given eight legions with 40,000 men, which with the addition of the allies means a total of 80,000. There is some doubt as to the exact figure, but clearly their army was very large.

Hannibal seized the strategically important position of Cannae in Apulia, and the consuls joined battle with him there. Hannibal's victory is the classic example of victory through encirclement. Surrounded on all sides, the Roman army was annihilated. Only 15,000 escaped death or capture. It is somewhat harder to assess the number of those killed, but it may have amounted to 50,000. One of the consuls was killed, along with an ex-consul from the preceding year, about half of the officers, and eighty other senators. Hannibal had rich men's gold rings collected in baskets to be poured out onto the floor of the Carthaginian senate as a sign of the extent of his victory. Hannibal once more released non-Roman prisoners.

Hannibal did not march on Rome. Though he is often criticized for this decision, it is hard to see how he could have done so, since he had no siege equipment. He did, however, finally bring about some revolts among Rome's allies. Some of the Apulian towns and most of the Samnites went over to Hannibal, but his major acquisition was Capua. This was one of the largest towns in Italy and the leading community of Campania. Capua's revolt led to the defection of a few small Campanian towns, but most stayed loyal to Rome.

Disaffection spread among Rome's Greek allies. In 215 B.C., Hiero, the tyrant of Syracuse and Rome's loyal ally since the First Punic War, died. His son was assassinated, and the town was induced to declare war on Rome in 214 B.C. Two years later, Hannibal captured Tarentum in southern Italy through betrayal, and in response to its revolt several other major Greek towns of southern Italy went over to him.

Once more the Romans responded to adversity with determination, making every effort to increase the number of legions. They raised new legions not only by releasing debtors and accused criminals from jail but even by freeing slaves (a very un-Roman thing to do). By 211 B.C., there were apparently twenty-five legions (in a normal year, there were only four). The coffers of the state were empty, and the armies in Sicily were told they had to provide for themselves. When Roman captives came to the senate after Cannae to arrange an exchange of prisoners, this was soundly rejected. Even as the Romans tried to maintain their manpower, it was all the more important to deny Hannibal any reinforcements.

The years 215–213 B.C. were marked in Italy by a whole series of campaigns, with Hannibal trying to take new towns, while the Romans recovered rebel towns. In 213 B.C., the Romans sent a force to besiege Syracuse, which capitulated two years later. By 212 B.C., they also began the siege of Capua, and the next year Hannibal tried to draw the Romans away with a feint on Rome, but the Romans did not raise the siege and the town soon capitulated. The year 211 B.C. thus marks the end of Hannibal's great hopes, the Romans having weathered the storm that followed Cannae. Once again their resources in manpower, the loyalty of their allies and their determination allowed them to overcome seemingly insurmountable disasters.

Now that the tide had turned in Italy, the Romans could undertake campaigns abroad to undermine Hannibal's strategic position while still fielding large armies against him. In order to prevent Hannibal from receiving any aid from Philip of Macedon, they began a somewhat desultory campaign in Greece in 211 B.C. (see pp. 77–78). Of more immediate effect against the Carthaginians, the Romans could send new forces to Spain, where, in 211 B.C., the troops that had marched there in 218 B.C. suffered a major defeat.

Back in 218 B.C., Gnaeus had taken the army of his brother the consul to Spain and established himself in northeastern Spain, thereby preventing any reinforcements from leaving to help Hannibal. The next year, the senate sent Publius to bring his brother reinforcements, and the two acted as joint commanders. There was indecisive fighting for some years, but a revolt in Africa in 214–213 B.C. led to many Carthaginian troops being diverted there. In 212 B.C., the Scipio brothers retook Saguntum. In this period, they not only prevented any assistance from reaching Hannibal but even established a major Roman presence in an area crucial to the Carthaginians.

The year 211 B.C. was disastrous for the Romans in Spain. In separate engagements, the Scipio brothers were defeated. Both were killed, and a non-senator actually assumed their *imperium* to command such of the Roman troops as had survived. This was completely unconstitutional, but what else was to be done? The Romans retreated to the Ebro.

By now Syracuse and Capua had been recaptured, so the Romans could afford to send reinforcements, which arrived in late 211 B.C. The next year, the Romans decided to elect a special commander for Spain instead of sending one of the regular magistrates or a promagistrate. P. Cornelius Scipio, son of one of the recently defeated commanders in Spain and nephew of the other, was chosen. He was only twenty-five years old and had never held a position of *imperium* before. This turned out to be a good choice: Scipio would first conquer Spain and then defeat Hannibal in battle.

In late 210 B.C. Scipio arrived with 30,000 troops. He planned a decisive stroke for the next spring (209 B.C.). Scipio took advantage of disunity among the Carthaginian commanders, and in a daring surprise assault, he seized New Carthage. In one blow, he seriously undermined the Carthaginian position. A number of nearby tribes went over to the Romans, and the Carthaginians withdrew to the interior and south.

The next year (208 B.C.) Scipio fought a battle with Hannibal's brother Hasdrubal at Baecula in southern Spain. Hasdrubal was tactically defeated but managed to extricate most of his force. He then abandoned Spain to march to the assistance of his brother in Italy. In 207 B.C., reinforcements were sent from Carthage, and in the following year, Scipio decisively defeated the Carthaginians at Ilipa. The Carthaginian position in Spain was now totally undermined. In 205 B.C., Scipio returned to Italy to be elected consul.

In 209 B.C., the Romans recaptured Tarentum and felt confident in their ability to put an end to Hannibal. For the next year, they elected as consul M. Claudius Marcellus, the man who had retaken Syracuse back in 211 B.C. He was the only general with the stomach to attack Hannibal directly, but he was killed in a minor skirmish. At this point, the Romans learned that Hannibal's brother Hasdrubal had slipped out of Spain with 20,000 troops and was going to spend the winter in southern Gaul. Above all, the Romans had to prevent Hasdrubal from reaching Hannibal.

In the spring of 207 B.C., Hasdrubal crossed into Italy. Hannibal dared not abandon his base in the far south to meet his brother at the Po (if he did so, the Romans were likely to seize his allies). Hence, Hasdrubal would have to move south either through Etruria or along the Adriatic coast. The Romans kept one army with Hannibal while the rest of their troops were kept divided until Hasdrubal's route became known. At this point, luck intervened.

The capture of a messenger revealed the brothers' plans, which allowed the Romans to concentrate their forces. At the river Metaurus along the Adriatic, the Romans launched their attack on an outnumbered Hasdrubal, who lost the battle and his life. Thus the only substantive attempt to reinforce Hannibal ended in failure, and his days in Italy were numbered.

In 206 and 205 B.C., Hannibal was kept hemmed in in the south. The Carthaginians landed another force in northern Italy, but it made no serious efforts to move south. In 204 B.C. the Romans continued to retake towns in the south, and in the following year both the northern force and Hannibal's were recalled to defend Carthage.

After Scipio was elected consul for 205 B.C., a vehement argument broke out in the senate as to what the next step should be. Eventually, he won the right to invade Africa but was not given much in the way of resources. In 204 B.C., he landed in North Africa, where he began to besiege Utica for use as a base but had to withdraw to winter quarters before the town was taken. In the next spring (203 B.C.), he renewed his siege of Utica and defeated a Carthaginian army, gaining control of the countryside. The Carthaginian commanders quickly rebuilt their forces and met Scipio in battle again. He completely outflanked them and destroyed the force. At this point, the Carthaginians recalled Hannibal from Italy and launched a final desperate naval attack on Scipio's fleet at Utica. Though there were some Roman losses, the Romans had clearly not suffered a major defeat.

At this point, the Carthaginians sued for peace. The Carthaginians at length accepted Scipio's terms, which were sent to Rome. They were approved after some delay in the winter of 203–202 B.C., but in the meanwhile Hannibal returned to Carthage.

When a Roman supply convoy was driven ashore near Carthage, it was seized by the hungry populace. When Scipio sent envoys to complain, they were attacked: under the influence of Hannibal's return, the Carthaginians repented of their surrender. Since it was already known that the senate had ratified the terms, the attack on the envoys was a deliberate rejection of the terms. As the matter turned out, the Carthaginians should have accepted them.

Scipio devastated the interior towns and waited for cavalry from Masinissa, a Numidian prince who had led a rebellion against the Carthaginians. Hannibal came to oppose Scipio but could not join battle before the arrival of the Numidians. Scipio and Hannibal met in a battle known (inaccurately) as Zama. The result was a complete defeat for the Carthaginians. Hannibal had now been defeated and fled the field.

The Carthaginians now surrendered again and received worse terms than before. The Carthaginians would lose all territory except for the immediate vicinity of Carthage, which would remain free. The Carthaginians' military was severely limited, they were prevented from waging war without Roman permission, and they had to pay 10,000 talents in fifty annual installments. In addition, Masinissa, who was recognized as king in Numidia, was given title to all the land of his ancestors, a vague provision that would cause the Carthaginians much trouble in the future. In effect, the broader Punic empire in the western Mediterranean was broken up, and the city of Carthage reduced to a Roman tributary. Hannibal had to persuade the Carthaginians to accept these harsh terms (there was really no alternative); in Rome the consul of 201 B.C. objected, wanting the war for himself, but the peace terms were accepted. After his triumph, Scipio received the title *Africanus* – "the conqueror of Africa."

Rome and Carthage remained at peace with each other throughout the next fifty years. This was the result of Roman engagement in the east rather than any lessening of Roman dislike of Carthage. In 191 B.C., the Carthaginians offered to pay off at once the annual tribute they owed for the next forty years, but the senate refused the offer, not wishing to allow the Carthaginians to cease to be obligated to Rome. The same year the Carthaginians offered a large amount of grain to help the Romans in their war in Greece, but the senate insisted on paying for the grain, again to avoid any Roman obligation. In effect, the Romans were refusing to engage in the kind of relationship involving the exchange of favors: if the Romans accepted a favor from their subordinates the Carthaginians, they would in some sense be beholden to them. By paying money for the grain, the Romans made sure that the exchange was a purely monetary arrangement without any further implications.

The Romans repeatedly allowed their ally, King Masinissa of Numidia, to take advantage of the terms of the treaty of 201 B.C. to harass the Carthaginians. According to the treaty, Carthage could not wage war without Rome's consent, and Masinissa was to recover the lands held by his ancestors without the nature of this claim being defined. Apparently the borders had been fixed by Scipio Africanus, but Masinissa repeatedly encroached upon Carthaginian territory, and the Carthaginians had no choice but to seek relief from the Roman senate. Though it is not true that the Romans actively incited Masinissa, they did generally favor him.

Masinissa's depredation occurred about every ten years, generally when Rome was occupied elsewhere (193, 182, 172, ca. 162 B.C.). In the first three instances, the senate's responses appear not to have been completely in Masinissa's favor. In 162–161 B.C., however, the senate made a major decision in his favor, which cost Carthage 500 talents per year in lost revenue. Throughout the 150s B.C., a series of equally unsuccessful Carthaginian embassies met with failure in Rome, and there was a notable souring of Carthaginian feeling towards Rome. At the same time, a leading senator named Cato the Elder, who had fought during the Second Punic War, ended every opinion he gave in the senate by stating, "Besides which, it is my view that we must destroy Carthage." Though Cato's opinion met with some opposition, there appears to have been a general shift in the direction of a belligerent attitude towards Carthage in the 150s B.C., when the fifty-year peace would expire. No doubt many Romans still harbored a great hostility toward the city as a result of Hannibal's depredations, and in any case, there was much booty to be had in seizing Carthage, whose economic prosperity had already been reviving in the 190s B.C. Finally, the Romans' many victories in the east had given them a confidence in their military prowess, which in turn made it seem that the conquest of Carthage would be easy. Hence, when war was declared, it was easy to raise troops for the campaign, which was not the case with wars in Spain. This confidence would prove to be mistaken.

The continued Roman support of Masinissa against Carthage led to the rise to power in Carthage of a "democratic" government that was opposed to the old oligarchy that had cooperated with the Romans. In 151 B.C., when Masinissa besieged a Carthaginian town, the new government sent 25,000 troops to relieve it. As it turned out, the inexperienced Carthaginian force was wiped out, but more importantly, the Carthaginians had violated the provision of the peace treaty that they should not wage war without Roman consent.

For some reason, war was not declared in 150 B.C. It was clear that war was coming, however, and the town of Utica immediately north of Carthage surrendered to the Romans. The Carthaginians themselves tried to negotiate with the Romans. In 149 B.C., Carthaginian envoys sailed to Rome, where they found that the Romans had already declared war but were willing to preserve the city if the Carthaginians turned over hostages and obeyed the consuls. The consuls then crossed over to Africa with a very large force – 80,000 infantry and 4,000 cavalry – and demanded the surrender of Carthaginian arms. After the Carthaginians complied, the consuls decreed that the Carthaginians had to abandon the town itself for destruction and could settle wherever they wanted in Carthaginian territory, provided that the new site was at least ten miles from the sea. Such a move was clearly impossible for a trading city, and the Carthaginians refused, declaring war on the Romans. The Carthaginians would prove once more that under desperate circumstances they would fight fiercely; they made huge numbers of weapons (presumably not having surrendered everything before) and freed their slaves in return for their military services.

The consuls of 149 B.C. did not accomplish much. Though one did temporarily breach Carthage's walls, a Carthaginian army outside the walls prevented any exploitation of the success. One consul returned to Rome at the end of the year to hold elections, and the other suffered losses in trying to find a base for his huge force in the winter of 149–148 B.C.

The consul of the next year (148 B.C.) was kept busy with attacks on various towns around Carthage, though at the end of the year another ultimately unsuccessful breach was made in the wall. At the consular elections for the next year, popular dissatisfaction with the slow course of the campaign broke out, and there was serious agitation that P. Cornelius Scipio Aemilianus, the adoptive grandson of P. Scipio Africanus, should be elected consul. Being underage and not having held the prerequisite junior magistracies, Aemilianus was doubly debarred from holding the consulship, but popular feeling ran so high that the senate arranged for the electoral law to be suspended in that year to allow Aemilianus to become consul.

In 147 B.C., Aemilianus spent much time restoring discipline to the Roman army. He also secured his rear, forcing the Carthaginian army in the field to withdraw into the city (this allowed the Romans freedom of movement in the countryside). In order to cut off Carthage totally he had a huge mole built to block the entrance to their harbor (the work is estimated to have involved the placement of about 15,000 cubic yards of large rocks in the sea). The Carthaginians cleverly built another exit for their harbor and improvised a new fleet from old parts. Their efforts were not rewarded: when the new fleet amazingly appeared, it did not immediately attack the unprepared Roman fleet due to inexperience, which allowed the Romans to recover. In the actual battle three days later, the Roman fleet won.

By the spring of 146 B.C., Aemilianus felt that Carthage was ready to be taken, and he launched an attack from the sea. After the Romans captured the walls, the Carthaginians burned the nearby streets. The Romans took permanent possession of the wall this time and now had to fight their way from the harbor district towards the citadel, being forced for six days to take one building after another. This sort of street fighting is virtually unheard of in antiquity (once the walls were breached, resistance was pretty much hopeless and surrender normally followed). The continuing resolve of the Carthaginians is a measure of their desperation.

By the seventh day, the Romans reached the citadel, and the Carthaginians offered to come out voluntarily if their lives were spared. Aemilianus agreed, and 50,000 emerged, but 900 Roman deserters refused to surrender and defended themselves in the precinct of the largest and most opulent temple in Carthage. Eventually, they set the temple on fire and died in the flames. The survivors were sold into slavery, and the town was stripped of its valuables and burned for ten days. The land was then cursed (the story that it was sown with salt is a later invention). Carthage ceased to exist.

It was decided to annex the territory of Carthage. Towns that had remained loyal to Carthage were destroyed, and those that had supported Rome were rewarded. A head tax was assessed on all adults in the province and a form of tribute based on land imposed. Though it was decided that a

Roman magistrate should now serve as the proconsul of Africa (as the annexed Carthaginian territory was called), no new position as praetor was created (see pp. 94–95 for an explanation). Africa would be a relatively peaceful province throughout the Republic, and hence we know little of its development during this time.

5

WARS IN THE EAST, 215 B.C.–146 B.C.

Strategic considerations led the Romans to become involved in the Greek-speaking east during the First Punic War, and over the course of the following half century, they engaged in a series of wars there that eventually resulted, rather against the Romans' will, in a permanent Roman presence and the creation of a province in Macedonia. Before discussion of these developments, it is necessary to begin with a general introduction to the Hellenistic world.

The Classical period of Greece (fifth–fourth centuries B.C.) was characterized by large numbers of city-states of various sizes that were very jealous of their independence and found it hard to cooperate. At this time, the Greek world in the east was restricted to the area of present-day Greece and the Aegean shore of Asia Minor. In the mid–fourth century B.C., Macedon under Philip II came to dominate the Greek city-states, and his son Alexander led them in the conquest of the Persian empire. Greek colonies were set up throughout the Near East, and the Greek language became the cultural lingua franca. These colonies became city-states in their own right and established various relationships with the monarchies in whose territories they stood.

Three major dynasties were set up in the fifty years of war that followed Alexander's death in 323 B.C. (The period of Greek history lasting from that date until the Roman victory at Actium in 31 B.C. is called "Hellenistic.") In Egypt, the Ptolemaic dynasty ruled (all the males were called Ptolemy). In the second century B.C., its rulers were fairly ineffectual. In the Near East was the Seleucid dynasty. By 200 B.C., it had lost control of Asia Minor, but Antiochus III (223–187 B.C.) gained the title "the Great" by reestablishing control over the areas east of Mesopotamia. Finally, the Antigonid dynasty ruled in Macedon. It had the difficult task of trying to maintain hegemony over the city-states of mainland Greece. These city-states continued to be just as jealous of their autonomy as they had been in the Classical period. Macedon entered into variance alliances, but crucial to Macedonian control of Greece were their garrisons in three towns which kept open the invasion route from Macedon into southern Greece: Demetrias in Thrace, Chalcis on the island of Euboea, and the Acrocorinth (the citadel of Corinth). These garrisons were known by the opponents of Macedon as the "three fetters" of Greece.

In addition to these major kingdoms, a small but important one grew up in western Asia Minor in the mid–third century B.C. There a dynasty arose that was at first subordinate to the Seleucids but later gained its independence. It is called "Attalid" after the first member of the family to claim the title "king" and ruled from the city of Pergamum.

By the time of their direct involvement in Greek affairs in late third century B.C., the Romans had been under indirect Greek cultural influence for centuries and had been dealing with Greek cities in southern Italy for about a century; Latin literature had been developing in imitation of Greek for about forty years. Thus, while the Romans had no great admiration for the Carthaginians, they were clearly culturally subordinate to the Greeks. This sense of cultural admiration alone was enough for the Romans to adopt a very delicate attitude toward the Greek states. Furthermore, unless the Romans were willing to commit large numbers of troops to the conquest and direct rule of the area, they initially needed to act in cooperation with at least some of the Greeks, which necessitated careful cultivation of Greek public opinion. Over time, Roman military victories would make them less solicitous of Greek opinion.

The first Roman involvement in Greece was the result of the Second Punic War. In 216 B.C., Philip V of Macedon began to interfere in Illyria. The Romans had been active there in the 220s B.C. but became distracted by the war with Hannibal. In the following year, the Romans intercepted a ship that turned out to have a draft treaty between Philip and Hannibal. The treaty was vague in detail but indicated that if Philip and Hannibal won, Rome was to be excluded from the eastern shore of the Adriatic. Given the perilous situation in which the Romans found themselves in the aftermath of the defeat at Cannae, it was imperative to make sure that Hannibal received no help from Philip. In 214 B.C., a Roman fleet made Philip withdraw, but the next year he returned with an army, which could not be opposed with only a fleet. The Romans clearly needed a land force to deal with the situation, and in 211 B.C., they formed an alliance with the Aetolians, who were old enemies of Philip. (The Aetolians were a comparatively primitive Greek population in west-central Greece, and their League was a dominant factor in Greek politics during the third century B.C.) The terms of the treaty were unusually unfavorable for the Romans: they agreed to provide naval help and to take some or all the moveable property when towns were taken, but the towns themselves were to belong to the Aetolians. The Romans clearly had no interest in acquiring permanent property across the Adriatic.

At first the alliance was successful, and the Aetolians captured a few towns, but 209 B.C. was the last year of major success. After that, not much happened, but neither the Romans nor the Aetolians had any interest in formally ending the war. When Philip invaded Aetolia in 207 B.C., the Romans provided their allies with no assistance, and despite Roman objections, the Aetolians sued for peace in 206 B.C. In the next year, the Romans belatedly sent a modest military force, but with the loss of the Aetolian alliance, the Romans could do little by themselves and reached an agreement with Philip that pretty much recognized the status quo.

This desultory war, dignified with the designation "First Macedonian War," had served its purpose of keeping Hannibal from receiving any reinforcements from the east. Immediately after the settlement of peace with Carthage, the Romans resumed the war in a much more vigorous manner.

Why exactly the Romans decided to declare war on Philip is not entirely clear. It used to be thought that the Romans were justifiably angry at him for his "stab in the back" in reaching an alliance with Hannibal, though it is not clear why he should not have done so and how this constituted a stab in the back. This was also considered another "defensive" war, in that he threatened the Roman "protectorate" in Illyria. This again is rather perverse: the Romans had no more right to it than he did, and in any case, they showed no great concern about the area. Yet another explanation is Philhellenism ("the love of Greece"). There is no real evidence for such an attitude, which seems to take at face value the propaganda made in support of the Roman cause during the war. Finally, there is yet again the possibility that the Roman magistrates were concocting a war for their own benefit. Certainly, the manner in which the centuriate assembly actually rejected the initial war vote suggests that the war was not at first very popular.

By 203 B.C., Philip had made some insignificant inroads in the Roman protectorate in Illyria, and once the Romans made it clear that they had taken notice, he turned his attention to the Aegean. In 201 B.C., he was at war with Pergamum, Rhodes (a large island off the southern coast of Asia Minor), and Athens, and late in that year an embassy from these opponents of Philip arrived in Rome to seek Roman assistance against him. Clearly, the Greek states were trying to get Rome involved for their own purposes. The senate determined on war, and envoys were sent east to demand that Philip stop waging war on the Greeks and make reparations to the king of Pergamum. The senate also voted Macedon as a province for one of the consuls of 200 B.C.: P. Sulpicius Galba, who had served there during the First Macedonian War, received the command.

Upon entering office, Galba asked the centuriate assembly to declare war. At a preliminary meeting a tribune argued against it, and for the only time in the entire history of the Republic, the assembly voted against a proposed declaration of war. Given the dominance of the well-to-do in the assembly, this vote demonstrates the weariness of most people after two decades of war with Hannibal and clearly shows that the war was generated by the magistrates in cooperation with the senate. Galba took some time arguing his position, and at a second assembly war was declared only when he promised that no veteran troops would be conscripted for service.

In late 200 B.C., Galba crossed over to the Balkans with two legions. He raided the Macedonian border area, gaining plunder and allies among the local princelings. The next spring, he operated in western Macedon, not doing much apart from plundering. After a minor Roman victory, the Aetolians (Rome's old allies in the First Macedonian War) were sufficiently encouraged to declare war on Philip, while the Achaean League (previously an ally of Philip) refused to get involved.

Galba was succeeded in the fall of 199 B.C. by one of the consuls of that year. There was little he could do once winter arrived, and in the spring of 198 B.C., the consul who received Macedon, T. Quinctius Flamininus, showed more energy than his predecessor had and arrived at the beginning of the campaigning season. Flamininus was less than thirty years old, and while he had seen a fair amount of military service in the war against Hannibal, he had only held the quaestorship. What led to such a young and inexperienced man being given such a command is not known. His appointment represented a change in Roman position. When he got to Greece, he negotiated with Philip, who offered to give up his conquests and pay reparations, but Flamininus now demanded that he should evacuate all of Greece (including Thessaly, which had been a part of Macedon for 150 years).

In 198 B.C., Flamininus managed to force his way into Thessaly, but was held up by sieges and decided to winter in Phocis, an area allied with Philip. Philip's military failure plus the propaganda value of Rome's new claim to be the defender of Greek freedom induced most of Greece to go over to Rome. Especially important was the defection of the Achaean League. In November, Flamininus and Rome's Greek allies met Philip to negotiate. Flamininus did not know yet whether he had been prorogued for the next year and was leaving his options open. If he was not prorogued, he would end the war to gain personal prestige. If he was, he could always break off negotiations. To avoid the talks stalling at once, he did not mention the "fetters." When the claims of the allies could not be resolved, Flamininus readily agreed to Philip's request to send an embassy to Rome. By the time it got there, Flamininus knew that he had been prorogued. Hence, as soon as Philip's envoys arrived, Flamininus' friends asked if he was prepared to abandon the fetters. Since this issue had not been raised at the earlier parley, they had no instructions about the question, and the embassy came to an end. This manipulation of events by Flamininus for selfish purposes shows the extent to which a Roman proconsul could dictate public policy to his own advantage.

In the spring of 197 B.C., Flamininus took his two legions and allied troops (mainly Aetolians) into Thessaly. After Philip came down with an army, battle was joined at Cynoscephalae. The fighting took place on rough ground that favored the looser Roman formation, and Philip's army was massacred. Philip now sued for peace and had to agree to whatever the Romans wanted. Their Aetolian allies wanted various towns that had been captured, believing that the old treaty of 212 B.C. was back in force. Apparently they had been led to believe this in 199 B.C., when they joined the Romans again. Flamininus quickly disabused them of this notion, declaring that the treaty had been abrogated when they made peace with Philip in 206 B.C. and that the towns that had voluntarily surrendered were in Rome's control. Since the Aetolians were despised by the other Greeks as uncouth, the latter were pleased at the Aetolians' discomfiture. Flamininus also refused the Aetolian demand that Philip should be deposed. Since Antiochus III (the Seleucid monarch) was at this time gaining territory in Asia Minor, the Romans wished Philip to remain as a counterbalance to him. Furthermore, getting rid of him would benefit only the Aetolians, something the Romans did not want to happen. Finally, Macedon served as a bulwark against the tribes to the north, and if Macedon was eliminated, chaos was likely to ensue. Philip offered to evacuate all of Greece, including the fetters. Flamininus accepted, collecting a small initial indemnity of 200 talents and sending word to the senate, which dispatched a commission of ten senators to assist Flamininus in drawing up a final settlement. It was decided that all Greek cities in Europe and Asia not garrisoned by Philip were to be free, while those garrisoned by him were to be handed over to the Romans by the time of the Isthmian Games (summer 196 B.C.), and that Philip was also to pay 1,000 talents, half immediately, the rest in ten installments. Particularly noteworthy is the inclusion of the Asian cities, some of which were already in Antiochus' hands. The intention was clearly to undermine Antiochus' position in Asia Minor, which indicates that influential Roman opinion was already in favor of intervening there.

The Aetolians, being disgruntled at not receiving much reward, claimed that only the Greek cities of Asia were really free and that the Romans would keep key positions, especially the fetters, for themselves; some of the legates did, in fact, urge that the Romans should keep them. Flamininus, however, successfully argued that Rome should not retain any permanent positions in mainland Greece. At the Isthmian Games in June and July of 196 B.C., the herald proclaimed to the assembled Greeks that the various areas that constituted Greece south of Macedon were to be independent, ungarrisoned, and tribute-free. The response among the Greeks was enthusiastic. For the next two years, Flamininus and the legates worked out the details of the new political arrangements, especially the creation of new leagues.

Why did the Romans act this way? Clearly, this move would, in addition to annoying the Aetolians, win great support for Rome in preparation for a showdown with Antiochus. It may also have reflected some philhellenic sentiment. Yet, it is hard to see what else the Romans could have done. If they had kept the fetters (and perhaps other key positions), then they would have been immediately and permanently involved in the chaotic mess of Greek politics. By letting the Greeks have their freedom, the Romans could win their favor without the trouble of constant supervision – or the difficulty of finding an available magistrate to do so. Furthermore, the Roman conception of freedom was different from that of the Greeks. While the Greeks thought that they were now literally free and could return to their old habits of squabbling with each other, the Roman idea was that the Greeks, while certainly retaining their internal freedom, would be obligated to the Romans for their benefits and would defer to their new Roman "patron" in the same way that a dutiful and grateful Roman client would. It would take some time for the Greeks to understand the full implications of Roman involvement in Greece and of the nature of their "freedom." In the meanwhile, the Romans could prepare for the coming conflict with Antiochus.

Antiochus III (223–187 B.C.) earned himself the title "the Great" by restoring Seleucid control over the eastern regions of Alexander's kingdom beyond Mesopotamia. At the same time that the Romans were proclaiming Greek freedom, he was about to turn his attention to the west and reassert Seleucid control over Asia Minor, which had been lost to the dynasty in the mid-third century. In particular, certain cities specifically mentioned in the Roman proclamation of freedom either already were or were soon to be controlled by Antiochus. He had also established himself in the abandoned town of Lysimachia on the Thracian coast in Europe and was subduing other towns in the area. In 195 and 194 B.C. Antiochus continued to campaign against the Thracians, and in 194 B.C., the Romans fulfilled their promise of freedom by withdrawing their army from Greece. In 193 B.C., Antiochus and the Romans engaged in a diplomatic struggle to gain support in Greece. Flamininus managed to outmaneuver Antiochus by portraying Rome as the beneficent guarantor of Greek freedom, though private statements to Antiochus show that this was an insincere stance. Meanwhile, in 193 and 192 B.C., Antiochus continued to operate in Thrace. The senate seemed to acquiesce in this as long as he did not advance further south. The Romans did not yet have cause to go to war, but the Aetolians would change this.

By now, the Aetolians were thoroughly disgruntled by the Roman presence in Greece: not only had the Romans duped them (as they believed), but their influence prevented the sort of marauding of which the Aetolians were fond. In 193 B.C., they entered into negotiations with Antiochus to persuade him to restore Greek freedom, but he was cautious in his response. In the following year, the Aetolians attempted to seize Sparta, Chalcis, and Demetrias, gaining control of only the last town. At this point, an Aetolian official visited Antiochus in Ephesus. He exaggerated Greek enthusiasm for Antiochus' cause, and this alone seems to have induced him to cross over to Greece in the fall of 192 B.C., with a clearly inadequate force of 10,000 men. Apparently, he decided that he would have to wage war with the Romans sooner or later, and if he neglected the opportunity provided by Aetolian hostility to the Romans and their capture of Demetrias, he might never get a better chance of success. He might also have calculated that with the withdrawal of the Roman army, the Roman threats were just bluster; if this was his calculation, he was wrong.

Antiochus' arrival in Demetrias meant war, and the conflict is known as the Syrian War. A praetor immediately crossed over to Epirus with two legions to give the Romans a base, and one of the consuls of 192 B.C. was instructed to raise an army immediately so that one of the next year's consuls could leave directly in the spring.

Antiochus soon discovered the falseness of Aetolian claims. Virtually no Greek cities voluntarily went over to him. Why should they? They now enjoyed more real freedom than they had in more than 150 years of Macedonian domination. By the time that the consul of 191 B.C. arrived in the spring, the praetor sent the preceding fall and Philip had already undermined the gains made by the Aetolians in Thessaly. Antiochus' position in the mainland was then completely undermined by the consul's arrival with 20,000 Italians (plus numerous Greek and Illyrian allies). All Thessaly surrendered, and Antiochus now had to choose between the humiliation of fleeing to Asia and an attempt to fight the Romans in a place where he could counterbalance their numerical superiority. Preferring the latter course, he tried to block the Roman advance from the north at Thermopylae. After he was outflanked, just as the Spartans had been 300 years before, and his entire army annihilated, he fled to Ephesus.

The Romans now determined to carry the war into Asia. Scipio Africanus' brother Gnaeus was elected consul for 190 B.C. and was given Asia as his province. Africanus himself could not be elected, since there was a prohibition against reelection within a ten-year interval, but he was to act as his brother's subordinate, it being expected that he would take actual command. First, the Scipios arranged for a six-month truce with the Aetolians, who were left in the lurch by Antiochus' precipitous withdrawal from Greece, and by October the Roman army had marched overland into Asia. At this point, Antiochus offered to give up his conquests and pay for half the cost of the war. The Romans demanded the evacuation of all of Asia Minor and the full cost of the war. Antiochus rejected these terms, and a decisive battle was fought in December at the city of Magnesia ad Sipylum. Although Antiochus had a two-to-one numerical superiority, his quickly assembled, rag-tag army was completely routed by the Romans. The Scipios now offered preliminary terms, which were accepted by Antiochus and ratified in Rome. He abandoned Asia Minor and paid a large indemnity (15,000 talents).

One of the consuls of 189 B.C. had already been granted the war in Asia as his province before news of the victory at Magnesia reached Rome. Hence, he moved east in 189 B.C. with the ten-man senatorial commission to settle affairs in Asia. As a "consolation prize," he was allowed to wage war against the Galatians (Gauls who had settled in central Asia Minor in the mid–third century B.C.), who had been Antiochus' allies.

The difficult question had been what to do with the Asian cities. The commission arrived in Asia with the senate's decision. They first divided Asia Minor into Greek and non-Greek areas. Of the non-Greeks, those north of the river Meander were to go to Eumenes, the king of Pergamum, those south of the river to Rhodes. The Greek towns were divided into two categories, those that had gone over to Rome before the battle of Magnesia being distinguished from the rest. The former alone would be free, while the rest were given to Eumenes or Rhodes.

The years after the settlement with Antiochus saw a perceptible hardening of Roman attitude toward the Greeks that had already begun at the end of the Syrian War. At the beginning of the Roman involvement in Greece, there was a strong tendency for the Romans to deal gingerly with the Greeks, soliciting their good opinion. As Roman military superiority became more apparent, some Romans adopted a less accommodating attitude. In addition, involvement in the squabbles of the wealthy Greek city-states engendered in certain members of the Roman senatorial class an insatiable greed and a willingness to use the force inherent in the Roman military for personal profit of a kind previously unimaginable.

In 189 B.C., after the failure of negotiations, one of the consuls of that year resumed war with the Aetolians and forced them to surrender. While he imposed a small indemnity upon them and restricted the composition of their league, the senate added two terms to make it absolutely clear that the Aetolians were subordinate to the Romans. In addition to having to keep the same friends and enemies as the Roman People, they had to "preserve the empire and sovereignty of the Roman People without deceit." By this the Romans now made explicit what they had thought the Greeks should have been able to figure out on their own: in terms of foreign policy, the Aetolians were to subordinate their own interests completely to those of the Romans – as the Romans understood them.

The Romans also showed themselves to be uncharitable towards their allies. They intentionally left unclear the exact nature of the control that Rhodes was to have over the cities on the mainland granted to the island, and a protracted war resulted. Once the Rhodians established their authority, the senate declared that the original intention had not been that the cities were to be directly controlled by Rhodes, thereby rendering all the Rhodians' efforts pointless. The only reasonable interpretation is that the Romans wished to subvert any strong neighbors, including their own allies. Not surprisingly, this series of events led to a lessening of enthusiasm for Rome among the Rhodians, but this was no longer of great importance to Rome.

The later relations of Philip of Macedon with the Romans were poor. They constantly (and it would seem unjustly) interfered in the 180s B.C. with his position on the Thracian coast and in Thessaly. They even tried to stir up Philip's younger son against him, but he was poisoned under mysterious circumstances. Upon Philip's death in 179 B.C., he was succeeded by his son Perses, who was the anti-Roman candidate for the throne. He seems not to have been as circumspect as his father, and during the 170s B.C., he undertook a number of actions to improve his position in Greece; while these moves were not inherently unreasonable, they increased Roman suspicions. In 172 B.C., Rome's ally Eumenes, king of Pergamum, came to Rome, making all manner of accusations against Perses and casting all his actions in the worst possible light. The consuls were chafing at the bit to declare war, but the senate was not yet ready. Although no effort was made to declare war openly until 171 B.C., already in the fall of the preceding year a praetor was sent with a force to Epirus to secure the invasion routes to Macedon. In addition, envoys were sent to various Greek communities to make sure of their loyalty.

In a meeting with Perses, a consular envoy encouraged him to defend himself against Eumenes' accusations and persuaded him to enter into a truce for the winter. This offer was completely dishonest. The Romans had no intention of negotiating in good faith and were simply stalling to allow themselves time to establish themselves in Greece before the start of the campaigning season the next year and to prevent Perses from making his own preparations. The envoy went on to destroy the Boeotian League, which had a strong democratic element and was hence unreliable from a Roman point of view. When he said he would deal only with the representatives of individual towns, the League fell apart, and only three towns took up Perses' cause.

The Third Macedonian War was finally declared in the spring of 171 B.C., and the consul P. Licinius Crassus moved to Thessaly, where he was worsted in a minor battle. Crassus blamed the Aetolians and arrested five leaders whom he accused of insufficient support of the Roman cause. Now mere lack of enthusiasm was a crime. Meanwhile, Crassus and one praetor of 171 B.C. and another of 170 B.C. happily went around making money by capturing towns – including some that were allies of Rome! When Greek embassies came to Rome to complain, the senate decreed that various steps to make amends should be taken. One of the praetors was by now back in Rome, and when the senate tried to hear complaints against him behind closed doors, he was accused before the assembly of the plebs by tribunes and convicted by all thirty-five tribes. Clearly the magistrates in Greece were out of control, and the senate unable to keep a rein on them; the Roman People were ready to act sternly with such magistrates – if they also failed to achieve victory.

The consul of 170 B.C. achieved nothing, and a commission was sent by the senate to find out why. Not surprisingly, they reported that the army was undisciplined. The consul of the next year brought the army into Macedon, but he, too, achieved little. Finally, in 168 B.C., an effective consul arrived – L. Aemilius Paullus, who had already been consul in 182 B.C. Paullus was as destructive, brutal, and greedy a Roman as they came, but because he was the father of the historian Polybius' friend Scipio Aemilianus, he did not receive his due share of opprobrium in antiquity. After taking the time to train his army properly, Paullus forced Perses to battle at Pydna in June of 168 B.C. The Macedonians fought on broken ground disadvantageous to the phalanx and were completely defeated; the Romans slaughtered 20,000, taking only 6,000 captive.

Following their decisive victory, the Romans had to decide what to do with Macedon. They clearly were still unwilling to establish a permanent presence there. They abolished the kingdom, dividing it into four republics. To prevent cooperation among these republics, they were denied *commercium* and *conubium* (see p. 50) with each other. The Romans also closed the royal gold and silver mines and kept for themselves the old royal taxes (halving the rate). The Roman state could now afford to stop collecting the land tax from Roman citizens.

Victory also meant that it was time to settle accounts with those who had not supported Rome to the fullest. In Aetolia, the pro-Roman faction killed 500 of its opponents and exiled more. Paullus then praised those who had carried out this act, thereby encouraging similar purges elsewhere. In addition, accusations were laid against many others, who were arrested and deported to Italy to be dealt with there. Among these were 1,000 members of the Achaean League, including Polybius, whose father was a leading member of the faction supporting Achaean independence (and hence implicitly opposed to the Romans). All Macedonians of any consequence were also deported to

Italy. Perses was humiliated by being paraded in Paullus' triumph and was kept in miserable circumstances in Italy.

The plunder made from conquering Macedon was immense, but apparently it was not sufficient to satisfy the avarice of Paullus, whose troops were discontented (they felt that Paullus had been keeping too much loot for himself). Accordingly, during his return to Italy in 167 B.C., he took advantage of a decree of the senate stating that Epirus, some of whose leaders had foolishly espoused Perses' cause, should serve as plunder. The area had already been subdued by a praetor, whose camp was near Paullus' and whom Paullus told not to interfere in his actions. He sent envoys to each of seventy towns to say that he would remove the garrisons if they collected all their gold and silver in their market place. When this was all arranged, he commanded his troops to attack all the towns suddenly at the same time on the same day. Through this act of treachery, 150,000 people were enslaved – so many, in fact, that the slave markets were glutted and the troops did not realize as much money as had been expected. This, of course, did no good to the enslaved thousands. It is reported that even a century and a half later, this once thickly populated area was deserted.

In the aftermath of the Third Macedonian War, action was taken against the island of Rhodes. The Rhodians had been a Roman ally for many years, but the senate's treatment of Rhodes after the Syrian War had made the Rhodians ambivalent about Rome. The ineffective consul of 169 B.C. had asked the Rhodians to attempt to negotiate an end to the war with Perses, but after the war turned in the Romans' favor, they claimed that the Rhodians' intervention had been an unfriendly act. Though the Rhodians had those responsible executed, an ambitious praetor tried to impel the Roman People to declare war on the island. Cato the Elder, an influential ex-consul, spoke against war in a famous speech, and the move was dropped. The senate, however, took measures that severely undermined the position of Rhodes. Not only were territories on the mainland taken away, but the Romans granted to Athens the Aegean island of Delos on the condition that it would be a free port (that is, that no duty would be charged on goods passing through). This resulted in a precipitous decline in Rhodian trade. Rhodes now ceased to be a major naval power, which no doubt served in the short run to enhance the image of Rome as the dominant power in Greece. However, the destruction of Rhodes' naval power had unintended consequences, as would often be the case with the irresponsible military victories of the Middle Republic, when the Romans initially took no steps to replace the peace-keeping functions that had been exercised by the powers they had overthrown. In this instance, the absence of the Rhodian navy allowed piracy to become rampant in the eastern Mediterranean, and eventually the Romans would be compelled to undertake major campaigns to rectify the disorders caused by their own actions. In addition, their shabby treatment of Rhodes further undermined the reputation of the Romans as the philhellenic champions of Greek liberty.

The artificial creation of four separate republics out of the kingdom of Macedon turned out in the long run not to be a great success. These states had no traditions of their own, and the peasantry appear to have retained a genuine fondness for the monarchy. A man called Andriscus claimed to be the son of Perses and eventually seized control of the old kingdom. It is indicative of the extent to which the Romans were reluctant to become directly involved in the management of their new empire that it is only at this stage (149 B.C.) that they reacted. A small force was sent under a praetor, and in an event that is fairly common in the history of the later Republic, an inexperienced, newly raised Roman army, led by a mediocre commander, was wiped out. In the following year, the praetor Q. Caecilius Metellus was sent out with another army. Metellus quickly defeated Andriscus and restored order in Macedon. He remained there with his army because trouble was brewing in the south.

Following the Third Macedonian War, 1,000 Achaean leaders were deported to Italy for questionable loyalty (no formal charges were ever laid), and it was only in 150 B.C. that the survivors, who numbered fewer than 300, were allowed to go. The resentment caused by this treatment was heightened by various moves that the Romans undertook in the 160s B.C. to undermine the Achaean League, in particular the removal of various cities from it. The man who controlled the League at this date was Callicrates, the very man who had informed on the 1,000 deportees. Similar "cooperative" Greeks were maintained in power in other Greek cities and leagues through the influence of the Romans. This situation led to the creation of a strong anti-Roman sentiment among those opposed to the leaders in power.

The immediate cause of war was the desire of Sparta to secede from the Achaean League. In the winter of 150–149 B.C., embassies were sent to Rome about the matter; during one of these, Callicrates died, and his loss gave a boost to the anti-Roman factions in the League. Because of the wars in Macedon and Carthage at this time, the senate decided to leave the matter alone temporarily, but an embassy was sent in 147 B.C. Now that the Macedonian revolt had revealed the extent of anti-Roman sentiment, the senate's decision was harsh. Not only was Sparta to be detached from the League, but so were four other towns that had not asked to secede. The reaction was a literal riot among the representatives of the Achaean cities who had been summoned to hear the decision. They attacked the Spartans, who had taken refuge in the lodgings of the Roman envoys. Another embassy was sent from Rome in an attempt to mollify the Greeks, though the decision to remove the cities from the League remained unchanged. The anti-Roman leader of the League prevented any real negotiations from taking place. He had apparently decided that a line had to be drawn somewhere against Roman interference and now resolved to bring matters to a head. It is hard to see what could have led him to believe that the Greek city-states were in a position to defeat the Romans militarily when Philip, Antiochus, and Perses had all tried and failed. In the spring of 146 B.C., the Achaean League refused to comply with the senate's decision and declared war on Sparta, which was tantamount to declaring war on Rome. The Romans made their own declaration of war against the Achaean League.

Metellus still had his army in Macedon and moved south. He also tried to negotiate a peaceful settlement before the consul of 146 B.C., L. Mummius, could arrive with his army. These negotiations proved futile, and Metellus defeated the Achaean forces north of the Peloponnesus at the battle of Scarpheia in Locris. Metellus had managed to advance as far as the Isthmus when Mummius showed up and took over operations. He routed the remaining Achaean forces and captured the city of Corinth.

A senatorial commission of ten was sent to assist Mummius in his settlement. They brought a decree that everything moveable in Corinth was to be sold or transported to Rome and that the city itself was to be razed to the ground. This move was intended to be a permanent example to the Greeks of the meaning of continued opposition to the senate's decisions.

It was finally decided to create a permanent province in Macedon. This would lead to extreme complications in terms of the administrative structure in Rome, because, when this province was created along with another new one in the same year for Africa, no new praetorships were created, as had been the case in the past when new provinces were established. This necessarily meant that prorogation would have to be used every year to provide propraetors or proconsuls to govern certain provinces.

The position on the mainland south of Macedonia was more complicated. The leagues of Greek cities were initially dissolved, though it seems that they were to some extent revived later on. A certain amount of territory among various hostile city-states (including all of the territory of Corinth) was directly confiscated by the Roman People. All the Greek states now had some formal relation with the Roman People, and while there was no permanent Roman magistrate stationed in the mainland, the governor of Macedonia was to intervene as necessary. Southern Greece as a whole was now known as Achaea but would not become a proper province with its own governor until the time of the emperor Augustus.

6

CONQUEST OF SPAIN,
218 B.C.-134 B.C.

During the Second Punic War, the Romans had subdued the Punic position in Spain ("Spain" being understood as the entire Iberian peninsula including modern Portugal). Once the Carthaginians were finally defeated, the Romans could conceivably have withdrawn from Spain, but this seems never to have been considered. The various local populations were by no means reconciled to the new Roman rulers, and throughout the second century (and well into the first), the Romans waged a long series of wars against various groups. While the Romans found it easy to defeat the military forces of the advanced communities of the Greek world, they had a much more difficult job subduing the primitive political organizations of Spain. The Romans also acted in a manner that can easily be characterized unflatteringly. Roman commanders were often guilty of waging war for little or no reason apart from their own greed, abusing their power, and acting in bad faith. Both the senate and magistrates on several occasions broke agreements made with locals. While the problems involved in maintaining Roman control may have been of fleeting importance in themselves, they would cause significant developments in Rome. The misconduct of commanders in the field led to the first efforts in Rome to establish permanent courts to deal with provincial misadministration. Furthermore, the reluctance of potential soldiers to be drafted for military service in the unremunerative and dangerous campaigns in Spain was a major motive behind Ti. Gracchus' proposal for land reform, which marked the beginning of the political turmoil of the Late Republic (see Chap. 8).

Like Italy before the Romans, Spain was at the time of the Roman conquest merely a geographic concept. There were Greek and Punic trading towns on the coast, and the interior was divided up among various linguistic groups. Within each group were local communities, generally centered around a permanent settlement. The linguistic communities sometimes united in times of war, but often did not. In dealing with the natives, the Romans treated with the individual "urban" communities as they surrendered. The inability of the local communities to cooperate expedited the ultimate Roman victory but also made it difficult to achieve a definitive "settlement."

Starting in 210 B.C., the Romans began to hold special elections to give a non-magistrate *imperium* to command the Roman armies in Spain. The exigencies of the war with Hannibal prevented any serious consideration of the long-term implications of Roman involvement, and these "ad hoc" commands show that the senate was not yet ready to make any permanent determination of what to do with the new conquests in Spain. Such elections of temporary commanders continued for more than a decade, but in 198 B.C., it was decided to create two new positions as praetor. One was to rule the areas along the Mediterranean coast (Hispania Citerior or "Nearer Spain"), the other the south (Hispania Ulterior or "Further Spain"); the interior was not yet subjected to Roman control. It was thus clearly decided to make the administration and conquest of Spain a permanent part of the Roman administrative system. In times of military crisis a consul could be assigned to one of the Spanish provinces.

By 199 B.C., the Romans had secured general peace in the areas controlled by them, and this presumably contributed to the decision to create the new praetorships. They also decided to withdraw the Roman legionaries, leaving Italian and local allies to maintain control. This was a bad idea, as revolts soon broke out. Roman legionaries had to be sent back; things became so bad that in 195 B.C., the consul M. Porcius Cato was sent out with additional troops to raise the number of legions from two to four. Because Cato wrote about himself, his achievements were exaggerated in the historical sources. While he did achieve some success, this was not much, given the size of his force. He also spread the war to the Celtiberian areas to the interior of the Closer province (the Celtiberians were a mixture of Celts and native elements). In 194 B.C., Cato returned to Italy with his two legions and celebrated a triumph. The wars continued under the command of praetors and extended to the west as far as the Lusitani on the Atlantic coast (more or less modern Portugal). The wars dragged on with minor Roman successes that were not decisive.

By the late 180s B.C., the Romans were making a serious effort to subdue Celtiberia. In 180 B.C., this campaign was taken over by the praetor Ti. Sempronius Gracchus. He managed to subdue most of Celtiberia and attempted to work out a permanent political settlement that would be acceptable to the various local communities. He apparently had more vision than most Roman commanders and was long after remembered for his integrity. From 175 to 155 B.C., there was peace in Spain. Presumably, the Romans were not yet ready to resume aggressive wars as they were consolidating their position, while the locals needed time to recuperate from the losses they had suffered at the hands of the Romans in earlier wars.

In 154 B.C., the Lusitani, who were still independent, invaded Roman territory, an attack that was to inspire revolt among the Celtiberians; there was uneven fighting for several years until 151 B.C., when Ser. Sulpicius Galba became governor of Further Spain.[1] After 8,000 Lusitani surrendered their weapons to him, he used the opportunity to slaughter them. This act of treachery was to have serious consequences. In Rome, it led to the passage of the first permanent court to try cases of provincial misadministration. One survivor of the massacre was Viriathus, who successfully led the Lusitani against the Romans for almost a decade. The Lusitani were not unnaturally incensed at their treatment, and Viriathus proved a very competent leader. He established a strong position in south-central Spain and defeated at least four Roman armies. In 145 B.C., the Romans began sending consuls against him. In 141–140 B.C., he surrounded a Roman army, which he released after its commander agreed to favorable terms (Viriathus could keep the territory that he held). Although this agreement was actually ratified by the Roman People, the senate incited the consul of 140 B.C., Q. Servilius Caepio, to renew the war. The next year, Caepio bribed some of Viriathus' associates to assassinate him, which brought an effective end to the war. The consul of the next year then subdued the northwestern corner of Spain.

Meanwhile, in Nearer Spain, the Aravaci, a Celtiberian people, revolted in 154 B.C., presumably as a result of the Lusitanian incursion. In 153 B.C., a consul was sent, but he achieved little. The next year another consul, M. Claudius Marcellus (descendant of the man who captured Syracuse in 212 B.C.), was sent. He offered reasonable terms, and an embassy was dispatched to Rome, where the senate thwarted the effort. The following year, Marcellus did arrange peace after some tribes surrendered. Upon his arrival, the consul of that year, L. Licinius Crassus, was annoyed to find peace and waged war on an innocent tribe, killing 20,000 adult males after the surrender of a town.

In 144 or 143 B.C., the Celtiberians, under the leadership of the town of Numantia, were led by the success of Viriathus to try their hand again at revolt. A series of unsuccessful consuls were sent out. Q. Pompeius, consul of 141 B.C., got himself into such trouble among the Aravaci that he offered them favorable terms, which the senate repudiated. C. Hostilius Mancinus, consul of 137 B.C., got into far worse trouble, being forced to surrender when the Numantines trapped his army in a pass. His quaestor Ti. Sempronius Gracchus, son of the praetor of the late 180s B.C., used his own good name to convince the Numantines of the Romans' good faith. The senate again repudiated the terms, and to make good the failure to ratify the agreement, Mancinus was turned over naked and bound to the Numantines, who refused

---

1 "Ser." is the abbreviation for the uncommon *praenomen* Servius.

to accept him, knowing that the blame for breaking the agreement did not lie with him.

As the war against Numantia dragged on without resolution, people at Rome became fed up. In 135 B.C., there was agitation to have Scipio Aemilianus, who had been illegally elected consul in 147 B.C. and presided over the destruction of Carthage, elected consul again. In the years since 152 B.C., however, a law had been passed prohibiting reelection. Once again, the law was suspended temporarily to allow the election of Aemilianus as consul for 134 B.C.

Service in Spain was so unpopular that Aemilianus had to use his own prestige to raise a force of volunteers to accompany him to Spain. As in Africa in 147 B.C., he first had to restore order to a demoralized army. Then he marched on Numantia itself and surrounded the town with a huge series of walls. Although the defenders numbered only 4,000 men against Aemilianus' 20,000 Italian troops and 40,000 Iberians, they held out for eight months, eventually resorting to cannibalism. Finally, in late summer of 134 B.C., Numantia surrendered.

This marked the end of major resistance to the Romans, but sporadic fighting went on until the middle of the next century, and full conquest was only achieved by the emperor Augustus. During the second century, however, the ongoing efforts necessary to pacify the country were a constant drain on Roman manpower, and the effort to provide armies for service there would demonstrate that the Middle Republic's method of military recruitment was inadequate for the permanent maintenance of imperial power.

7

EFFECTS OF THE CONQUESTS ON ROME

The Hannibalic War saw great constitutional anomalies as the Romans attempted to cope with many simultaneous military demands in disparate locations. During the second century B.C., the senatorial oligarchy worked out a system of office holding that was meant to regularize the personal competition in the interests of the stability of the overall oligarchy. At this point, we have sufficient contemporary information to have some sense of how the system worked in practice. It was this system that the senatorial oligarchy would attempt to defend in the last century of the Republic, when military and political pressures eventually brought about its collapse. For the conquest of the Mediterranean basin that had been carried out in the period from 264 to 146 B.C. entailed unforeseen consequences that made the Republican system of government unmanageable.

During the Hannibalic War, competent military leaders were often elected to repeated consulships, and members of prominent families were elected directly to high office at a young age. In the early part of the second century, the pattern for office holding was regulated. By the *lex Villia annalis* of 184 B.C., the offices of quaestor, praetor, and consul were made obligatory in that order, and minimum age requirements were set down for each (thirty-nine for the praetorship and forty-two for the consulship; there is some uncertainty about the quaestorship, but the minimum for it seems to have been twenty-five). The tribunate of the plebs and aedileship were optional (normally held at the ages of thirty and thirty-six). A law was also passed making it illegal to hold the same office again without an interval of ten years, which in practice restricted reelection to the consulship, and at some point after 152 B.C., any reelection was prohibited. Finally, the office of dictator fell into abeyance. The motive behind these measures must have been a collective desire on the part of the oligarchy to give all its members a single chance to gain prestige and power through office holding by preventing prominent individuals from "hogging" office.

This hostility towards excessive prominence did not, of course, mean that individuals did not continue to strive for personal prestige – far from it – but those considered to be excessively influential could be the focus of attack. The most conspicuous examples of this are Scipio Africanus and his brother Gnaeus, who were brought low through legal accusations in the 180s B.C. On the whole, the senate was able to regulate its members fairly handily during the second century down to 133 B.C. The only major example of a member of the oligarchy asserting himself against the senate is provided by Africanus' adoptive grandson, Scipio Aemilianus. In 147 B.C., the voters demanded that Aemilianus, who was merely a candidate for the aedileship, should be returned as consul in order to bring the seemingly mismanaged war against Carthage to a successful end. The presiding magistrate refused, and rioting eventually resulted in a temporary abrogation of the *lex Villia* so that Aemilianus could be elected consul, though he was underage and had not held the praetorship. In 135 B.C., the new law against repetition of office had to be suspended, again in the interest of Aemilianus, so that he could take over the disastrous war with Numantia. It is noteworthy that this rioting happened in connection with the centuriate assembly, which was dominated by those who held land and were liable to military service. These potential soldiers were dissatisfied with their commanders and demanded a particular general to lead them. Overall, however, the soldier-electors were happy enough to choose the magistrates from among the members of the oligarchy. This would eventually change.

During the second century B.C., the administrative and military require-ments of the overseas conquests began to strain the Republican system. The permanent acquisition of foreign territory dictated the creation of new mag-istracies with *imperium*, but the oligarchy was very disinclined to this. With the creation of the first two provinces in 227 B.C., the number of praetors was double that of consuls. Since there was not much attrition in war and most praetors could be expected to seek the consulship, this situation would result in a surplus of thwarted praetors, who might feel compelled to seek illegal or immoral ways to reach the consulship. Thus, it was nearly a decade after the final conquest of Spain that two more praetorships were created to govern that area in 197 B.C. That this was an uncongenial move is indicated by a law passed in the late 180s B.C., which provided that the number of praetors to be elected should alternate between four and six. Even this restriction proved unmanageable, and the number reverted to six. Even so, special assignments for various praetors meant that prorogation was a standard practice, and this was even more the case when the provinces of Africa and Macedonia were cre-ated in 146 B.C. without any increase in the number of praetors. There were now eight praetorian provinces (including the two legal positions in Rome) for only six praetors. The fundamental problem was the inconceivability of increasing the number of consuls beyond the traditional pair: any increase in the number of thwarted ex-praetors was thought to threaten the stability of the oligarchy, yet the system clearly needed more than eight magistrates with *imperium* every year. This problem would soon get much worse.

As the power of the Roman People spread throughout the Mediterranean basin, it proved to be impossible to maintain any sort of control over the activities of Rome's magistrates. It was physically impossible for the senate to have any immediate knowledge of distant events, so magistrates were sent off to fulfill some assignment, and one simply had to hope for the best. There was often a conflict between the personal interest of the magistrate and the "general good." Sometimes, magistrates would thwart negotiations if they wished to continue with a war. On the other hand, magistrates coming to the end of their term would sometimes make agreements that would then not be honored at Rome, presumably at the behest of the incoming magistrates, who wished the war to continue. It is true that when a settlement was necessary at the end of a war that had a definitive conclusion (like those against the advanced polities of the Greek East), a senatorial commission would be sent out to assist the magistrate in charge. Such a commission, however, could operate only under limited circumstances, when there was a relatively clear-cut issue to be decided in a comparatively peaceful setting. It was not possible to use such commissions for the conduct of war or for general administration. As the Romans unwillingly took on further permanent territorial obligations overseas, the lack of coordination in the administrative system and the institutional inability to direct the behavior of magistrates would lead to increasing problems.

Much of the difficulty with magistrates overseas derived from two basic considerations: the absolute right of the magistrates to use their *imperium* without restriction and the greed that developed among the office-holding class. Since Roman law did not grant foreigners any inherent rights, a magistrate could not be accused of murder for killing foreigners by virtue of his *imperium*. Even if it had been legally practicable to restrict *imperium* under certain circumstances, the necessities of warfare dictated that magistrates should have full use of their *imperium* against foreigners. Yet, not only did Roman magistrates in the second century often seem to view war as simply an opportunity to enrich themselves, but they began to take advantage of their powers to extort money in peaceful provinces. Starting in late 170s B.C., there were various ad hoc attempts in Rome to set up courts to deal with such malfeasance, but none were particularly successful. In 150 B.C., one governor in Spain, Ser. Sulpicius Galba, attacked a tribe that had surrendered (see p. 91) and this led to an attempt to set up a special court to investigate the matter. When the proposed legislation was being debated, Galba made an emotional appeal to the voters, and the law was rejected. In response, a tribune had a law passed to establish a permanent court for complaints by foreigners against extortion on the part of Roman governors. This court was comparatively mild. It operated according to the procedures of civil law and merely restored the stolen property without any further penalty. The juries consisted of senators, who in practice found it difficult to convict fellow senators, but the establishment of this court at least indicates the recognition of the need to curb the abuse of power in the provinces.

While one can disparage the behavior of Roman magistrates as "greedy," they were merely behaving in accordance with the traditional practice by which the commander had control of the booty from victory, giving some to the soldiers and officers, depositing some in the treasury, and keeping a large share for himself. Now, however, the power of the Roman state meant that this practice resulted in vast sums of money entering the pockets of the office-holding class. In the past, the magistrates had not been hugely wealthier than the regular small holders, the difference between the fifth and first census classes being only a factor of ten (a minimum of 100,000 sesterces' worth of property versus 11,000).[1] An anecdote suggests that as late as the First Punic War, even consuls were not terribly wealthy. When M. Atilius Regulus was assigned the task of keeping the army in Africa in the winter of 256–255 B.C., he asked to be relieved on the grounds that the slave who managed his property had run away and his wife was not up to the job. In the later Republic, even a minor senatorial family would own large numbers of slaves, so that the family's business affairs would hardly be dependent upon a single individual, and their holdings would be worth far more than ten times the value of the minimum qualification for the lowest census class.

The wealth that poured into Rome did not simply wind up with senators. The Roman state had large contracts for services to let out (like collecting taxes in the provinces and building projects), and these were bid on by wealthy non-senators, called "equestrians." Socially, the senators and equestrians were indistinguishable, the term "senator" simply designating those members of the wealthiest class who held office. The term "equestrian" derives from the fact that owning a horse was expensive, and thus the Roman cavalry had in the past been raised from among the wealthiest citizens. The Romans eventually found that their cavalry was not very good and adopted the practice of using cavalry supplied by allies. They then began to use those Romans who met the requirement for serving in the cavalry as junior officers in the army. Thus, the term "equestrian" was used loosely of the wealthy Romans

---

1 Though the Romans often calculated sums in terms of the *denarius*, a dime-sized silver coin, they did so more frequently in terms of the *sestertius*, a large copper coin worth one quarter of a denarius.

who could theoretically serve in the cavalry (the earliest official requirement is unknown; by the Late Republic it was possession of property worth 400,000 sesterces). Among the broader category of equestrians, the most important were those who resided in Rome and belonged to the companies that were formed to bid on state contracts for public services (this group was to some extent equated with the members of the eighteen special equestrian centuries in the centuriate assembly, but the exact relationship between these two influential groups is rather unclear for the second century B.C.). These state contractors were called "publicans," and already in 169 B.C. their political influence was so great that when one of the censors angered them, they could have secured his conviction for malfeasance (only the counterarguments of the other censor prevented this). Pretty much by definition, these equestrians consisted of the nonpolitical members of the upper class, but in the Late Republic, their defense of their own interests would at times be politically destabilizing.

The wealth of both senators and equestrians consisted for the most part of landowning, which was the only form of reliable, long-term investment in Greco-Roman antiquity.[2] It is not surprising, then, that much of the wealth acquired in the wars of conquest was used to buy land. The wealthy did not so much put together vast compact estates (which would later be the case) as hold many estates in various locations. These estates would then be cultivated by means of the large numbers of slaves captured during the wars. The acquisition and use of such slave labor is one of the ugly aspects of the Republic, but this very important institution is dimly understood, since such an unseemly business is seldom mentioned in the ancient sources. While L. Aemilius Paullus' outrageous enslavement of 150,000 on a single day in Epirus in 167 B.C. is hardly typical, the event nonetheless shows something of the scale of the enterprise.

The output of these large estates presumably would have undercut the produce from small holdings in the open market, though it is not known to what extent smallholders depended on selling grain on the open market for their livelihoods. What is known for sure is that the wealthy made an (economically reasonable) effort to buy out small holdings, sometimes pressuring their neighbors into selling. The position of the smallholders was further undermined by the fact that the male head of the household, whose labor would have been crucial to the economic success of a small parcel of land, would often be away on military duty. If he returned comparatively soon from a victorious war with some wealth derived from plunder, then his absence may not have been so detrimental. If he died on campaign or returned from a war

2 The Carthaginians, of course, were mainly traders, but this activity was frowned upon among the Romans.

in Spain where there was little plunder to be had, then the family holding would become untenable, and a wealthy buyer could easily be found.

The demise of these small holdings had two consequences. First, the old occupants were likely to emigrate to Rome, which grew greatly in population. In any case, whether resident in Rome or elsewhere, these dispossessed small-holders were often desirous of regaining land and would eventually make their wishes known in the assemblies in Rome. The desire on the part of a large segment of the electorate to have land distributed to them would become a destabilizing factor in Roman politics.

Second, the decline of the class of smallholders had serious implications for the Roman military. Since the soldiers had to provide their own equipment, only those with a sufficient amount of property to afford this were recruited into the army. The majority of the soldiers would have come from those who met the minimum qualification for the fifth (bottom) census class, and these were exactly the category of farmers most likely to sell out to the wealthy. While there were no economic statistics in antiquity, anecdotal evidence shows that there was reluctance to serve in unremunerative and dangerous wars. While it had proven easy to raise a large army for what was expected to be an easy (and profitable) war against Carthage in 149 B.C., by 138 B.C. some tribunes of the plebs issued restrictions on the consuls' method of selecting recruits for a war in Spain and arrested the consuls (an unheard-of procedure) when they refused to adhere to these restrictions. Again in 134 B.C., the senate forbade Scipio Aemilianus to conscript recruits forcibly for the war against Numantia.[3] Thus, the wars that led to the territorial expansion had the unexpected consequence of leading to a decline in the very class of people who provided the bulk of the soldiery. The attempt to remedy this situation would result in the beginning of bloodshed in Roman politics.

The vast wealth and power of the senatorial class led, not surprisingly, to a fair amount of arrogance on their part. In 168 B.C., a senatorial commission was dispatched to tell Antiochus IV of Syria to halt his campaign against Egypt, and when given the news, the king said he would respond after consulting with his advisors, whereupon the senior envoy drew a circle around the king in the sand and told him that he had to answer before leaving it. Antiochus then capitulated. If this is how kings behaved before senators, it is not surprising that Roman magistrates behaved haughtily in the states of the Italian allies. During the second century B.C., several laws were passed that forbade Roman magistrates to execute or even flog Roman citizens who were not enrolled in the army, but the non-Roman allies enjoyed no such protection and at times even leading men of such communities were flogged to

---

3 This prohibition may reflect resentment at Aemilianus' illegal election to the consulship, but it could not have been implemented if there had been no complaints.

death for trivial reasons. Furthermore, while the Italian allies provided half the troops for Roman armies, they got a smaller share of the plunder, and when the Roman state did distribute land, they again got smaller lots than citizens. Since such communities were also increasingly adopting Roman ways, it seemed unreasonable by the latter part of the century that Italian allies should have no say in the electoral process in Rome, no right to hold office themselves, and no protection against the caprice of Roman magistrates. The desire of the allies to be granted Roman citizenship would be a very divisive issue at Rome.

Why, then, was it not granted? Presumably, because the nobility knew how to work the present political system in Italy and preferred not to endanger their control of the state in order to mollify the allies. In 242 B.C., the creation of two new tribes raised the number to thirty-five, and there would be no further additions. The Roman state covered most of central Italy, and this situation became more or less permanent throughout the second century B.C. The only real change was that any remaining communities holding citizenship without voting rights were granted full citizenship. There would be several unsuccessful attempts in Rome to satisfy the allies, but this issue would cause much trouble until a revolt among the allies forced the Romans to grant them citizenship.

Thus, the great wars of the Middle Republic brought with them much more than glory and plunder. The Roman oligarchy was eventually compelled to take on territorial and military commitments that placed great strains on the Republic's administrative system. The wealth that poured into Italy and Rome created many internal problems. Once the office-holding class had acquired vast sums of money, such wealth became a necessary requirement for running for office, which in turn contributed to the tendency of magistrates to take advantage of every aspect of office that could make them more money. In addition, there arose a new class of wealthy non-senators, who had provided services for the state and whose influence would cause the senatorial oligarchy much trouble. The wealth invested by senators and non-senators in land acquired from smallholders and cultivated with slave labor led to a serious decline in the class of smallholders who provided the bulk of the Republic's soldiery. Finally, the treatment of the Italian allies as inferiors led to a demand on their part for Roman citizenship. The senatorial oligarchy would show itself to be incapable of dealing with these problems, which would eventually overwhelm the Republican form of government.

PART THREE

———

COLLAPSE OF THE REPUBLIC,
133 B.C.–27 B.C.

A s we have seen, the conquest of the Mediterranean basin brought a number of problems for the oligarchy to solve. Though it proved tenacious
in the defense of its privileges and control of the political system in Rome, the
oligarchy ultimately proved to be incapable of dealing with these problems,
and the Republican form of government fell victim to the violence that became progressively more common. The breakdown of the oligarchy's control
can be divided into four periods.

The first began in 133 B.C., when, as a result of a tribune's increasingly
reckless efforts to legislate and then implement a program of land reform, the
oligarchy resorted to an illegal act of violence to ward off what was perceived
as a threat to the senate. The oligarchy was to find, however, that the use of
violence was a double-edged weapon that could just as readily be used against
it. The next fifty years were a period of political turmoil in Rome, with much
popular agitation against perceived abuses of the senatorial oligarchy; while the
oligarchy refused to allow any reform of the political system, various members
of the oligarchy acted as champions of the discontent to further their own
careers. Two issues dominated this conflict:

1. land reform, which began as an attempt to remedy the inadequacies of the
    traditional methods of raising troops but came to be an end in themselves,
    and
2. the desire of the Italian allies to be granted Roman citizenship.

In the last decade of the second century B.C., perceived senatorial incompetence in dealing with various wars led first to the election of C. Marius to the
consulship against the will of the oligarchy and then to his being repeatedly
reelected, contrary to regular legal practice. Marius' career foreshadowed the
situation in the last century of the Republic, when various prominent senators would gain extended military commands and use them to advance their

careers against the interests of the oligarchy. Marius also contributed to this further development when he changed the method of military recruitment by allowing the landless to enlist: these new troops had no stake in preserving the old political system and every reason to support their commanders. This new loyalty would eventually be the decisive factor in ending the long series of armed conflicts that broke out in 91 B.C. when, at the failure of the last of a series of vain attempts to grant citizenship to the Italian allies, they went into revolt. The Romans won this war after a number of military disasters, but only by granting the allies their desire. The oligarchy's attempt to restrict the political rights of the new citizens resulted in further conflicts in the 80s B.C., and the eventual winner was L. Sulla, who used his veterans from a war in the east to impose his dictatorial control over the entire state. In a mere half century, the political stability of the second century was completely destroyed, and despite the fact that Sulla posed as the defender of the senate, real power was now shown to rest with the man who was ruthless enough to seize control of the state through use of the military.

The second period comprises the three decades that followed Sulla's attempt to restore senatorial control of the political system: these years demonstrated that the military needs of the overseas empire acquired over the preceding two centuries were incompatible with maintenance of the old political system: it was necessary to bestow huge commands of long standing on men who could then use their power to control the political scene in Rome.

During the third period, the traditional system of senatorial government broke down completely. By the 50s B.C., three men could dominate politics at Rome, where the voting system degenerated into a chaos of rioting gangs and flagrant bribery. Finally, in 49 B.C., a civil war broke out between C. Julius Caesar and Cn. Pompeius, and the Republican form of government would never function properly again. Caesar emerged victorious, but was assassinated by disgruntled Republicans when it became clear that he had no intention of restoring the traditional Republic, something that would have been impossible even if Caesar had wished it.

The final period of the demise of the Republic took place in the fifteen years that followed Caesar's assassination in 44 B.C.: the ultimate victor in a prolonged conflict among various warlords was Caesar's great-nephew and adopted son, who demonstrated his political acumen by adopting autocratic powers while at the same time assuaging senatorial opinion through a sham restoration of the Republic, thereby establishing the position of Roman emperor.

The Late Republic is by far the best-attested period of antiquity. The years from 133 to 31 B.C. attracted much attention from ancient historians, both Greek and Latin, and the last decades of the Republic were considered the golden age of Latin literature, so that many contemporary works survive.

This does not mean, however, that the evidence is at all complete. In particular, the loss of the later books of Livy means that there is no complete narrative of the period, and the attestation for the earlier years is particularly spotty. The attestation for the events down to the Social War consists mostly of the activities of famous individuals: Plutarch's *Lives* recount the careers of prominent senators, while the first book of Appian's *Civil War* concentrates on more or less the same careers but with an emphasis on violence in contrast to the moral aspect of Plutarch's biographies. Fragments of the annalistic historian Dio Cassius are also preserved. All these Greek authors of the Imperial period (the first two lived in the second century A.D. and Dio in the third) had little understanding of the Republic, but their information often goes back to well-informed sources. The last decades of the Republic are amply attested in the many surviving works of the orator Cicero. His speeches and philosophical treatises often allude to earlier as well as contemporary events, and large numbers of letters both to and from him give a lively picture of the events that was never intended for publication. The dictator Julius Caesar wrote two rather contentious narratives, of his campaigns in Gaul and the first two years of the civil war that he started in 49 B.C., and other writers added contributions about his later campaigns; the Imperial biographer Suetonius (early second century A.D.) provides much information about the end of the Republic in his *Lives* of Caesar and of Augustus. While all these sources have faults in perspective and they hardly present a complete picture, there is a vividness to the preserved information about the fall of Republic that no other period of Roman history possesses.

8

ASSAULT ON THE OLIGARCHY,

133 B.C.–81 B.C.

The tribunate of Ti. Sempronius Gracchus is important for a number of reasons. As several ancient sources indicate, it marks the first time that bloodshed had been practiced in Roman politics since the early days of the Roman Republic centuries before. The second century B.C. had been one of comparative domestic peace, and Ti. Gracchus' tribunate marks the beginning of the spiral of violence in the Late Republic that would eventually kill thousands and bring down the Republic. It was the "optimates," the supporters of the ruling oligarchy, who felt so threatened by Ti. Gracchus that they resorted to this violence. Eventually, they would reap the rewards of this action, since they were to be the principal victims of the violence. They killed Ti. Gracchus because they felt threatened by his use of the powers of the assembly of the plebs against the will of the oligarchy. Tiberius' tribunate thus marks the first major example of the use, by a member of the oligarchy, of popular discontent to further his own career, though he actually stumbled into his conflict with the oligarchy unintentionally while trying to assist with legislation that he thought would address a pressing issue: problems in military recruitment. Later writers interpreted his career in light of his own and his brother Gaius' deaths and conceived of them both as "democrats" (that is, men who upheld the right of the people as a whole to have the decisive role in government, as was the case in Greece), but this is inaccurate. The Gracchi belonged to one of the most prominent families in the oligarchy, and their goal was not to undermine the senate but to reform the system on its behalf. Both died when the oligarchy resorted to violence in the defense of what it perceived to be its own interest. In addition, the demise of the Gracchi at the hands of senatorial violence saw the creation of a self-conscious political movement that opposed the senatorial oligarchy as a whole, though its leaders for the most part came from it.

In the decade before Tiberius' tribunate, there seems to have been some movement in the direction of the assemblies asserting their independence from the oligarchy's control. In 139 B.C., a tribunician law was passed over the senate's strong objections to mandate voting in elections by ballot. Before this reform, votes had been cast orally, which assisted the oligarchy and their friends in making sure the people voted "correctly." In 137 B.C., the ballot was introduced in the voting for most trials conducted before the assemblies. Clearly, there were people who did not wish to have their votes "controlled," though the nature of the sources is such that we have no real access to what the "average" voter thought. In any case, Tiberius would take advantage of this more "independent" frame of mind in the assembly of the plebs.

The main problem that Ti. Gracchus wished to deal with was the trouble in finding enough smallholders to enroll in the army (some sources suggest that the Gracchi intended to help the poor as an end in its own right, but this view is colored by political perceptions derived from the Greek world). In 138 B.C., some tribunes had imposed restrictions on the consuls' levying of troops and arrested them for violating these restrictions; in 135 B.C., when Ti. Gracchus' own cousin Scipio Aemilianus was elected consul to deal with the situation in Spain, the senate refused to let him levy new troops. There was a sense that the large estates that the wealthy cultivated with slave labor were a cause of the decline in the numbers of smallholders, and this feeling would have been exacerbated by a major slave revolt that broke out in Sicily in 135 B.C.: a number of praetors were actually defeated because of the inexperience of their armies, and the revolt was not finished off until 132 B.C. When Ti. Gracchus became tribune for the year 133 B.C., he had a proposal to solve the crisis of the smallholders that included a redistribution of public land.

The Roman state owned large amounts of land, especially in southern Italy as a result of confiscations imposed as penalties on towns that went over to Hannibal during the Second Punic War. In the early second century B.C., the censors were happy enough simply to have anyone bring this land back into cultivation. At some point, a law was passed stating that no one could possess more than 500 *jugera* of this land (one *jugerum* equals about two-thirds of an acre).[1] This law was apparently generally obeyed in 167 B.C., when Cato the Elder alluded to it in a speech, but by 133 B.C., it was largely ignored. The law had no mechanism for enforcement and many people held large amounts of public land, which they treated as their own. Tiberius' proposal was to elect a three-man commission that would make a survey of the public land, seize amounts held in excess of the old law, and redistribute it to Roman citizens in small parcels. This land would allow the new occupants to become subject to

---

1 The annalistic sources ascribe such a provision to the fourth century B.C., but while some restriction is conceivable, the figure of 500 *jugera* is far too large for such an early date and presumably reflects the common habit in the annalistic tradition of giving contemporary usage an early and anachronistic origin.

the levy, and to avoid the problem of purchase by the rich, the parcels could not be sold at will. Ti. Gracchus' proposal enjoyed support among certain very influential senators, including his father-in-law, the *princeps senatus*,[2] and P. Mucius Scaevola, one of the consuls of 133 B.C. It turned out, however, that there would be grave opposition to the law.

While Tiberius' proposal was irreproachable from a strictly legal point of view, there were practical objections. No one had, apparently, minded when the ownership of the land was usurped, and it would be unfair to ask for it back after people had improved it with their own money. In any case, the land had often been distributed in unequal ways among the heirs of the person who first took it: why should one son lose his inheritance of supposedly public land, while another retained his inheritance of private land? And what of daughters whose dowries consisted of public land? The argument was also made that the Roman People relied upon these rich people to carry out public functions and would therefore suffer if the well-being of the wealthy was undermined (a self-serving but plausible position). Whatever the merits of their case, those threatened by the proposal enlisted the help of one of Tiberius' tribunician colleagues, M. Octavius, who vetoed the law when it was to be put to the vote. Tiberius then allowed the senate to debate the matter, hoping that Octavius would be made to back down in light of the great popularity of the bill (back in 139 B.C., a tribune had been convinced under similar circumstances to stop opposing the first bill introducing voting by ballot). Octavius refused to back down, however, and Tiberius reacted in an extreme way. He proposed a bill deposing Octavius from office on the grounds that while a tribune was supposed to be upholding the interests of the plebs, he was instead opposing a law they strongly supported. When the bill was put to the vote and was about to pass, Tiberius still begged Octavius to relent, but he would not, and the bill was passed.[3] Tiberius had nothing in mind but the immediate goal of having his land law passed, ignoring the troubling implications of the move. A replacement for Octavius was elected, and the land law was duly passed.

The senate had another trick up its sleeve, however, and refused to grant the money necessary to fund the activities of the commission. At this point, a fortuitous event happened: the king of Pergamum died and left his kingdom to the Roman People.[4] Traditionally, the senate was to deal with matters affecting

---

2 Each year, this title was given to the ex-consul whose opinion was the first to be asked in the first session of the senate in that year.

3 Why Octavius did not veto this bill is unknown. Perhaps he feared violence if he did, or he may have claimed that the proposal was unconstitutional and refrained from lending it credibility by vetoing it.

4 The purpose of such a bequest was to remove any benefit if someone assassinated him in the interest of a different claimant for the throne. There are several other instances of Hellentistic kings naming the Roman People as their heir.

foreign and military policy, but Tiberius quickly had a law passed accepting the inheritance and providing that the royal treasures were to be used to fund the land commission. Tiberius was now having the People intrude on the senate's prerogatives.

By now, there was much opposition to Tiberius among the oligarchy. It was pointed out that if a tribune could be deposed for an unpopular veto, then the veto basically meant nothing, and one of the basic principles of the Roman constitution, the right of one magistrate to thwart the actions of another, fell away; his law accepting the Pergamene inheritance marked an unwanted intrusion into the oligarchy's sphere. Then Tiberius took another unprecedented step when he sought direct reelection to the tribunate. Since Roman magistrates were exempt from prosecution during their term of office, it was normally not the case that one could run for a new office while already in office. Otherwise, continuous tenure in public office would result in permanent legal immunity. While there was no specific law prohibiting such reelection, no one had, in fact, been reelected in this way in centuries, and the practice was for all practical purposes unconstitutional. But there was no authority to decide what in fact was constitutional, and "constitutionality" simply meant what was accepted practice. Hence, when he saw that he would certainly be prosecuted, Tiberius sought reelection.

It was argued that he was seeking *regnum* or "kingship," the Roman expression for an unacceptable domination of the political scene by one individual. Tiberius had his followers seize control of the Capitol (either to hold the tribunician elections or to pass a law to authorize this). A meeting of the senate was held, and P. Cornelius Scipio Nasica, one of the leading consulars, asked the consul Scaevola what action he would take against this. When Scaevola replied that he would tolerate no illegality but would not act until something illegal had actually been done, Nasica stated that those who desired the Republic's preservation should follow him, and led a mob of senators and equestrians to the Capitol, where Tiberius was beaten to death along with 200 to 300 of his supporters. Nasica presumably thought that once Tiberius secured reelection, it would be impossible to overturn it, and if he was reelected once, what was to prevent him from being reelected for the rest of his life? This unofficial action was the first step in the introduction of violence into the politics of the Late Republic, and not only would it become increasingly common, but it would soon be used against the oligarchy that had initiated it.

That the opposition to Tiberius did not primarily derive from the content of the land law is shown by the fact that it continued to operate for four years after Tiberius' death. His death had long-term consequences through the creation of a permanent political program that was opposed to the oligarchy. Because Tiberius and his followers used the powers of the assemblies against the oligarchy, those opposed to the oligarchy were called *populares* ("men of the People"), while the supporters of the senate were called the "optimates" (or "best men," from the Greek notion that the wealthy oligarchs were "better" than the common people). The *populares* had no fixed program but regularly sought support in the assemblies against the senate. Furthermore, the *populares* were not literally "men of the People," but members of the oligarchy who used popular discontent with the oligarchy for their own purposes, especially early in their careers. The optimates, on the other hand, upheld the prerogatives of the senatorial oligarchy to control the political system.

The consuls of 132 B.C. undertook to persecute those who had supported Tiberius, and this led to much resentment. The senate took advantage of possible troubles in Asia (the name for the newly acquired territory of Pergamum) to get Nasica out of the way by sending him there to investigate matters; his fortuitous death then prevented him from being accused of murder. As it turned out, a usurper claiming to be a member of the Attalid royal family began a revolt (mostly among the poor) against Roman rule in Asia. In 131 B.C., P. Licinius Crassus Mucianus (natural brother of P. Scaevola, the consul of 133 B.C., and father-in-law of Ti. Gracchus' brother Gaius) first thwarted the assignment of subduing this revolt to his colleague on account of taboos associated with an obscure priesthood held by the colleague (Mucianus held the most important priesthood in the state religion and could decide such matters), but when he was himself prevented from taking up the job (probably by tribunician veto), he had a law passed authorizing an election to choose the commander. Similar elections had been held during the Second Punic War, but the procedure had fallen completely into abeyance in the second century B.C. and violated the principle of senatorial control of provincial assignments. In effect, Mucianus was appealing to the People to assert his own will against the senate. Such behavior boded ill for the oligarchy's long-term control of the administrative system. Mucianus won, but as so often was the case, an untested Roman army was initially unsuccessful, and Mucianus was killed in a major defeat. The consul of 130 B.C. put down the revolt, and one of the consuls of 129 B.C. spent several years settling the affairs of the new province. As had been the case with the two new provinces set up in 146 B.C., no new position as praetor was created to provide governors: the empire of the Roman People was seriously overtaxing the ability of the traditional city-state to govern it.

The functioning of Ti. Gracchus' land commission was brought to a halt in 129 B.C., when the non-Roman Italian allies complained to the senate about the unfairness of taking Roman public land from them. The senate assigned the decision in this matter to one of the consuls, who promptly left on a minor military campaign, at which point land distribution ceased. It would seem that public land held in excess of the legal limit by Romans was now used up, and if distributions were to continue, some sort of settlement with the allies was necessary. M. Fulvius Flaccus, one of the consuls of 125 B.C., tried to have a law passed granting these allies citizenship, but there was major opposition, and the effort lapsed when Flaccus was called to campaign in Gaul. One Latin colony actually went into revolt and was destroyed by a praetor, L. Opimius.

Southern Gaul was the natural route for Roman armies to take when being sent to Spain, but the Romans had not wished to take over permanent control. They had an ally in the Greek colony of Massilia (modern Marseilles), and troubles between the city and Celtic tribes to the interior resulted in a series of consular campaigns that lasted until 120 B.C. From then on there would be a permanent military presence in the area, which came to be known as the province of Narbonensis. It is not clear exactly when it was set up as a proper province, but the Roman state had taken on yet another assignment for the praetors without increasing the number of praetors.

Ti. Gracchus' younger brother Gaius became tribune for the year 123 B.C. He cherished the memory of his brother, and it was clear from the start that he intended to take up where his brother had left off. First he proposed a law that would prevent anyone who had been removed from office from being elected to another. This was aimed at M. Octavius, but C. Gracchus withdrew it, ostensibly at the request of his mother, the daughter of Scipio Africanus. Whether this was true or merely an excuse, C. Gracchus seems not to have held any particular rancor against Octavius and was willing to drop the matter once he had made his point of legitimizing his brother's attempt at reelection when it was clear that the bill would have passed.

Next, C. Gracchus passed a law that prohibited the passing of judgment on Roman citizens without the authorization of the People. This was aimed at those who had persecuted his brother's supporters in 132 B.C. The two consuls had used the traditional right of relegation in a nontraditional manner. Relegation meant that by decree a consul could force someone to stay in one place or not enter a given place, and such a decree had no long-term meaning. The two consuls of 132 B.C. had held investigations into the conduct of Tiberius' supporters and, after a quasi-legal decision, passed a "sentence" of relegation against some people. At this point, no Roman citizen was normally executed after being convicted of a capital offence but would instead go into exile, so if these "relegations" were considered legal by later consuls and those convicted were prohibited from returning to Rome to exercise their rights as citizens, they would be tantamount to a capital sentence, despite the fact that no magistrate had such a power. In effect, the regular short-term "relegation" was converted into a new form of trial in contravention of the normal idea that only the People could pass such sentence or authorize a court to do so. Once C. Gracchus' law was passed, P. Popilius Laenas, the sole surviving consul from 132 B.C., went into exile to avoid being tried.

The chronology and details of C. Gracchus' two terms as tribune are by no means certain, but he passed a large amount of legislation. Some laws benefited common citizens. He set up a grain law that authorized state sale of grain at $6\frac{2}{3}$ sesterces per measure, which in effect set a maximum price in the free market. He also prohibited the magistrates from enrolling soldiers below the old traditional minimum age of seventeen. In another move intended to revive his brother's program, he restored the distribution of land in Italy and authorized the establishment of colonies both in Italy and abroad. He benefited the wealthy equestrians (those Romans with enough money to serve as junior officers in the army) through building projects that they could carry out for the state. In particular, he passed legislation that modified in favor of the wealthiest equestrians resident in Rome the procedure for giving out the contracts for collecting the taxes owed by the wealthy new province of Asia. Those who purchased these contracts were called tax-farmers, and by having a law passed to have the bidding for these contracts carried out by the censors in Rome instead of by the governor in Asia, C. Gracchus ensured that equestrians who dominated the centuriate assembly would be in the best position to win these lucrative tax-farming contracts.[5] In return, C. Gracchus could expect the cooperation of the equestrians for his other projects.

One law was seen to be antisenatorial, but such was not C. Gracchus' intent. He first proposed that the juries on the panels that tried cases of provincial extortion should be a mixture of senators and equestrians. He then changed this proposal, perhaps because at this time Manius Aquillius, who had flagrantly accepted large bribes when settling the province of Asia in the aftermath of its unsuccessful revolt, was acquitted. In its final form as passed, the law provided that the juries would now consist exclusively of equestrians, and the penalty for conviction became punitive: the simple restitution to the plaintiffs that the old law provided continued, but in addition anyone convicted had to turn over an equal sum to the treasury. These new jury panels

5 The system of tax-farming seems odd to modern notions of government, but the leasing of public functions to private individuals is a commonly attested procedure in primitive states. This practice allowed the rudimentary administrative setup of the Republic, which had no permanent bureaucracy to manage a complicated operation like tax collection, to call upon the expertise and capital of wealthy individuals to exercise this public function in the name of the Roman People. The bidding would theoretically force the potential tax-farmers to pay the state the highest amount possible for the taxes while at the same time leaving themselves a surplus for profit. The procedure had the additional benefit of putting the state's share immediately in the treasury, while the tax-farmers then took the time and effort to recoup their purchase price from the provincials. The governors were expected to oversee the workings of the tax-farmers and to make sure that the provincials paid the taxes they owed without being overtaxed, but the system was obviously open to abuse.

were dominated by the heads of the equestrian companies that bid on contracts in Rome, especially those for collecting provincial taxes. Hence, there was an inherent conflict of interest between the tax-farmers and their friends who sat on the juries on the one hand and the governors whose fate they decided on the other. Yet, it was not till thirty years later that this conflict manifested itself. The jury panels provided under this law did, however, provide the jurors for special courts, which would be set up to prosecute what was considered senatorial misconduct in subsequent decades, and this led to the erroneous idea that C. Gracchus had intended this sort of antisenatorial behavior from the start. In any case, once the senatorial juries had shown themselves to be incapable of convicting other senators, C. Gracchus chose the wealthiest group of nonpolitical Romans to judge them. It is hard to see how he could have predicted that in later years the tax-farmers who dominated the equestrian order would make use of their control of the courts for their own purposes or that the struggle for control of the panels would drive an artificial wedge between the senators and equestrians, whose interests were fundamentally the same. In addition, the law provided that a praetor was to preside over the court of extortion. Here is yet another praetorian responsibility without any increase in the number of praetors.

That C. Gracchus' intentions were not antisenatorial is proven by his law on the consular provinces. This dictated that the senate had to select the provinces for the next year's consuls before they were elected, which meant that the decision would be made on the basis of more or less objective needs rather than the influence of the newly returned consuls. Most strikingly, the law prevented any tribunician veto, since otherwise a friendly tribune could be used to thwart the matter until after the elections. The aim was not to destroy senatorial influence but to keep the influence of important senators from affecting policy-making.

In 123 B.C., C. Gracchus succeeded where his brother had failed, securing (apparently without much trouble) reelection for the following year. His second tribunate was a disaster, however, because of C. Gracchus' decision to propose citizenship for the Italian allies. This matter was considered so important – and controversial – that the M. Flaccus who had sought to pass similar legislation as consul in 125 B.C. now got himself elected tribune to help in the effort, despite the fact that it was unheard of for an ex-consul to run for tribune. The opposition was led in 122 B.C. by one of the consuls and by M. Livius Drusus, one of the tribunes. They played on the fears of the common voters, arguing that any increase in the number of citizens would necessarily reduce the benefits of the present ones. Drusus also impugned C. Gracchus' honesty in overseeing building projects set up by his own laws, and he proposed additional colonies. When met with such opposition, C. Gracchus left for forty days to oversee the new colony being established on the site of Carthage, leaving Flaccus to lead the drive for the proposed law. Flaccus, however, was outmaneuvered by the opposition, and when C. Gracchus returned, the cause was lost. The proposal was rejected, and he was defeated in an attempt at a third tribunate.

In 121 B.C., the opponents of extending citizenship dominated the political scene, one of the consuls being the L. Opimius who had destroyed the Latin colony that revolted in 125 B.C. Some of C. Gracchus' legislation was repealed, and when a vote was to be taken to repeal the law establishing the colony at Carthage, C. Gracchus' supporters gathered at the voting place in large numbers at dawn. One of the presiding tribune's attendants who was taking part in a preliminary religious ceremony said something offensive to the Gracchans, who stabbed him to death with the pens used to mark ballots. At this violence, the assembly broke up and, in fear of meeting a fate similar to that of Tiberius' supporters in 132 B.C., C. Gracchus' adherents seized the Aventine Hill, which was associated with the plebs in their conflict with the patricians centuries earlier. The Gracchans wished to negotiate a settlement, but Opimius would hear nothing of it. In this chaotic situation, he summoned the senate and had it pass a decree stating that the consuls should make sure that no harm came to the state. This was the first time the so-called *senatus consultum ultimum* or "final decree of the senate" was passed.[6] On the basis of this decree, Opimius used an army that was camped outside of the city in preparation for a triumph to attack the Gracchans. During the assault thousands were killed, including the ex-consul Flaccus, and C. Gracchus himself fled but committed suicide when about to be captured. In effect, Opimius took the final decree as authorizing him to take whatever steps necessary to restore order, even if this meant violating the normal legal protections of Roman citizens. His acquittal the following year on a charge of murder implicitly endorsed this view, though it was some years before the validity of the decree was generally accepted, and even then it was at times called into question.

Secure in its victory, the oligarchy returned to its regular control of the state. The colonies promised by Drusus were never set up, and during the next decade or so, several laws were passed to undo the Gracchan land legislation and allow the law's beneficiaries to sell their allotments. The oligarchy had developed a visceral dislike of any form of land legislation, while the Gracchi were now revered in certain quarters as men who had been killed while serving the common people. Though land distribution was for a time at an end, the problems with the levy that had been the initial cause of the Gracchan legislation remained unsolved.

---

6 This term is used in a later source, and while there it is probably just a general description rather than a technical term as it is sometimes taken to be, this is a convenient way of referring to this important decree.

The next step in the decline of the oligarchy came as a result of a number of military disasters that took place under the military leadership of the oligarchy. First, in 113 B.C., a consul in Macedonia launched an unprovoked attack on a Germanic people called the Cimbri in the Balkans and suffered a major defeat. The Cimbri would soon inflict a series of defeats on the Romans, but first a war in Africa became a major embarrassment for the oligarchy.

Numidia lay to the west of the Roman province of Africa, and there King Masinissa had been a loyal ally since the Romans helped install him during the Second Punic War. He was succeeded in 148 B.C. by his son Micipsa, who had no legitimate heir. Micipsa relied on the services of his illegitimate nephew Jugurtha, who commanded the Numidian forces sent to help the Romans in the 130s B.C. during the war against Numantia. There Jugurtha entered into friendship with a number of noblemen serving in the Roman army. Later, Micipsa had two sons of his own, and upon his death in ca. 118 B.C., the kingdom was to be divided among Jugurtha and these sons by the decision of a senatorial commission. Jugurtha ignored this, murdering one of his cousins and waging war on the other, Adherbal. In defeat, Adherbal fled to Rome, where the senate decided to send a commission headed by L. Opimius, the killer of C. Gracchus, to settle the matter. Adherbal was granted the wealthier eastern half of the kingdom, while Jugurtha received the western half. Ignoring this ruling, Jugurtha resumed the war and paid no attention to yet another commission sent by the senate. Adherbal was surrounded in his capital, where he had to rely on the fighting prowess of Italian merchants to keep Jugurtha at bay. Eventually, these Italians tired of the war and insisted that Adherbal surrender, claiming that the protection of the Roman People would guarantee his safety. Not only did such protection not keep Jugurtha from torturing Adherbal to death, but he also executed the Italian merchants. At this point, the senate could not avoid declaring war on Jugurtha.

In 111 B.C., the consul L. Calpurnius Bestia took to the field, making use of L. Opimius' services as a subordinate. Soon Bestia reached an agreement with Jugurtha, but at Rome this was rejected as too lenient. It was thought that bribery was the cause of this leniency and a tribune, C. Memmius, actually had a law passed granting Jugurtha safe conduct to come to Rome and reveal whom he had bribed. When he got there, another tribune forbade him to speak, which only heightened the feeling that there was something to be concealed. As consul in 110 B.C., Sp. Postumius Albinus resumed the war without much success, and when he returned to Rome in the fall to conduct the elections, he left his brother Aulus in charge. Aulus rashly decided to go on campaign and managed to get himself surrounded, at which point he had to surrender.

Outrage broke out when news of this latest example of noble incompetence reached Rome in 109 B.C. The oligarchy's reputation was not helped when one of the consuls launched another attack on the Cimbri, who by this time had migrated to Gaul, and suffered another catastrophic defeat. It seemed as if the ruling senatorial oligarchy was no longer capable of producing effective magistrates, and since the apparent bribery was thought to be the reason for this situation, a tribune had a law passed authorizing a special court to investigate charges of bribery arising from the war in Africa. The jurors were to be chosen from the album of the jurors for the extortion court, that is, of equestrians first enrolled under C. Gracchus' legislation. Cicero claimed that the panels consisted of Gracchan jurors, which suggests that they were motivated by a spirit of revenge, but this seems to be a simplistic explanation. These men may well have been satisfied at the downfall of Gracchus' opponents, but it seems much more likely that the motivation for the convictions was complete dissatisfaction with the military incompetence of the oligarchy. Among those convicted were the ex-consuls Sp. Albinus, L. Bestia, and L. Opimius.

The other consul of 109 B.C., Q. Caecilius Metellus, continued the war against Jugurtha. Metellus belonged to one of the most prestigious families of the time. His father had subdued the revolt in Macedon in 148 B.C. and nearly ended the Achaean War in 146 B.C., and many Caecilii Metelli held the consulship in these years (123, 119, 117, 115, 113 B.C.). Metellus began a methodical campaign of subduing Numidia in order to deny Jugurtha any support or refuge, but such a slow method of warfare, while the only reasonable course of action, was not likely to satisfy outraged public opinion in Rome.

Among his subordinates, Metellus had brought along C. Marius, a man who would rise to unprecedented heights because of dissatisfaction with the oligarchy. Born in 157 B.C. to a prominent local family in the city of Arpinum in southern Latium that had only been raised to full Roman citizenship in 188 B.C., Marius served under Scipio Aemilianus in Spain and then began a not very spectacular political career in Rome. He was helped in this in that his family was traditionally associated with the Metelli, a circumstance that must have been particularly helpful for a "new man," that is, someone whose family had never held office in Rome before. Barely reaching the praetorship in 115 B.C. (and barely escaping conviction for electoral corruption), he served as propraetor in Spain and gained a triumph. Presumably, he had no expectation of reaching the consulship, though he was important enough to be given as wife a member of the Julii Caesares, a not very prominent patrician family (she was the famous Caesar's aunt). Hence, Marius was presumably happy enough to offer his military knowledge to the consul Metellus.

The disrepute of the nobility and his own military success in Numidia led Marius to consider running for the consulship. At first Metellus refused to let him return for this purpose, but Marius turned to soliciting the support of the troops and local Roman merchants. Metellus eventually relented, presumably realizing that an unwilling subordinate was of no use. On the basis of his claim that he could do a better job at ending the war, Marius was returned in 108 B.C. as consul for the next year. Provincial appointments, however, were the prerogative of the senate, which renewed Metellus' command. Therefore, a tribune passed a law directing that the command should be bestowed by election, and not surprisingly the voters chose Marius. Metellus shed bitter tears at the news, and as a snub to Marius, the senate bestowed on Metellus the title Numidicus as if he had won the war. These sour grapes notwithstanding, this turn of events again showed the oligarchy losing control of the political process in Rome.

Marius was to levy fresh troops to take as reinforcements to Africa, and in this he instituted a procedural change that was to be of fundamental importance in the fall of the Republic. In recent years, it had proven difficult to recruit troops only from among those who possessed enough property to qualify for at least the fifth census class, and Marius abandoned this requirement, recruiting troops from any free Romans. Thus, the old militia system that drew the state's soldiery from the comparatively well-to-do citizens who dominated the centuriate assembly was now abolished. The military would eventually become an institution that had little interest in the assemblies in Rome, or in their laws and elections. Instead, the troops' main interest would be to support their commander, who alone would be in a position to make sure that they were granted land upon discharge. While it is true that the troops of the Late Republic were not uniformly self-centered and did at times show themselves disinclined to engage in civil war, it is also true that their patriotism would center on not wishing to shed the blood of other Roman soldiers; loyalty to the state as embodied in the traditional prerogatives of the senatorial oligarchy was of little concern to them. Marius himself never exploited the new army in this way, but within less than twenty years its potential would become all too clear.

As it turned out, Marius' method of waging war against Jugurtha was little different from that of Metellus. By 105 B.C., Jugurtha was boxed into the territory of his father-in-law, the king of Mauretania, who handed Jugurtha over to Marius' quaestor, L. Sulla. Though at the time it would have been clear that all credit for ending the war in this way went to Marius as the commander with *imperium,* in later years Sulla would dispute this.

Meanwhile, the nobility continued to bungle military affairs. In 107 B.C., Marius' nobleman colleague as consul suffered yet another defeat in Gaul at the hands of the Cimbri, who by now were joined by another Germanic tribe, the Teutoni. Q. Servilius Caepio, consul of 106 B.C., continued to command in Gaul as proconsul in 105 B.C., when he was joined by one of that year's consuls, another new man, Cn. Mallius Maximus. Caepio refused to cooperate with his low-born colleague. A senatorial commission eventually persuaded Caepio to keep in the vicinity of Maximus, but he still refused to join forces. The result was a tremendous defeat at the battle of Arausio on the river Rhone in late 105 B.C., where first Caepio's, then Mallius' armies were overwhelmed. Supposedly the losses amounted to a staggering 80,000 men.

After all previous evidence of senatorial ineptitude, the news that the latest disaster had been caused by the arrogant refusal of a nobleman to cooperate with a new man resulted in even greater hostility to the oligarchy. Despite the fact that since the middle of the century it had been illegal to be reelected as consul, Marius was not only returned in absentia for the year 104 B.C. (he was still in Africa), but would hold the office continually down to 100 B.C. His consular colleagues were elected on the basis of Marius' approval. Marius thus achieved a level of personal political dominance that was unprecedented.

Marius took over the troops who had been raised in 105 B.C. and prepared them for a showdown with the Cimbri, who had in the meanwhile marched into Spain, and the Teutoni, who were milling around in northern Gaul. It was not until 102 B.C. that these Germans undertook to invade Italy. They conveniently divided their forces, which allowed the Romans to attack them separately. At Aquae Sextiae in Gaul, Marius overwhelmed the Teutoni. His colleague, Q. Lutatius Catulus was not so successful, allowing the Cimbri to enter northern Italy. The next year, Marius (with the assistance of the prorogued Catulus) wiped out the Cimbri at the battle of Vercellae. Marius now reached the pinnacle of glory as the savior of the state, being awarded the consulship of 100 B.C. simply as an honor. In that year, however, political crisis would seriously undermine Marius' prestige.

The political situation in Rome had continued to be tumultuous after Marius departed for the war in Africa. In 106 B.C., the consul Caepio had passed a law putting senators on the jury panels for the extortion court and by extension on those of all the other courts, which used the same jury panels (the details are not clear, but a likely guess is that two-thirds of the jurors would be senators and one-third equestrians). In 105 B.C., Caepio's *imperium* was revoked by law (an unheard-of action) after the defeat at Arausio, and in 104 B.C., a number of young noblemen serving as tribunes instituted legal action against various commanders implicated in the defeats in Gaul. The assault on the nobility would only increase the following year.

In 103 B.C., L. Appuleius Saturninus, son of a family of praetorian rank, held the tribunate. He had Cn. Maximus, the defeated consul of 105 B.C., convicted of treason, while a colleague had Caepio convicted. Saturninus also had a law passed that established a special court to try the charge of "lessening the majesty of the Roman People." While it was doubtful that Caepio's subjective conduct could be characterized as treason, there was no question that he had objectively harmed the prestige of the Roman People, and this new court would allow the members of the jury panels to convict senators on such grounds. Once the courts were restored to the equestrians, this would allow for a more "popular" venue for overseeing senatorial behavior, though in fact this court never became very prominent in the Late Republic. Saturninus also had a law passed, no doubt at Marius' request, granting land to the veterans of Marius' African campaign. It was the desire for similar legislation that would henceforth bind troops to their general.

In 102 B.C., Saturninus tried unsuccessfully to have a man of dubious background enrolled in the census as the son of Ti. Gracchus; Saturninus was apparently trying to associate himself with those who held the memory of the Gracchi dear. Saturninus had another associate in C. Servilius Glaucia, the son of another family of praetorian rank. In some capacity (most likely as tribune), Glaucia had a law passed restoring the jury panels to the equestrians. In 101 B.C., when presumably tribune, Glaucia also assisted in the reelection of Saturninus as tribune for the following year. The exact details are not clear, but to bring this about, one of the regular candidates was murdered to make room for Saturninus. It is even said that Marius' troops were responsible for the act. Whatever the truth of this, Marius wanted Saturninus returned to office because he needed a vigorous man to pass land legislation for his Gallic veterans.

In 100 B.C., when Glaucia was praetor, Saturninus acted on Marius' behalf. First, to secure the support of the urban plebs, he had a new grain distribution law enacted. Next, he had the land law passed. At this point, Marius had gotten from Saturninus what he wanted, but Saturninus had plans of his own, though what exactly they were is not known. First, he gained reelection for himself at the same time that the supposed son of Ti. Gracchus was also returned as tribune. The next move was to have Glaucia elected directly to the consulship for the following year. Strictly speaking, this was illegal, but given Marius' repeated consulship, such a move was not to be excluded out of hand. Nonetheless, Marius discussed the matter with a council of leading senators and ruled that Glaucia's candidacy would not be accepted: Marius could gain nothing from the combination of a tribunate for Saturninus and for the sham Gracchus under the consul Glaucia. Saturninus and Glaucia had two options, and accepting defeat gracefully was not to their liking. In the consular elections, M. Antonius, who had just come back from a successful campaign against pirates in Asia Minor, was returned first, and when it was clear that C. Memmius, the man who had as tribune in 109 B.C. summoned Jugurtha to Rome, was about to be returned, someone murdered him in the middle of the electoral assembly. The intention was to gain the consulship for Glaucia by the same means that had gotten Saturninus his second tribunate, that is, through a special election after the murder of one of the regular candidates; they seized the Capitol, presumably to pass a law allowing Glaucia's candidacy.

If they hoped that Marius would acquiesce in this move, they were wrong. Marius' sole aim now was to secure a respected seat among the leading ex-consuls, and he wished to put behind him his (to the oligarchs) disreputable past. Marius had the senate pass the so-called Final Decree just as it had in 121 B.C., and when he brought an armed force to the Capitol, Saturninus and his associates realized that the game was up and surrendered. Despite the fact that Marius had guaranteed their safety, mobs went wild and murdered them. First, in 133 B.C., the sacrosanct person of a tribune of the plebs had been violated by a senatorial mob; then in 121 B.C. a decree of the senate was used as justification when a consul attacked an ex-tribune and his supporters; now this same decree was used by the most prominent representative of opposition to the oligarchy to suppress a tribune and a praetor, who were then murdered. The oligarchy had thus had the use of violence in the defense of its interests fully ratified but would soon find that such violence could easily be used against the oligarchy. As for Marius, this violent end to his fifth consulship ruined all his hopes for respect. His complicity in the deaths of Saturninus and Glaucia caused a rupture with the opponents of the oligarchy, but the senate was not about to welcome him with open arms. Instead, the savior of Rome would stew in bitterness for a decade.

As already noted, M. Antonius was sent as praetor in 102 B.C. to deal with pirates in Cilicia, the southeastern corner of Asia Minor. The navy of Rhodes had in the past kept the pirates in check in the Aegean, but in 166 B.C. the Romans had ruined the island's economic prosperity by opening the free port at Delos (see p. 86). From then on, the problem of piracy gradually increased, and Antonius' mission was to put an end to it. Although he did temporarily subdue the area, such an ad hoc policy was no long-term solution, and the pirates would continue to cause trouble. In addition, in Cilicia the Romans had taken on yet another provincial responsibility without any increase in the number of praetors.

The early to mid-90s B.C. were comparatively calm in Rome. The ongoing problem of the desire for Roman citizenship on the part of the Italian allies was highlighted by a measure of the consuls of 95 B.C., who set up a court of inquiry to strip of Roman citizenship Latins and allies who had usurped it. While this move was irreproachable from a strictly legal perspective, it was to be disastrous politically. It was already clear enough that Rome would not grant citizenship formally, but now any process of gradual acceptance through enrollment of noncitizens in the census was to be prohibited.

This is a convenient place to examine why the allies wanted citizenship, and why the Romans refused to grant it. The leading families of the Italian communities, who had close connections with prominent Roman families, wanted the right to influence elections through voting and to run for office themselves. Lower-class Italians wanted equal benefits from military service: half of all Roman armies consisted of Italian allies, yet they received lesser shares of booty. Also, they either received lesser allotments in land distributions or were totally excluded. Finally, during the second century B.C., laws were passed prohibiting Roman magistrates from executing or even flogging Roman citizens not on military service, but a Roman magistrate could kill any foreigner he pleased at will. Since the Italian allies had over the years adopted Roman ways and even the Latin language, it seemed reasonable to them that they should share the benefits provided by the Roman state just as they shared its burdens. As for the oligarchy at Rome, which was primarily responsible for the refusal to grant citizenship, the attitude seems to have been that since they knew how to ensure their control of the Roman state under present circumstances, there was no reason to endanger this satisfactory situation. Who was to know what effect such expansion of citizenship would have on the political process? While many members of the nobility clearly recognized the inevitability (and perhaps the fairness) of the grant of citizenship, their opponents were able to play upon the greed of the common voters by claiming that an increase in the number of citizens would result in the diminution of the benefits falling to the present citizens. The result of this short-sighted intransigence would be a civil war that ushered in a decade of unprecedented violence.

The trigger for this war started in an unlikely source. While governors were supposed to act impartially in deciding disputes between the communities of the provinces who owed taxes to the Roman People on one hand and the equestrian tax-farmers (see p. 112) who collected those taxes on the other, in practice it was both less troublesome and politically beneficial to decide in favor of the tax-farmers. In the three decades since Asia's establishment as Rome's richest province, the favoritism shown towards the tax-farmers had resulted in much economic distress. Hence, the senate assigned Asia to Q. Mucius Scaevola, son of the consul of 133 B.C. and a man of notable integrity. It is not clear when this governorship took place; it was most likely after his consulship in 95 B.C., although perhaps after his praetorship. In any case, Scaevola spent only nine months in settling the affairs of Asia in a governorship that would serve as a model for excellent administration. Until his successor arrived, he left in charge his subordinate P. Rutilius Rufus, who had been consul in 105 B.C. In 92 B.C., the angered tax-farmers, who resented Scaevola's decisions against them but felt unable to attack him directly, accused Rufus of provincial extortion for his few months in command. The attack was agreed to be outrageous, but Rufus played into his accusers' hands by refusing on principle to engage in the sort of emotional appeals to the jurors that were customary in Roman courts, and thus he was convicted. This manifest injustice led to outrage and calls for reform of the courts.

M. Livius Drusus, son of the man who had subverted C. Gracchus in
122 B.C. and one of the wealthiest members of the oligarchy, took up the
challenge. He devised a program of reform that was meant to solve many
of the problems of the state in one fell swoop. He apparently conceived of
himself as the patron of the senate and as acting in its interests, but those who
accepted the by this time traditional notion that the excessive dominance of any
individual was dangerous to the senate as a whole opposed him on principle.
In practical terms, his proposals offended more people than they benefited.
First, like a good popular politician, he passed legislation instituting a grain
dole to gain the support of the urban plebs. Next, he passed a land law for the
rural plebs. To solve the dispute over the courts, he proposed transferring the
jury panels to the senate but enrolling the most prominent 300 equestrians in
the senate (which theoretically numbered 300). But the equestrians did not
want the responsibility of being senators (otherwise they would have run for
office themselves!), while the senators resented the equestrians being granted
for free the status for which they had worked so hard. Drusus used violence to
have his laws passed, and for support in the senate relied on L. Licinius Crassus,
whom Cicero considered the best orator before him and who had instituted
the court of citizenship as consul in 95 B.C. In September, Crassus died, and
Drusus' support in the senate evaporated (an indication of the huge influence
that one prestigious senator could wield). Drusus' laws were invalidated on
the grounds that they had been passed through violence, but Drusus did not
object. He must have learned from the fate of the Gracchi and of Saturninus
and Glaucia the futility of tribunician violence, and he may have still hoped to
pass legitimately the crowning element in his program: the grant of citizenship
to the allies. One day, while meeting with visitors, he was stabbed to death.
No one was ever caught, but whoever was responsible had the blood of far
more men on his hands: the death of Drusus was the last straw for the Italian
allies, who now went into revolt.

Even before the death of Drusus, the Italian allies seem to have been
making preparations to force the Romans to grant them citizenship, and
the senate sent magistrates and senators around Italy to keep an eye on this
dangerous situation. When in late 91 or early 90 B.C. a praetor learned of a
conspiracy in the city of Asculum and made threats, he was killed along with
other Romans. After this, open warfare broke out. This conflict is known as
the Social War (from *socius*, the Latin word for "ally"), the major areas of
revolt being those closest to Rome in language and culture. In effect, these
groups were the most aggrieved at the Roman refusal to grant them citizenship
because they felt themselves to be most entitled to it. The very nature of the
revolt doomed it to failure in that the only unity of the rebels lay in their wish
to be Roman. They set up a collective state with magistrates and institutions

modeled on those of Rome, but this was a completely artificial creation. Their long experience in the Roman army gave them a potent military force that inflicted several major defeats on newly raised Roman armies, but the allies never really stood a chance.

Realization of the extent of dissatisfaction among the allies came as an unpleasant surprise to the Romans, who went into official mourning. The courts were closed apart from a special court set up to try the Romans "responsible" for the outbreak of the revolt. Accusation before this court merely served as a weapon for infighting among the oligarchs, and farcically the tribune who set up the court was convicted in it in 89 B.C.!

The Romans created two military commands in 90 B.C. The consul P. Rutilius Lupus (not to be confused with P. Rutilius Rufus) held command in the east and north. He was killed in battle, and C. Marius, a relative whom he had appointed as a subordinate, saved the situation. The senate then insulted him by granting to Q. Servilius Caepio, the son of the consul of 106 B.C. and much inferior in rank to Marius, a command equal to that of Marius. Caepio then showed his ineptitude by being killed in an ambush. Marius now assumed full command and routed the Italians again. Meanwhile, another subordinate of Lupus, Cn. Pompeius Strabo, eventually inflicted a major defeat on the Italians and began the siege of Asculum, which turned out to be a nasty, protracted affair.

Meanwhile, the other consul, L. Julius Caesar, managed to keep the revolt in check with a victory over the allies, and at the end of the year returned to Rome to hold the elections, leaving in charge his subordinate L. Sulla, Marius' quaestor back in 107 B.C. In Rome, Caesar passed a law granting the Italian allies citizenship. Now the revolt was pointless, but it took some years to subdue areas that would not yield.

In the command arrangements for 89 B.C., the senate continued to exact its vengeance on Marius. Cn. Strabo was elected consul and continued in command of the siege of Asculum. One might have expected the other consul, L. Porcius Cato, to take over in the south, but instead he was given Marius' command to the east while Sulla was retained in the south. Sulla was no more a magistrate than Marius at this time and was much inferior in seniority, but the senate took the opportunity to favor Sulla, who was about to run for the consulship, and at the same time snub the upstart Marius. This may have seemed great fun at the time, but Marius' bitterness would soon be instrumental in unleashing a far more dire civil war.

As it turned out, Cato, who denigrated Marius' successes of the preceding year, got himself killed in a defeat. Strabo took over his army and defeated a huge force coming to the aid of Asculum, which then surrendered. This broke the back of the revolt in the north. Meanwhile, Sulla began the assault on Samnium and was elected consul for 88 B.C., when his subordinates would continue the conquest. Though the Roman forces suffered a few more defeats, the revolt was mostly over.

When the regular courts resumed functioning in 89 B.C., they did so with a new regime for the jury panels. A law was passed that provided for the election of the jurors by the tribes, each choosing fifteen for a total of 525. The courts used this system throughout the 80s B.C., but we have no information on how it worked in practice. This interesting attempt to solve the long-standing dispute over control of the jury panels through popular election would be swept away in Sulla's conservative reforms of the late 80s B.C.

Meanwhile, a major foreign entanglement arose in the east. Mithridates was the king of the partially Hellenized kingdom of Pontus in the northwest of Asia Minor and got involved in a dispute with the Romans over who should be king of a territory in central Asia Minor. By 90 B.C., the senate had dispatched a three-man commission headed by Manius Aquillius, the consul of 101 B.C., to find a solution. Aquillius was a greedy man and persuaded the king of Bithynia, a territory in the northwest that was allied with Rome, to attack Mithridates as a way for the king to pay off his debts to influential Romans (presumably including Aquillius). Given the seriousness of the situation in Italy at this time and the absence of a significant Roman military force in the east, this was a rash move indeed, especially when it was taken without any authorization from Rome. In any case, it proved to be disastrous. A three-pronged attack on Pontus was easily thrown back by Mithridates, who seized all of Asia Minor. Aquillius and a propraetor were captured, while another propraetor was driven to the island of Rhodes. (Aquillius was killed by having molten gold poured into his mouth as punishment for his greed.)

The precipitous collapse of the Roman position in Asia Minor must have come as a surprise both to the Romans and to Mithridates, and clearly a major force would have to be sent east from Italy to deal with this situation. In 88 B.C., Mithridates tried unsuccessfully to capture Rhodes and then sent armies into Greece, where the inadequate Roman forces were again driven back. To cement his support in the province of Asia, Mithridates ordered cities there to carry out simultaneously the slaughter of all the resident Romans, and supposedly 80,000 were massacred in this way. While there was clearly much resentment against Rome in the Greek cities, many communities did remain loyal to Rome. In any case, as consul in 88 B.C., L. Sulla was assigned the task of waging war against Mithridates, but Sulla would be prevented from moving east until the following year because a series of political disputes resulted in a full-scale civil war in Italy.

Sulla had done well in his career in the 90s B.C. and became a leading member of the oligarchy. In 91 B.C., as he looked forward to a run for the consulship, Sulla had had the king of Mauretania set up a monument on the

Capitol that portrayed the surrender of Jugurtha to Sulla, as if Sulla had been responsible (see p. 117). The supporters of Marius were so offended by the implied disparagement of Marius, who had been legally responsible for the surrender, that they were on the point of using violence to tear it down when the Social War broke out. Though Marius had had good relations with Sulla during the war against the Cimbri and Teutoni, there was now a bitter rupture between him and his former quaestor.

While granting citizenship to the allies had been easy enough to authorize in practice, determining exactly how to enroll them in the Roman state was a rather more contentious issue. The sources are not entirely clear, but it seems that the plan was to create eight tribes (voting districts) specifically for the new citizens, who would then be outvoted by the thirty-five tribes of the old citizens. The tribune P. Sulpicius Rufus wished to pass a counter-proposal that would have distributed the new citizens evenly among the thirty-five old tribes. Among the steps he took to gain support for the bill, he promised to pass a law to authorize an election to choose the commander for the eastern campaign, it being expected that Marius, who still had much influence among the voters, would be elected in place of Sulla. By this point, Sulla was in the Campanian city of Nola preparing his troops for transit to the east, and he returned to Rome to thwart Rufus. A riot broke out and Sulla was forced to take refuge in Marius' house. There, he apparently swore to allow Rufus' proposal to go through in return for their protection and then returned to his troops. Rufus proceeded to pass both his citizenship bill and a second one authorizing the election for the eastern command, which was then bestowed on Marius.

At this point, Sulla took a step that would seal the fate of the Republic, even though it would continue to function (more or less) for another four decades. Having returned to Nola, he informed his troops that if they tolerated the transfer of command, which he characterized as having been illegally implemented through violence (which was probably true enough), Marius would release them and take other troops to the east, which seemed likely to provide the troops with plenty of plunder. Sulla then led his troops to Rome, which he seized without trouble. Rufus was killed and his laws repealed, while Marius fled and, with difficulty, made it to Africa. It had never apparently occurred to them that Sulla would use his troops against the political process in Rome, a step that was unprecedented. In fact, only one of Sulla's officers (his quaestor) cooperated in the action. Sulla had some conservative reforms passed (the sources are not clear on their exact content), and after seeing to the election of the consuls for the next year, who had to pledge to support his reforms, Sulla returned to his army and crossed over to Greece in early 87 B.C.

Thus, Sulla was the first commander to take advantage of the natural loyalty of his landless soldiers to control the political process in Rome. While he may have had some legal justification in doing so, his actions represented an increase in the level of violence at Rome that was far more dangerous to the traditional oligarchy than the disorders associated with tribunes. The landless troops raised since the time of Marius' consulship in 107 B.C. had no particular loyalty to the assemblies in Rome, unlike the smallholders who used to form the bulk of the soldiery and who had an important say in affairs at Rome, especially in the centuriate assembly. Though the oligarchy would retain control for some years, the military needs of the empire would make it increasingly common for generals to have under their command large numbers of troops whose loyalties were mostly focused on the general. The civil wars that resulted would ultimately necessitate a radical revision in the structure of the state.

The lesson of Sulla's march on Rome was quickly learned. His colleague as consul in 88 B.C. was sent to take over the army with which Cn. Strabo had captured Asculum, but Strabo convinced the troops to mutiny and kill the consul, which left Strabo in command. There was not much Sulla could do about this, and he left Strabo undisturbed with his army to the north of Rome.

After Sulla's departure for the east in 87 B.C., civil war resumed in Rome. One of the consuls, L. Cornelius Cinna, renounced his adherence to Sulla's reforms and declared that he would have a bill passed distributing the new citizens evenly in the old tribes. He was opposed by his colleague Cn. Octavius. When rioting broke out, Cinna was driven from the city, and the senate declared his consulship void (he was replaced by a nonentity, which left Octavius in charge).

Octavius had apparently not learned Sulla's lesson and had no proper forces at his command. Meanwhile, Cinna took over some Roman troops who were still suppressing holdouts from the Social War and enrolled large numbers of new citizens, while Marius returned from Africa with troops raised from among his veterans, landing in Etruria to the north of Rome. As these forces marched on Rome, Octavius belatedly tried to gather support for himself. The main force available was that of the treacherous Cn. Strabo, who played both sides for a while, but eventually decided to support Octavius. Strabo died in an outbreak of disease in his army, however, which left Octavius defenseless. The forces of Marius and Cinna now seized the city, and Octavius was killed.

Marius now had his vengeance on those whom he considered responsible for the shabby treatment that he had received from the senate. In total, fourteen senators are known to have been killed. While by later standards the number of deaths was small, those killed were among the most prominent senators, and such slaughter was unprecedented. The oligarchy was now beginning to feel the violence they themselves had unleashed forty-five years before with the murder of Ti. Gracchus. Marius and Cinna were elected consuls for 86 B.C., but Marius died soon after taking up his seventh consulship. This must have been a relief for Cinna, who had tried to restrain the bitter violence of his colleague. Though Cinna's reputation would be blacked by the sources, which were written in the aftermath of Sulla's triumph in the late 80s B.C., it would seem that Cinna was an energetic and basically reasonable man who held together the opposition to Sulla. While these sources maintain that Sulla provided a refuge for the persecuted nobleman during the "reign of terror" instituted by the followers of Marius and Cinna, an unbiased reading of events shows that, in the mid-80s B.C., the oligarchy considered the political process in Rome to be legitimate, and it was Sulla, whose command in the east was now declared legally void, who was the renegade. Virtually no one fled to Sulla, and the ex-consuls were content to remain in Rome. Though the leading men of the oligarchy were no doubt not terribly happy with Cinna's control of the political scene, there was equally no doubt that the consuls elected in Rome were the authorized magistrates of the Roman People. This view would retroactively change after Sulla's ultimate victory.

Once Sulla arrived in northern Greece, he took over command of the local Roman forces, which had been driving Mithridates' troops south. Sulla launched a major assault on Athens, but this was a failure. After numerous setbacks, Sulla finally captured the town in early 86 B.C. By now another Mithridatic army had overrun Macedonia and marched south. Sulla met this force at the Boeotian town of Chaeronea, where he won an overwhelming victory. At this point, a new army arrived from Italy under the command of L. Valerius Flaccus, who had been elected to replace Marius as consul. This army stayed in the north, apparently with the intention of avoiding a direct confrontation with Sulla. Meanwhile, another Mithridatic army landed in Boeotia, and Sulla destroyed it too at Orchomenus. Greece was now securely back in Roman hands, and Sulla's prestige gave him the unshakeable loyalty of his troops.

Flaccus moved towards Byzantium to cross over to Asia Minor, but a subordinate named C. Flavius Fimbria undermined the troops' loyalty to Flaccus, who maintained tight discipline. In the resulting mutiny, Fimbria had Flaccus killed and took over command in another demonstration of the uncertain loyalties and greedy tendencies of the landless troops. Fimbria moved his army into the Roman province of Asia but failed in an attempt to capture Mithridates because Sulla's forces refused to cooperate. While one would have thought the destruction of the man responsible for murdering many thousands of Roman citizens would have been paramount, Sulla had other ideas. He preferred to cut a deal with Mithridates in order to have a free hand to deal with his Roman opponents. In the Peace of Dardanus of 86 B.C., Mithridates was allowed to keep his ancestral lands so long as he withdrew from Roman territory and provided Sulla with money and ships for an invasion of Italy.

Sulla crossed over to Asia and pursued Fimbria, who committed suicide after his army defected to Sulla. Sulla's troops were not very happy with the lenient terms given to Mithridates, but he assuaged their discontent by billeting them among the wealthy disloyal cities of Asia, where they could extort money from the locals to their heart's content. Sulla knew that money was the best way to assure his troops' loyalty in the uncertain struggle that lay ahead.

As Sulla was waging the war, both he and Cinna's supporters warily kept an eye on each other and awaited the outcome of events. Though Sulla was officially an outlaw, no direct move was taken against him (note how Flaccus tried to avoid contact in 86 B.C.). For his own part, Sulla apparently allowed new governors to be sent out from Rome for some of the recaptured areas. Cinna held the consulship continuously down to 84 B.C., having as his colleague in 85 and 84 B.C. Cn. Papirius Carbo, whose family had supported the Gracchi. The enrollment of the allies as citizens was still unresolved, and in order to avoid causing trouble at home, nothing was done about this until right before Sulla's invasion of Italy.

By 84 B.C., Sulla's position as the reconqueror of the east was secure, and Cinna decided to take an army to Illyricum (the eastern shore of the Adriatic). His exact intentions are unclear, but at the very least a campaign here would allow him to train his troops in an area that would threaten any invasion route into Italy from the east. The crossing of the Adriatic was bungled, however, and mutinous troops killed Cinna, whose death entirely changed the situation. Sulla had been in negotiations with him to try and find some compromise, but when envoys from Sulla who were traveling to Rome to negotiate a deal heard news of Cinna's death, they hurriedly returned to Sulla. All bets were now off, and Sulla resolved to end the stalemate by force.

Upon the death of Cinna, there was no clear leader for the opposition to Sulla. Carbo apparently did not have the same force of character and was not returned as consul in 83 B.C. Instead, two men who were presumably thought to be more congenial to Sulla were chosen. Sulla nonetheless landed in southern Italy with his army that year. The two consuls moved south to oppose him, but after one was defeated twice, L. Cornelius Scipio Asiagenus entered into negotiations with Sulla. Scipio made some sort of agreement with him, but his army defected to Sulla. When released by Sulla, Scipio reneged on the deal, and Sulla reacted bitterly. He declared that he would forgive those who had opposed him before Asiagenus broke his word but would pursue to the end those who continued to fight against him after that date. And an unpleasant end it would be.

At this point, it was reasonably clear who would emerge victorious, and various members of the oligarchy began to raise troops in Italy for Sulla, the most prominent of these being Cn. Pompeius, the young son of the consul of 89 B.C. Sulla's opponents were now desperate: Carbo was reelected as consul for 82 B.C. along with C. Marius, the twenty-six-year-old son of the famous general; and the slaughter of a number of prominent senators of doubtful loyalty was carried out in Rome. Meanwhile, much confusing campaigning ensued. Marius was put under siege in Praeneste and Sulla managed to capture Rome, driving the consul Carbo to Africa in the process. Sulla could not, however, achieve a decisive victory to subdue his opponents, and a huge army was raised against him in Samnium. After three unsuccessful attempts to raise the siege at Praeneste, this army marched on Rome but was wiped out by Sulla at the battle of the Colline Gate outside of Rome. Marius then died in an attempt to escape from Praeneste, and Sulla sent the young Cn. Pompeius (known traditionally in English as "Pompey") to subdue Sicily and Africa, where he executed a number of senators including the consul Carbo, earning himself the title of "young butcher."

After the victory at the Colline Gate, Sulla convened a session of the senate during which he had large numbers of prisoners noisily executed nearby. He told the not unreasonably disturbed senators to pay no attention as he was merely doing away with troublemakers. The message was clear. Sulla was in undisputed control of the state and would ruthlessly wipe out all his opponents. This was the point at which the myth began that most members of the oligarchy had secretly yearned for Sulla to deliver them from the oppression of Cinna. Sulla graciously went along with this falsehood.

Once the consuls were disposed of, Sulla had an election held to appoint him to the office of dictator, which had not been held for more than a century. A law was passed at the same time declaring that whatever he decided to do was legally valid. The oligarchic system of government that had seemed so stable only fifty years before now lay in shambles. The oligarchy had introduced violence into the political system with the murder of Ti. Gracchus, and over the years the use of violence became increasingly acceptable as various political disputes in Rome led to more and more bloody discord. The refusal of the oligarchy to grant citizenship to the allies had eventually resulted in an armed revolt and then in civil war that saw a senatorial commander use the loyalty of his landless troops to seize control of Italy and to wreak on his enemies – and others – a form of vengeance that brought domestic violence to unheard-of levels. As dictator, Sulla would try to restore senatorial control of the state, but the military needs that had allowed him to amass so much power in his hands would merely increase, and within thirty years the senatorial oligarchy's political control would collapse in another civil war.

9

RESTORED OLIGARCHY,
81 B.C.-59 B.C.

A s the self-appointed guardian of the senate, Sulla now sought to reform the constitution in order to restore the oligarchy's political control. It is hard to overestimate the importance of Sulla's reforms for the final thirty years of the functioning Republic. He was a strong believer in the adage that one should help one's friends and hurt one's foes, and the acts he carried out to this end would still be disputed twenty years later. In addition, he introduced a large number of major governmental reforms. Though some were eventually repealed, Sulla's reforms provided the basic framework of the operation of the final years of the Republic.

By the time that Sulla fought his way back to victory in Italy, he was clearly a vindictive man. He had Marius' physical remains scattered into a tributary of the Tiber and wreaked vengeance upon his still living opponents. In the midst of the indiscriminate violence that followed the victory at the Colline Gate, it was decided to "regularize" the process by drawing up lists of people who could be legally killed with impunity and whose property would then be confiscated. This procedure, which was duly enacted by law, was termed "proscription." The children of the proscribed were prohibited from holding office in the future, a measure that would later cause much strife. The property was sold at public auction and was won at cheap prices by Sulla's associates (who would be stupid enough to bid against them?). (Sulla supposedly freed 10,000 confiscated slaves, who, receiving the name Cornelius, presumably cherished the memory of their namesake.) The first proscription list consisted of the magistrates who had fought against him, but soon the lists were expanded to include large numbers of rich equestrians, including those from the Italian countryside. The sources are contradictory about the numbers involved, but something like 200 senators and 2,000 equestrians were killed. Political violence had now been institutionalized. The proscriptions were halted on June 1, 81 B.C.

The war in Italy did not end promptly with the victory at the Colline Gate. Fighting against holdouts continued into 80 B.C. Sulla had a particular antipathy for the Samnites, who were suppressed with much savagery. Sulla punished the cities that had opposed him, confiscating territory from many and even stripping some of their Roman citizenship. Sulla is said to have disbanded twenty-three legions, and he founded many colonies of his veterans in Italy on the sites of towns that had opposed him.

These were acts designed to help Sulla's friends at the expense of his enemies. He also attempted to enshrine the supremacy of the senate that was his excuse for engaging in civil war. Put together, these reforms drastically changed the appearance of the governmental system in Rome and are referred to as the Sullan constitution (though Rome, of course, had no formal constitution).

- The tribunate was emasculated. Tribunician legislation was (apparently) prohibited, and their right to intervene against the actions of magistrates restricted. In addition, to prevent the use of the office by members of the oligarchy like C. Gracchus, anyone who held the tribunate was debarred from further public office.
- The number of praetors was raised to eight, for a total of ten magistrates with *imperium*. From now on, it was the normal practice that the regular magistrates spent their year in office in Rome, the praetors presiding over a series of courts set up by Sulla, and that these men would then govern a province the following year. With ten provinces, this scheme could theoretically have worked, but already in the 70s B.C., special functions that distracted various magistrates led to certain provincial assignments lasting for three years, and in any case the addition of new provinces would ruin the plan.
- Governors now needed the authorization of the senate or People to leave their province, wage war, or enter an allied kingdom. These measures were meant to curb the independence of the governors, who were to be subordinated to the central authority of the senate and the legislation passed at its behest. It would soon turn out that mere laws were unable to restrain a determined governor with the will to use military force, as Sulla himself could have foreseen.
- To make up for the losses of the past decade and to provide for the senate's new responsibilities, Sulla enrolled large numbers of new senators, raising the total to 600. These new senators were mostly of equestrian standing. The larger total was necessary for the manning of the large jury panels, which were turned over exclusively to the senate. Election to the quaestorship now automatically conferred membership in the senate.

Sulla passed these reforms over the course of several years as dictator, while consuls continued to be elected. When Sulla resigned the dictatorship in 79 B.C. and allowed the regular offices of the Republic to return to full operation, he must have thought that he had ensured the continued control of public life by the senatorial oligarchy. Two things soon militated against this happy outcome. First, the bitter way in which he avenged himself on his enemies left many people extremely hostile to his memory and opposed to his arrangements. Even some like Cicero, who thought that the whole of Sulla's arrangements had to be defended since the abrogation of one would lead to the unraveling of the whole system, felt somewhat uneasy about the situation. The eventual "received opinion" about Sulla was that while his victory over his opponents was desirable, the way in which he exercised power afterwards was deplorable. Thus, his constitutional arrangements had an aura of "original sin" about them. Furthermore, the types of men who actively supported Sulla in exacting his revenge were greedy, murderous thugs. Among the members of the aristocracy who went over to Sulla and became the bulwark of his system, those who were not themselves corrupt were certainly guilty by association.

Second, it is a truism of modern scholarship that Sulla could not undo the precedent that he himself had set. He had shown that it was possible to use violence to overthrow the "legitimate" government and that those who assisted such an attempt could make a large amount of money in the process. While many learned the lesson about violence, most failed to note that it was ultimately the veteran legions that assured Sulla's success. There would be several unsuccessful efforts in the next two decades to use "private" violence to overthrow the state, but it was only with Caesar's willingness in 49 B.C. to lead his Gallic legions against Rome that Sulla's example would finally destroy the Republican government.

The attack on Sulla's constitution had already begun during his lifetime. While still dictator in 79 B.C., he presided over the consular elections for the following year. Both men were apparently supporters of Sulla's arrangements. Q. Lutatius Catulus was definitely a Sullan man: his father had been Marius' colleague as consul in 102 B.C. and committed suicide in 87 B.C. after Marius' capture of Rome. His colleague, M. Aemilius Lepidus, belonged to a prominent patrician family and had prospered as a result of Sulla's return, but he chose to advance himself through championing those hostile to Sulla's arrangements. During the course of 78 B.C., Sulla died an unpleasant natural death, and Lepidus immediately began to pursue a policy of opposition to the Sullan settlement. Not surprisingly, Catulus opposed this, and the year ended without the election of new magistrates. In late 78 B.C., some locals in Etruria rose up against the settlers placed on confiscated property, and when Lepidus, who already held Cisalpine Gaul as his province through a legate, was sent to suppress these rebels, he instead joined them. In 77 B.C., the senate passed its "Final Decree," entrusting the proconsul Catulus with the suppression of Lepidus.

Lepidus marched on Rome, hoping to win a second consulship. Catulus in the meanwhile sent Pompey north as his legate to attack Lepidus' legate in Cisalpine Gaul. This legate fell into Pompey's hands and was treacherously killed. When news of this reached Rome, Lepidus' resolve (or support) collapsed, and he fled to Sardinia, where he soon died a natural death. At this point, one of Lepidus' supporters, M. Perperna Veiento, son of the consul of 92 B.C. and grandson of the consul who suppressed the revolt in Asia in 130 B.C., took the remains of his forces to Spain, an area under the control of Q. Sertorius, a man who had been opposing Sulla since the civil war.

Q. Sertorius was a man of equestrian background who had commanded troops in support of Marius in 87 B.C. He was elected praetor for 83 B.C. and first supported the consuls against Sulla, then took up command as governor in Spain. He was then driven out by an army sent by Sulla and fled to Africa. In 80 B.C., Sertorius returned at the request of the Lusitani, a tribe of Further Spain. When Sertorius defeated the Sullan governor, the senate decided to send the consul Q. Caecilius Metellus Pius against him. Things did not go well for Metellus at all, his forces suffering several defeats in 79 B.C.

Sertorius now set himself up as an alternative to the Sullan settlement in Rome, establishing his own "senate" and having magistrates elected. He also actively enlisted the support of the natives. Sertorius' position was further strengthened in 77 B.C. by the arrival of the remains of Lepidus' army under Perperna, but ultimately, the anti-Sullan position in Spain depended on his own personal charisma and prestige.

Meanwhile, Pompey took advantage of the situation to extort a command for himself. Following the defeat of Lepidus, the proconsul Catulus, for whom Pompey served as legate, commanded him to disband his troops. With various excuses, Pompey avoided doing so. With Metellus faring poorly in Spain, he wished to be sent there as a proconsul, and given Pompey's military force, the senate had no choice but to comply, though the appointment was totally unconstitutional, Pompey never having held even the quaestorship and possessing no *imperium* of his own. Pompey had succeeded where death had cut short his father, that is, in using an army to extort a command for himself. He would go on to show himself to be totally unconcerned with constitutional niceties, acquiring one command after another in a completely unprecedented manner. Though support for Pompey was associated with the tradition of the *populares'* opposition to the senate, his career had little in common with the policies of the Gracchi and of Saturninus, who had championed popular discontent with the senatorial oligarchy's management of public affairs. Pompey stood for nothing but the accumulation of personal power, and he is the first of a series of "warlords" who followed Sulla's lead in using military command to gain political power in Rome.

Once he arrived in Spain to work alongside the unwilling Metellus, Pompey showed himself no more capable of bringing a swift end to Sertorius, the years 76–73 B.C. being spent in an indecisive series of maneuvers and sieges. The end came in 73 B.C., not through victory but treachery. Sertorius seems to have become tyrannical toward the end, and he was assassinated by Perperna, who succeeded to his command but lacked the charisma and authority to hold together the old coalition of anti-Sullan and local forces. Pompey lured Perperna's army into a trap, and after defeating it he captured and executed Perperna. By the time Pompey returned to Italy in 70 B.C., he was able to put the finishing touches on the suppression of a major slave revolt.

In the third century B.C., the Romans picked up an unpleasant fondness for gladiatorial shows, probably from the Samnites. Gladiators were captives who were to fight to the death as a funerary offering. Under the Republic, gladiatorial shows were never put on by magistrates in an official capacity, but magistrates would offer such shows privately as a way of gaining popularity. Soon the numbers of gladiators that were presented swiftly increased, and schools were established for training slaves (often military captives) as gladiators. Campania was a favorite site for such schools, and in 73 B.C. a revolt broke out at such a school, led by two Gauls and a Thracian called Spartacus. The rebels spread out in the countryside, and large numbers of rural slaves joined them, raising their numbers to the tens of thousands. They organized themselves militarily and defeated several raw armies sent against them. The rebels defeated a praetor and then moved into southern Italy, where their numbers increased further and they spent the winter.

In 72 B.C., the servile army was large enough to divide in two. While Spartacus realized that defeat was inevitable in Italy and wished to escape across the Alps, another leader foolishly continued to plunder southern Italy. A propraetor wiped this force out, but the rebels under Spartacus held out, in the process defeating not only three commanders of praetorian rank, but both the consuls! At this point, when they were so close to escaping from Italy, Spartacus' army foolishly turned back south. After the defeat of the consuls, the senate ordered them out of the war, and command was turned over to M. Licinius Crassus, who had been praetor the preceding year. After some maneuvering, the rebel force split in two once more, and Crassus defeated them separately, Spartacus falling in battle. All that remained was the task of rounding up fugitives. Pompey, who had recently returned from Spain, aided in this task, and to Crassus' huge annoyance, claimed that he had put the final end to the slave war. As a mark of victory, Crassus had 6,000 slaves crucified on the Appian Way between Rome and Capua. Spartacus himself is often taken as a symbol of revolt against oppression, but he had no principled objections to slavery as an institution. He simply did not want to be one himself and showed remarkable qualities of leadership in organizing other rebellious slaves and attempting to escape Italy.

When Pompey returned to Italy with his victorious army in 71 B.C., he was intent on securing the consulship, despite being underage and having held none of the prerequisite offices. Under the circumstances, the senate had no choice but to suspend the operation of the *lex Villia* (see p. 93) to indulge him. Crassus was elected consul with him, but given the way that Pompey had dimmed the lustre of Crassus' victory over Spartacus, it is not surprising that they found it hard to cooperate. They did, however, manage to pass a law restoring the tribunate to its full powers (back in 75 B.C., the prohibition against holding any other public office after the tribunate had already been repealed). It was an indication of the consuls' inability to cooperate that it was a praetor who passed a law dividing the jury panels evenly between senators, equestrians, and a class of people called "tribunes of the treasury."[1] This restoration of the tribunate and the ending of the senatorial monopoly of the jury panels were the only revisions of Sulla's constitution before civil war ended the Republic. After his disappointing consulship, Pompey would soon find new laurels for himself as a result of a war that had broken out several years earlier.

In 74 B.C., King Nicomedes of Bithynia (an area to the northeast of the Roman province of Asia) died, leaving his kingdom to the Roman People. It was clear that acceptance of this inheritance would lead to war with Mithridates (he and Nicomedes had a dispute about an area between their kingdoms), and the consuls contrived to get commands in the east. One consul would have limited participation in the war, but the other, L. Licinius Lucullus (Sulla's quaestor and right-hand man[2]), would eventually receive command of all Roman forces in Asia Minor and embark upon a major campaign far to the east.

The consuls were still in Rome in late 74 B.C., and the conflict, known as the Third Mithridatic War,[3] began with the spring of 73 B.C., when they were already in their provinces. Mithridates attacked Bithynia, cutting off the other consul, but Lucullus marched from Cilicia to help and forced Mithridates to raise the siege by cutting off his supply lines to Pontus, thus achieving a strategic victory without open battle. A Roman naval victory in the spring

---

1 The tribunes of the treasury used to be involved in tax collection, but what exactly the title signified at this time is unclear. At any rate, they were close to the equestrians in monetary qualification.
2 He was the only officer who had remained loyal to Sulla during his march on Rome in 88 B.C.
3 The Second Mithridatic War was begun in 83 B.C. by a man whom Sulla had left in command in Asia while Sulla was off engaging in civil war. Sulla wanted no trouble from the east and quickly curbed his overly enthusiastic subordinate.

of 72 B.C. then forced Mithridates to withdraw into Pontus. In preparation for an advance into Pontus, the other consul undertook a long siege of the town of Heraclea on the north coast, returning to Rome in 71 B.C. after its fall. When Lucullus decided to move east in 72 B.C., this move would entail a great expansion of Rome's commitments, and he took the decision on his own without consulting the senate.

In the spring of 71 B.C., Lucullus took a position by the town of Cabira, where he and Mithridates watched each other for a while without joining battle. Eventually, Mithridates decided to retire further east, but his army lost cohesion as it withdrew, and Lucullus destroyed it. Lucullus now set about subduing Pontus and Lesser Armenia to the east, while Mithridates retained control only of the Crimea and Colchis (western Caucasus).

After Cabira, Mithridates had fled to his son-in-law Tigranes, the king of Armenia. In ca. 96 B.C., Tigranes had come to the throne of the small Armenian kingdom and took advantage of a power vacuum caused by dynastic chaos in the Parthian and Seleucid kingdoms to seize northern Mesopotamia and northern Syria. (The Parthians were an Iranian dynasty whose territory stretched from Mesopotamia to the borders of India.) Thus, Mithridates' son-in-law was the most important king in the Near East. With the conquest of Pontus complete in 70 B.C., Lucullus demanded that Tigranes should turn over Mithridates or face war. (That this threat of war was made without any authorization from Rome shows the extent to which Roman generals now felt comfortable about acting without consulting the senate – not a surprising attitude from Sulla's quaestor!) Tigranes refused, and in 69 B.C. Lucullus invaded Armenia. To force Tigranes into battle, Lucullus invested his newly founded capital, and while Lucullus won a decisive victory, it did him no good. Lucullus destroyed the capital, and many vassals of Tigranes made their submission to the victorious Roman general, but final victory was elusive: as was the case with Jugurtha, the enemy simply withdrew into the barren interior. In 68 B.C., Lucullus invaded northern Armenia, but Tigranes refused battle and harassed Lucullus' supply lines. The early onset of bad weather in the mountains forced Lucullus to give up his campaign and withdraw to the far south, where he spent the winter of 68–67 B.C. Tigranes then returned to southern Armenia, throwing out the garrisons Lucullus had left behind. Thus, while Lucullus retained military superiority, he could not permanently occupy enemy territory.

Meanwhile, in 68 B.C., Mithridates took advantage of Lucullus' retreat to the south to invade eastern Pontus, where the locals welcomed his return. Lucullus had left a small garrison in Pontus while off on his exploits, and in the following year, Mithridates managed to defeat the Roman forces at the battle of Zela. After learning of his subordinates' troubles, Lucullus marched quickly to bring relief, but he arrived too late. After meeting the shattered remnants of the defeated army, Lucullus' troops, who were already annoyed at the tight rein he kept on them, mutinied. Refusing to march east again, they insisted on taking a position in Cappadocia, where they agreed to prevent any Mithridatic attack on Roman territory.

This was the end of Lucullus. His position of great power in the east had been a source of resentment in Rome, and in 67 B.C. the tribune A. Gabinius passed a law assigning Pontus and Bithynia to one of the consuls of the year. The revolt of his troops meant that Lucullus would have no opportunity to finish the war before the new commander arrived in 66 B.C. As it turned out, command against Mithridates would go not to the consul of 67 B.C. but to Pompey, who was in the area with a special command against the pirates. Lucullus may be considered the last Republican general in that he voluntarily relinquished command when replaced through the legal process at Rome. Yet his huge command, which lasted for six years, encompassed several provinces and led to a war undertaken hundreds of miles from the old Roman border with no consultation of the senate, shows how the geopolitical circumstances of the Roman People's empire could not be dealt with by the institutions of the old Republic.

The inability of the regular magistracies of the Republic to handle imperial concerns is illustrated by the events that led to Pompey receiving the command in the east. Already in 102 B.C., M. Antonius had been sent during his praetorship to subdue the pirates operating out of Cilicia in southeastern Asia Minor. The turmoil of the First Mithridatic War had led to an upsurge in their depredations, and from 78 to 75 B.C. a proconsul subdued much of the south coast of Asia Minor. Despite the triumph bestowed on the proconsul, the pirate problem continued. In 74 B.C., the praetor M. Antonius (son of the praetor who had campaigned there in 102 B.C.) was given the unprecedented task of subduing the pirates throughout the Mediterranean, receiving proconsular *imperium* that covered the coasts of all provinces. To some extent, this novel command overcame the problem caused by the geographically restricted provinces – namely, that if a Roman magistrate operated against the pirates in one area, they could simply sail off somewhere else. However, Antonius' personal presence was still needed for operations, which restricted his effectiveness. At first he attacked pirates in the western Mediterranean but then attacked their strongholds on Crete, where he suffered a major defeat in 71 B.C. The necessary principles to defeat them were already known, but what was needed was the right commander.

The consul of 69 B.C., Q. Caecilius Metellus, continued the campaign in Crete, but elsewhere the pirates were out of control. They even attacked Ostia, the port of Rome itself, and took many prominent Romans captive. By 67 B.C., the situation had become intolerable. Clearly the ad hoc solutions employed until now were unsatisfactory, and in that year the tribune A.

Gabinius proposed a law authorizing a completely novel form of command, this new position to be filled by an election. After much dispute, the law was passed, and Pompey was immediately elected to the new command.

Though in 74 B.C. M. Antonius had been allowed to exercise his *imperium* throughout the Mediterranean, it still basically had to be exercised by him in person (his legates derived their use of *imperium* from his, possessing none of their own). Under the *lex Gabinia*, Pompey was empowered to appoint fifteen legates who had their own *imperium* (*legati pro praetore*). In effect, the People were delegating to an individual their exclusive right to bestow *imperium*, which by normal constitutional principles could be done only through election. This completely new procedure would eventually allow the emperors to control all militarily significant provinces through *legati pro praetore*. Pompey was given *imperium* equal to that of all provincial governors to a distance of fifty miles from the coast. He also received the power to raise huge numbers of troops (more than 100,000) and vast sums of money for the purpose. This command was to last three years. As it turned out, the pirates could be dealt with in a much shorter period of time once Roman resources were coordinated. Within forty-nine days, Pompey and his legates swept the Mediterranean from west to east, and the pirate threat was finally ended with a major naval victory off Cilicia.

Thus, Pompey was now conveniently available in 66 B.C., when the full extent of Lucullus' setback in Asia became known in Rome: a tribune proposed a law to transfer the provinces of Asia, Cilicia, and Bithynia and Pontus to Pompey and to give him vast resources to prosecute the war against Mithridates, including the express right to wage war at his discretion. There was senatorial opposition to giving such a huge command to one person, but the law was easily passed. Pompey soon took over in Asia Minor and quickly marched from Bithynia into Pontus. Though Mithridates still had much money in his treasuries, he could not translate this into troops. For once, he was outnumbered by a Roman army, and at Dastira Mithridates' army was annihilated. Finding Tigranes unwilling to receive him, Mithridates withdrew to his territories north of the Black Sea (he was assassinated by a son in 63 B.C.).

Pompey made no serious effort to pursue Mithridates and earned some criticism for this. Pompey had other plans in mind: the establishment of a permanent Roman presence in the Near East. In late 66 B.C., Pompey advanced toward Armenia. Realizing that it was pointless to resist, Tigranes met Pompey and placed his diadem (crown) at Pompey's feet as a sign of submission. Pompey replaced the crown on his head, thereby allowing Tigranes to reign by his own (and the Roman People's) permission. Theoretically at any rate, Tigranes was now a client king, that is, one who owed his power to the Roman People and could be replaced at their will. Rome was entering into a new phase of foreign relations. For a century and a half, the Republic had been able to destroy any king it chose to. Now the Romans were coming into permanent relations with states on their boundaries that they could not take over themselves. The client kings would serve as a way for the Romans to control intractable foreign territory without ruling it directly, and large numbers of such kings would be set up in the Near East from now on until the first century A.D., by which time the Romans established direct rule in such territories. Pompey left Tigranes in control of his "ancestral kingdom" but on behalf of Rome took his conquests in Mesopotamia, Cilicia, and Syria. (Tigranes' submission would ever after serve as the basis of Roman claims to control over Armenia, which were constantly rejected by the Parthians and then the Persians.)

After campaigning in the Caucasus in 65 B.C., Pompey retuned to Asia Minor, where he organized the new province of Bithynia and Pontus. In an act typical of the Republic's method of indirect provincial administration, he abolished the centralized bureaucracy of the Pontic kingdom and established a number of Greek-style city-states to administer the country side. He also established permanent relations with a number of local dynasts in the barbarous upcountry of eastern Asia Minor.

In late 64 B.C., Pompey appeared in northern Syria.[4] This region was theoretically under the control of what was left of the Seleucid dynasty, but since 129 B.C. there had been no powerful king. For reasons not clearly known, Pompey decided to end the Seleucid dynasty and annex Syria as a Roman province. Presumably, Pompey felt that this wealthy area could not be left in a vacuum, with the Parthians ready to move in now that Tigranes' power had been eclipsed. He also seems to have decided to establish a permanent boundary with the Parthians. At any rate, when war broke out between them and Tigranes in 64 B.C., he offered to arbitrate and awarded Mesopotamia to the Parthians. He could have seized the opportunity of a dispute with Rome's "ally" Tigranes to embark on a new campaign, but he must have felt that Rome had absorbed enough territory, for the moment at least. Finally, in 63 B.C. he intervened in a dynastic dispute in the dynasty ruling Judaea, going so far as capturing Jerusalem. (The cities of Phoenicia and the kingdom of Judaea were allied territories overseen by the governor of Syria without being directly annexed.)

Pompey basically established where the eastern limit of Roman expansion would lie. Although there were various attempts to attack the Parthians, the

---

4 In the broadest sense, ancient Syria is the area populated by various Semitic populations and bounded by the Tarsus mountains in the north, the Mediterranean in the west, the desert west of the river Euphrates in the east, and the Sinai peninsula to the south. The narrow strip of habitable land along the southern stretch of the eastern Mediterranean littoral is generally distinguished as Phoenicia to the north and Judaea to the south.

eastern border of the Roman empire would lie along the northern Euphrates and the Syrian desert to the south for the next two centuries. Even when the Romans became more aggressive in the second century A.D., they merely advanced into northern Mesopotamia (and even that was fleeting). Before the Third Mithridatic War, direct Roman control was limited to the western and southern shores of Asia Minor. Now the Romans were directly responsible for all of Asia Minor, establishing the province of Pontus and Bithynia in the north and setting up a complicated system of subordinate kingdoms in the interior and west. In addition, the Romans took over control of northern Syria and directly confronted the Parthians with four legions and two proconsuls in the immediate area (in Cilicia and Syria). Thus, the decade between the outbreak of the war and Pompey's settlement saw the entire situation in the Near East change dramatically. Rome was now in more or less control of the entire eastern Mediterranean.[5] When Sulla raised the number of praetors to eight, there had been an equal number of provinces and of magistrates with *imperium*. Now the demands of the Roman empire began once again to outstrip the resources available to the Roman state to manage it.

The areas conquered by Pompey were very wealthy, doubling the income of the Roman state. Pompey was said to have recovered 36,000 talents from the Mithridatic treasures.[6] Though the exact total is not known, Pompey emerged from this war with vast sums in his pocket and distributed nearly 400 million sesterces to his subordinates and troops. He received extravagant honors from the Greeks of the east, who treated him as they had their royalty. Pompey himself adopted the cognomen Magnus ("the Great") as a latter-day Alexander, though many in Rome refused to recognize this very nonoligarchic name. Once it became clear in the late 60s B.C. that Pompey was quickly finishing off the war against Mithridates and Tigranes, everyone in Rome had to wonder what the conqueror of the east would do upon his return – would he act like another Sulla? This uncertainty overshadowed all decisions and is crucial to an understanding of the course of Cicero's famous consulship in 63 B.C.

Though Cicero's political importance can be overestimated because we know so much about him, he is an important figure in the political events of the last decades of the Republic. He came from one of the leading families of

---

5 In 74 B.C., Cyrene in north Africa (equivalent to modern Libya) was established as a province, to which Crete was added in the early 60s B.C. The kingdom of Cyrene had actually been bequeathed to Rome by its last king back in 96 B.C., but with its usual reluctance to set up a new province, the senate had allowed the local cities to run their own affairs. Chaos resulted and eventually forced the creation of yet another provincial command.

6 A talent weighed nominally about eighty pounds, and was worth 6,000 drachms = 6,000 denarii = 24,000 sesterces. It took about two talents to finance the operation of a ship for a year.

the town of Arpinum in southern Latium, and, despite having no ancestors who had held office at Rome, he rose to the consulship on the basis of his talents as an orator. He was considered the greatest Latin author in antiquity, and for this reason large numbers of his speeches, philosophical treatises, and letters were preserved; these allow us to have a much clearer picture of the years from the mid-60s B.C. to his death in 43 B.C. than is the case with any other period of antiquity.

Cicero was related by marriage to Marius, but he consistently ignored this connection in his political allegiance: his loyalties were completely with the senatorial oligarchy, and all he wished for was to be accepted by the nobility. For their part, the nobles were happy enough to make use of Cicero's oratorical skills but never really accepted this new man into their ranks. Talent, hard work, and good fortune did, however, bring it about that he not only reached the consulship, which was itself a remarkable achievement for a new man, but held every office in the first year allowed by law.

The trouble of Cicero's consulship revolved around L. Sergius Catilina (Catiline in English), who belonged to a patrician family fallen on hard times and who had gained wealth in his youth through acting as Sulla's henchman after the civil war – he represented the worst of those who had come to prominence through adherence to Sulla. To some extent, he is hard to judge, as all the sources disparaged him after his failure, but there seems to have been little good in him. Eventually, he tried to seize power through violence, though this may have been an act of desperation after his regular career was thwarted. Defeated in his run for the consulship in 64 B.C., he made a last, unsuccessful effort in 63 B.C., which Cicero did his best to block. In the fall of that year, there were reports of men collecting arms in Etruria for an uprising – supposedly these were veterans of Sulla who had failed at farming and wished for more illicit gains through civil war. In late October, the senate passed its "Final Decree," authorizing Cicero to secure the safety of the commonwealth. On November 7, Cicero delivered a masterful speech (the *First Catilinarian*) in which he implicated Catiline in illegal plotting for which Cicero had no real evidence. Whatever the truth of the matter, Catiline withdrew from the city, supposedly to go into voluntary exile, but he soon turned up to lead the uprising in Etruria. This was a pathetic effort that was presumably intended to repeat Marius' capture of Rome in 88 B.C., but its lack of proper preparation doomed it to failure like the efforts of Lepidus in 78 B.C. Cicero's consular colleague led a force against Catiline, who died in battle when his forces were suppressed early the following year.

More momentous was the revelation of a related conspiracy in December of 63 B.C. Some of Catiline's associates attempted to persuade envoys who were in Rome representing a tribe in Roman Gaul to convince their tribe to go into revolt, with the intention that the distraction caused by this revolt would assist Catiline's revolutionary activities. The Gauls reported this harebrained scheme to Cicero, who had the Gauls insist that the conspirators make their proposal in writing. Once this was done, Cicero had the conspirators arrested, and in a dramatic meeting of the senate made them acknowledge their part in the affair. Then their immediate execution was ordered on the basis of the "Final Decree" passed back in October. This act was of dubious legality, since the Final Decree had not been passed in connection with these events, and in any case it was normally an emergency measure taken during times of rioting. In this instance, it would have been perfectly possible to respect the legal rights of the accused and bring them to trial before the regular courts. Why, then, the need for such haste? Cicero was presumably in such haste in order to prevent Pompey from having any excuse to "intervene" in civil disturbances in Italy when he returned from the east with his victorious army. Cicero's questionable actions would eventually lead to his exile.

As it turned out, despite much fear as to his intentions, Pompey was not another Sulla. When he returned with his army in late 62 B.C., he promptly dismissed all his troops apart from a few who would take part in his triumphal entry into Rome. Like Marius, Pompey simply wanted to be a respected member of the senate now that he had achieved such glory, and, like Marius, Pompey would find that the oligarchy was hostile to a new man who had risen to such prominence against the will of the senate. This was all the more the case with Pompey, who had acquired numerous commands without having held any of the regular magistracies apart from the consulship (which he extorted illegally), who had seemed to go out of his way to offend senior senators like Crassus and Lucullus and who had in his youth executed a number of senators including a consul. Once he disbanded his army, Pompey found the senate to be obdurate in its refusal to grant him the two things he needed most: distribution of land to his veterans and ratification of his acts in the east.[7] All efforts made in 61 and 60 B.C. to secure these two ends proved fruitless, and to get what he wanted, Pompey was forced to form an alliance that would result in the demise of the Republic.

---

7 Though ratification was not necessary to validate his decisions, it would make it harder to question them, and his prestige demanded that they should be upheld.

IO

CAESAR AND THE END OF REPUBLICAN
GOVERNMENT, 59 B.C.-44 B.C.

Although this was by no means clear at the time, Caesar's consulship in 59 B.C. marks the beginning of the end of the Republic. From that date on, the normal form of government began to become unmanageable, and the issues arising from his consulship led directly to the civil war that followed a decade later. C. Asinius Pollio, a friend of Caesar's and an important political figure after his death, began his history of that civil war with the year 60 B.C., since an account of that year was necessary to understand the consulship to which he dated the start of the decline of the Republic.

C. Julius Caesar belonged to a patrician family that was moderately successful in the second and early first centuries B.C. Caesar's aunt had been married to Marius, and throughout his earlier career, Caesar did his best to play up his connection with Marius. Hence, he was not exactly a respected member of the senatorial establishment in the years of the Sullan constitution. In the debate about the Catilinarian conspirators, he spoke against their execution and in his praetorship the next year was involved in turbulent doings that were meant to set the stage for Pompey's return by violence (Caesar gave up these activities when it became clear that the situation was not ripe for intervention on the part of Pompey). After a successful governorship in Spain, Caesar was back in 60 B.C. to seek the consulship. In Caesar, Pompey saw just the man to solve his problems.

In addition to Pompey's concerns, there was another problem that helped Caesar gain the consulship. The tax-farmers who had recently bid to collect the taxes of Asia had not been aware of the extent of the economic dislocation caused by the war with Mithridates, and now that they realized that they could not make a profit, they wanted a refund of part of the money that they had paid for the privilege of collecting those taxes. Cato steadfastly blocked any compromise on this issue, which drove the tax-farmers and their equestrian friends to support Caesar. Among their chief supporters in the senate was

M. Crassus, Pompey's old consular colleague. Crassus was a man who was fond of "behind the scenes" maneuvering, and Caesar offered to solve the tax-farmers' problems if Crassus supported his run for the consulship. Caesar also secretly reconciled the two enemies Pompey and Crassus.

The man who led the opposition to Caesar and his associates was M. Porcius Cato, who was the great-grandson of the consul of 195 B.C. and was related to many of the leading families of the oligarchy. Cato had a strong reputation for personal integrity and did not care whom he offended in strictly upholding what he considered right. His main concern was to attack all those who he thought threatened the institutional integrity of the senate. His fanatical devotion to what he took to be matters of principle often led him to lose sight of the bigger picture and to force into opposition those who could have been won around to being acceptable members of the senate through judicious compromise. It was the Republic's misfortune that its most prominent defender was an uncompromising man whose inflexibility would result in civil war.

Caesar won the election, but the oligarchs managed to get Cato's son-in-law Bibulus elected, thinking that he could successfully obstruct Caesar. They misjudged both men.

After an unsuccessful effort to win the senate around to his proposals and enact them in an acceptable manner, Caesar had to resort to violence, and Pompey and Crassus openly revealed their support. The alliance of Pompey and Caesar was then cemented by the former's marriage to the latter's daughter. The astonished opposition was now routed, and Caesar passed laws ratifying Pompey's acts and reducing the tax-farmers' bid, as well as two agrarian laws that gave land to Pompey's veterans and to the urban poor. In addition, a tribune voted Caesar a five-year command in Gaul.

The influence of Caesar, Pompey, and Crassus was invincible, and until Crassus' death in 53 B.C., the combination of the three was sufficient for complete domination of the state, to the outrage of optimate opinion. This alliance is traditionally called the "First Triumvirate," but the term is incorrect and misleading. While the "Second Triumvirate" later formed in 42 B.C. was a proper magistracy authorized by law, the so-called First Triumvirate, so named by analogy with the second, was an informal, private arrangement. Caesar, Pompey, and Crassus had no officially recognized title and dominated the state purely by virtue of their various forms of influence. Furthermore, the title suggests a greater degree of unanimity than there really was. In 60 B.C. the interests of the three happened to coincide, and their cooperation went on for some years. Yet each, while tied to his companions, was willing to cooperate only to the extent that this benefited his own interests. The limited nature of their cooperation is shown by the fact that their agreement was couched in negative terms: they swore not to do anything opposed by another of them. However, so long as the oligarchs under Cato's leadership were united in the opposition to the three, they would have to stick together. The death of Crassus would eventually lead to a reconciliation of Pompey and the oligarchs against Caesar.

For the next decade, one of the major questions would be how to view Caesar's legislation. All his laws had been passed under clearly dubious circumstances, but if any single bill was invalidated, then the validity of them all would be impugned. Thus, anyone who benefited from one of the laws had to support them all. Therefore, the hostility of the senate under the influence of Cato and others necessarily forced Pompey to continue to support Caesar, despite the fact that Pompey was clearly unhappy with this situation and did not at all relish the ill will of the oligarchs.

Even though Caesar's present and later difficulties with the senate led to the retrospective conclusion that he was inherently opposed to it, this is clearly not so. In the spring of 58 B.C., before going off to seek glory in Gaul, Caesar stayed near the city, offering to submit his own acts for the senate's approval. Once more, he met with nothing but obstruction. Presumably he felt that he would be able to secure acceptance of his measures as a whole, and his opponents blocked any discussion through fear of this outcome. Caesar gave up and left for what turned out to be ten years' fighting in Gaul. When he returned after a decade, he found the same obstruction, but this time his opponents forced him into actions that would end the Republic.

There had been troubles in Gaul in the late 60s B.C., but by the time of Caesar's arrival, things were quiet. Caesar, however, was not about to let any outbreak of peace stand in the way of his quest for glory. He turned out to be a very good general, and in the interest of his own reputation, he spent the next decade waging war right and left with little justification. Caesar expanded the area of Gaul controlled by the Romans, which had been restricted to the south, to include all territory between the Pyrenees, Alps, and Rhine. In the process, he and his lieutenants made vast amounts of money from plunder and the sale of captives into slavery. Hundreds of thousands of people, if not more than a million, were killed, but since they were merely Gauls and Germans, nobody pays much attention to them. Caesar sent annual reports ("commentaries") of his activities to Rome, and later worked these up into a literary composition that survives. Not surprisingly, Caesar's self-serving account presents a flattering picture of himself and his actions, and the elegance of his style wins esteem today as it did in antiquity. This should not, however, blind us to the hypocrisy, duplicity, and savagery he exhibited in his campaigns.[1]

---

1 At one point, Cato proposed that Caesar should be turned over for punishment for his unjustified savagery against a German tribe. Naturally, Cato's proposal was based on

In 58 B.C., Caesar provoked war with two tribes outside of the Roman provinces (by his own reckoning, killing 258,000 out of 368,000 of one group). This firmly established his presence far beyond the old Roman province in the south, and he spent 57 B.C. subduing the Belgae in the area of the modern Low Countries. Caesar was masterful at the judicious use of savagery or moderation as the situation dictated (to intimidate the locals, he enslaved the entire population of one obstinate tribe – 53,000 people). At the same time, a subordinate subdued the territories along the English Channel. The year 56 B.C. was taken up with further conquests in Brittany and the southwest, which effectively brought all of Gaul under Roman control.

In 55 B.C., Caesar treacherously wiped out an entire German tribe that was trying to cross the Rhine and reconnoitred on the far side of the river for a few days. In the fall, he led a preliminary scouting expedition across the Channel to Britain and followed this up with a major invasion the next year (his command having been extended for another five years; see p. 148). The campaign in Britain proved less than successful. As the Romans would later find in Germany, it was difficult to subdue sparsely populated areas living at a low level of subsistence: the natives simply ran away, and it was dangerous and unrewarding to garrison such areas. Though Caesar claimed to have conquered the island, the Romans would not return for a century.

Meanwhile, there was discontent in Gaul. Caesar had to favor his allies, and their enemies naturally became anti-Roman. While he was off in Britain in 54 B.C., a Gallic tribe threatened a Roman garrison of a legion and a half, and when the Romans withdrew under a truce, the Gauls wiped them out. (Caesar uncharitably pins the blame for the debacle on one of the commanders, though by Roman standards Caesar should, as the commander with *imperium*, receive both the credit and blame for the actions of his subordinates.) Upon his return, Caesar attacked the tribe so savagely that they disappeared from history.

The year 53 B.C. was spent putting down more revolts, and the next year saw the last major resistance to the Romans. As in Italy during the Social War, the dominant position of the Romans had brought their diverse enemies together in a form of artificial unity. This revolt was one of "national" feeling, as even those whom Caesar had favored were carried along by the anti-Roman revolt. Though the revolt eventually encompassed most of the tribes of Gaul, it centered around the tribes to the immediate north of the Roman province. Presumably, they were most familiar with the Romans and least inclined to fall under their sway. Caesar's comparatively small forces came close to defeat several times, but eventually he hemmed the main Gallic force in at the town

---

his unflagging hostility towards Caesar, but this does show that Caesar's actions were questionable even by Roman standards.

of Alesia, and while he was besieging it, he had to construct a second set of siege works facing outward in order to beat off the attack of a relief army. In a monumental act of military skill, he defeated the relief force and then compelled the surrender of the town. Since his position was still insecure, Caesar decided to treat the surrendered rebels leniently.[2] When they went over to the Romans, the revolt pretty much collapsed. The winter of 52–51 B.C. and the following summer were spent in suppressing various holdouts. On the whole, Caesar continued to be lenient. The major exception to this was in the stronghold of Uxellodunum. When it was captured, he had the defenders' hands cut off as a permanent warning to those who would oppose Rome.

By the fall of 51 B.C., Caesar had exhausted Gaul into submission. He added 200,000 square miles to the empire of the Roman People. The amount of tribute he imposed on the conquered territory (40 million sesterces) was comparatively small, which indicates how weakened the area was after ten years of warfare. No tribe revolted again until 46 B.C. In his triumph he claimed to have killed 1,192,000 people, and he had seized so much gold that its value dropped by a quarter in Italy. Apart from benefactions throughout the Mediterranean, he paid 100 million sesterces just for the land for his new addition to the forum in Rome. The years in Gaul had been very successful – for Caesar at any rate – but now the question was whether the victorious Caesar could return to Rome in spite of the opposition of his enemies.

Meanwhile, the 50s B.C. had seen the breakdown of the traditional voting process in Rome. One factor in this was the introduction of permanent gangs to influence and disrupt voting by P. Clodius Pulcher. Younger son of the patrician family of the Claudii, Clodius seems to have enjoyed making trouble for its own sake. He generally sided with the opposition to the oligarchy, and the low-class pronunciation "Clodius" was emblematic of his professed sympathies. Clodius had a vendetta against Cicero, who had ruined his alibi in an earlier incident, and wishing to destroy him for the execution of the Catilinarian conspirators, Clodius tried to get himself adopted by a plebeian in order to seek the tribunate. Eventually succeeding, Clodius became tribune in 58 B.C. and organized gangs among the lower classes to dominate the electoral process. After first passing various laws to gain support and to avoid trouble (one law authorized the annexation on questionable grounds of the island kingdom of Cyprus and got Cato out of the way by appointing him to the task), he passed another that exiled anyone who executed Roman citizens without the People's approval. Though Cicero was not mentioned by name, this measure was clearly directed at him. Most of the nobles he consulted

---

2 Though the leader Vercingetorix was kept in prison for six years until Caesar's triumph, after which he was strangled.

recommended that he not oppose the measure by violence, and once it was passed, he departed for exile. This was perhaps premature, since he had not yet been convicted. In any case, the next year was occupied with disputes concerning his recall. Clodius used his gangs to intimidate his opponents, and in turn P. Sestius and T. Annius Milo organized gangs to oppose him in the name of the oligarchy. (Though supposedly fighting for the senate, Milo seems to have been a ruffian of Clodius' stripe.) Finally, in mid-57 B.C., legislation recalling Cicero was passed after much turmoil. Cicero interpreted the many efforts that went on throughout Italy on his behalf (Pompey organized a campaign in which the communities of Italy passed decrees calling for his recall) as a sign of his own popularity, but while there was no doubt an element of personal favor in it, the affair had taken on a symbolic significance. Cicero's exile was seen as a reflection of the violence prevalent in Roman politics, and the demands for his recall were indicative of a desire to see a return to normal conditions. This wish was to go unfulfilled.

The other factor leading to the breakdown of regular government was the ongoing dispute about the validity of Caesar's legislation. Many efforts were made to undermine Caesar, but so long as he held a legitimate command, he could not be prosecuted. The law appointing him in Gaul prohibited his replacement before 54 B.C., and in 56 B.C. a plan was hatched to separate Pompey from Caesar. Pompey had been given a special appointment in 57 B.C. to deal with a grain shortage, and Cicero made a proposal to fund this office through overturning Caesar's second agrarian law, which conveniently would not affect Pompey's veterans. Perceiving Pompey's general unhappiness with the situation and his alienation from Crassus, Caesar called a meeting at Luca in his province.[3] There, the threatening rift was settled, and it was decided that Pompey and Crassus would hold a joint consulship in 55 B.C. As a result, to his humiliation, Cicero had to abandon his plan. In the meanwhile, five months of violence were necessary to prevent the holding of elections under the hostile consuls of 56 B.C. until a cooperative *interrex*[4] could oversee the proceedings at the start of the next year.

The new consuls, who had been elected through violence, now stood for law and order, passing various ineffectual measures intended to restore order. More ominously, all three members of the alliance were granted military commands: Caesar's position in Gaul was extended for another five years, while

---

3 It is indicative of the vast influence wielded by Caesar, Pompey, and Crassus that 120 senators attended, among whom were many magistrates with *imperium*.

4 The *interrex* was an ancient position that presumably dated back to the Kingdom (the term means "in between king"). Only patrician senators could hold the position, whose sole purpose was to elect the consuls when there no longer were any to hold elections. Each *interrex* held office for five days.

Pompey received the two provinces of Spain, and Crassus was appointed to the governorship of Syria (both for five-year terms). Having no need for more glory, Pompey did not go to Spain himself and instead ruled his provinces through his legates while staying in Italy. (This novel method of governance was ultimately to be used on a much greater scale by the first emperor.) Crassus, on the other hand, was thirsty for glory equal to that of his colleagues and hastened off to Syria with the intention of winning laurels against the Parthians. This campaign turned out to be a disaster, and the death of Crassus entirely changed the dynamic in the relationship between Caesar and Pompey.

The Parthians were an Iranian people, who gained control of the eastern section of the Seleucid kingdom starting in the mid–third century B.C., and by the middle of the next century, they had taken Mesopotamia from the declining Seleucids. During his praetorship in Cilicia in the 90s B.C., Sulla was the first Roman magistrate to come into contact with the Parthians, and they played a comparatively minor role in the Third Mithridatic War. At that time, Pompey decided against continuing the war against them, settling on the Euphrates as the boundary between Roman and Parthian territory. Politically, the Parthian kingdom was organized on a sort of feudal basis. The king was not terribly strong, and under him was a powerful aristocracy that provided troops in time of war. The Iranian peoples were traditionally very effective in cavalry, and this was also true of the Parthians, whose cavalrymen were able to shoot arrows from horseback (they also had armored cavalry). The Romans had never had to deal with an enemy equipped in this way.

There had been dynastic disturbances in Parthia during the mid-50s B.C., but by the time Crassus arrived, these had been settled. Crassus invaded Mesopotamia in the summer of 54 B.C. but had not gotten very far when he decided to halt for the winter, which he spent plundering the allies. (The sources are rather hostile to him and greed was supposedly one of his faults. Whether he was any worse than the average governor is open to question.) In the spring of 53 B.C., Crassus resumed his attack. The king of Armenia advised an invasion route along the foothills of northern Mesopotamia in order to reduce the effectiveness of Parthian cavalry, but Crassus preferred a direct march through open country towards Seleucia (the Parthian capital on the Tigris in southern Mesopotamia).

At Carrhae in northern Mesopotamia, the Parthians met him. Crassus advanced immediately with his tired troops against the Parthian force in a broad, thin front with cavalry on the flanks. When the Parthians approached, the Romans formed a square; when the Parthians attacked, the Roman skirmishers and cavalry withdrew within the square. Now the Romans were surrounded, and the Parthians rained arrows in on them. Crassus sent his son Publius out with a large force (about 4,000 men) to drive them away. After drawing this force forward with a feigned retreat, the Parthians surrounded and annihilated it. The Parthians cut Publius' head off to display it to Crassus. At this point, Crassus became lethargic, and the Roman retreat soon became a rout, as the army broke into various contingents. Crassus was eventually tracked down and wiped out with the troops accompanying him. At this point, the Roman army as a whole lost all cohesion. Some surrendered on the spot, others tried (for the most part vainly) to fight their way back to Syria. Of 42,000 men, about half died, a quarter (12,000) made it back to Syria, and the remainder were taken alive by the Parthians (who settled them in distant areas, where some still survived in A.D. 1).

Crassus' quaestor Cassius (who was later to be one of Caesar's assassins) escaped with some Roman cavalry to Syria. There were great fears of a Parthian invasion, but the victorious general was murdered by his ungrateful king, and the situation in the east stabilized. The Romans had learned a rough lesson in the difficulty of invading Mesopotamia, a task that would frustrate many emperors.

Meanwhile, the civil order continued to break down in Rome. The consuls of 54 B.C. were committed enemies of Caesar, but could accomplish nothing. A scandal involving electoral corruption among the consular candidates meant that 53 B.C. again began without consuls. Though there were rumors that Pompey would be made dictator, nothing came of this. Finally, in July of 53 B.C. (the normal time for the elections for the following year!), the consuls for that year were elected. The year 52 B.C. began with yet another *interregnum*. Milo, who had organized gangs to counter those of Clodius during the period of Cicero's exile, was a consular candidate, while Clodius himself was running for the praetorship. By accident, the two met on the Appian Way south of Rome while escorted by their gangs. A brawl began in which Clodius was killed. The body was brought back to Rome, and major rioting ensued; eventually Pompey was voted sole consul with the agreement of the oligarchy (after several months, he had his new son-in-law elected as his colleague), and he used troops to suppress the rioting. The persistent failure to elect consuls in due time and the unprecedented election of a sole consul (presumably Sulla had tarnished the office of dictator sufficiently to rule it out) show the extent to which the regular government in Rome was dysfunctional. The cooperation of Pompey with the oligarchs led by Cato shows that in the aftermath of Crassus' death, Pompey was returning to his original intention of becoming a respected member of the senate, while the oligarchs were happy to use him as a tool against Caesar.

The alienation of Pompey from Caesar took place over the course of several years. Julia, Caesar's daughter who was married to Pompey, died in childbirth in 54 B.C. The child soon died, and the course of the Republic's demise may have been quite different if it had not. Pompey refused to enter into another marriage alliance with Caesar. Then the death of Crassus at Carrhae entirely changed the situation. Now there was a direct opposition between Caesar and Pompey without a third party to act as a balance. Pompey made his general intentions clear enough by marrying the daughter of a senior member of the oligarchy: he was aligning himself with the senatorial opponents of Caesar led by Cato.

As the 50s B.C. drew to a close, the question that loomed ominously was how to deal with Caesar once his command in Gaul expired. Pompey and he were apparently on a collision course. Caesar's command was soon to expire, and if he could not manage to secure a second consulship before giving up his command, he was likely to be condemned in a trial (magistrates were exempt from prosecution during their office). There was some talk of Caesar being reelected in absentia, but nothing came of this, presumably because the oligarchs would thwart the attempt. In 50 B.C., it became legally permissible to discuss Caesar's replacement in the senate, but he purchased the services of one of the consuls and a tribune to thwart this. The situation would change in 49 B.C., since both of the new consuls were known to be anti-Caesarian.

The simplest interpretation of the very complicated legal situation is that Caesar could be replaced on March 1, 49 B.C., at which point he would be without office and subject to prosecution. In his account of the civil war, Caesar claims that all he wanted was to be allowed to run for the consulship in absentia, as a law of 52 B.C. had allowed him to do. This claim is disingenuous on his part, because he also needed to block any replacement of him as governor, because otherwise he would have no protection from prosecution until January 1, 48, and he could be reasonably certain that before then his enemies could have him condemned for his clearly illegal activities as consul in 59 B.C. By the start of 49 B.C., he had been outmaneuvered by his opponents, and the question was whether he would allow them to use the legal process to end his career (he faced no worse punishment than exile). The answer was no – he preferred to begin civil war and cause the deaths of thousands in defense of his own personal interests. And the final destruction of the Republican form of government resulted.

In December of 50 B.C., the senate as a whole showed its disinclination to resolve the situation by violence when it voted 377–20 that both Caesar and Pompey should give up their armies. Nonetheless, both Pompey and the senior members of the oligarchy under the leadership of Cato were set on war. Pompey knew that Italy could not be defended against Caesar's veteran army with the available troops and planned to withdraw to the east upon the outbreak of war in order to gather forces there and return as a latter-day Sulla. Though unaware of this strategy, his oligarchic allies were keen on dividing up the spoils they foresaw from their defeated enemies. Thus, as soon as the senate could convene in January of 49 B.C., the matter of replacing Caesar was raised, and it was promptly vetoed by two tribunes acting in Caesar's name. The Final

Decree of the senate was then passed, and the tribunes, against whom nothing had, in fact, been done, fled to Caesar, who was waiting with one legion on the Rubicon River, the boundary between his province of Cisalpine Gaul and Italy proper.

The arrival of the tribunes gave Caesar all the excuse he needed to begin the war, and a few days later he crossed the river, advancing as far as the city of Ancona, where he halted. When news reached Rome, the magistrates fled to Campania and an embassy was dispatched to Caesar to protest his actions and find out exactly what he wanted. He basically agreed to give up his command in Gaul and run for the consulship in person so long as Pompey left for Spain. His terms were pretty much accepted by the senate, and the same embassy was sent back to tell him as much. It appears that by the time he received the second embassy in late January, he had decided to seek a military solution (he continued to negotiate, though in questionable faith). Though Caesar's own account of the matter has done much to confuse matters by distorting the chronology of events, it seems that the initial advance was meant to make the senate realize the seriousness of any move to destroy Caesar. Yet, when it gave in, he resumed military operations, having by this time found out that a bid for domination through civil war had a good chance of succeeding. While in 88 B.C. Sulla had been abandoned when he marched on Rome by all but one of his officers, now only one of Caesar's failed to stick with him. Furthermore, it was clear that his arrival was not unwelcome among the Romans in the areas occupied by him. He had much prestige, he was apparently not going to harm their property, and by now the landowners were more interested in being on the winning side of civil war than on upholding the traditional oligarchy – the experience of Sulla's invasion of Italy showed the dangers of choosing the wrong side. Since it had also become clear that his enemies were totally unprepared, Caesar decided to launch a swift action to seize control of Italy while delaying and confusing his enemies with peace negotiations. At first, he posed as the defender of the constitution, pointing to the expulsion of the tribunes and other supposedly nontraditional actions on the part of the senate. Increasingly, he was forced to rely on his own resources, and this plus the success of his actions led to the abandonment of any "constitutional" stance and its replacement by a more autocratic attitude.

During the lull of late January of 49 B.C., garrisons had been established by various magistrates in the towns surrounding the area where Caesar had halted his initial advance. When Caesar resumed operations in late January and quickly overran these garrisons, numerous important Republicans fell into his hands, and he now began his policy of *clementia Caesaris* ("Caesar's mercy") by which he released any captured citizens. Caesar was consciously avoiding the bloody policy of Sulla, and as a result of this and of the obvious fact that he had a better force than Pompey did, the towns of Italy generally went over to him voluntarily. Pompey now declared that Italy could not be held and announced his decision to cross over to Greece in order to marshal the resources of the east. He withdrew his forces in Italy to Brundisium for the passage to Greece, and Caesar pursued him, arriving on March 1. Caesar tried to prevent Pompey's departure by force, but by March 17, Pompey had managed to escape with his remaining forces.

Once Pompey managed to escape to Greece, Caesar marched on Rome to try to put his position on a more secure footing. Though most senators had fled with Pompey, a few remained. In particular, Caesar wanted the cooperation of Cicero, who had not gone east. In the end, he could secure the assistance of only a very few reputable senators, and in June Cicero crossed over to Greece. The visit to Rome also showed that Caesar's defense of the rights of the tribunes was a fraud. When forbidden by a tribune to set foot in the central treasury, Caesar ordered his soldiers to throw the tribune to the side and remove the vast wealth within. So much for the rights of the tribunes that Caesar was supposedly defending.

Pompey's abandonment of Italy left it in Caesar's control, and the question was what to do next. Clearly an immediate invasion of Greece was out of the question (Caesar had no fleet yet), so he decided to attack Spain, where three legates of Pompey controlled seven legions. By April, Caesar reached Massilia in Gaul, which had gone over to the Republicans and admitted the ex-consul who was the senate's legitimate replacement of Caesar in Transalpine Gaul. After a few weeks of unsuccessful attacks on the town, Caesar left the siege in the hands of a subordinate and took most of his army to Spain.

Two of Pompey's legates joined forces (five legions) to oppose Caesar, but he soon outmaneuvered their army. The morale of the Pompeian troops was dubious, and when Caesar cut off their water supply, these legates capitulated, the third soon following suit. In only forty days, Caesar had completely undermined Pompey's position in Spain. Pompey's legions there were dissolved, and the men released from their military oath. Caesar left Q. Cassius Longinus, one of the tribunes who had fled to him on the Rubicon, in charge of Spain. Not only was this to prove a poor choice, but Cassius' position was completely unconstitutional: an inscription describes him as "tribune of the plebs *pro praetore*," that is, a tribune functioning with pro praetorian-rank *imperium*. But only the Roman People could grant *imperium*, either by law or by election. Now it was the military commander who could bestow authority by virtue of the loyalty of his troops. The spirit of the Republic was clearly dead.

As Caesar, who had in the meanwhile been appointed dictator, returned to Italy, Massilia was captured and stripped of its own privileges as a punishment for defending itself against Caesar in the name of the legitimate governor of the province. Back in Rome in late 49 B.C., he had himself elected consul for the following year and tried to handle major disturbances in Italy with a plan for debt reduction (it had been feared that he would cancel debts). In addition, a substantial force that had been sent to Africa under the command of the man who had served Caesar well as tribune in 50 B.C. but otherwise had no claim to official authority was wiped out when Juba, the king of Mauretania, cooperated with the Republican governor.

In 48 B.C., Caesar once again demonstrated his initiative and luck. First, he managed to bring his forces across the Adriatic, despite adverse weather and Republican control of the seas, to face Pompey in Greece, where he was gathering the forces for his intended return to Italy. After much maneuvering around the site of Caesar's initial landing, Pompey actually pierced Caesar's lines and could have inflicted a major defeat upon him if he had realized the extent of his success. As it was, Caesar managed to escape to Thessaly in northern Greece, where he had a city sacked and plundered in order to mollify his troops and to make the Thessalians toe the line. Pompey brought up his army and camped near Caesar's position at Pharsalus.

The Battle of Pharsalus can be taken as the death blow of the Republic. Gathered there were the united forces of the legitimate government against those of the military leader Caesar. Never again would there be a military force loyal to the Republican government instead of its general. The battle took place on August 9, 48 B.C., and resulted in a complete victory for Caesar. Pompey's whole army retreated in defeat, and the next morning the remnants surrendered. Pompey himself fled for Egypt, leaving 15,000 dead. Suetonius reports that when Caesar saw them, he remarked, "This is what they wanted. After all my achievements, I, Gaius Caesar, would have been condemned if I had not sought assistance from my army." While not entirely unreasonable, this sentiment does leave out of account the readiness with which he pursued the military option once his opponents pushed him into the corner. In any case, what his enemies wanted was to punish him for his excesses in his consulship, not the death of thousands of Romans. It was Caesar who decided that his own safety was more important than any other consideration.

After the battle, no one officially surrendered on behalf of the Republican forces, and Caesar would have to find some sort of accommodation with the traditional ruling class. He generally continued the policy of clemency, refusing it only to those whom he had already pardoned. The first person to take advantage of the clemency was Cato's nephew M. Junius Brutus, who would later lead the conspiracy against Caesar. Many others fled to Africa, which was still in Republican hands.

Pompey decided to flee to Egypt, since he had restored the previous king to power in the 50s B.C. and was still owed a large sum of money for this. If he expected gratitude from the young king Ptolemy XIII, who was married to his own sister Cleopatra, he was mistaken; and he was murdered upon arrival.

Caesar arrived with a small force after occupying Asia and claimed not to be pleased by the gift of Pompey's head and signet ring.

Caesar, who was probably fifty-two years old, quickly fell in love with the twenty-one-year-old Cleopatra, Ptolemy's sister and consort, and became embroiled in dynastic squabbles.[5] After he was besieged in the palace, help finally arrived, and in the spring of 47 B.C., Caesar stormed the royal camp. Since Ptolemy had drowned in the Nile during the fighting, Caesar now made Cleopatra queen with her younger brother, Ptolemy XIV (whom she later murdered in 44 B.C.). Caesar remained in Egypt for several months, despite the fact that there were serious problems to deal with. Disorders resulting from the debt problem continued in Italy, while the Republicans were gathering their forces in Africa. Caesar did nothing about these problems as he idled away the months touring Egypt in the company of his young new girlfriend, who bore him a son that summer.

Finally, in about late June, Caesar left Egypt for Asia Minor. Mithridates' son Pharnaces, who had retained control of the Crimean territories, took advantage of the civil war to overrun his father's old kingdom in 48 B.C. Caesar apparently decided to wait until the start of the campaigning season (June by the calendar was March by season) to quash this invasion. He quickly put together an army, and met Pharnaces at Zela in early August of 47 B.C. He completely routed the royal army in four hours. In writing back to Italy, he used the famous phrase "I came, I saw, I conquered" (*veni, vidi, vici*), which was also displayed on a placard in his triumph. Caesar snidely commented that Pompey was lucky to have gained his reputation from defeating such enemies.

By September, Caesar was back in Italy and suppressed the violence that continued because of the debt crisis. He also took measures to deal with his own need for money: he had the property of his fallen enemies confiscated and auctioned off, accepted gold crowns from Italian communities, and secured loans from the wealthy. While Caesar was no Sulla, he was clearly beginning to behave in a manner by no means in accordance with Republican virtues.

Caesar primarily needed this money to pay for his planned invasion of Africa, but he was also facing problems from his own troops. They were now tired of fighting and wanted to be discharged and to receive tangible rewards. After numerous subordinates proved unable to restore order, Caesar himself had to intervene. His personality alone sufficed to end the troops' complaints. When he called them "citizens," the soldiers instantly repented and sought his forgiveness. This shows the extent to which real power now depended on the charismatic relationship that a leader could establish with his troops.

---

5 The Ptolemaic dynasty had adopted the Egyptian practice of sibling marriage, which in this instance would preclude difficulties that might arise from the marriage of a powerful individual to the king's sister.

In December of 47 B.C., Caesar sailed for Africa, where he found that a new Republic army commanded by men who had escaped from Pharsalus had been reinforced by King Juba of Mauretania. After much indecisive maneuvering in early 46 B.C., Caesar, who needed a quick victory, induced the enemy to accept battle at Thapsus by putting himself in a seemingly disadvantageous position; as usual, Caesar emerged victorious. His troops were in a bad mood, and when the Republican army tried to surrender, they refused to accept this and slaughtered 10,000 Romans. Some Republicans committed suicide, while others, including Pompey's sons Gnaeus and Sextus, fled to Spain, where there was discontent with the man Caesar had left in charge.

Caesar was generally clement, but some of his intransigent enemies were executed. Cato, however, refused to seek mercy, committing suicide. Caesar later lamented his death and claimed that he would have pardoned him. No doubt, but the unacceptability of this from Cato's point of view was the whole point. Caesar had no business "pardoning" fellow aristocrats whose sole crime had been opposition to Caesar in defense of the traditional government (or so Cato saw it). There was no denying Cato's integrity (even his enemies had to concede it), and his principled refusal to accept autocracy was to set a destructive pattern for the attitudes of later aristocrats towards the monarchical form of government that eventually replaced the Republic.

Caesar annexed Juba's kingdom as the province of Africa Nova. He also confiscated the property of local Romans who had served his enemies as centurions and imposed tribute on towns that opposed him. In June he set sail for Italy, stopping in Sardinia to collect more fines from supporters of the Republican (anti-Caesarian) cause. Whatever Caesar's original justification for the war, he now clearly judged people simply on the grounds of whether they supported or opposed him.

In the fall, Caesar celebrated triumphs over Gaul, Egypt, Pharnaces, and Juba. He passed over the campaigns against citizens in Spain and Greece in silence, but claimed that the Republicans in Africa were serving Juba (later, Caesar's heir would similarly misrepresent the war against M. Antonius and Cleopatra). After the triumph, the soldiers present received 20,000 sesterces, while the spectators received 400 sesterces as well as a distribution of free grain and oil. Gifts to the soldiery and populace of Rome would come to be one of the major elements supporting the power of the emperors.

In November of 46 B.C., Caesar was forced to leave Rome for Spain, where the subordinates to whom Caesar had delegated the task of dealing with the Republican forces, under the overall command of Pompey's son Cn. Pompeius, had proved unable to do so. When Caesar began to force his opponents back, Cn. Pompeius decided to fight because he was beginning to lose prestige among his supporters. The final battle took place at Munda in March of 45 B.C. The Republicans fought desperately, because up until now Caesar had been executing those whom he captured as rebels. Things went so badly for Caesar that at one point he contemplated suicide. Instead, his personal intervention in the fighting saved the day, which saw 30,000 of his opponents die. During mopping-up operations, Cn. Pompeius was killed, but his brother Sextus survived to cause trouble for Caesar's heir. With this victory, military opposition to Caesar was at an end. The question now was what Caesar would do with his power.

Already by the time of his arrival in Italy in September of 47 B.C. it was clear that Caesar held greater power than anyone since Sulla. Changing expectations in the intervening thirty-five years meant that it was natural to grant Caesar honors that went far beyond Sulla's. The defeat of the main remnants of the Republicans at Thapsus the next year only heightened the sense that Caesar was far superior to any other mortal, and the senate granted him completely unprecedented powers and honors. Further and greater honors followed the victory at Munda. These honors associated him with the gods, the Greek kings of the East, and the Roman kings of the past. In the process he alienated not only surviving Republicans but also important senatorial supporters of his. These disgruntled men then entered into a conspiracy against his life. The assassins thought that the murder of the dictator would be sufficient to ensure the revival of the Republic. What they did not realize was that the concept of personal autocracy was now irrevocable and that the personal prestige of Caesar could be used by others to recreate his position for themselves.

It is sometimes stated that Caesar had plans to reform Rome, but it seems clear that he had no idea of what to do next. He settled many veterans in Italy and also established numerous colonies throughout the Mediterranean basin for them. He restricted the number of recipients of free grain, reformed the court system in Rome, and replaced the clumsy lunar calendar of the Republic with essentially the 365-day calendar still in use. But he had no idea of how to find a position for himself within the traditional constitution or how to replace it.

When Caesar was in Italy between the African and Spanish campaigns, there was a feeling that the Republicans and he could come to some sort of understanding and that he would restore the Republic. Caesar "magnanimously" allowed the return to public life of certain men who had strongly opposed him in the late 50s and fought against him during the civil war. As it turned out, however, the hoped-for reconciliation was not really possible.

Perhaps out of a sense of desperation caused by this impasse, Caesar decided to campaign along the Danube before moving east to avenge the defeat of Crassus by invading the Parthian kingdom. In preparation for his absence, a law was passed authorizing him to make electoral arrangements for the years 43–41 B.C. Caesar assigned provincial governors himself, and in December of

45 B.C., he was given the right to appoint directly half of all the magistrates below the consulship (there were now sixteen praetors and forty quaestors). This was definitely not how the restored Republic was supposed to work. The last straw came in February of 44 B.C., when the increasingly high-handed Caesar was declared dictator for life. In a ceremony that is widely reported in the sources and somewhat hard to interpret, the consul M. Antonius put a diadem (a royal symbol) on his head in public, but Caesar removed it and had it dedicated to the gods. Presumably, this event was prearranged, the intention being that Caesar would accept the kingship if the crowd insisted, which it did not.

Whatever Caesar's intention, this appointment as lifetime dictator was the last straw for anyone with Republican sentiments, and a widespread conspiracy was soon formed. While many had supported Caesar from the beginning of the civil war and others had gone over to him after various defeats suffered by the Republican forces, none had done so from a desire to see Caesar installed as king. It seemed that the only solution was to kill the tyrant. The leaders of the conspiracy were Cato's nephew M. Junius Brutus and C. Cassius Longinus, who had served as Crassus' quaestor and saved the situation after the disaster at Carrhae. Both were Republicans who had been pardoned by Caesar and appointed as praetors in 44 B.C. In addition to being Cato's nephew, Brutus was supposed to be a descendant of the L. Junius Brutus who headed the conspiracy to expel the last Roman king.[6] Eventually sixty men were involved, though Cicero was not asked to join. Caesar received hints of a conspiracy but refused to take precautions, apparently trusting fatalistically in his good fortune. For once it failed to protect him, and on the Ides of March (March 15) in 44 B.C., he was stabbed twenty-three times just before a session of the senate, falling dead in front of a statue of Pompey. His assassination showed that hostility to the kingship among the senators was even greater than he suspected. It would take the cunning of his heir and the brutal experience of another thirteen years of bloody civil war to reconcile the ruling class to the inevitability of a permanent autocracy (and even then it had to be introduced covertly).

---

6 There are problems with the identification since the regicide was a patrician and the later Junii were plebeian, but that does not affect the fact that Brutus thought himself to be the tyrannicide's descendant.

II

CONFLICT OF THE WARLORDS,

44 B.C.–27 B.C.

Caesar's assassins acted on the assumption that Caesar himself was the sole obstacle to the restoration of the function of traditional Republican government, and for this reason Brutus refused to allow the assassination of M. Antonius (known in English as Mark Antony), Caesar's colleague as consul. The conspirators expected the Republic simply to start functioning again. In this they completely misread the situation. All the governors had been appointed by Caesar, and he had arranged the consuls for some years ahead. These and many other decisions by Caesar that benefited various individuals and groups could not be rescinded. In addition, there was the persona of Caesar. He was widely popular because of his successful exploits, and whoever could become heir to that persona would gain many adherents, most importantly his many veterans. Hence, the assassins were greeted with much popular indignation.

The first and most obvious candidate for filling Caesar's shoes was the surviving consul, Mark Antony. Grandson of M. Antonius the consul of 99 B.C. and son of the same-named praetor of 74 B.C. who had unsuccessfully attempted to defeat the pirates, Antony was distantly related to Caesar, served him as quaestor in the late 50s B.C., and attempted with middling success to govern Italy in 47 B.C. while Caesar was away. Caesar was pleased enough with Antony to name him as consul (despite his not having held the praetorship) for the year of his departure for the east. After the assassination, Antony tried to reach an accommodation with the perpetrators while at the same time assuming control of all the interests represented by Caesar. But he did not count on Caesar's heir.

In his will, Caesar had adopted C. Octavius, the nineteen-year-old grandson of his sister. The young man's father was the first man in the family to enter politics in Rome, reaching the praetorship but dying as governor of Macedonia. Thus, in his attempt at power, Caesar's heir had no tool to use but the name of his adoptive father, but he was eventually able to use it to become the first emperor. By Roman convention, the adoption gave him the name C. Julius Caesar Octavianus, and hence he is generally known in modern scholarship as Octavian. He never used the last part of the name, which would be a reminder of his humble origins, and hence it is best to call him "young Caesar" for the first years after the dictator's death.

Caesar's great-nephew had accompanied him to Spain in 45 B.C., but at the time of the assassination, he was studying on the eastern shore of the Adriatic. He hurried back to assume his inheritance and to attempt to become the leader of his adoptive father's followers. Naturally, Antony resented his presence but could do nothing to get rid of him. Antony now faced an insoluble problem. Any attempts to promote the image of the dead dictator alienated the supporters of the Republic, while he ran the risk that the supporters of the dead dictator would go over to young Caesar if he tried to suppress the enthusiasm for the dictator's memory that his heir was exploiting. In particular, Antony tried to downplay the games that were to be given in July in honor of Caesar's victories, but the young Caesar borrowed large sums to put them on in style. Fate intervened in the form of an unusually prominent comet, which was taken as a sign of the dictator's soul being accepted among the gods. The soldiery demanded that Antony and young Caesar be reconciled. This in turn led to a public dispute with Brutus and Cassius, whom Antony got out of the way by having the senate vote them the governorships of insignificant provinces of Crete and Cyrene.

By early October Antony had had enough of Rome. Back in May he had had a law passed giving him control of Cisalpine Gaul, which would allow him to intimidate Italy, in exchange for his previous province of Macedonia, whose legions he was allowed to keep. He now left for southern Italy to take command of four legions crossing over from Greece. His intention was to lead them north to seize Cisalpine Gaul from D. Junius Brutus. A relative of M. Brutus, D. Brutus had been appointed by Caesar as governor of Cisalpine Gaul just before his death; after participating in the assassination, D. Brutus had taken over the province in April.

In the meanwhile, young Caesar decided to take military action himself. He resolved to raise troops of his own and to undermine the loyalty of Antony's. Deciding not to attack Antony directly, young Caesar marched on Rome, arriving on November 10. Here his plans fell apart. None of his senatorial supporters would come out for him openly, and the veterans, many of whom had served under Antony, refused to march against him. When Antony marched on Rome, young Caesar realized that he did not have sufficient resources to oppose him and withdrew to Etruria with the troops loyal to him. Antony then left for Cisalpine Gaul, and by the end of the year had D. Brutus under siege in the town of Mutina (modern Modena).

This is a convenient point at which to consider the attitude of Cicero. He was a deeply dissatisfied man. Ever since his consulship nearly twenty years earlier, his oratorical skills had counted for little amidst the violence that dominated political life. Upon the death of Caesar, however, he saw his chance to use his talents in defense of the Republic. In particular, he developed an almost pathological hatred for Antony, whom he took to be the embodiment of all that was wrong with the commonwealth, and in his reckless determination to find any force to suppress Antony, he would adopt policies that were both inherently unconstitutional and in any case doomed to failure. First, he argued for granting some official standing to young Caesar, who had raised troops without any public authority. M. Brutus and Cassius were opposed to this course, realizing that there was no way that the heir of Caesar could cooperate with his assassins. While Cicero's course of action is objectively wrong-headed, the many speeches and letters of his that survive from this period have been influential in coloring modern judgments.

On January 1, 43 B.C., the two new consuls who had been appointed in 45 B.C. by Caesar assumed office. Neither had any senatorial prominence but had served Caesar well. As it turned out, they were moderate Caesarians who acted in defense of the Republic. Cicero persuaded the senate to legitimize young Caesar with the status of an ex-praetor. It is indicative of how unusual young Caesar's position was that the permission that was at this time granted for him to hold the consulship ten years earlier than allowed by law would still not let him hold that office until thirteen years later. Despite a willingness on Antony's part to compromise, negotiations broke down, and by April the two consuls were in the north with young Caesar in an effort to raise the siege of Mutina. A series of battles took place in short order, and Antony was forced to break the siege and withdraw to Transalpine Gaul.

At first Cicero rejoiced at the result, but fate intervened. One consul died in a battle and the other soon succumbed to his wounds. At this point, an attempt was made by the senate to shunt young Caesar aside. This was a fatal mistake, which showed a failure to grasp the situation. Along with other slights, the senate voted to transfer his troops to D. Brutus. Ominously, they refused, and young Caesar refused to cooperate with D. Brutus in prosecuting the war against Antony any further.

Antony, meanwhile, entered into an alliance with M. Aemilius Lepidus, son of the consul of 78 B.C. and governor of Transalpine Gaul. Lepidus had been a strong supporter of Caesar during the civil war, and it was obvious to him that if Antony was done away with, his turn would come next. Lepidus was declared a public enemy by the senate in late June, but there was not much the Republicans could do for the moment.

Meanwhile, there was upheaval in the east, which resulted in large numbers of troops coming under the command of the assassins. After the assassination of Caesar, Antony had allowed the next in line for the consulship, Cicero's disreputable ex-son-in-law, the young patrician Dolabella, to assume office, and he was appointed governor of Syria, departing for the east with troops in the fall. When in January of 43 B.C. C. Trebonius, whom Caesar had appointed as governor of Asia at the beginning of 44 B.C. and who had participated in the assassination before taking up his command, assisted Dolabella's army in its march, Dolabella showed his thanks by seizing Trebonius and torturing him to death. Dolabella then continued his march to Syria, where in the meanwhile Cassius had illegally seized control. For at the start of the year, when it seemed that armed conflict with Antony was likely, both Brutus and Cassius had decided to seize provinces for themselves. Cassius had saved Syria back in 53–51 B.C. as quaestor in the aftermath of Crassus' defeat at Carrhae, and because of his prestige from this past success, the eleven legions in the area soon went over to him. Hence, when Dolabella foolishly resolved to challenge Cassius with his own smaller force, he was easily defeated.

For his part, M. Brutus had already seized Macedonia when Dolabella was passing by on his march to the east. In late 44 B.C., M. Brutus had first gone to Athens to study philosophy instead of governing Crete, but when the governor of Macedonia left the province in early 43 B.C., he turned over control of it to M. Brutus. Back in April of 44 B.C., when Antony exchanged Macedonia for Cisalpine Gaul, it had been decided that the former would be turned over to Antony's brother C. Antonius, who was praetor in 44 B.C., but when C. Antonius entered Macedonia in January of 43 B.C., he was quickly defeated and captured by M. Brutus.

M. Brutus' seizure of Macedonia was promptly recognized by the senate, but Cassius' position in Syria was legitimized only after Antony's defeat in April. At the same time, when Sex. Pompeius, Pompey's son who had remained in armed opposition in Spain since the defeat at Munda and who was no friend of young Caesar, offered his services in defense of the state, he was rewarded with the novel position of "commander of the fleet and shore." While the proponents of the traditional constitution now controlled significant military resources, their counsel was divided. Cicero was still in favor of continuing the fight against Antony hammer and tongs and of maintaining the alliance with young Caesar, but M. Brutus and Cassius remained dubious about any alliance with the dictator's heir and refused to burn their bridges with Antony. Seeing that there was no chance of attack from the west for the time being, M. Brutus and Cassius conquered Asia Minor in the latter part of 43 B.C. Cassius in particular was energetic in seizing money from those who had supported Dolabella in order to buy the loyalty of his troops with it after the fashion of Sulla.

Back in Italy, a certain inertia took root in the senate following the defeat of Antony and the death of the consuls. Young Caesar continued to press for the consulship, and when his demands went unsatisfied, he marched on Rome in July. Resistance soon collapsed, and he was duly elected along with a cousin, who passed a special law authorizing a tribunal to try those who had murdered Caesar. Young Caesar seized the treasury to give rewards to his troops.

Meanwhile, all the governors of Spain and Gaul joined forces with Lepidus and Antony, and D. Brutus was killed while attempting to flee to M. Brutus. The time was now ripe for the Caesarians to unite, and young Caesar traveled to northern Italy for a conference. There it was agreed that Antony, Lepidus, and young Caesar were to be elected *triumviri rei publicae constituendae* ("board of three for setting the state in order") for a period of five years. (Analogy with this official triumvirate gave rise to the erroneous designation of the earlier coalition of Caesar, Pompey and Crassus as the "First Triumvirate.") The triumvirate was to have wide-ranging powers to control the state, and the consulship never again retained any substantive powers though it continued to bestow prestige. Antony retained Cisalpine and the newly conquered parts of Gaul as his provinces, while Lepidus received all of Spain and Narbonensis. It was a mark of his inferior position that young Caesar had to give up the consulship and received as provinces Africa and the islands of Sicily, Sardinia, and Corsica, which would have to be taken by force. Needing money, the triumvirs raised funds by adopting Sulla's invention, the proscriptions. A few hundred minor senators died, along with a few thousand men of equestrian rank (the sources disagree on the numbers). The only consular to die was Cicero, who thus paid the price for his ill-advised policies. In retaliation, M. Brutus had Antony's brother Gaius executed.

Many of the proscribed fled to Pompey's son Sex. Pompeius in Sicily. After his appointment as a naval commander by the senate in 43 B.C., Sex. Pompeius had seized Corsica, Sardinia, and Sicily, establishing his main position on the last island. An attack launched against him late that year by a general of the young Caesar was a failure, and Sex. Pompeius was to cause young Caesar much grief the next years. Young Caesar could, however, console himself with the senate's vote on the first day of 42 B.C. proclaiming the adoption of the dead dictator as an official god of the Roman state. Young Caesar could now style himself as "son of the god."

It was not until well into 42 B.C. that Antony and young Caesar were prepared to move east, and in September M. Brutus and Cassius moved back to the Balkans with their troops. After a certain amount of maneuvering, in October Antony provoked the Republican forces to battle near the city of Philippi in northern Greece. When his forces were defeated by Antony's, Cassius rashly committed suicide, unaware that M. Brutus had triumphed over young Caesar. M. Brutus now assumed sole command of the forces, but was not the general that Cassius had been. He offered battle in mid-November and was completely defeated. It is debatable when exactly the Republic ended, but certainly the battle of Philippi was a bloodbath for the nobility. Most of the prominent men from the period before Caesar were already dead, but large numbers of their descendants died at Philippi. The dictator's assassins and the proscribed committed suicide, but many escaped to Sex. Pompeius in Sicily.

As for the victors, Antony proceeded to subdue the east, while young Caesar returned to Italy, where he undertook the thankless job of distributing land to the veterans. They were never satisfied with what they got, while the dispossessed were obviously aggrieved. In 41 B.C., Antony's brother L. Antonius played a rather dishonest game trying to undermine young Caesar. While championing the cause of the dispossessed, he also tried to rouse indignation at young Caesar's handling of Antony's veterans by claiming that he was short-changing them. After open hostilities broke out, L. Antonius was eventually forced to seek refuge in the Etruscan city of Perusia (modern Perugia), but received no help either from the governors loyal to Antony in the north or from Antony himself. When compelled to surrender in late February of 40 B.C., L. Antonius was pardoned, but young Caesar rather uncharitably had the town councilors executed. Antony's attitude is a little hard to understand. Presumably, he was content to leave his brother to act independently against young Caesar: he stood to gain if L. Antonius succeeded, while he could deny any responsibility in the event of failure. But if this was his plan, he gained nothing in the end, and the governors of Gaul went over to young Caesar.

By 40 B.C., things looked bad for young Caesar, who was hated by the Republicans and whose actions during the proscriptions in 43 B.C., the seizure of land for the settlement of veterans after Philippi, and the war with L. Antonius in 41 B.C. had devastated Italy. While no one of importance recognized young Caesar's legitimacy, Antony had just made an accommodation with the Republican navy and was cooperating with Sex. Pompeius, whose naval forces could cut off the food supply of Rome. Now it seemed that Antony was in a position to crush young Caesar. Late in the year, Antony landed in southern Italy, but when young Caesar came to oppose him, Antony's Caesarian troops once more refused to attack the dictator's heir and forced Antony to reach a new agreement with him. Antony and young Caesar agreed to divide the Roman world basically in two at Macedonia: Antony held Macedonia and the east, while young Caesar controlled Europe to the west. Sex. Pompeius was left in possession of Sicily, and Lepidus (the now unimportant third triumvir) was given Africa.

It turned out not to be so easy to control Sex. Pompeius. He was dissatisfied with the agreement and promptly resumed his operations. It was clear that a permanent arrangement would have to be made with him, so a meeting took place in 39 B.C. Sex. Pompeius had imagined that he would be made a triumvir in place of the ineffectual Lepidus. In this he was mistaken, but he was to be consul the next year, and his control of the islands was recognized. In addition, his supporters (apart from surviving assassins) were allowed to return to Italy. Since neither young Caesar nor Sex. Pompeius had much interest in adhering to it, the agreement soon broke down. For his part, Antony gave young Caesar no assistance.

Around this time there was a change in young Caesar's status. He was beginning to gain prestige simply through the passage of time. By 38 B.C. he began to use a bizarre name, which, while having some precedent in previous practice, was extraordinary: *Imperator Caesar divi filius* or "General Caesar, son of the god." The form *imperator* represents the use as a personal name of a hereditary title voted to the dictator, and eventually this name would form part of the titulature of the emperors and become a term for that office. This new name marked the young Caesar out as a super-human individual with a separate identity from that of his adoptive father, and for the rest of this chapter he will be designated as Imp. Caesar. Around this time it became evident that Sex. Pompeius' cause was in decline, and while most of those who defected went over to Antony, a number transferred allegiance to Imp. Caesar.

In 38 B.C., Imp. Caesar launched an assault on Sicily that was wrecked by a storm. The next year was spent preparing a new force, Antony agreeing to contribute ships for it and to strip Sex. Pompeius of his consulship. In addition, the triumvirate, which had legally expired at the end of 38 B.C., was renewed retroactively for a term lasting until the end of 33 B.C. It is indicative of the extent to which legal niceties were now irrelevant that in the interval until the belated legal renewal of their powers the triumvirs had continued to hold the same powers as before, even though their office was already expired.

After meticulous preparations, Imp. Caesar's right-hand man M. Agrippa led a full-scale invasion of Sicily, with Lepidus bringing up additional forces from Africa. At the battle of Naulochus Sex. Pompeius' fleet was finally wiped out. (He fled with the remains to Asia. There he reestablished himself and entered into negotiations with Antony but was defeated and executed in 35 B.C.) After the victory, land forces being besieged by Lepidus wished to surrender to him, and when Imp. Caesar forbade this, Lepidus accepted the surrender anyway and, feeling that it was time to assert himself, demanded that Imp. Caesar leave the island to him. Imp. Caesar entered Lepidus' camp, and his prestige was such that Lepidus' troops went over to him (this bit of public drama was prearranged with the help of bribery). Imp. Caesar was already foreseeing the need to shed his reputation as a "teenage butcher" and allowed Lepidus to retire to ignominious exile in Italy, where he survived for more than thirty years. Now it was time for a showdown with Antony. Imp. Caesar spent the years 35 and 34 B.C. campaigning in the interior of the Balkans, presumably to season his troops for the impeding conflict with Antony.

After the victory at Philippi in 42 B.C., Antony moved east to take control of the defeated Republicans' provinces, in the process making the acquaintance of Cleopatra, the queen of Egypt, who bore him children. In 40 B.C., while Antony was in Greece to keep an eye on activities in Italy, the Parthians (in cooperation with a renegade Republican) seized the opportunity to overrun Syria and Asia Minor. Antony sent against them a general who first expelled the enemy in 39 B.C., and when the Parthians invaded Syria again in 38 B.C., he annihilated their army at the battle of Gindarus.[1] In effect, just as the battle of Carrhae had halted Roman expansion to the east into northern Mesopotamia, Gindarus showed that the Parthians would not be able to oust the Romans from Syria.

After further distraction during Imp. Caesar's struggle with Sex. Pompeius, Antony decided to attack Parthia in 36 B.C. In an attempt to avoid mistakes made by Crassus in his disastrous invasion, Antony decided not to march straight down Mesopotamia and instead moved to the east in order to travel through country less favorable to Parthian cavalry. He advanced quickly to the capital of Media, where he besieged the Parthian king, but in the meanwhile the Parthians wiped out his siege train, which was following at a slower pace. With the approach of winter and no sign that the siege would end soon, Antony was compelled to withdraw. Unlike Crassus, Antony did not lose heart in adversity and managed to return to Roman territory with his force still effective despite the loss of a quarter of the troops. To regain prestige, the next year he invaded Armenia and deposed its king, who had left Antony in the lurch during the Parthian campaign. Now, with the removal of Lepidus, the stage was set for a showdown with Imp. Caesar. Unfortunately for Antony, the way in which he had chosen to exercise power in the east did not help him in the coming conflict.

The invasion of 40 B.C. showed that the system of client states set up in western Asia Minor and Syria after Pompey's conquest more than twenty years earlier was unreliable, and Antony made some major readjustments in Asia Minor. In 36 B.C., he made further arrangements in favor of Cleopatra, with whom he entered into a permanent personal relationship of sorts. Antony had married Imp. Caesar's sister back in 40 B.C. and had two daughters by her, but he treated her poorly and sent her back to Italy in 35 B.C., Cleopatra having born him another son in 36 B.C. In 34 B.C., Antony celebrated a Roman triumph in Alexandria and soon ordained a thoroughgoing rearrangement of the east, both acts making a bad impression in Italy. Cleopatra herself adopted the Oriental title "queen of kings," and was given control of territories

---

1 It is a sign of the Romanization of Italy that this general had as a child been displayed in the triumphal procession of Cn. Pompeius Strabo back in 89 B.C. during the Social War.

that had been held by the Ptolemaic dynasty in the past. Her and Antony's young children were given titles implying that they would be given power over further territories in adulthood, and Cleopatra's son by Caesar the dictator was recognized as Cleopatra's co-regent. While there was nothing unprecedented in giving Roman territory to eastern potentates, the extent of these grants was unheard of. Furthermore, traditional Roman client kings were normally proven men who could serve the Roman interest in some way, but these grants to minors were clearly dynastic in purpose, serving the interest of the Ptolemaic dynasty of Egypt, which now had the blood of Roman generals in its veins.

To some extent it is difficult to understand exactly what Antony's intentions were because the preserved accounts are fairly hostile. It seems that from 37 B.C. on he was increasingly operating in the guise of a Greek monarch. While no marriage with a foreigner was recognized in Roman law, his actions suggest that he was trying to establish himself as an eastern potentate through his relations with Cleopatra. The offence caused to Roman sensibilities by Antony's eastern activities may have been exaggerated after his defeat, however, and it seems not to have caused immediate alienation among his supporters. At any rate, the desertions from his cause began only after it became likely that he would suffer military defeat. Nonetheless, this association with Cleopatra certainly did him no good in Roman opinion, and it offered Imp. Caesar a convenient excuse for war.

The triumvirate legally expired on the last day of 33 B.C. The consuls for the year 32 B.C., who were both partisans of Antony, had documents from Antony in which he sought official recognition of his dispositions in the east. Imp. Caesar wished these to be made public in order to discredit Antony. After a certain amount of negotiation about this, one consul attacked Imp. Caesar in the senate in early 32 B.C. At this point, Imp. Caesar summoned the senate, though he no longer had any official position. Sitting in his seat between the consuls, Imp. Caesar attacked both Antony and the offending consul. No one dared raise a voice against Imp. Caesar, and the consuls promptly left Rome to join Antony in the east with 300 senators in tow. Clearly, the person of Imp. Caesar was all-powerful in Rome, despite the expiration of his triumviral office.

Now Imp. Caesar was in a bit of a quandary. It was obvious that war would soon follow, but he needed to rally public opinion in Italy first. He received the necessary grounds for war when he learned of Antony's will from defectors and then had it read out in the senate. In it, Antony recognized the legitimacy of Caesarion (the son of Cleopatra whose father was supposedly Caesar the dictator), left large legacies to his children by Cleopatra, and directed that he be buried alongside Cleopatra in Alexandria. Though substantively this was not terribly objectionable, the official line in Rome was that it showed that the drunken, degenerate Antony had now completely fallen under the sway of the wanton queen of Egypt, who was the antithesis of the chaste and modest values of Italy. Imp. Caesar could thus claim to be defending Italy against the threat of decadent eastern despotism rather than waging civil war. Antony was stripped of his consulship for the next year, but was not declared a public enemy. Such a declaration would have meant an overt war against Antony, something that Imp. Caesar wished to avoid. Instead, he portrayed the matter as one involving only the foreigner Cleopatra.

Italy was in turmoil. While Imp. Caesar's interpretation of events was clear, many still supported Antony or, at any rate, had no great desire to go to war again simply for Imp. Caesar's sake. Imp. Caesar, who, to judge by the staged takeover of Lepidus' legions in 36 B.C., had a flair for public drama, hit upon the idea of turning the outrage supposedly caused by Antony's activities into a national cause. Clearly the decrees of the subservient senate and the laws passed under compulsion in the assemblies no longer signified much. Instead, a campaign was orchestrated in which the municipalities "voluntarily" expressed their will that Imp. Caesar should take command. On this basis, all of Italy, as Imp. Caesar later claimed in his autobiographical summation of his life, swore an oath of personal loyalty to him and demanded him as their "leader" (*dux*) in the upcoming struggle. This oath not only served as an excuse for the war and a rallying point, but it also gave Imp. Caesar a (nonofficial) political position to mask the fact that his power was based on control of the military. With this outpouring of public support for a national war, Imp. Caesar had war declared on Cleopatra in the fall of 32 B.C.

Antony's war plan was to gather his forces in Greece to oppose the advance of Imp. Caesar into the east. When he heard that Imp. Caesar's fleet was threatening a detachment of his own fleet in the northwest of Greece, Antony hastened there with his whole fleet but found himself stuck in a very disadvantageous position. While Antony's land forces may have been the equal of Imp. Caesar's, he had no experience in naval matters and was now cut off from his main lines of communications by Imp. Caesar's naval superiority. While Imp. Caesar refused to fight on land, Antony was unwilling to fight at sea. During the summer, Antony's situation deteriorated as his troops were weakened through malaria, and his supporters began to go over to Imp. Caesar. By late August, it was clear that something drastic had to be done.

On September 2, 31 B.C., Antony attempted to fight his way out with his naval forces in the battle known as Actium. As it turned out, his and Cleopatra's naval forces were totally routed, though they themselves managed to escape separately and sailed to Egypt. When the commander of Antony's land forces in Greece, who had been ordered to bring them to Asia, abandoned the troops, they promptly went over to Imp. Caesar. While the battle of Actium may not itself have been a major military engagement, it was politically decisive. Though it took another year to get rid of Antony and Cleopatra, they were already doomed. Troubles with veterans in Italy delayed Imp. Caesar temporarily, but by the summer of 30 B.C., he was invading Egypt from both east and west. Antony committed suicide, and after a few weeks Cleopatra followed suit, perhaps to avoid being paraded in a triumph. Imp. Caesar was proclaimed pharaoh, though legally Egypt became a possession of the Roman People. He had no choice but to kill Caesarion, his rival as son of Caesar the dictator, but otherwise spared Antony's children.

Imp. Caesar was now the undisputed ruler of the Roman world and its chosen leader. Any restoration of the Republican form of government was by now out of the question, and it remained to be seen whether Imp. Caesar, unlike his adoptive father, would be able to establish a permanent form of power for himself without offending senatorial opinion and suffering the fate of the dictator.

12

POLITICS IN THE LATE REPUBLIC

The fall of the Roman Republic is a topic that has always attracted much attention. Not only is the precipitous collapse of the traditional political system and its replacement by an autocracy inherently fascinating, but this is also the best-attested period of antiquity in terms of literary history. Nonetheless, the ancient sources concentrate primarily on the major personalities, and the amount of information about the practical functioning of the political system is limited. Hence, modern discussions of the politics of the Late Republic are necessarily rather theoretical, and differences of interpretation generally result from emphasizing varying items among the limited evidence rather than from any essential disagreement about the evidence itself.

In the nineteenth century, Roman politics of the Late Republic were understood to revolve around two "parties," the "optimates," whose pro-senatorial stance led them to be considered equivalent to conservatives, and the "*populares*," whose antiestablishment sentiment seemed to resemble European liberals of the nineteenth century. This conception was rooted in the ancient sources, which tended to view the politics of the Late Republic in terms of the Greek opposition of oligarchs and democrats. Two trends in scholarship in the early twentieth century rejected this conception. First, in 1912, M. Gelzer published a revolutionary study (the English translation is entitled *The Roman Nobility*) in which he demonstrated that the consulship of the Late Republic was dominated by a limited number of families that held the post over several generations. He showed that the term "nobleman" in Latin referred specifically to someone who had an ancestor who had held the consulship, and he explained the dominance of these families in social terms. These families had vast wealth, and Roman social relations were structured in such a way that those lower down the social ladder naturally sought assistance from their "betters," who in their capacity as "patrons" would both assist their "clients" in dealing with both legal and governmental difficulties, and expect the clients to lend their electoral support to the patron and the candidates supported by him. In addition, the term "friendship" had little to do with personal affection and was used to designate the institution by which upper-class Romans exchanged "favors" with one another (in effect, such instrumental relationships were described with the terms of personal affection). This institution was the means by which the members of the oligarchy "got things done." Next, in 1924, F. Münzer published the book known in English as *Roman Aristocratic Parties and Families*. This work was the fruition of the biographical notices of Roman individuals he made for an encyclopedia on antiquity. Münzer examined in detail the cooperation of members of various families over generations and argued that such cooperation corresponded to the "factions" mentioned in the ancient sources. This work was fundamental in establishing the scholarly method known as prosopography, that is, the study of the interrelationships among the ruling families over time.

The studies of Gelzer and Münzer were greatly elaborated in the following years. It was demonstrated that the optimates and the *populares* were nothing like modern political parties with fixed programs, and instead represent "methods of operation." While the *populares* championed the powers of the assemblies against the senate and often supported land legislation, the optimates defended the interests of the senatorial oligarchy in the guise of upholding the traditional constitution and opposed land reform as a matter of principle. The popular leaders were always wealthy individuals and mostly advocated popular programs during the lower stages of their careers, becoming more optimate in their policies as they advanced up the scale of office. Thus, politicians would support political causes not out of ideological conviction but on the basis of shifting considerations of career. It was also noted how the patron-client relationship was extended into foreign affairs, as foreign communities dealt with the oligarchy by means of hereditary patrons in the senate.

The notion of prosopography has been treated in various ways. Some viewed families as fairly consistent "factions" that were reasonably consistent in cooperating with or opposing other families over time (this view was mostly applied to the period of oligarchic continuity in the years between the Hannibalic War and the tribunate of Ti. Gracchus). Others viewed "factions" as groups led by a prominent senator at a given time and sought to delineate such factions through the examination of marriage relations (it being common practice in antiquity to cement political alliances through marriages). It was also thought that the procedures of the criminal courts of the Late Republic made it possible to discern "factional" relationships. There being no public prosecutor, for the most part the man who made an accusation also presented the pleadings against the accused, and the ancient sources provide a great deal of information about the cases of important accusers and defendants. Hence, it was considered that detailed examination of who prosecuted whom could illuminate the rivalries of various "factions."

In recent years, this conception of Roman politics has come under attack. It is argued that the followers of Gelzer and Münzer unjustifiably ignored the role of substantive issues in the political disputes of the Late Republic through a perspective that viewed politics as merely a series of conflicts among various ruling families whose marriages are thought to reveal the true nature of political associations. In effect, some scholars feel that an interpretation of Roman politics based on social structure and the study of prosopography rules out *any* role for a conflict of ideas, and these scholars generally feel that they must reject its conclusions in their entirety. In particular, a tendency to lump together the distinct interpretations of Gelzer and Münzer has the unfortunate consequence that rejection of the excesses of the prosopographical method associated with Münzer has often entailed a concomitant depreciation of Gelzer's undeniable insights into the social underpinnings of upper-class control of the regular electoral process.[1] In place of older interpretations that viewed events from the perspective of the machinations of the oligarchy, there has recently been a tendency to adopt a very democratic view of the political scene of the Roman Republic.[2] This view has some validity for the last decades of the functioning Republic, but even then the traditional role of social relations in determining political activity continued to be dominant. While it is true that it would be wrong to deny the importance of real political issues in the late Republic, it is equally wrong to deny the role of social relations as the foundation for the dominance of the senatorial oligarchy. Basically, there is no reason why the situation has to be viewed in an "either/or" fashion. It is perfectly possible for a public debate about issues to take place against a background in which men often adopt political stances on the basis of social rather than political considerations. It is no doubt incorrect to interpret the findings of Gelzer and Münzer as implying that public issues were an irrelevant façade that concealed the social structure that "really" determined political events, but it is equally fallacious to believe that the issues were all that mattered and that social

---

1 In the English-speaking world, the attack against the views of Gelzer and Münzer began with a series of essays by P. A. Brunt that are collected in his *Fall of the Roman Republic*. His reinterpretation was primarily motivated by a rejection of the prosopographical analysis of the fall of the Republic in R. Syme's *Roman Revolution*, and, in attacking Syme's analysis, Brunt rejected the methods of both Gelzer and Münzer, often in a rather vague way.

2 This democratic interpretation was implicit in Brunt's rejection of Gelzer and Münzer, but he never laid much emphasis on it. It was left for others to draw out the implications of Brunt's work, the clearest example being F. Millar, *The Mob in Rome in the Late Republic*.

considerations did not play an important role in determining the course of events.

To some extent, the debate about the extent to which Rome was "democratic" is a sterile argument over terminology. The revisionist criticism leveled against the followers of Gelzer and Münzer is most effective in showing the limits of the old interpretation of the concept of a client system (Lat. *clientela*). It is false to imagine that the noble houses of Roman politics had large numbers of lower-class clients who voted for their patrons and the candidates recommended by their patrons. In the context of social influence in the electoral process, the "client" model seems more applicable to the ways in which the office-holding class could gain support from the moderately well-to-do voters who dominated the centuriate assembly, which down to the end of the Republic almost exclusively elected members of the leading families of the nobility to the consulship. Who exactly determined the votes in the more "democratic" tribal assembly and assembly of the plebs, however, is not at all clear. The number of voters in all forms of voting was always a small fraction of the overall electorate, and the Roman assemblies seldom represented in any straightforward way the views or interest of the poor. While it is clear that in the period from Ti. Gracchus down to the Social War, various members of the office-holding class (e.g., the Gracchi, Marius, Saturninus, M. Livius Drusus the younger) championed popular discontent against the oligarchy and in the process passed legislation opposed by the oligarchy, it remains unclear why at this time in particular it became possible to use the legislative assemblies against the interests of the oligarchy as a whole. Given the lack of any concrete information about the relative numbers and voting patterns of various social groups in any particular electoral assembly and the swiftness with which the circumstances of politics in the Late Republic changed (e.g., the apparent increase in the population of the city of Rome itself, the increasing acceptability of the use of violence in politics, and the effect of the enfranchisement of Italy during the Social War), it will probably never be known what led to the sudden upsurge of independent political activity in the legislative assemblies in the late second century B.C.[3]

Within the context of the scale by which events are studied here, it is perhaps better to consider the developments in the basis of political power in Rome. In the Middle Republic, the political scene was one in which the landowners (the majority possessing small-scale holdings) would vote in Rome to determine who among the wealthiest landowners would be the leaders of

---

3 The introduction of the secret ballot, which Cicero associated with the nobility's loss of control over the electoral process, is probably not the root cause but a by-product of it. At any rate, it was only in 131 B.C., two years after the tribunate of Ti. Gracchus, that the procedure was implemented for voting on legislation.

the state. These leaders would then command the armies raised from the less wealthy landowners in wars whose main purpose was to win booty. The troops did profit, but in the process, the office-holding families became hugely wealthy, and this widening differential led to a conflict of interest between the senate and the increasingly hard-pressed smallholders. The half century from the tribunate of Ti. Gracchus to the consulship of Sulla represents a period when certain members of the office-holding classes championed the discontent of the many against the senatorial oligarchy. In the process, violence soon became an accepted tool in getting one's way.

A second factor contributing to the demise of the second-century consensus was the growth of a large and unruly populace in Rome. Since all our accounts are written by upper-class Romans who presented their own views, it is hard to determine what exactly the aspirations of the urban plebs were, but they came to dominate the electoral process in Rome. Those who wish to emphasize the importance of public issues in the politics of the Late Republic point to numerous statements from antiquity that recognize the right of the Roman People in their assemblies to control public affairs. This is no doubt true in the abstract, but the question was, whom did the assemblies represent? As the urban plebs came to play an increasingly dominant part in determining the decisions of the assemblies (certainly in legislation, to a lesser extent in elections), the decisions made in Rome came to be viewed as having less legitimacy in the broader sense among the wealthy men throughout Italy who dominated society and who, according to Roman concepts, should have the greatest say in public affairs.[4] The assemblies completely lost legitimacy when, in the course of the 50s B.C., they became the playthings of the rival gangs of Clodius and Milo. At that time, the way to the future was shown when the municipalities of Italy sent petitions to Rome (asking for Cicero's recall from exile and pledging support for Pompey before the showdown with C. Caesar). The Roman People were no longer represented in the assemblies dominated by the urban plebs but now consisted of the entire population of Italy, whose views were represented by the local elites of the municipalities. Caesar's heir, Imp. Caesar, brought this trend to fruition when he was acclaimed the leader of the Roman People by these municipalities and everyone swore personal allegiance to him.

That Imp. Caesar was in a position to receive such allegiance was the result of two other related trends that undermined the political consensus of the Middle Republic. First, the old political structure was intimately connected with the system of military recruitment. Armies were raised from the small

4 This idea is no doubt uncongenial to modern sensibilities, but there is no more reason to consider the urban plebs any more representative of the "Roman People" as a whole than the traditional office-holding class.

landowners for temporary campaigns, and it was these men who had the largest say in the decisions of the assemblies. In effect, the soldiery picked their military leaders by electing the magistrates and thus had a clear interest in maintaining the Republican electoral system. By the late second century B.C., it was clear that this system of recruitment was no longer capable of providing the necessary number of soldiers, and the efforts of the Gracchi and others to solve the problem through land distribution resulted in failure. When in 107 B.C. Marius for the first time ignored the traditional property qualifications and enrolled the landless in the army, he severed the old connection between military service and control of the electoral process in Rome. Although it took some time for the full implications to be realized, this meant that the soldiery would look to their generals to provide them with a plot of land upon discharge. Since the oligarchy had a dislike for land distribution on principle and in any case wished to deny generals the political rewards of benefiting their soldiers in this way, the landless soldiers were generally disposed to follow their generals against the senate and the electoral system in Rome. Sulla also showed that an easy way to secure the loyalty of the troops during civil conflict was the lavish distribution of booty, whether taken from foreigners or political enemies.

Furthermore, because of the strategic needs of the conquests of the Roman People, it was necessary to grant commands of a nature without precedent in the Middle Republic. The only possession of the second century B.C. that needed an ongoing military presence was Spain, and even it put unbearable pressure on the system for military recruitment. During the first half of the first century B.C., there were huge campaigns in both east and west that spanned many years and stretched for hundreds of miles and that resulted in the granting of unprecedented power to commanders who thereby acquired the resources to dominate the political scene in Rome. The new annexations also brought the need to provide armies of occupation on a permanent basis. The Republican form of government, based on the short-term tenure of governors holding restricted territories, was inherently fragmented, and the ad hoc passage of laws and senatorial decrees in Rome could not provide any sort of rational management of military resources. The special commands covering the entire Mediterranean that were established to deal with the pirate threat showed the need for some sort of overall military command to oversee the empire of the Roman People in its entirety.

Finally, the resources made available by the military necessities provided unprecedented scope to the ambitions of the office-holders. The competitive ethos had been just as strong in the Middle Republic, but then it had literally been inconceivable for someone like T. Flamininus to lead his troops against Rome if he had been superseded against his will. During the civil disorders that began with the assassination of Ti. Gracchus, violence became first acceptable and then common in domestic politics, and the use of the troops for political purposes in the 80s B.C. did away with any restraints on those who were willing to gain power by any means. The outbreak of the civil war in 49 B.C. marked the demise of the dysfunctional political system of the Republic. What now mattered was retaining the loyalty of the troops. Brutus and Cassius may have posed as defenders of the traditional constitution, but having seized their provinces illegally and secured the allegiance of their armies through the bountiful distribution of plunder, they were fundamentally no different from the other warlords competing for power in the aftermath of the death of Caesar the dictator. Even if these "Republicans" had prevailed at Philippi, they would have found it impossible to restore the old Republic. While traditional-minded Romans looked back with wistful nostalgia at the consensus of the second-century oligarchy, the old constitution had worked under circumstances that no longer held true. Basically, some way had to be found to curb the elaborate military setup necessary to maintain control over the vast territory held in the name of the Roman People. It was the genius of Caesar's heir to establish the necessary autocracy within the framework of a sham restoration of the Republic that found more or less universal acclaim.

Figure 1. These holes dug in the ground on the Palatine Hill to support the wooden beams for primitive mud-and-daub dwellings provide some of the earliest evidence for the occupation of Rome in the early Iron Age. (Photograph: Scala/Art Resource, NY.)

Figure 2. The "She Wolf" of Rome. When this wolf of Etruscan workmanship from the Regal period was discovered during the Renaissance, it was instantly associated with the story of Romulus and Remus, and the two boys were added underneath. The ancient meaning of the statue is unknown, but it is certainly suggestive of an early date for the foundation myth. (Musei Capitolini, Rome. Photograph: Scala/Art Resource, NY.)

Figure 3. The beard and toga show that this bronze bust portrays a Roman of the Middle Republic. (The custom of shaving was adopted in the second century B.C., but there is no way to know when exactly the bust was made.) This is probably the portrait of a particular individual (it is traditionally identified, for no good reason, as Brutus, the founder of the Republic), and the work was perhaps meant to convey the earnest gravity thought to be characteristic of the men who dominated public life in the period before the popular strife that characterized the last century of the Republic. (Musei Capitolini, Rome. Photograph: Scala/Art Resource, NY.)

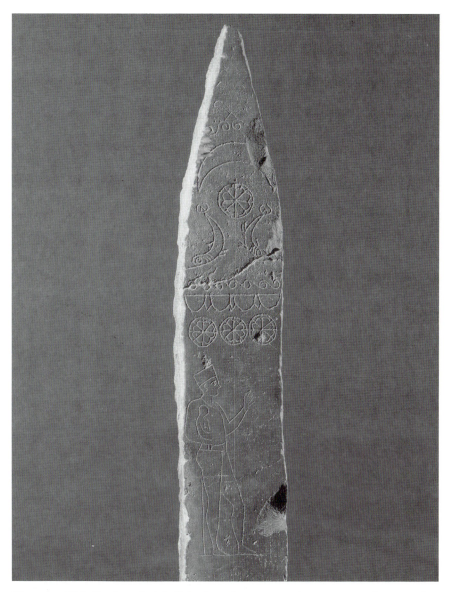

Figure 4. This Punic stele (obelisk-shaped monument) portrays a priest carrying a child and was found in the "tophet" of Carthage, that is, the site where large numbers of urns containing the burned bones of children were found. While some scholars deny that the Carthaginians engaged in child sacrifice, the archaeological and literary evidence supporting this practice is overwhelming. There is no way to tell what exactly the priest here is going to do with this child. (Musee National du Bardo, Tunis. Photograph: Erich Lessing/Art Resource, NY.)

Figure 5. This galley of the Imperial period is probably not much different from the vessels used by the Romans and Carthaginians in the naval battles of the First Punic War. (Museo Pio Clementino, Vatican Museums, Vatican State. Photograph: Scala/Art Resource, NY.)

Figure 7. This coin of ca. 110 B.C. commemorates the right of *provocatio,* which prevented a Roman magistrate from flogging or executing a Roman citizen. The figure in the center is a Roman magistrate with *imperium,* who is wearing military attire and is making a threatening gesture towards the man wearing a toga on the left (the toga being the characteristic garment of the Roman citizen); the figure on the left is the magistrate's attendant, who is carrying the rods with which the civilian is to be flogged. The word *provoco* ("I appeal" to the Roman People) is supposed to be enough to prevent the infliction of physical harm. (Other evidence shows that the words "I am a Roman citizen" were supposed to have the same effect.) The desire to gain this protection against the capricious violence of Roman magistrates was one of the reasons why the Italian allies wished to be enfranchised. The junior magistrate who had this design made (P. Porcius Laeca) was a direct descendant of a man who had had one of the laws passed in the second century B.C. that extended the right of *provocatio* beyond the *pomerium;* in the last century of the Republic, it became increasingly common for the "moneyers" (mint officials) to use the reverse designs of the coinage to commemorate the achievements of their ancestors. (© Copyright The British Museum.)

Figure 6 (*facing page*). This bronze tablet preserves a decree of a magistrate affecting the status of a local population: "Lucius Aemilius, the son of Lucius, decreed that the slaves of the Hastenses who lived in the Lascutane Tower should be free. He ordered that they should possess and hold the land and town that they had possessed at that time, so long as the Roman People and Senate wished." Roman governors had wide-ranging powers to make such decisions, and gained for themselves and their families the gratitude of those whom they favored. These powers also provided the unscrupulous with the means of making large sums through bribery. The magistrate here is probably L. Aemilius Paullus, who served as proconsul in Further Spain in 190–189 B.C. and later proved to be rapacious after his defeat of Macedon in 168 B.C. (Louvre, Paris. Réunion des Musees Nationaux/ Art Resource, NY.)

Figure 8. Cn. Pompeius (Pompey) rose to the highest offices through untraditional means, but he eventually wanted merely to become a respected leading member of the senatorial oligarchy. During the civil war with Caesar, he proved to lack vigor as a general. (Louvre, Paris. Photograph: Réunion des Musées Nationaux/Art Resource, NY.)

Figure 9. This late Republican bronze statue (of an otherwise unidentified Aule Metelle, the Etruscan form of the Roman name Aulus Metellus) shows a man engaged in oratory. Cicero and other Roman speakers would have addressed the Roman People in a similar stance. Surviving orations of Cicero show that such speeches could be quite long and elaborate, but the exact effect they had on the electorate is debatable. (Museo Archeologico, Florence. Photograph: Scala/Art Resource, NY.)

Figure 10. C. Julius Caesar let nothing and no one stand in the way of the pursuit of his own interests. After subduing all opposition in a civil war, he could find no way to reconcile his personal autocracy with the traditional constitution, and was assassinated by those who expected a return of the Republic. (Uffizi, Florence. Photograph: Alinari/Art Resource, NY.)

Figure 11. M. Tullius Cicero was a new man who gained the consulship through his powers as an orator. The information provided by his many literary works help make the last two decades of the Republic the best attested period of classical antiquity. Cicero had little practical political sense, and, in his blind hatred of Antony, he proposed gross violations of the traditional constitution that he was supposedly defending, thereby expediting the early career of Caesar's heir, the man who would finally replace the Republic with a monarchy. (Museo Archeologico Nazionale, Naples. Photograph: Scala/Art Resource, NY.)

Figure 12. This coin of ca. 112 B.C. shows the voting process. A man on the left receives from the smaller figure below a ballot on which he is to indicate his choices for magistrates (probably by writing their initials), and the man on the right has crossed the intervening gangway ("bridge") and is about to cast his ballot into the urn that would contain the votes from one voting unit. The candidates who won the votes of that one unit would receive its single vote, and those who won the most units were elected. The unequal membership of the units was one of the institutional devices intended to reduce the influence of poorer voters. The lines at the top of the design may indicate the barriers that separated this unit (perhaps a tribe whose name began with "p" if the symbol in the top left is a sign bearing that letter) from the others. (© Copyright The British Museum.)

Figure 13. This coin of ca. 63 B.C. shows a voter casting a ballot in an election about legislation. The ballot that he is about to drop in the voting urn displays the letter "u" for *uti rogas* or "as you ask," indicating that the voter approves of the legislation proposed by the presiding magistrate. A negative ballot would show the letter "a" for *antiquo* or "I reject." (© Copyright The British Museum.)

Figure 14. The Altar of Peace was voted to Augustus by the senate in 13 B.C. The monument was dismantled in Late Antiquity, and the mostly intact pieces were discovered in the 1930s. The work consists of an enclosing wall around the altar itself (*top*), and the enclosure was decorated with many symbols of peace, including a frieze portraying the arrival at the altar of various state priests and the family of Augustus. The detail (*bottom*) shows a panel featuring a female representation of *telus* ("the earth") or Italy. The children at her breast and the animals at her feet represent the abundant fertility that is to be attributed to Augustus' restoration and maintenance of peace. (Photographs courtesy of Steven E. Hijmans.)

Figure 15. The Prima Porta statue of Augustus (*above*) was excavated in the ruins of a huge villa (in the modern town of Prima Porta) that probably belonged to Livia, the wife of Augustus. On the breastplate (*right*) is a scene portraying the return of military standards lost by Crassus at the battle of Carrhae (presumably to Augustus' son-in-law Tiberius). This surrender was officially represented as a great military victory, but the fact that it was secured through negotiation (and the threat of force) illustrates Augustus' decision not to engage in war in the East. The scene on the breastplate also contains cosmic imagery, which perhaps suggests that Augustus has restored order to the world, but the exact interpretation is by no means certain. Even though the garb here is military, the effect is to show Augustus as the preserver of peace. (Photographs courtesy of Steven E. Hijmans.) (*Continues*)

Figure 15. *Continued.*

Figure 16. Gaius (Caligula) was raised under the gloomy days of Tiberius' autocracy and was mentally unbalanced. The new young emperor soon betrayed everyone's great expectations of him, and his abuse of Imperial powers finally revealed for all to see the loss of traditional liberties and the absolute control of the emperor. (Louvre, Paris. Photograph: Réunion des Musées Nationaux/Art Resource, NY.)

Figure 17. Statue of Claudius. This image clearly equates the emperor with Jupiter, the chief god of the Roman state, an aggrandizing form of portrayal that was necessitated by the emperor's physical deformities and lack of dynastic legitimacy. (Museo Pio Clementino, Vatican Museums. Photograph: Scala/Art Resource, NY.)

Figure 18. Vespasian's seizure of Imperial power is the culmination of the process by which the aristocracy of the cities of Italy came to dominate the government under the Julio-Claudians. Vespasian's unprepossessing nature is clear in this portrait, yet his comparatively humble background and lack of dynastic legitimacy forced him (and his sons) to pile up civic honors in a way that had been unnecessary for the descendants of Augustus. (Museo Nazionale Romano delle Terme, Rome. Photograph: Scala/Art Resource, NY.)

Figure 19. The Arch of Titus, voted to him by the senate to commemorate the triumph (victorious entry into the city of Rome) that he celebrated after his capture of Jerusalem in A.D. 70. (Photographs: main view; © Scott Gilchrist; details, courtesy of Steven E. Hijmans.) (*Continues Overleaf*)

Figure 19. *Continued.* The details show Titus in his triumphal chariot and the great menorah that had adorned the temple of Yahweh being carried in the procession. (Photographs: main view; © Scott Gilchrist; details, courtesy of Steven E. Hijmans.)

Figure 20. The Flavian Amphitheater (also known as the Coliseum, after a colossal statue of the sun god that stood nearby). Mostly built by Vespasian, this was the venue for the bloody spectacle put on by emperors for the entertainment and edification of the populace of Rome. Many thousands of animals and men would die during special events like the games commemorating Trajan's conquest of Dacia, but considerable (though smaller) numbers were slaughtered every year. (Photograph courtesy of Steven E. Hijmans.)

Figure 21. Trajan's Column was a novel form of monument, whose height indicated the amount of the Quirinal Hill that had to be excavated during the construction of the forum that the emperor built out of the proceeds of the conquest of Dacia. (*Continues*)

Figure 21. *Continued.* The column was covered with a spiraling visual documentary of the campaign, which could be viewed from the surrounding porticoes in the forum. To what extent this visual narrative would have been comprehensible to the average viewer is open to question. (Photographs courtesy of Steven E. Hijmans.)

Figure 22. The Pantheon (*top*), the temple to all the gods that was the brainchild of the amateur architect Hadrian. The original pantheon was build by Augustus' companion Agrippa, but dates on the bricks in the building show that the present structure was built under Hadrian, who modestly repeated Agrippa's original dedication on the porch. While the front of the building looks like a normal Roman temple, this façade conceals an amazingly original interior, which is a vast open area made possible through the use of a cement dome. The detail (*bottom*) looks up at the ceiling with its opening to let in light. (© Scott Gilchrist.)

Figure 23. The emperor Hadrian's philhellenism is manifested in his beard. The Romans gave up wearing beards towards the end of the Republic, and in growing a beard Hadrian was following Greek practice. Wearing a beard became customary for emperors until the Christian Constantine returned to shaving. This bronze statue was excavated in modern Israel, where the philhellenic emperor's policies led to a destructive second revolt. (Israel Museum, Jerusalem. Photograph: Erich Lessing/Art Resource/NY.)

Figure 24. A column was set up to commemorate the German campaigns of Marcus Aurelius in imitation of Trajan's column. The literary tradition for Trajan's Dacian Wars, while far from complete, nonetheless make it possible to make reasonable conjectures about the events portrayed on his column, but the much poorer record of Marcus' war makes it much harder to understand the events portrayed here. (Photograph courtesy of Steven E. Hijmans.)

Figure 25. This majestic bronze statue of the emperor Marcus Aurelius on horse-back survived through the Middle Ages only because of the erroneous belief that it portrayed the first Christian emperor, Constantine. The rather emotionally cold portrait is appropriate for the Stoic philosopher, but such treatment is typical of the middle second century. (Photograph: Art Resource, NY.)

Figure 26. The megalomania of Commodus is apparent in this bust, which represents him as the hero-god Hercules wearing the skin of the Nemean lion. Such a guise is appropriate for an emperor who killed animals in the Coliseum, a degrading act by normal Roman conceptions. (Musei Capitolini, Rome. Photograph: Scala/Art Resource, NY.)

Figure 27. This arch in the Roman Forum was dedicated by the senate to Septimius Severus to commemorate his triumph in civil war. Note how much larger this monument is than that of Titus (Fig. 19), which is indicative of the inflation of Imperial honors and titles under the insecure Severans. The arch is also representative of Severus' overtly vindictive attitude towards his foes: civil war had been thought unworthy of commemoration through triumphs under the Republic. (Photograph courtesy of Scott Gilchrist.)

Figure 28. Sculptors of the early to mid–third century often made remarkably vivid portraits of various emperors. In this bust of Severus' son Antoninus (Caracalla), the angry expression and the violent turning of the head to the left seem to confirm the seriously disturbed personality attributed to him in the literary tradition. (Louvre, Paris. Photograph: Réunion des Musées Nationaux/Art Resource, NY.)

Figure 29. A group of praetorian guardsmen. For the most part, they had little to do, but the praetorians' central encampment gave them a crucial role when a dynasty failed. (Louvre, Paris. Photograph: Erich Lessing/Art Resource, NY.)

NERO CLAVDIVS DIVI CLAVDI F GERMANICI CAESAR
N TI CAESAR I S AVG PRON DIVI AVG ABN CAES
AVG GERMAN PONT MAX TRIB POT VII IMP VII
COS IIII   PEDITIB ET EQVITIB QVI MILIT IN
COH VII QVAE APPELLANTVR PASTVR ET CAL
LAECOR ET I HISPAN ET I ALPINOR ET I VSI
TANOR ET II ALPINOR ET I HISP ET V LVCENS
ET CALLAECOR ET SVNT IN ILLYRICO SVB L SAL
VIDIENO SALVIANO RVI QQQ QVINA ET VICENA
STIPENDIA VT IVRA MERVER QVOR NOMIN
SVBSCRIPTA SVNT IPSIS LIBERIS POSTERISQ

EORVM CIVITATE M DEDIT ET CONVBIVM CVM
VXORIB QVAS TVNC HABVISSENT CVM EST
CIVITAS IIS DATA NAVT IS IOV I CAELIB ESSENT
CVM IIS QVAS POSTEA DVXISSENT DVM TAX
SINGVLI SINGVLAS AD VINON IVLGN PI
DANIO SALINATORE L VELL IO PATERCVLO
COS COH II HISPAN CVI PRAEST C CAESIVS
APER IOV II IANTVMARO ANDEDVNIS F
VARCIANO DESCR ET RECOGN EX TABVIA
AENEA QVAE FIXA EST IN CAPITOLIO ADIA
TVS SINISTR AEDIS THENSAR   EXTERISECVS

Figure 30. "Military diploma" is the modern term for documents that were provided to non-Roman soldiers who had been enfranchised (along with their wives
and children) after fulfilling twenty-five years' service. Every year, a large tablet
was erected in Rome for each province to record the grants given to all the men so
discharged from all the units in that province, and there was a service to provide
individuals with extracts that could serve as proof of their citizenship in their
homes. This one records a grant made by Nero on July 2, A.D. 60, to the caval-
ryman Iantumar the son of Andedunis, who had served in the Second Cohort of
Spaniards in Illyricum. (Kunsthistorisches Museum, Vienna; Photograph: Erich
Lessing/Art Resource, NY.)

Figure 31. This frieze from a private funerary monument shows a chariot race in progress in the Circus Maximus, the huge race course that could seat nearly 250,000 spectators. The chariots ran eight laps around the central spine. Presumably the man who was fond enough of these races to wish to take them with him into the next world was duly grateful to the emperors who oversaw the system that provided the shows. (Museo Archeologico, Foligno. Photograph: Scala/Art Resource, NY.)

Figure 32. *Caption Overleaf.*

Figure 33. An altar to the *lares* ("household gods") of Augustus: by fostering the worship of his *lares* and *genius* (a sort of personification of the soul) Augustus could provide an outlet for the wish to treat him as a god among the general public without overtly provoking upper-class sensibilities as his adoptive father Caesar had. (Uffizi, Florence. Photograph: Alinari/Art Resource, NY.)

Figure 32 (*overleaf*). This inscription preserves a complete list of the members of the city council of the southern Italian city of Canusium in A.D. 223. Analysis of the names indicates that the city government was managed by a comparatively stable oligarchy of rich men, but the legal provisions passed by various emperors show that even at this date, many of the members of the rich classes who had previously held municipal office in the empire were beginning to find office holding an irksome burden that was to be avoided, and the disasters of the mid–third century would only aggravate the situation. (Photograph: Christopher S. Mackay.)

Figure 34. Panel portraying the apotheosis (assumption as gods) of Antoninus and his wife Faustina from a column raised by Marcus Aurelius and Lucius Verus to commemorate their predecessor. During the Principate, the bodies of emperors who had died in good grace were generally cremated in the Campus Martius, an open area outside of Rome, and a caged eagle was released from the flaming pyre to symbolize their ascension to the heavens. Here, the souls of Antoninus and his wife are represented both by portraits (which have iconography associating them with Jupiter, the chief Roman god, and his wife Juno) and eagles. The male figure in the lower left represents the Campus Martius, while the female opposite him is Rome. The identity of the winged young male carrying new gods aloft is unclear, but he may represent the "golden age" (*saeculum aureum*) brought about by the deceased emperor and his consort. (Photograph courtesy of Kathryn Andrus.)

Figure 35. In another vivid portrait, the anxiety of Philip the Arab is palpable in his nervously wrinkled brow. Is he wondering when he, too, would suffer the violent end that had befallen every emperor since the death of Septimius Severus, more than three decades before? (Braccio Nuovo, Vatican Museums. Photograph: Scala/Art Resource, NY.)

Figure 36. The Ludovisi Sarcophagus (so named after its first owner) is the finest example of a theme of sarcophagus decoration that appropriately started in the reign of Marcus Aurelius: the portrayal of Roman soldiers engaged in confused combat with barbarians. The work is dated to the 250s or 260s, though there is no overt indication of the identity of the man in the center, a youthful Roman commander whose body was presumably held within. For the most part the helmeted Romans are individually victorious, but there is no sense of triumph, just chaotic, endless violence. (Museo Nazionale Romano (Palazzo Altemps), Rome. Photograph: Scala/Art Resource, NY.)

Figure 37. This massive relief on a rock face in Iran commemorates the Persian king Shapur's victories over various Roman emperors. Perhaps, the one raising his arms in supplication is Philip, while the one held by the arm is Valerian. In a less well-preserved frieze, a figure, presumably Gordian III, lies under the hooves of the Persian king's horse. (Roud-i-Shapur, Iran. Photograph: Art Resource, NY.)

Figure 38. Gallienus is generally treated with contempt by the literary sources, but it was quite an accomplishment for an emperor to stay alive for fifteen years in the mid–third century. (Louvre, Paris. Photograph: Réunion des Musées Nationaux/Art Resource, NY.)

Figure 39. This panel from Palmyra was once thought to portray Zenobia, the queen who ruled in the east during the collapse of Roman authority, but it probably shows one of the goddesses worshipped in this area where Semitic and Greek influences comingled until Aurelian's sack ruined the city in A.D. 273. (National Museum, Damascus, Syria. Photograph: Giraudon/Art Resource, NY.)

Figure 40. The walls built by Aurelian around Rome, which had not been fortified since the construction of walls during the aftermath of the Gallic sack ca. 386 B.C., graphically symbolize the dangers of the period. Who could have imagined during the Principate that armed bands could descend upon the city from the north? (Photograph: Werner Forman/Art Resource, NY.)

Figure 41. Statue of Trajan. An easy way to identify Christians (and to check the sincerity of a recantation) was to make them perform the civic rite of offering some incense to the divine emperor. This procedure is first attested in a famous inquiry that the governor Pliny the Younger made to the emperor Trajan about the procedures to be followed in prosecuting Christians (who were told to make sacrifice before a statue like the one portrayed here). Pliny subtly suggested that while their religious beliefs were, in his opinion, perverse, the Christians did nothing criminal that merited execution. Trajan ignored the hint, and the persecution became fixed policy. (Louvre, Paris. Photograph: Réunion des Musées Nationaux/ Art Resource, NY.)

Figure 42. This rather crude sculpture portrays very directly the unity of the emperors under the tetrarchy. The two Augusti (Diocletian and Maximian) and their two Caesars (Galerius and Constantius) each hug each other, the latter pair respectfully behind the former. This artificial system worked only once (after the abdications of A.D. 305), then collapsed the following year under the claims of Imperial offspring (the sons of Maximian and Constantius) who had been left out of this picture. (S. Marco, Venice. Photograph: Scala/Art Resource, NY.)

Figure 43. This head is a fragment of a colossal statue of Constantine that once graced a basilica (court house) in Rome. The blank expression is indicative of the formal Imperial ceremonial instituted by Diocletian. (Palazzo dei Conservatori, Rome. Photograph: Scala/Art Resource, NY.)

Figure 44. The arch built for Constantine to commemorate his "liberation" of the city in A.D. 312 is a further indication of how the once mighty capital had fallen in importance. Much of the arch's decoration was pilfered from the monuments of earlier rulers, as a result, presumably, of either poverty or lack of talent. In a gesture towards the new emperor's known support of Christianity (and perhaps even as an allusion to the vision he supposedly saw the night before the Battle of the Milvian Bridge), the senate vaguely described him as having acted "through divine inspiration." (Photograph: Scott Gilchrist.)

Figure 45. The philhellenic pagan allegiances of Julian the "Apostate" are made clear by his return to the bearded look first sported by his philhellenic predecessor Hadrian (see figure 23). In this Julian was making a very physical indication of his break with his Christian precessors, since Constantine had resumed the practice of imperial shaving. (Louvre, Paris. Photograph: Réunion des Musées Nationaux/Art Resource, NY.)

Figure 46. Valentinian I, another uncouth Pannonian who became emperor as a result of military competence. (Barletta, Italy. Photograph: Scala/Art Resource, NY.)

Figure 47. The Porta Nigra ("Black Gate") protects the fortified entrance to the Imperial capital of Trier (Germany), which often served during the fourth century as the capital of emperors stationed along the Rhine. (Photograph: Erich Lessing/Art Resource, NY.)

Figure 48. Stilicho is portrayed on one panel of a diptych (a set of joined ivory panels that were created to commemorate consulships in Late Antiquity). The demeanor of this general of German origin who dominated Honorius in the west and apparently subordinated all other interests to his desire to assert control over the eastern half of the Empire, is surprisingly mild. (Treasury, Duomo, Monza, Italy. Photograph: SEF/Art Resource, NY.)

Figure 49. Little remains of the civic amenities set up by the Eastern emperors in Constantinople, but one that does survive is the Column of Theodosius I. The base shows various imperial scenes, and here the emperor, flanked by his heirs Honorius and Arcadius and surrounded by court officials, presides over the chariot races. The emperor's role in these games was a self-conscious imitation of practices in Rome. (Photograph: Christopher S. Mackay.)

PART FOUR

THE PRINCIPATE,
27 B.C.–A.D. 235

Caesar Augustus, as Imp. Caesar came to be called, succeeded where his adoptive father had failed by managing to set up a military autocracy that controlled the military without offending Republican sensibilities. He ostensibly restored the Republic, but many of the traditional offices were drastically changed in their operation, and he retained within his hands a collection of unprecedented powers that gave him overall command of the armies and allowed him to intervene in the traditional institutions of the Republic. This meant that, in practice, he had absolute power, though he strove mightily to conceal this. Hence, there was no official proclamation of the Empire, and indeed official policy denied any such thing. Yet, when Augustus died, there was absolutely no choice but to have a successor, and in fact Augustus had expended much effort over the years to mark out an heir.

From the time of Augustus on, Rome would always be ruled by an emperor, and power would be passed down through a series of dynasties. Though many men believed erroneously that effective authority could be seized in Rome, Imperial power ultimately rested upon control of the provincial armies, and for the two and a half centuries from the granting of the title of Augustus to Imp. Caesar in 27 B.C. down to the end of the Severan dynasty in A.D. 235, the armies normally remained loyal to the legitimate heir of the dynasty. This was a time of relative peace on the borders, and the emperors generally did not take part in military affairs and instead remained in Rome. One of the many titles of the emperors was *princeps* or "leading man," and it is from this title, which emphasizes the nonmilitary aspect of the emperor's position, that the period 27 B.C.–A.D. 235 is known as the "Principate." The role of the emperor would change greatly during the middle years of the third century A.D., when much warfare on the borders and a general breakdown of dynastic legitimacy would bring about great changes in the role of the emperor.

In the discussion of the Principate, there will first be several chapters that narrate the Augustan foundation and the successive dynasties. Since unlike the Republic, which had no permanent administrative system, the Principate had a whole series of institutions through which the emperor exercised his power and that granted him legitimacy, there will be separate treatment of this Imperial system.

Writing in the third century A.D., the Greek historian Dio Cassius (book 53, chap. 19) contrasted the ease of discerning the reasons for decisions taken under the Republic, when there was public discussion of policy, with the secrecy of the Empire, when decisions were made by the emperors in private. While Dio may have overestimated the translucency of decision making under the Republic, it is true that there is much more guesswork involved in assessing the motives of the emperors. This period is covered unevenly by the literary sources. Dio Cassius' annalistic treatment is preserved in larger excerpts, which cover many of the years in question. They are particularly useful for the reign of Augustus, which is treated specifically by no narrative source. The surviving portions of the *Annals* of the historian Tacitus cover most of the reigns of Tiberius, Claudius, and Nero, while his *Histories* treats the civil war of A.D. 69 and the first two years of Vespasian, at which point it breaks off. Tacitus is considered one of the greatest historians of antiquity and is generally reliable, though his strong personal opinions about various emperors seem to have colored his narrative. Suetonius provides biographies of the emperors down to Domitian, though his treatment is thematic rather than narrative and he treats his sources uncritically. There are preserved from this period many other works that are not historical sources but nonetheless provide much historical information about the years down to the emperor Trajan (e.g., the essays of Seneca the Younger, Tacitus' *Agricola*, the letters of Pliny the Younger, and the poetry of Martial). A change in taste in Latin literature set in during the reign of Hadrian, and the result is that there is much less literary evidence preserved for the Principate from his time on (what was written did not appeal to the people in Late Antiquity, whose judgments largely determine what was written in the manuscripts that would survive into the modern period). Dio continues to be a valuable source in the surviving fragments, but there is much less in the way of illustrative material. A work from late antiquity called the *Historia Augusta* (see p. 264) provides Imperial biographies starting with Hadrian, but these are of dubious value. For the period from Commodus to Septimius Severus, there is a continuous narrative by the Greek historian Herodian, but it is careless in detail and marred by excessive distortion for rhetorical effect.

One area in which the Empire has much more attestation than the Republic is epigraphy. The peace and prosperity of the Empire fostered a strong tendency to preserve various texts in inscriptions that survive to today (or were transcribed in the past before being lost). Many inscriptions commemorate the careers of Imperial officials, and hence it is possible to undertake careful studies of individuals and of patterns of office holding. Soldiers were fond of setting up funerary monuments, which make it possible to study the distribution of units as well as individual career patterns. The workings of the Imperial government are also illustrated by numerous decisions preserved in inscriptions. While such documents are not a complete substitute for historical narratives, they do facilitate the examination of the institutions of the Principate and often provide a useful check on the literary sources.

13

AUGUSTUS AND THE ESTABLISHMENT

OF THE PRINCIPATE, 31 B.C–A.D. 14

With the defeat of Antony and Cleopatra, Imp. Caesar was the sole and undisputed power in the Roman state and the question was, now what? The first thing to deal with was the troops. He had taken over Antony's soldiers and now had about a half million in service. He dismissed about 300,000, providing land for them, both in Italy and through the establishment of a large number of colonies abroad, and with the remaining troops he set up the military on a permanent basis (see p. 249). By confiscating the treasury of the Egyptian kings, he had a huge amount of money available, which made it rather easier to acquire all this land without bloodshed.

After spending two years settling affairs in the east, he returned to Rome in late 29 B.C., where he celebrated a hugely expensive triumph and distributed vast sums to the troops and the inhabitants of the city. In 28 B.C., he began to give up some of his untraditional powers and otherwise set the stage for a permanent political settlement.

The Romans had a traditional loathing of kings, and it was thus impossible to set one up overtly. Julius Caesar had been assassinated for merely acting in some ways like one. Yet, recent history had shown that if the armies were left in the control of the annual magistrates, one would eventually gain enough power to use his troops against the government. Many thousands had died during the civil wars, and clearly there was no going back to the Republic. But how could order be maintained without appointing someone as king?

Imp. Caesar went before the senate in January of 27 B.C. and laid down all his powers. Although this was undoubtedly what any good member of the senate would theoretically desire, everyone must have known that such a move would only lead to a renewal of the civil wars that had cost so many lives during the preceding two decades. Therefore, a compromise was proposed whereby the old system would be restored in a limited way, but Imp. Caesar would retain great power, particularly control of the military. Imp. Caesar must have had the details worked out in advance and coached various senators in the proposals they were to make once he ostensibly gave up all his powers. Thus, whereas Caesar the dictator was assassinated for not restoring the Republic, his heir theoretically did so and was then granted powers that nullified that restoration. In gratitude, the senate voted Imp. Caesar the title Augustus (see p. 184), by which he will be referred to from now on.

The electoral system seems to have been fully restored at first, and there was proper competition for office. In fact, there were difficulties throughout the 20s B.C. because of electoral corruption. Augustus did have the right to "commend" men whose election would be automatic, but he used this right very sparingly (it became more commonly used by his successors after the elections had been removed from the People and given over to the senate).

It seems that Roman contemporaries honestly believed in the restoration of the Republic, perhaps because of a sincere gratitude they felt for the ending of the bloodshed of the civil wars. Yet it was all a fraud, as was perfectly clear to Greeks of the time. The contemporary geographer Strabo called the restoration a sham and refers to Augustus as a *basileus,* the Greek word for king that was commonly used of him in Greek inscriptions. How, then, was it possible for him to possess regal powers while still ostensibly restoring the functions of the Republic?

The answer is through the retention of military force. Virtually all provinces that had legions in them were given to Augustus. While the peaceful, ungarrisoned provinces had a senatorial proconsul, the unruly provinces and those along the border were commanded by Augustus through "legates." Legates had been regular deputies of proconsuls under the Republic, and in 55 B.C., Pompey had set a precedent by ruling his two Spanish provinces through legates for years without leaving Rome, and Augustus used a similar system to rule the provinces that had legions. Furthermore, because the troops had sworn personal allegiance to him, all the legions were likewise commanded by a legate appointed by Augustus. Thus, there was no possibility of civil war resuming since virtually no one commanded troops apart from Augustus and his representatives, and in any case all the troops were loyal to Augustus. At first Augustus paid their discharge bonuses out of his own funds, but eventually the cost proved to be too high even for him, and in A.D. 4 a special treasury was set up under Augustus' care to provide for the troops through a tax on the manumission of slaves and on inheritances.

Because Augustus now held the ultimate command over all troops, the legates who commanded them were not in legal control (they operated under the emperor's auspices), and therefore their victories were ascribed to him and it was he who was hailed *imperator* ("victorious general") for their victories. Furthermore, proper triumphs came to be reserved for the emperor and his relations, and victorious generals were merely given the triumphal insignia (the decorations worn by those who had celebrated a triumph).

In addition to his command over the troops in the provinces, Augustus also established a very large personal bodyguard near Rome called the praetorian guard. This arose from the bodyguard of provincial governors but was much larger. Nine cohorts of them (nearly the size of a whole legion) were created in 27 B.C., three near Rome and the rest scattered throughout Italy. This was a novelty since under the Republic there had been no permanent military or police force in Rome or Italy. Augustus kept personal control of the praetorians until 2 B.C., when he established the position of praetorian praefect. These troops did not cause Augustus any problems, but the praetorians and their praefects wielded great influence under later emperors.

In addition to the traditional provinces of military significance that Augustus ruled through legates of senatorial rank, he was in charge of a number of smaller provinces that were ruled in his name by governors of equestrian rank then called praefects (the title was later changed to "procurators," and this is the form by which the position is known in scholarship). During the Empire, new provinces of whatever size were generally governed after this pattern. The only province with an equestrian governor that did not follow the normal pattern was Egypt. Because of its large garrison (several legions), it ought to have had a senatorial governor, but Augustus believed that because it was easily defensible if seized by an outsider and had great strategic importance as the source of the grain for Rome, it had to be treated separately. Though it was legally a regular possession of the Roman People, Augustus was treated like the traditional pharaoh there, and a praefect of equestrian rank ruled in his name. Augustus was so jealous of Egypt's wealth that he forbade any senator to set foot there without his permission, and the position of praefect was considered in his day the highest position attainable by a man of equestrian rank (later it was placed in second position behind the post of praetorian praefect).

Meanwhile, ten traditional provinces that lacked a proper garrison continued to be governed by ex-magistrates (two of consular and eight of praetorian rank). These governors were normally appointed by lot to a one-year term several years after their term of office in Rome. The number of these senatorial provinces was fixed, and if one was transferred to Imperial control, a less important Imperial province was given in return.

The nineteenth-century German scholar Theodor Mommsen argued that there was a genuine and legitimate division of provincial responsibility between the emperor and senate, and he termed this dual form of government a "dyarchy" (rule of two). Even at that time this conception was dubious, as some ancient sources indicated that in the senatorial provinces Augustus had a form of *imperium* greater than that of its governor, and the inaccuracy of the dyarchic conception was fully demonstrated with the publication in 1927 of decrees preserved in inscriptions in the North African city of Cyrene. Some of these decrees show Augustus directly interfering in the administration of justice in the senatorial province of Cyrene after he was appealed to by locals. He politely couches his decisions in the form of wishes, but there could have been no doubt about the governor's compliance. Though the Republic was ostensibly restored and Augustus avoided making his powers overt, nonetheless he clearly had the ultimate say over everything.

The clever title "Augustus" both suggested and concealed the power that had been bestowed on Imp. Caesar. This new title was derived from the Latin adjective borrowed into English as "august," and it means basically the same thing. While grand-sounding with its religious overtones, the new title had the advantage of lacking any specific political signification. Thus, the title set him apart from everyone else without specifying how exactly. All later emperors adopted this honorific, and it was reserved for the ruling emperor (as opposed to the heir apparent).

There were further refinements of Augustus' power. To retain control over this newly restored Republic, Augustus held the consulship every year from 27 until 23 B.C. This would cause obvious problems, since it was the ambition of any Roman senator to become consul, and those with illustrious consular ancestors considered it their right. Thus, if Augustus hogged half of the positions available, there would be some unhappy senators who might try to solve the problem through assassination. The solution was that Augustus would cease to be elected consul on a regular basis and would be given tribunician power instead. As a holder of a tribune's powers for life (actually the power had to be renewed every five or ten years, but this was a formality), Augustus could preside over the senate and quash the actions of any magistrate. The power was more symbolic than functional. In effect, it allowed him to interfere in the regular operations of the senate and magistrates without seeming to be autocratic. Yet, it was held to be an important power, and all emperors retained reference to it in their titulature. From this point on, most emperors held the consulship only on special occasions.

In 20 B.C., there was electoral strife in Rome while Augustus was off campaigning in Spain. Eventually he was forced to return to restore order. As a further power he received consular *imperium* for life. The exact significance of this is not clear, but it would seem that up until this time he had had *imperium* in his own provinces and *maius* (superior) *imperium* in senatorial provinces but none in Rome. Now he had the *imperium* of a consul in Rome without actually holding the consulship.

In 12 B.C. M. Aemilius Lepidus, Augustus' old colleague as triumvir who had been forced into retirement in 35 B.C., finally died. Lepidus held the post of *pontifex maximus* or chief of the state priests. As an expression of loyalty, people from all across Italy came to Rome to elect Augustus to the position, and from then on this title always belonged exclusively to the ruling emperor. In 2 B.C. Augustus was acclaimed *pater patriae* ("father of the fatherland"). Apart from his immediate successor Tiberius, all later emperors adopted this title.

The proconsular *imperium*, tribunician power, and positions as *pontifex maximus* and *pater patriae* effectively delineated Augustus' supreme status within the state, and the possession of the totality of these honors constituted the new position of emperor, though it was never officially instituted as such. The granting of this title would thus mark the accession of his successors.

Another, less obvious, element in Augustus' power was his control of men's political careers. He always had the right to "commend" anyone as a candidate at election time, which guaranteed his election, and when, towards the end of his life, Augustus found the strain of canvassing for such men in person too physically demanding, this commendation was turned into a procedure by which he was allowed to commend a fixed number of candidates, who then directly assumed office without election. The electoral process itself was heavily modified in the last decade of his life, but the exact details are poorly understood because of contradictory and incomplete evidence. At first, special electoral units consisting of senators and of the equestrian members of the jury panels in Rome would hold preliminary elections that were then ratified by the regular assemblies. It seems that by early in the next reign, the elections were simply carried out in the senate. This procedure reduced the chance of anyone inappropriate being elected, since the senate would not wish to displease the emperor. Once a man entered the senate, his future career was determined by the emperor; the most significant positions were now the legateships controlled directly by the emperor. Thus, no senator who wished to advance in his public career would do anything that he knew would offend the emperor.

Alongside the traditional senatorial career, Augustus opened a parallel career for men of equestrian status. They held lower-level commands, managed the extensive properties owned by Augustus in the provinces, governed lesser provinces with garrisons, and superintended various functions in the emperor's control such as the grain supply of Rome and the praetorian guard. Though the monetary requirement for equestrian status was less than that for the senate and the traditional prestige of senatorial status was theoretically higher than that of the equestrian officials, many men preferred to work directly for the emperor rather than hold the old magistracies, and in effect Augustus established an additional source of manpower to run the permanent administrative system that he created.

Since Augustus not only was never officially proclaimed emperor but strove to conceal the autocratic nature of his rule with a façade of Republican constitutionality, it was impossible for him to overtly proclaim an heir to a position that did not in law exist. Yet, if civil war was not to resume, his position had to be passed on to a successor. In trying to find himself an heir, Augustus was hindered by one simple biological fact: he had no son. While women in the Republic were not entirely bereft of influence, they could not vote or hold public office, and thus a daughter was in no position to act officially. Under the Empire, numerous women did acquire great power through their ability to influence the emperor, but this was not an official function. Never throughout the course of the Roman Empire would a woman reign in her own right. It was thus imperative to find a male successor, who had to be directly marked out as heir through marriage to Augustus' daughter Julia. While Augustus enjoyed much luck in his life, fortune did not smile on his dynastic efforts, and he left what today would be termed a dysfunctional family.

The first man whom Augustus attempted to mark out as his successor was his nephew Marcellus. In 25 B.C., when Marcellus was seventeen years old, his special position was indicated by a decree of the senate allowing him to hold the regular magistracies at an abnormally young age, and the next year he was married to Augustus' fourteen-year-old daughter. Nothing came of this plan since Marcellus died without issue the next year.

Next, Augustus married Julia to his right-hand man M. Agrippa, the victor at Naulochus and Actium, who had already been given a very important position when he was sent to the east to operate independently with proconsular *imperium*. The union with Julia was a fruitful one, resulting in three sons who reached adulthood and two daughters. In 18 B.C., Agrippa was clearly marked out as the heir apparent when he, too, received the tribunician power, something no one but Augustus held, and Augustus adopted two of Agrippa's sons, who now became known as Gaius and Lucius Caesar. Thus, Augustus would eventually be succeeded by sons of his own blood, and in the meanwhile Agrippa their father could be trusted to run things for them until they came of age.

In 12 B.C. this scheme was wrecked when Agrippa died. Now, Augustus was left in a difficult situation in that his grandsons were mere boys, and the only adults in his household were his stepsons, who at this moment were engaged in campaigning for him. The obvious solution was to marry Julia to the elder stepson, Tiberius. Unfortunately, abstract logic and the realities of human relations do not always coincide: the somber Tiberius and the gay-spirited Julia soon came to loathe each other, and the marriage was childless. It was clear that the favor shown to Tiberius was only a stopgap measure, as Augustus still wished his adopted sons Gaius and Lucius to succeed despite the fact that Tiberius had his own son. In 6 B.C., Tiberius was granted the tribunician power for five years and was to go to the east like Agrippa on a diplomatic mission, but some event that is not well understood intervened.

Apparently unhappy with his marriage and his second-rate status, Tiberius withdrew to exile on the Greek island of Rhodes.

The years of Tiberius' exile would shatter Augustus' domestic tranquility. Julia's sexual escapades became so notorious that they were finally brought to her father's attention, and she was exiled to a small island. Both his grandsons were marked out as heirs by receiving extraordinary honors upon reaching adulthood, but his plans were soon ruined. A natural death removed Lucius in A.D. 2, and in A.D. 4, Gaius, who two years previously had been sent to the east with proconsular *imperium,* died of a lingering wound that he had received during an assault on a town. Augustus was bitterly disappointed by the deaths of his adoptive sons and now had no choice but to rely on Tiberius, who had been allowed to return to Rome in A.D. 2 as a private citizen. Augustus adopted Tiberius, who was immediately given both proconsular *imperium* and the tribunician power. Hence, Tiberius automatically succeeded to Augustus' position upon his death in A.D. 14.

Augustus was not done with his efforts to secure succession through his own blood, however. Despite the fact that Tiberius had a son from an earlier marriage, Augustus had him adopt his own nephew Germanicus. Not only was Germanicus thus related by blood to Augustus (he was the grandson of Augustus' sister), but he was married to Agrippina, a daughter of Augustus' daughter Julia by Agrippa. Thus, if Tiberius was succeeded by Germanicus, Germanicus' children would be the great-grandchildren of Augustus. Clearly Augustus considered that the most important element in ensuring the succession was a relationship with him by blood, and the future history of the dynasty would prove him correct.

One major advantage provided by the new system set up by Augustus was that the concentration of power in one man's hands allowed for a systematic assessment of the military needs of the Empire. Out of the large number of legions in existence at the end of the civil wars Augustus retained twenty-eight, and he deployed them in permanent positions along the borders and in unruly provinces. With this military force, he then set about filling out the borders of an empire that had been haphazardly acquired under the Republic.

Augustus spent the years 26 and 25 B.C. subduing northwest Spain, the last area in the peninsula not under Roman rule. There were a few revolts subsequently, but these were the last gasps of local resistance, and the garrison of three legions was soon reduced to one, as the process of Romanization quickly advanced.

The Roman East was a rather untidy area, and Augustus made many readjustments in the territories controlled for the Romans by local client kings. The most important of these was Amyntas, king of Galatia in central Asia Minor, who was granted large amounts of territory in this unruly area. When he died in 25 B.C., most of his kingdom was annexed as the new province of Galatia. This was part of the general trend by which direct Roman rule was extended eastwards towards the Parthian border.

The only organized threat to the Roman Empire came from the Parthians. There was much talk at Rome about avenging Crassus' disastrous defeat at Carrhae. Augustus realized that such an invasion would be needlessly risky, but also felt compelled to do something. The Armenian king had reverted to Parthian allegiance in the 30s B.C., and in 20 B.C. Augustus' threat of invasion compelled the king to return the standards and some of the captives taken at Carrhae. While this was presented in Rome as a military triumph, Augustus refrained from opening hostilities. He must have considered that, given the results of Crassus' and Antony's campaigns, the likelihood of permanent military success against the Parthians was remote. The Roman border in the east would not move for two centuries.

There was some campaigning to the south of Egypt, but it was soon clear that it was impractical to advance in towards Arabia or Ethiopia. The area of the greatest expansion was on the borders to the north. There, Augustus occupied the interior of the Balkans up to the Danube, but disaster in his attempt to hold Germanic territory across the Rhine led to the realization that the Romans did not have the resources to support any further expansion.

In addition to Greece and Macedonia, the Romans had long controlled the Adriatic coast of the Balkans, but the interior was occupied by various independent tribes. Already in the early 20s B.C., the governor of Macedonia advanced northwards to the Danube, but the permanence of the conquests he made is not clear. An incursion into Macedonia in 16 B.C. resulted in a prolonged effort to subdue the area starting in the following year. After the initial conquest of the interior, a major revolt broke out and was not extinguished until A.D. 9. The eventual result was the creation of several important military provinces: Illyricum, which encompassed Dalmatia (the area to the interior of the Adriatic coast); Pannonia, which extended northwest towards the Danube; and Moesia on the lower Danube. The savagery of the Roman conquest cowed the locals into temporary submission. In connection with these operations, the minor provinces of Raetia and Noricum were established north of the Alps and south of the Danube. In this way, Roman control of the Balkans was extended to the Danube, from the river's mouth to its headwaters. There it was to remain for more than a century.

In 12 B.C., Augustus' stepson Drusus undertook an attempt to conquer territory beyond the Rhine. In four campaigns down to 9 B.C., he subdued various tribes and extended Roman control to the river Elbe. At the same time, his brother Tiberius was subduing Pannonia. Upon Drusus' death in an accident, Tiberius took over the German campaign, operating there until 7 B.C. The next year Tiberius fell into disgrace for a decade, and while efforts to subdue Germany continued under senatorial subordinates of Augustus, later sources, which were written by authors wishing to flatter Tiberius, tend to ignore these campaigns. After being restored to favor in A.D. 4, Tiberius resumed campaigning in Germany the next year; in A.D. 6, he moved to Pannonia for a planned campaign that was intended to destroy an important Germanic kingdom, but this plan was thwarted by a major revolt in the Balkans.

The Marcomanni, a Germanic tribe that had lived in the area recently conquered by the Romans, had withdrawn to the area corresponding to modern Bohemia on the upper Elbe, and the conquest of this area would open communications between the new conquests in Germany and those along the Danube. Tiberius was to attack from the south while another general attacked from Roman Germany in the west. After Tiberius had already advanced far into the Marcomanni's territory, news arrived of a widespread revolt in Pannonia, and Tiberius quickly returned there after concluding a peace treaty.

Twenty years after the savage Roman conquest, all of Pannonia rose in revolt when a new generation of warriors reached adulthood and made a final attempt at expelling the Romans. Although the hard-pressed Romans did manage to prevent the capture of any towns by the rebels, Tiberius decided to withdraw to the southwest of the province and to use scorched-earth methods and compel the rebellious areas into submission through starvation. The Pannonian tribes were by no means unified, and some soon returned to Roman allegiance. The fighting was hard, but by A.D. 9, the revolt was over. Roman resources were pushed to the limit in dealing with the revolt. Back in Italy, Augustus had so much trouble raising new troops that he had to resort to drafting not only freedmen (ex-slaves) but even slaves freed specifically for this purpose. Just when the revolt in Pannonia was put down, an even greater debacle occurred in Germany.

While leading three legions from summer to winter camp in Roman-occupied Germany, the commander was ambushed in the Teutoburg Forest by German tribesmen, and all three legions were wiped out. This defeat eliminated nearly half of the troops along the Rhine, and the Romans withdrew to the Rhine, abandoning all the newly conquered territory. Tiberius immediately assumed command, and despite some punitive campaigns to restore Roman prestige, no attempt was made to recover the lost territory. Augustus encountered even more trouble recruiting new troops than he had during the Pannonian Revolt.

The prospects for the conquest of Germany that had seemed so bright only three years before were now dashed. The Romans simply did not have sufficient resources to risk them in the attempt to conquer the barbarous areas of Germany. While it was comparatively easy to control the settled agricultural populations around the Mediterranean, it was difficult for the Romans to impose their will among the primitive Germans. Their low level of existence allowed the Germans simply to move on if they found things unpleasant, and the Romans were reduced to moving their troops around from camp to camp without being able to establish permanent control over this new territory without urban centers. Just as Augustus had decided not to attempt to expand eastwards against Parthia, strategic considerations forced him to give up his hopes of expansion into Germany.

Upon his death, Augustus left a memorandum advising his successors to be content with the Empire's boundaries and not to engage in aggressive wars. This advice was for the most part followed for the next two centuries, and those emperors who acted otherwise generally demonstrated the wisdom of Augustus' counsel. The military establishment was large enough to defend the Empire but had no strategic reserves, so that it was very difficult to raise additional troops quickly, as the events of A.D. 6–9 demonstrated. The potential gains from military adventures were simply not worth the risk of a major defeat (the losses at Teutoburg eliminated more than ten percent of the legionary forces). The expansion of the Empire was thus effectively at an end.

Augustus seems to have become somewhat bitter in the last years of his life, after his dynastic schemes had come to naught and his conquests in Germany had been thwarted. Towards the end, he also exhibited an intolerance of behavior he found unacceptable, having certain men exiled for remarks of which he disapproved. Such actions hinted at the absolute and autocratic power that was at his disposal. Nonetheless, Augustus exercised that power with moderation for the most part, and in the four decades after the sham restoration of the Republic the Romans became accustomed to the idea of one man holding such unheard of powers. It was only under the successive members of his dynasty that the realities of Imperial autocracy dawned upon them. As it was, when he died of old age in A.D. 14, everyone was grateful to him for having restored the blessings of peace, and he was duly enrolled among the gods by the senate.

14

JULIO-CLAUDIAN DYNASTY,

A.D. 14–A.D. 68

Augustus was succeeded by four emperors related to him in various ways, and this dynasty is called Julio-Claudian because the first two successors belonged to Augustus' family, the Julii, while the last two were Claudii. Under the Julio-Claudians, the Romans would discover the real cost of ensuring peace by transferring autocratic power to one man. With his talent for manipulating public opinion, Augustus had done his best to conceal the true nature of his absolute power. His successors were either unable or unwilling to engage in the charades necessary to hide the true nature of their power, and their indulgence in despotic behavior proved traumatic to senatorial opinion.

Augustus was succeeded by Tiberius. Before discussing the events of his reign, it would be useful to consider how emperors are assessed. There was an ancient literary tradition about the emperors, arranging them into the categories "good" and "bad." This list was ultimately determined by the senatorial class, whose evaluation was largely based on the emperor's relationship with the senate. In the case of Tiberius, this assessment is further colored by the biases of the senatorial historian Cornelius Tacitus, who lived in the early second century A.D. Tacitus wrote a history of the Julio-Claudians starting with the death of Augustus (*Annals*), and his portrait has had a great influence. Having lived under Domitian, whom he viewed as a secretive hypocrite, Tacitus modeled his view of Tiberius on Domitian. He also had a "unitary" interpretation of human character, taking it to be unchanging, so that if there are indications of good behavior on the part of someone who was later bad, these signs are taken as reflecting and attempt at concealment of the "true" character.

Tacitus' interpretation seems to be a misreading of Tiberius, who apparently began well enough as emperor, but was ill suited to the position. He lacked the finesse that Augustus had possessed in getting his way without seeming to be autocratic. Tiberius, who in some ways might be called the last Republican, tried to get the senate to assume substantive responsibility for policy such as it had held under the Republic, but this was fundamentally impossible given Tiberius' powers. It did not help that Tiberius was a reticent man and refused to spell out clearly what he wanted. He thus became embittered because of what he viewed as sycophancy on the part of the senate. Tiberius also came to take an active dislike of his quarrelsome relations and behaved towards them in a way that can only be characterized as monstrous.

Modern historians tend to adopt a different perspective. Tiberius was a reasonably efficient administrator, and this is the criterion by which modern assessments are often made. Thus, a number of emperors like Claudius and Domitian, who were disastrous in terms of "human resource management" (i.e., getting along with the members of the upper class whose cooperation was necessary to run the Empire), are considered to be "successful" in the broader perspective. To some extent, there is some validity to this view, and the sole criterion cannot be upper-class attitudes in Rome. Yet, getting along with the senate was certainly a requirement for effective rule.

When Augustus died in A.D. 14, Tiberius already possessed the same powers as Augustus had (proconsular *imperium,* tribunician power, and control of the praetorian guard stationed near Rome), and he had been acting as Augustus' equal in the years since his adoption. After dealing with the honors of Augustus, the senate was convened to discuss Tiberius' role in government. Tiberius claimed to want to share some of his powers with the senate, but this was impossible. The powers of Augustus were absolute and indivisible. There was no such thing as being a partial emperor, and eventually Tiberius had to give in. He took on the title Augustus and assumed the office of *pontifex maximus,* but throughout his reign he refused the title *pater patriae,* being the only emperor to do so.

The real basis of Imperial power was soon revealed by separate mutinies that broke out in Pannonia and along the Rhine when news arrived of Augustus' death. Already in the time of Augustus there had been dissatisfaction with the allotments of land given to soldiers and with delayed discharges, and the armies seized upon the opportunity provided by Augustus' death to demand better terms of service. Drusus, Tiberius' natural son, was sent to the Danube, where he made use of the soldiers' superstitions about an eclipse of the moon to induce their return to obedience. Germanicus, Tiberius' nephew and adopted son, was in Gaul at the time and had a much harder time restoring order there. The soldiers actually urged him to lead them in revolt against Tiberius. This he refused to do and took advantage of guilty feelings created among the soldiers by a theatrical withdrawal of his family to bring them back to obedience. He then led them on a campaign into Germany to distract them.

During these tumultuous events, Tiberius himself remained in Rome, where he was criticized for not intervening personally. Yet, there is no doubt that he was right not to become directly involved. If the troops rejected him in person, military and dynastic chaos would have resulted. For the most part, the emperors of the Principate would not take personal command of the troops, who would stay loyal to a legitimate emperor whom they virtually never saw. In the future, a regular procedure in the accession of a new emperor was the prompt distribution of a sum of money ("donative") to every soldier to ensure his loyalty.

Germanicus campaigned for several years in Germany, where he seems to have entertained some notion of making good the losses suffered after the defeat at the Teutoburg Forest. If so, Tiberius shared no such illusions, and some of the perilous situations into which Germanicus got himself demonstrated once more how risky such aggression was. In A.D. 16, he was awarded a triumph, and this was a subtle way of telling him that the campaign was over. Germanicus did not comply, believing that he could soon subdue Germany, and returned only after receiving a number of importunate letters from Tiberius. The sources are uniform in suggesting that Tiberius viewed the supposed victories as futile and ruinous to the state, an assessment that was basically correct.

In A.D. 17, there were problems on the eastern border, and like the heirs apparent under Augustus, Germanicus was sent east with *maius imperium*. As it turned out, the diplomatic problems were transient, but Germanicus' proconsulship revealed serious flaws in Tiberius' methods. When the youthful Gaius Caesar had gone east, an ex-consul was sent along as an assistant to keep him out of trouble, and in a similar way, Tiberius sent a friend of his, Cn. Calpurnius Piso, to be governor of Syria, seemingly with some sort of mission to keep an eye on Germanicus. At least that is what Piso thought. He quarreled bitterly with Germanicus and seems to have thought that he would have Tiberius' support in this. Relations between the two became so bad that when Germanicus fell ill in Syria in A.D. 19, he believed that Piso had poisoned him and ordered him to withdraw. Germanicus soon died, and Piso nearly started a civil war when he attempted to return to his province, but he was persuaded to return to Rome. There he was accused of treasonable activities and was tried before the senate, committing suicide when it became clear that Tiberius would not rescue him. He was then convicted of treason (the charge of poisoning being ignored). The whole sordid affair seems to have derived from Tiberius' inability to express his wishes clearly, which left people to make up their own minds in ways that he did not necessarily approve of. Furthermore, Germanicus' widow Agrippina was completely alienated from Tiberius as a result of the affair, and this would have serious repercussions in the Imperial household.

In A.D. 23, Tiberius' own son Drusus died, leaving behind a minor son. Tiberius' heirs were the two elder sons of Germanicus, but the malignant influence of one of Tiberius' associates intervened. L. Aelius Sejanus was praetorian praefect, and in this capacity won the emperor's affection. In A.D. 25, Tiberius, who was tired of dealing with his public and private responsibilities, withdrew to the small island of Capri off the Bay of Naples, never to return to Rome. Sejanus thus controlled Tiberius' access to information and proceeded to acquire seemingly unbounded power in Rome. Any senator who wished to advance in his career had to seek Sejanus' favor, and he arranged to destroy his opponents through accusations before the senate. In addition, Sejanus sowed discord between Tiberius and Germanicus' family, eventually securing the arrest of Agrippina and her elder sons (the heirs apparent). It would seem that Sejanus wished to secure power for himself through an amorous relationship he had formed with the widow of Tiberius' son, who was thus the mother of Tiberius' young grandson. By removing Germanicus' family, Sejanus may have felt that he could rule in the name of the young man once Tiberius died.[1] In A.D. 31, Sejanus seemed about to get everything he wished for. Tiberius allowed him to become consul despite being of only equestrian rank and was poised to adopt him. Then, in an act that served in antiquity as a prime example of the fleeting nature of success, Tiberius had him stripped of his command as praetorian praefect and executed. What motivated this sudden loss of favor is not known, but Tiberius is said to have been very anxious about the loyalties of the praetorian guard and was very circumspect in his actions against Sejanus. Later history would prove that the soldiery were doggedly loyal to the house of Augustus, and it is highly unlikely that they would have rejected the legitimate emperor in favor of an outsider. The career of Sejanus shows both how far it was possible to advance oneself through manipulating the emperor as well as the extent to which such power depended solely upon the will of the emperor.

The downfall of Sejanus did nothing to ameliorate the lot of Tiberius' imprisoned relations, who were abused in prison until they were executed or starved to death. He made no further provision for the succession, though he kept in his company the youngest son of Germanicus, who duly became the next emperor when Tiberius passed away in A.D. 37. Rumor had it that the emperor was assisted (either by his successor or by the praetorian praefect

---

1 After his downfall, Sejanus' ex-wife actually claimed that he had induced Tiberius' son's wife to poison him, though it is hard to see how she could have known this. Since her own children had just been executed as a result of her husband's fall from grace, her accusation could have been a concoction motivated by rancor.

in the heir's interest) in departing from this life, and if people had known this for a fact, it is unlikely that they would have objected.

Tiberius' relations with the senate were just as bad as those with his family. Though in the beginning, he appears to have been reasonable in his actions, eventually he lost control of the situation, allowing accusations of treason against prominent individuals to be made on the flimsiest of grounds. The form of treason set up in the later Republic is called *maiestas*, more properly *maiestas laesa*, literally "reduced greatness" (i.e., of the Roman People). Though the charge of harming the "greatness" of the emperor (as surrogate for the Roman People) is attested under Augustus, such charges first became widespread under Tiberius. A procedural aspect of Roman criminal law was an important factor in this development. There was no public organ of prosecution, and those who lodged an accusation would prosecute the accused before the senate. Since the successful prosecutor got a share in the condemned man's property (as an encouragement to assuming the burdens of prosecution), there was a strong pecuniary motive not only to lodge legitimate prosecutions but to concoct them through entrapment or simply lying. While Tiberius made some effort to restrain *maiestas* trials in the first few years of his reign, things got out of hand in later years, particularly once Tiberius was out of Rome and could be manipulated by Sejanus. The death of Sejanus did nothing to remedy the situation, as it was now possible to face accusations on the grounds of having been his supporter in the past. Among modern biographers, there is a strong apologist tendency, and there is a trend to discount the "terror" under Tiberius by pointing out that comparatively few people were executed. This neglects to note that in terms of the number of potential victims, the number of victims was large, and in any case this view misses the essential point. Under Tiberius, people often came to a bad end through no fault of their own, and the random nature of such prosecutions led to a large degree of uncertainty in the lives of the senatorial class. Finally, it must be borne in mind that under the Republic only slaves and foreigners were subject to execution, and Roman citizens convicted of a theoretically capital offence were allowed to go into exile. That a member of the senatorial class should be executed and his body exposed for public abuse before being dragged by a hook to the Tiber and tossed in was a disgrace literally unimaginable under the Republic, but such a fate became a very disturbing possibility for those convicted of *maiestas* under Tiberius. This unpleasant situation was fundamentally attributable to Tiberius' refusal to recognize that his guidance was necessary to make the system of concealed autocracy function smoothly. Instead of managing the senate so that it reached the "right" decision, Tiberius claimed to want it to operate independently, but then criticized the results, sometimes faulting it for laxness, sometimes censuring it for harshness. Under such circumstances, it was not unreasonable for the senate to err on the side of severity, without any consideration of Sejanus' baneful influence.

Tiberius also showed himself to be incapable of managing the senate in its administrative capacity. The only senatorial province with a legion stationed in it was Africa, and during Tiberius' reign much trouble was caused there by a local warlord named Tacfarinas, who had served in the Roman military and applied the military training he had acquired to leading a minor revolt. Tiberius apparently expected the senate to choose the governors to carry out this campaign on its own, but it declined to do so on several occasions and insisted on leaving the decisions to Tiberius. He complained about the senate's constant practice of referring all important matters to him, but under the circumstances what else could be expected of them? If they made the wrong decision, they could expect only complaints from Tiberius, who ought to have indicated what he wanted to the senate in a diplomatic way, as Augustus would have done. As it turned out, the rebellion was eventually suppressed without too much trouble. This was the last war during which a senatorial proconsul held an independent command, and henceforth all generals would be subordinates of the emperor.

Tiberius may have kept a careful eye on governors, but his salient characteristic was inertia. He hated to make decisions. For instance, as long as a governor was not actively incompetent, Tiberius left him in place. One man was appointed by Augustus in A.D. 12, reappointed in A.D. 15, and left in place until his death in A.D. 35. Such a long tenure is unheard of in other reigns. This again shows that Tiberius failed to understand that one of the main requirements of his position was that he should manage the personnel who manned the administration.

Whatever the merits of his administration, his appalling treatment of his family indicates a lamentable failure as a human being. While Augustus apparently could not bring himself to kill a relative during his lifetime, Tiberius did so several times, in savage ways. Tacitus' conception that Tiberius was evil from the start is simplistic, but there can be no doubt but that Tiberius was ill suited to handling autocratic power inherent in the Augustan Principate.

Tiberius was also irresponsible in the arrangements he left for the succession. Upon his death, his adoptive grandson Gaius, the sole surviving son of Germanicus and Agrippina, was promptly hailed as emperor. Tiberius' will did not make the succession clear, naming both Gaius and Tiberius' grandson Ti. Gemellus, who was seven years younger than Gaius. The senate quickly agreed to invalidate the will, although Gaius did adopt Gemellus as his heir. Gaius also unenthusiastically suggested the deification of Tiberius, but this was soon dropped. Later, emperors who were approved of were normally deified and their acts upheld, while the memory of those disapproved of was condemned (which happened only when a dynasty fell). Tiberius represents an exception in that while his acts were considered valid, he was not deified. Gaius (generally known in modern works by his nickname "Caligula"[2]) ostentatiously claimed that he would return to the ways of Augustus, but he would soon reveal the true nature of the Imperial autocracy.

In the fall of A.D. 37, Gaius nearly died of an illness, and after his recovery began acting tyrannically. The biographer Suetonius claims that the illness deranged him; whatever the truth of this, his unsuitability to be emperor became increasingly clear. One of his first acts upon recovering was to demand that someone who had made a vow to give up his own life if Gaius survived his illness should make good on his promise. During the following winter, he secured his position by disposing of various people who threatened him, including his supposed heir Ti. Gemellus.

Gaius became increasingly erratic and cruel in his behavior. He stole other men's wives (twice), and the treason law was revived. Supposedly, he once burst out laughing during a party, and when the consuls who were dining with him politely asked if he would share the joke with them, he commented that it had just occurred to him that if he wished, he could have them executed, an idea that may have provided amusement to the emperor but was not surprisingly unsettling to everyone else.

He came to have delusions of grandeur, squandering vast sums of money having a bridge built across the Bay of Naples in some sort of gesture of oriental kingship.[3] By the time that he returned to Rome in the spring of A.D. 40 following a visit to the legions along the Rhine in which he showed himself to be increasingly irrational, he seems to have become fully convinced of his own divinity, dressing in the attributes of various gods and berating his colleague Jupiter. He went so far as to order the governor of Syria to erect a statue of him as god in the Temple in Jerusalem, an act that would have caused a major revolt in Judaea. The governor delayed long enough that Gaius was dead before he was obliged to carry out this clearly insane command.

Despite the fact that many senators were condemned for treason, no emperor was ever assassinated by a senatorial conspiracy. Tyrants were always murdered by those in their household who felt threatened. In the case of Gaius,

---

2 This name means "little boot" and is a diminutive of the designation for the typical footgear worn by soldiers. As a child he accompanied his father to his command on the Rhine, and the name derives from a mock uniform made for him by doting soldiers.

3 This is reminiscent of a famous incident reported by the Greek historian Herodotus. Supposedly, the Persian king Xerxes had the Hellespont bridged when he was setting off to enslave Greece, and when the bridge was broken by a storm, he had the sea flogged. This act would thus be emblematic of the ruler's supreme and untrammeled power, which even extended to control of the natural world.

this meant various members of the praetorian guard, whose exact motives are not known (Gaius apparently was prone to mock one of them who was a officer in the guard, but this does not explain why others should undertake such a perilous course of action.) In January of A.D. 41, as he was returning to the palace from a public ceremony through an underground passageway, he was stabbed to death by the conspirators, who proceeded to kill his wife and two-year-old daughter, presumably to remove anyone likely to seek revenge. That the sole motive for the assassination was hatred or fear of the emperor is shown by the fact that the conspirators seemed to have made absolutely no plans for the succession.

There was an attempt on the part of the consuls to reinstate the Republic. This effort is generally derided by modern historians as being totally unrealistic, but one can hardly blame them for trying when news suddenly arrived of the death of the monster. Such an attempt was fundamentally unrealistic, however. While the magistracies of the Republic still existed in name, they were mere shadows and the emperor possessed all real power through control of the army. Even if the senate had been unanimous in its sentiments, it is hard to see how it could have taken over control of the troops, who had been personally loyal to the house of Augustus for more than seventy years. Furthermore, the senators were not unanimous. Certain prominent members wished to take advantage of the situation to try and seize the Imperial dignity for themselves. This course was likewise unrealistic. Imperial history would show that while it was possible when a dynasty was extinguished to seize the Imperial titulature in Rome through a coup d'état, men who seized power in this way were soon pushed aside by the commanders of provincial armies.

While there were no adult male descendants of Augustus alive (Gaius having murdered them), neither the direct lineage of Augustus nor his house in the broader sense were extinguished, and it was completely unrealistic to think that there was any alternative to giving the Imperial power to someone else who belonged to the dynasty and thus had a natural claim to the soldiers' loyalty. The only real candidate was Gaius' uncle Claudius. When the praetorians heard of Gaius' murder, they went on a rampage and one soldier found Claudius cowering behind a curtain in the palace. Claudius apparently expected to be killed and was somewhat taken aback at being hailed emperor and taken to the camp of the praetorians. There was a bit of a farce with negotiations going on between the new emperor in the camp and the consuls, but the latter soon realized the impossibility of standing up to the praetorians (apart from considerations of the dissension in the senate itself) and gave in.

The assessment of the emperor Claudius to some extent resembles that of Tiberius. Whereas the ancient sources are almost uniformly hostile, modern interpreters are rather more generous. Claudius had been born with various physical defects and for this reason had been kept out of the public eye. He seems to have had a reasonable intelligence and something of an academic bent (he wrote several historical works now lost). This side of his personality naturally appeals to modern academics, as do his somewhat chaotic interventions in administration, where he regularized a number of trends from earlier reigns (for example, formalizing the pattern of various military careers). Thus, there is a common tendency to discount the bias in the sources against him. And the sources hate him. Apart from his physical deformities, he was derided for being controlled by his wives (bad enough from an ancient perspective) but also by his freedmen (outrageous to the ancients). An objective assessment of his behavior shows him to have been a weak individual who was easily manipulated by those around him and who found it easy to get him to authorize executions, even of his own relatives. While an improvement on his nephew, Claudius was still ill suited to managing the Augustan Principate.

He adopted the nomenclature of the house of Augustus, even though he did not actually belong to it, calling himself Ti. Claudius Caesar Augustus. (Caesar was now an Imperial title rather than a family name.) This nomenclature was intended to assert his membership in the dynasty and thus his claim on the troops' loyalty. This was tested in A.D. 42 by a military revolt against the new emperor. At the instigation of a number of senators, the governor of Dalmatia persuaded the two legions under his command to rise in revolt against Claudius. The actual revolt was rather pathetic, and within four days the troops returned to their loyalty. This demonstrates how difficult it was to succeed in revolting against an established dynasty. Nonetheless, the event showed that Claudius was in need of further personal prestige, and a major campaign was planned for the next year to acquire greater glory for the new emperor. At the start of his reign, Claudius had already realized the need for military prestige and annexed the kingdom of Mauretania, whose king had been murdered by Gaius. Perhaps spurred on by the revolt in Illyricum, in A.D. 43, he violated Augustus' precept against military expansion by invading Britain with four legions from the northern borders. Although the governor of Pannonia exercised real command, Claudius was present for the first sixteen days of the campaign to allow him to take personal credit. The Romans quickly established control over England as far as the Midlands and Wales. Though there were several campaigns under later emperors to extend their control to the north, the Romans were never able to occupy the north of England or Scotland. As a finale, in A.D. 46, he converted the client kingdom of Thrace into yet another province.

Naturally, the succession was a matter of importance. Upon his accession Claudius already had an adult daughter from a youthful marriage, and he had her married to a senior aristocrat. In A.D. 39 or 40, he himself married the fourteen-year-old Valeria Messallina, the daughter of a leading family of the Republican aristocracy and a great-granddaughter of Augustus' sister Octavia on both sides. In A.D. 40, she bore him a daughter named Octavia (the name is indicative of the dynastic nature of the marriage) and the next year a son, who in A.D. 43 received the name Britannicus in honor of his father's conquest.

Messallina abused her ability to sway Claudius by favoring her friends and harming her enemies. She was apparently a young woman of strong sexual energy, and not surprisingly did not find her deformed husband very attractive. Her debauchery became legendary, but even she went too far in A.D. 48, when she fell in love with C. Silius, consul designate for the year and grandson of one of Augustus' generals. She seems to have celebrated an open marriage with the young and beautiful Silius while Claudius was off at Ostia. It is hard to imagine what good she could have imagined would come from such brazen activity. In any case, his freedmen took counsel and eventually persuaded Claudius' favorite concubine to break the news to him. He was heartbroken and could not summon up the spirits to do anything, but eventually, the freedmen prevailed upon him to sign her death warrant.

With Messallina dead, it seemed that Claudius needed a new wife, and in A.D. 49, after a debate among his three most powerful freedmen, each of whom had a candidate, Claudius married his niece Agrippina the Younger (Gaius' surviving sister, the daughter of Agrippina the Elder and Germanicus). She had previously been married to a member of one of the most important Republican families, and by him she had given birth in A.D. 37 to a son, L. Domitius Ahenobarbus, who was thus the great-great-grandson of Augustus. Ahenobarbus was four years older than Claudius' son Britannicus, and in A.D. 50 Agrippina persuaded Claudius to adopt her son, who thus became Nero Claudius Caesar and took precedence over Britannicus. Claudius' daughter was already betrothed to a member of the aristocracy, and in order to make her available for Nero, Agrippina had a prosecution launched against the fiancé: she was clearly a determined woman who would let nothing stand in the way of her own power (she had one of the other candidates for marriage to Claudius exiled and driven to suicide).

One of Messallina's victims had been Agrippina's sister Julia, who had been exiled in A.D. 41 for supposedly having an affair with the literary figure Seneca. He languished in exile on the miserable island of Sardinia until A.D. 49, when Agrippina secured his recall. She wished him to be the tutor of her son Nero, and thought that his mistreatment at the hands of Messallina would make him ill disposed to Messallina's son Britannicus. Seneca exerted much influence at court, toadying to Claudius' freedmen and to the emperor himself, whom he apparently loathed. In A.D. 51, Agrippina had an equestrian official, Sex. Afranius Burrus, appointed both as praetorian praefect and as a second tutor of Nero. Thus, in the early A.D. 50s, Agrippina managed to put in chief positions in the Imperial administration men loyal to her (and her son).

In A.D. 53, Agrippina secured the marriage of Nero to Claudius' thirteen-year-old daughter Octavia. (This marriage was not a success, as the couple loathed each other). Agrippina now had everything she could want, the emperor's son holding second place after her own, who was married to his daughter. Fate could only wreck her arrangements, and thus it was best (from her point of view at least) that Claudius should die now. Since he would apparently not cooperate, he needed to be helped along, and in October of A.D. 54, he died during a feast. It is generally thought that he had been served poisoned mushrooms by Agrippina. Seneca and Burrus, whose complicity in the act is not known, quickly won over the praetorians in favor of Nero, who was duly hailed emperor in place of Britannicus. Claudius was deified and remained in the official pantheon, though his cult was rather neglected under Nero.

For the most part, Nero has not received in modern historical scholarship the kind of revisionist apologies one finds for the other Julio-Claudian successors of Augustus, though he does not seem to have been any worse than Gaius. He succeeded to the throne at the age of seventeen, and in the beginning, he was guided toward good government by his advisers. Gradually he came to assert himself and fell under the influence of "bad" friends. Basically, Nero took little interest in government and seems not to have been an inherently bad person, but he was both insecure and susceptible to manipulation by those around him. Eventually, a number of conspiracies against him arose, and he finally fell from power through his own ineptitude.

It was generally agreed that Nero's first five years were exemplary, mainly because the affairs of state were managed by Agrippina, Seneca, and Burrus. Agrippina sought to hold power equal to that of her young and inexperienced son, however, and Seneca and Burrus endeavored to stir up personal conflict between Nero and his mother to weaken her influence. During an argument in early A.D. 55, Agrippina suggested that she have Britannicus, who would reach adulthood the next day, installed as emperor in Nero's place. That night, Britannicus was poisoned at dinner. Agrippina became even more uncivil to her son, and relations between them deteriorated. To undermine Agrippina, Burrus and Seneca encouraged him in his excesses, which she tried to curb.

Around this time Nero fell in love with Poppaea Sabina, the granddaughter of a prominent senator under Tiberius. She was the wife of Otho, who was one of Nero's drinking companions (and would later seize the throne after Nero's death). When Nero became infatuated with Poppaea, Otho obligingly let Nero have his way with her. By A.D. 58, the affair was fully established, and when Agrippina objected (she was apparently personally affronted by the failure of the marriage with Octavia, which she had taken such pains to arrange), Nero finally resolved to get rid of his bossy mother. Knowing that Seneca and Burrus would be of no use in this project, he enlisted the help of a freedman tutor of his who was now employed as the praefect of the fleet stationed at Misenum (a town on the Bay of Naples). Since it was considered too risky to poison her outright or to lodge an open accusation, it was decided to construct a special collapsible boat that would be sunk with her on board. Unfortunately, this clever plan came to naught when it turned out that she could swim, and she had to be killed the old-fashioned way. The death of Agrippina marked a major step in Nero's independence, as he would increasingly ignore Seneca's and Burrus' advice, despite their help in providing excuses for his murder of his mother (it was claimed that she was plotting against him).

Meanwhile, there was major trouble in the east, where the king of Parthia had succeeded in installing his brother as king of Armenia in place of the king recognized by the Romans, thereby breaking the traditional agreement by which the king of Armenia had to rule with Roman consent. In late A.D. 54, the experienced general Cn. Domitius Corbulo was sent to take a special command in Asia Minor to deal with the situation. Corbulo found that the troops stationed in the east, who had not seen battle for years, were in a poor state of training, and he spent a number of years restoring their readiness. Finally, after fruitless negotiations with the Parthians, major campaigning began in A.D. 58, and Corbulo would engage in a series of campaigns over the next six years. While he repeatedly overran Armenia, it proved much more difficult to keep the Roman candidate on the throne in the face of Parthian opposition. After several abortive attempts at negotiations, it was finally decided that the Parthian candidate would receive his crown from Nero, which he eventually did in A.D. 66. Nero treated the whole affair as a great triumph of military force and trumpeted his restoration of peace, but the whole matter confirmed the wisdom of avoiding fruitless campaigning in the east.

While the war in the east dragged on, Nero increasingly asserted his independence, as he fell under the sway of his girlfriend Poppaea and other bad influences. When Burrus died in A.D. 62, Nero replaced him as praetorian praefect with Tigellinus, one of his disreputable companions; at this point, Seneca apparently foresaw that he would no longer be able to exercise any control over Nero and requested that he be allowed to withdraw from public life and to turn over to the emperor the vast sums of money that he had made through his influence on the government. The emperor refused the request, but in fact Seneca never did enjoy Imperial favor after this. Seneca realized too late that ultimately his policy of acquiescing in the emperor's crimes to maintain his moderating influence was a self-defeating course of action.

In A.D. 62, Tigellinus played on Nero's fears of various collateral members of the Imperial family, who were driven to suicide. In the following years Tigellinus (and others) would increase Nero's suspicions to maintain their own power (and in the process cause real sources of fear to arise in the form of conspiracies). In A.D. 62, Nero also finally got rid of his wife Octavia and the pregnant Poppaea realized her ambition to marry him. An initial attempt to have Octavia convicted of adultery failed, and she was divorced on the grounds of sterility. Popular demonstrations in her favor persuaded Nero to reinstate the charges, and after being exiled to an isolated island, she was murdered.

One aspect of Nero's personality (apart from his proclivity to murder) that earned him the disfavor of the upper class was his fondness for the arts. Already in A.D. 60, he instituted a new series of Greek-style artistic contests in Rome under the name *Neronia* ("Neronian games"). He wished to perform himself at that time, but the senate managed to avoid this by offering him victory crowns ahead of time; at the second celebration in A.D. 65, he did perform. This participation was disgraceful in terms of Roman values, since performers were normally people of low social standing. Nero made matters worse by encouraging men and women of both equestrian and senatorial standing to perform. This sort of behavior began to undermine his personal prestige. Murdering his mother was one thing; acting like a Greek musician was quite another.

His reputation for artistry got him into further trouble when the center of Rome burned in A.D. 64. The city possessed something of a fire brigade, but without forced water, there was little to be done once a fire got out of control. Rumor had it that the emperor had availed himself of the opportunity to use the fire as a backdrop while he recited poetry to the accompaniment of the lyre. (He would later start work on an extravagant palace complex in the area freed up by the fire, but that does not prove that he started it.) This story is probably false, but to get himself out of this unpleasant situation, he needed culprits.

He found them in the form of adherents to a new cult, Christianity, which had a small following among the Greek-speaking populace of Rome.[4] As a result of popular misconception of their practices, malicious rumors abounded and were difficult to verify (at that time most people had doubtless never set eyes on a Christian). Accordingly, these people, whose rejection of the pagan gods was misconstrued as a hatred of mankind, could readily be blamed for starting the fire, and a number of Christians were executed publicly in a sort of parody of the crime they were charged with (they were bound to stakes and set alight as human candles). While this event is not terribly significant in its own right, it does indicate that within thirty-five years of the death of Jesus, the new cult had already spread to Rome itself.

---

4 Many easterners moved to Rome to take advantages of the opportunities for employment in the Imperial capital, and large numbers of manumitted Greek-speaking slaves also wound up there. For the early development of Christianity, see Chapter 20.

The year A.D. 66 saw the outbreak of the only major failure in Roman provincial policy. While most population groups that had some sense of self-identity, like the Greeks and the Punic settlers of the western Mediterranean, found it possible to operate politically within the framework of Roman hegemony, the Jews did not. Their sense of nationhood was based upon the special relationship with their god that was laid out in the books of the Hebrew bible. These books indicated that this relationship would be manifested in the secular success of their state over its enemies, and thus the Jews found it difficult to accept foreign rule. In particular, the notion arose that a man anointed by God (the "messiah") would free God's people from their oppressors and restore them to their independence. Such notions were obviously hard to reconcile with subordination to the Roman emperor.

Though the Romans had assisted the Jews in their revolt against the Seleucid dynasty in the mid–second century B.C., it was only from the time of Pompey's establishment of the province of Syria in 64 B.C. that they became directly involved in the affairs of Judaea. On the whole, the Romans preferred to rule the area through client kings. The dynasty that had been established after the revolt against the Seleucids was ended in 37 B.C., when a local general named Herod took over the throne with the permission of the triumvirs. He managed to transfer his allegiance in time to Imp. Caesar in the aftermath of Actium and survived until 4 B.C., when his kingdom was divided among three sons. The one who ruled around Jerusalem proved not to be a success, and when he was deposed in A.D. 6 the area was organized as the province of Judaea, which was ruled through equestrian-rank governors (procurators) under the oversight of the governor of Syria.

We are comparatively well informed about Roman administration in Judaea, and the governors on the whole attempted to accommodate local religious sensibilities, especially concerning Jerusalem and its great Temple to the Jewish god around which all cultic practice was centered. Since Jewish opinion was in many ways divided, however, there was always a good possibility that any given decision would offend someone. Perhaps it was the difficulties inherent to Roman administration that motivated Claudius to give the Roman province plus other territory that had been held by descendants of Herod to his childhood friend Agrippa, a grandson of Herod who had grown up in Rome and had already been installed by Gaius as ruler of a small portion of the old kingdom. Upon Agrippa's death, most of his territory reverted to government by Roman procurators, though his son inherited a small territory and was allowed to oversee the administration of the Temple in Jerusalem.

The Jewish historian Josephus, a commander in the revolt who was captured by the Romans and wrote an extensive history of it, tries to blame the outbreak of the revolt on the malfeasance of the last procurators, but their behavior seems not to have been markedly more wicked than that of the average Roman governor. Rather, in the years leading up to the revolt, there was apparently an upsurge in expectations of the imminent arrival of the messiah, and several prophets attempted to lead the masses in revolt against the Romans and were suppressed by them. While it may well be true that the efforts of the procurators to curb this activity were unsuccessful and may have led to increased anti-Roman sentiment, it is hard to see how they caused the revolt. Clearly within the Jewish community there was much internal ferment against the Romans, which resulted in a breakdown of public order.

The outbreak of the revolt began with a minor incident that got out of hand. In the spring of A.D. 66, the procurator Florus seized a large sum of money from the Temple treasury. The reason for this was that tax receipts were in serious arrears, but the seizure was taken to be an act of theft. After initial skirmishes with angry crowds, a major riot broke out, which forced the procurator to withdraw to his capital at Caesarea, since he had insufficient forces to deal with the situation.

The Jewish landowning class and their allies, the priestly class that administered the Temple, opposed the revolt, foreseeing that it was futile to oppose the Romans, but by mid-summer the rebels had seized most of the major defensive positions in Jerusalem, including the huge precinct of the Temple. By September, the single Roman cohort left behind by Florus was forced to surrender; the troops left the city under safe conduct but were slaughtered. This act guaranteed that there was no turning back. After these successes in Jerusalem, the rebels seized defensible positions in the countryside. Roman control in Judaea was at an end.

Meanwhile, P. Cestius Gallus, the governor of Syria, had gathered a large force to restore order, and in October he marched on Jerusalem with a large army of about 30,000 troops.[5] After an eight-day assault on the heavily defended city, the peace party within the walls was about to open the gates to him, but Gallus suddenly abandoned the siege and withdrew. Unaware of how close he was to success, Gallus had decided that since he did not have a full siege train with him and winter was approaching, he had no choice but to give up his attack for the time being. This decision was a disaster on two accounts. In the first place, the Jewish rebels were elated at their victory, and their attacks on the retreating army turned the withdrawal into a rout in which several thousand Roman troops died. Far worse was the overall effect. The withdrawal seemed to show God's approval of the revolt, and now the war party held full ascendancy over those who realized that the overwhelming military superiority of the Roman forces was bound to crush the revolt in the end.

---

5 The procurators of Judaea had a few cohorts at their disposal, but major unrest generally had to be quelled by bringing troops down from Syria.

When news of Gallus' defeat was brought to him, Nero put T. Flavius Vespasianus ("Vespasian" in English) in charge of suppressing the revolt, and a force totaling about 60,000 men was gathered from various provinces for this purpose. By the spring of A.D. 67, Vespasian's army approached from Syria, and after much hard fighting the north of Judaea was back in Roman hands. In the spring of the following year, some of his advisers suggested to Vespasian that because of internal dissension among the rebels Jerusalem could be stormed, which would bring the revolt to a quick end. Vespasian preferred to subdue central Judaea, allowing the quarreling of the defenders of Jerusalem to weaken them further in the interim. By June, Vespasian was ready to prepare for the siege, but when news of Nero's death arrived, he suspended military operations to await the outcome of the turmoil at Rome. In the meanwhile, Nero had lost control of the political scene in Rome and been overthrown.

A major deterioration in Nero's relations with the senate came as the result of a conspiracy to assassinate him. It was formed by a number of senators and equestrians, whose aim was to replace Nero with C. Calpurnius Piso, a popular member of a family of the Republican nobility. The plot was betrayed by the freedman of one of the senators involved, and when this betrayal was discovered by the conspirators, Piso hesitated to throw caution to the wind and appeal to the city and praetorians, despite the fact that a number of officers of the guard were involved. Thus, the plot came to nothing. A major investigation revealed the large size of the conspiracy, and Nero was shocked at the extent of disloyalty not only in the senate but also among the praetorians. Nero came to fear the old aristocracy in particular, and from A.D. 65 on there were many trials for treason in the senate. His insecurity also led to the slaughter of the remaining descendants of Augustus.

Despite the clear signs of dissatisfaction with his rule, Nero decided in the fall of A.D. 66 to cross over to Greece, the land of culture. There he intended to display his artistic skills (the Olympic games had even been postponed for his visit). Nero apparently competed honestly, but it should come as no surprise that he won whatever competition he entered. In honor of his reception, Nero restored the province to the semi-independent status it had had under the Republic. Nero had a great time, but his days were numbered.

While Nero was away in Greece, affairs slipped out of control back in Rome, where the freedman Helius had been left in charge with the power to do as he saw fit. Helius sent letters warning Nero of the growing discontent in Rome, but he ignored them. As the emperor savored his artistic triumphs, his sycophantic retinue endeavored to keep distracting bad news from him. Finally, in late A.D. 67, Helius had to travel to Greece to retrieve Nero. As it turned out, it might have been a better idea to keep the emperor away from Rome.

When he returned to Rome in early A.D. 68, he celebrated a sort of parody of a traditional military triumph, entering the city in the manner of a victorious Greek athlete rather than as a Roman general. He rode in Augustus' triumphal chariot, but instead of passing through a triumphal arch he did so through a breach in the walls as was the custom of the victors in the Greek games. He was accompanied by placards displaying the names of the games at which he had won prizes instead of the names of the military enemies whom he had vanquished, and he was attended not by soldiers but by his artistic companions. Finally, instead of winding up at the temple of Jupiter Optimus Maximus, where victorious generals fulfilled their vows by dedicating plunder, he rode to the Palatine temple of Apollo, the god of artists. Nero was going out of his way to flout Roman sensibilities, and to sober-minded Romans it must have been clear (if it had not already been) that the emperor was totally unsuited to his position. Certainly, such self-indulgence was no way to retain the loyalty of the military.

Things had gotten so bad that C. Julius Vindex, governor of the militarily insignificant province of Gallia Lugdunensis, sent letters to other governors asking for their support in a revolt. Most passed on the offer to the Imperial chancery in Rome. Despite this lukewarm response, in about mid-March of A.D. 68 Vindex proclaimed his revolt. In early April, the governor of one of the Spanish provinces, P. Sulpicius Galba, decided to support the revolt and declared himself to be the legate of the senate and People of Rome. The legate of the single legion in Spain supported Galba, as did M. Salvius Otho, the governor of Lusitania (modern Portugal), who had lent his wife Poppaea Sabina to Nero.

When news of this reached Rome in mid-April, Nero reacted with surprising vigor. He assumed the office of consul himself, summoned units from Illyricum, Germany, and Britain, raised a new legion from the fleet stationed in southern Italy, and had Galba declared a public enemy. At some point soon after, news reached Rome that L. Clodius Macer, the legate of the one legion in the province of Africa, had likewise declared for the Republic. For some reason Nero stayed at Rome. Since his exercise of the Imperial dignity had for the most part been limited to signing death warrants and performing in artistic competitions, he may well not have known what else to do.

Meanwhile, L. Verginius Rufus, the governor of Upper Germany, remained loyal to Nero and led his troops against Vindex. At the battle of Vesontio in May, he crushed such troops as Vindex had managed to raise, and Vindex committed suicide. This victory ought to have saved the situation for Nero, but ironically it caused him more trouble. Rufus' victorious troops wished to proclaim him emperor. Rufus refused the honor, but word of the troops' attitude spread, and units in Illyricum hailed Rufus as emperor. When rumors of these events reached Rome, Nero panicked, thinking that the troops were disloyal. He decided to flee to Alexandria in Egypt, but this decision undermined the loyalty of praetorians, whose officers refused to follow. When he fled anyway, the praetorian praefect Nymphidius Sabinus persuaded his troops to declare their support for Galba as the new emperor. (His colleague Tigellinus pleaded illness as an excuse for inaction, but he had perhaps decided that there was no hope for Nero.) The senate now declared Nero a public enemy. He took refuge in the villa of one of his freedmen outside Rome, and as horsemen approached to arrest him, he somehow managed to commit suicide.

Through his own foolishness, the last Julio-Claudian emperor was now dead. His disregard of public opinion in acting as a performer had squandered the loyalty that he could rightfully claim as a legitimate member of the dynasty, and his ineptitude and indifference had resulted in a complete loss of control in late A.D. 67 and 68. He could have saved the situation with even the least bit of initiative in rallying the military, whose natural attitude was loyalty to the Imperial house. Nero truly was an artist rather than an emperor. It was not so much that the dynasty was deserted by the forces loyal to it as the other way around. Since he had finished the process of eradicating the entire line of Augustus that had been begun by his predecessors, the dynasty died with him. The Romans would now have to go through the difficult process of establishing a new dynasty.

15

CIVIL WAR AND THE FLAVIAN DYNASTY,

A.D. 68–A.D. 96

With the end of the Julio-Claudian dynasty, it remained to be seen how someone would establish himself as emperor and set up a new dynasty. As Tacitus famously remarked, the events of the year following Nero's death revealed the secret that an emperor could be made elsewhere than at Rome. This was because Imperial authority was ultimately based on control of the military. Thus, to retain power it was necessary to establish control over the provincial armies, which in turn meant that those armies could impose their own choice. The events of the so-called Year of Four Emperors (A.D. 69) showed that even if an emperor gained recognition in the city of Rome, this counted for nothing in the face of opposition from the provincial armies. It took a year of civil war and the death of three Imperial candidates before the fourth could establish a new dynasty.

Even before the death of Nero, the praetorian praefect Nymphidius Sabinus had been arranging to have the praetorian guard recognize Galba, the rebellious governor of Spain, as emperor, and after Nero's suicide the senate promptly acquiesced in his proclamation as emperor by the praetorians, voting Galba all the Imperial titles including not only the title "Augustus" but also the family name "Caesar." The nearly seventy-year-old Galba was an unremarkable, childless senator who had a reputation for old-fashioned Republican severity. For many years previously he had been known by a different name that he had assumed as a condition for accepting an inheritance, but as emperor he reverted to his original name. The motivation for this reversion was that the Sulpicii Galbae had been prominent in senatorial politics for more than two centuries, and Galba's claim to the purple was at least in part based on belonging to this famous family. If he thought that the prestige of a musty old name would count for much, the events of the next few months would disabuse him of this misconception.

Even before he got to Rome, Galba's position was already being challenged. The praetorian praefect Nymphidius Sabinus ineptly conspired to have himself made emperor. Though the plot was promptly betrayed and Sabinus executed, these events showed that Galba's hold on power was not very tight. During the summer of A.D. 68, Galba made his leisurely way to Rome, and once he got there, it turned out that his dour demeanor and old-fashioned virtue would not win him any friends. Despite the fact that it had become traditional that, upon his accession, the new emperor would give donatives to the inhabitants of Rome, the provincial soldiery, and (perhaps most importantly) the praetorian guard, Galba refused to give any. Though theoretically laudable given the financial straits in which the treasury had been left by Nero's profligate ways, this decision did nothing to gain him popularity, especially among the praetorians, who were used to being treated with indulgence. Galba also acted vindictively toward those who had supported Nero, who had after all been the legitimate emperor. In addition, Galba ordered the return of gifts made by Nero to his favorites. Because much of this property was now in the hands of third parties who had legitimately purchased it but were now being compelled to surrender it, this act, too, won him no popularity and much hostility. Finally, Galba had two important governors assassinated, including L. Clodius Macer, the governor of Africa who had, like Vindex, rebelled against Nero. While there was some justification for these acts, this sort of behavior reminded people of the bad old days of Nero. As a practical matter, Galba was winning few friends and making many enemies. There was more to being emperor than simply having an impressive lineage and a sour expression.

Surprised at the swift end of the old dynasty, the provincial governors and armies followed Rome's lead and swore allegiance to the new emperor. It soon dawned on others, however, that if Galba could become emperor, then so could they. In particular, a revolt broke out among the German legions in the name of A. Vitellius, whom Galba had appointed as governor of Lower Germany after assassinating the old governor. Vitellius was the son of a senator who had enjoyed the highest favor under Claudius. Vitellius comes off poorly in the sources – since he was ultimately overthrown by Vespasian, the historians who wrote under Vespasian and his dynasty denigrated Vitellius, whom they reviled as an inept glutton interested in nothing but food. This judgment seems hard to reconcile with the loyalty that he quickly acquired in his short reign and the fact that his governorship of Africa in A.D. 60 was so highly thought of there that many volunteered to enter his service after his proclamation as emperor eight years later.

The revolt began on January 1, A.D. 69 in Upper Germany, where two legions refused to renew their oath of allegiance to Galba. At first the revolt seems to have been merely negative, and the troops would swear allegiance only to the Senate and People of Rome. When news reached Lower Germany, a legionary commander who felt that Galba had not rewarded him sufficiently for his previous actions in suppressing disloyalty towards Galba impelled Vitellius to proclaim himself emperor, and all the legions along the Rhine promptly took up his cause. Clearly, mere recognition as emperor in Rome was not sufficient to secure the obedience of the provincial armies.

When news reached Rome of trouble on the Rhine, Galba thought that the cause of this discontent was his old age and childlessness, and in an effort to secure dynasty loyalty, he decided to adopt L. Calpurnius Piso Licinianus, who was a descendant of several of the highest families of the Republican nobility. Galba still seemed convinced of the magical powers of descent from the Republican nobility. Piso was apparently a rather dour character like Galba himself, and the latter continued in his failure to recognize the true nature of Imperial power, refusing to offer the traditional donative in celebration of the adoption.

The adoption of Piso came as a shock to M. Salvius Otho, who like Vitellius was the son of a father who had reached the highest senatorial positions under Claudius. When Otho obligingly surrendered his wife Poppaea Sabina to Nero, the emperor had rewarded him with the governorship of Lusitania (modern Portugal) in A.D. 58 at the age of twenty-six. Still there in A.D. 68, Otho supported Galba and accompanied him to Rome. He expected that as a reward for his early loyalty he would be adopted by Galba and was bitterly disappointed when Piso became the emperor's heir. Following the adoption of Piso, Otho quickly resolved to seize power through a coup d'état and found that the praetorian guardsmen were none too fond of Galba, who had given them no donatives and caused the execution of their most recent commander. In the vicinity of Rome, there were a number of units that had been gathered by Nero in his final days and treated unfavorably by Galba. On January 15, Otho proclaimed himself emperor, and the praetorian guardsmen quickly espoused his cause. Piso belatedly promised a donative, but it was too late. Galba was abandoned by those around him and committed suicide, while Piso was hunted down and killed. The crowds in Rome were enthusiastic about the change, and the senate duly bestowed the Imperial titles upon Otho.

Given Otho's unsavory background, many people were not unreasonably apprehensive about how he would behave. The senators' appreciation was therefore all the greater when Otho showed himself to be a mild and temperate man, who would personally intervene several times to prevent the praetorian guardsmen from killing senators they disliked. His moderation earned Otho a very favorable presentation in the sources, though he probably was no better (or worse) than Vitellius, who had the misfortune of opposing the ultimate victor.

While Otho seized the Imperial titles in Rome through a coup d'état, Vitellius was on the Rhine, resting his claim on his acclamation by the seven legions stationed there. The provinces of Gaul, Britain, and Spain declared for Vitellius, while Otho received the allegiance of Africa and the east. The question now became how to resolve these conflicting claims.

Vitellius and Otho at first addressed each other by letter in a courteous way, but it soon became obvious that there could be no peaceful resolution. On paper, Otho had more troops, but Vitellius' forces were concentrated and ready for action, while most of Otho's legions were scattered across the Mediterranean. Otho needed to hold Vitellius at bay until he could marshal his forces, especially the legions in the Balkans.

In mid-March, Otho departed from the city to take command of the defense of northern Italy, while Vitellius dispatched forces to the south by two separate paths (one column was delayed while it plundered towns that had been loyal to Vindex the previous year). The two opposing armies faced each other near Cremona, but it was decided that Otho should remain at nearby Brixellum to avoid ruining his prestige in the case of defeat. This was a mistake, as his presence might have stiffened his troops' resolve, and defeat would in any case be fatal. On April 14, battle was joined at a location where the Vitellians were attempting to bridge the Po (the engagement is called the Battle of Bedriacum, though it was really closer to Cremona), and after a long and confused struggle, the Vitellian forces carried the day. Supposedly 40,000 men died in the battle and pursuit. Once the magnitude of the disaster was clear, Otho committed suicide, first destroying any correspondence that would have incriminated others in the eyes of Vitellius.

At Rome, Vitellius exercised his victory with moderation. Though he discharged Otho's praetorians, he gave them rewards, and then created a new guard from his own legionaries from Germany. In his capacity as emperor, he adopted a stance of constitutional restraint. He always refused the title of "Caesar" and called himself "Augustus" only after this title had been duly bestowed on him by the senate. He also ended the use of freedmen in the highest positions in the chancery at Rome and began the practice of employing free Romans of equestrian status in their stead. The sources accuse him of being a cruel glutton. If he ate too much, this was no different from other upper-class Romans of the time. As for cruelty, only two executions of prominent Romans were attributed to him, and neither of these were prominent partisans of Otho. Under the circumstances, such behavior is not very bloody. On the whole, it seems the very bad portrayal of him in the sources derives from the inherent hostility of the Flavian writers and the manner of his demise, which would not be as edifying as Otho's.

The legions of the east swore allegiance to Vitellius, but without much enthusiasm. A conspiracy against him was formed by the two eastern governors with the largest number of troops under their command. T. Flavius Vespasianus was in command of the forces suppressing the Jewish revolt that had broken out in A.D. 66. He was the descendant of sturdy, frugal equestrian stock from the Italian countryside, he and his brother being the first members of their family to attain senatorial standing. Sabinus, the elder brother, had been praefect of the city for twelve years under Nero and Otho, and continued to hold this position under Vitellius. At the time of Nero's suicide, Vespasian was ready to assault Jerusalem, but decided to halt operations to await the outcome of events in Rome. The governor of Syria was childless, and when news of Vitellius' success reached the east, he suggested to Vespasian that they should cooperate in making Vespasian emperor, pointing out that they had six legions and could count on the support of the two in Egypt and that it was unlikely that the Danubian legions would support Vitellius, since they had recently fought against him on behalf of Otho. Vespasian was hesitant, but plans continued anyway. On July 1, A.D. 69, he was proclaimed emperor by the praefect of Egypt, and soon all the east went over to him. Since the new claimant controlled Egypt, the breadbasket of Rome, the policy adopted by his eastern supporters was one of caution: they would marshal their forces while Vitellius' position in Rome was undermined by means of cutting off the grain supply from Egypt. As it turned out, this plan was overtaken by the enthusiasm of Vespasian's adherents on the Danube.

When news reached the Balkans of the revolt in the east, the legions stationed there quickly went over to Vespasian. The governors were cautious, older men who warily and unenthusiastically went along with the troops' decision. Leadership was seized by the young and ambitious legionary commanders, especially Antonius Primus, who commanded a legion that had been raised by Galba and was thus hostile to Vitellius. At a council of commanders in the Balkans, he won the day for a plan to invade Italy as soon as possible instead of waiting for the troops from the east. After the acquiescence of the tribes across the Danube had been secured, he set off without even waiting for the more distant legions in Moesia to arrive.

By September, news arrived in Rome that advance forces had moved from the Balkans into northern Italy. Vitellius still had large forces in Italy and sent north four entire legions plus detachments from seven others. Of the two generals who had held command in the campaign against Otho, one was ill, so the other was sent. This proved a bad choice, as he was so eaten with jealousy of the other that he attempted to subvert the troops' loyalty and to go over to Vespasian. This plan came to nothing, and he was arrested, but before the other commander, whose health had in the meanwhile improved, could arrive to take command, Primus seized the opportunity to attack Vitellius' forces while their command was in disarray. Vitellius' forces were divided in two, and Primus attacked them separately. First he defeated the forces camped near

Cremona on October 26 and compelled them to retreat, then defeated the other force, which had just arrived by forced march. This whole engagement is known as the Second Battle of Bedriacum (though again it was really closer to Cremona). The next day Primus actually managed to seize the Vitellian camp after a perilous direct assault, and the eight German legions surrendered. The victors also mercilessly plundered the blameless city of Cremona.

When news of the debacle at Cremona arrived in the south, most of Vitellius' forces went over to Vespasian. There was clearly no longer any hope for Vitellius, and as Primus approached Rome, he promised Vitellius money and undisturbed retirement if he would give up power peacefully. Vitellius entered into negotiations with Vespasian's brother Sabinus, who was still acting as praefect of the city. They reached an agreement and swore an oath to uphold it.

It turned out not to be so easy to stop being emperor. When Vitellius made a public declaration of his intentions, rioting broke out, and when Sabinus used the troops under him to try and suppress this, they were forced to take refuge on the Capitol. Unfortunately, Vitellius had no control over his forces, who were loyal to him whether he wanted this or not, and the next day the praetorians stormed the Capitol, in the process burning to the ground the temple of Jupiter Optimus Maximus, the main shrine of the state religion. Sabinus was captured and brought to Vitellius at the palace. Vitellius received him civilly and tried to calm the mob, but they thrust him aside and tore Sabinus limb from limb.

In mid-December, Primus' forces received word of the attack on Sabinus and promptly marched on the capital, arriving the next day. Some resistance was made against their entry into the city, but it was quickly overcome. For some reason, Vitellius refused to commit suicide and remained in the palace. He was soon found and forced to march bound and naked through the city, to the derision of the mob that had recently refused to let him abdicate. He was eventually executed, and Vespasian was proclaimed emperor by the senate.

With the death of Vitellius and the recognition of Vespasian as the emperor, the war in Judaea could resume in A.D. 70. When Vespasian set off for Italy, he left his son Titus to finish the war. Now that all the surrounding countryside had been subdued and Jerusalem reduced to dire straits through lack of food and infighting among the besieged defenders, Titus decided to launch an assault on the heavily fortified city, which enjoyed the protection of both rough terrain and well-built defensive works. First, by May the outer wall in the north was taken after heavy resistance. Next, nine days of attack were necessary to capture the inner wall. The defenders of the fortress called the Antonia refused to give up; a month was spent building a vast rampart in preparation for the assault, but the defenders managed to make it collapse through undermining. After a monumental effort to build four more ramparts, the Romans captured the Antonia and were finally ready to attack the huge precinct surrounding the Temple. Again, a huge effort was needed to capture the precinct, but this was eventually achieved and the great Temple destroyed (July-August). The siege was still not over, and a further attack was necessary to capture the inner city. Those inhabitants not killed were sent to the mines or kept for gladiatorial combat, and the remains of the once-great city were razed. The rebels still held a few fortresses in the countryside, but these were mopped up without much trouble in the next few years.

The war had a devastating effect on the life of the Jewish community. The Jewish population of Judaea was clearly much depleted as a result of the war, and a number of Roman colonial settlements were established. Though the Jews were not specifically expelled, large numbers fled abroad. In addition, now that the great Temple that had been the center of Jewish religious life and the priestly class that had administered it were gone, Jewish religion would take a new line of development that was focused on local synagogues, abandoning the blood sacrifice that had previously been a central aspect of cultic practice at the Temple.

Meanwhile, Vespasian had to secure his newly won position and make sure that he did not go the way of his predecessors. He was of comparatively humble origins, and his accession represents the final triumph of the men of municipal Italian origin who had become increasingly prominent in Roman politics since the Late Republic and especially under the Julio-Claudians. While there were other elements in Vespasian's victory in the civil war, it nonetheless turned out that the ability to command the respect of such men was more important than having a good Republican pedigree like Galba's. Vespasian now had to reestablish the sort of dynastic loyalty that Nero had so needlessly squandered.

The most important task facing Vespasian after the death of Vitellius was the establishment of his authority over the whole empire. Since the German army's defeat at the Second Battle of Bedriacum meant that the most powerful component of the army had been compelled to recognize him, it was easy to gain the support of the rest of the legions. Vespasian dismissed Vitellius' praetorian guard and enlisted a new one. Large numbers of troops had been raised during the turmoil of A.D. 68–69, and Vespasian founded many colonies for those discharged. These activities cost a lot of money, and the poor state in which the treasury had been left by Nero compelled Vespasian to be tardy in paying debts and to raise taxes, which gave him a reputation for being ungenerous.

It was also necessary to establish legitimacy for the new dynasty, which is called "Flavian" from the emperor's *nomen*. A major theme in the self-image of the new dynasty was the restoration of peace, and the associated idea that maintenance of the dynasty was necessary for the preservation of order. Numerous altars survive in Rome celebrating the victory of Vespasian, with inscriptions celebrating notions like *pax Augusta* ("imperial peace") and "the permanent peace brought by the house of Vespasian and his sons." Similar themes are celebrated on the coinage, and Vespasian built a new forum with a temple to the goddess Peace in it.

There was also an attempt to establish a constitutional legitimacy for the Imperial powers. Chance has preserved in Rome the last in what must have been a series of bronze tablets on which was inscribed the text of a law bestowing powers upon Vespasian. The preserved section gives Vespasian various specific powers, exemption from the laws, and the right to do whatever he thinks beneficial. In effect, by passing this law the Roman People gave over to the new emperor the powers that are theoretically theirs, and this act formed the legal basis of the emperor's powers. The powers of the earlier emperors (especially Augustus) had never been neatly laid out in such an overt way, but grew up gradually over time as the emperors' autocratic position resulted in their gradual usurpation of the functions of the state. Only with the establishment of a new man who had no dynastic claim to earlier prerogatives was it thought necessary to spell out his position in an explicit enactment.

Vespasian's relations with the senate were not without difficulty. First, there was the troublesome problem of how to deal with those senators who had profited from prosecutions against those disfavored by Nero. Already under Nero an outspoken senator named Thrasea Paetus had spoken out publicly against abuses in the senate and was eventually forced to commit suicide. Soon after Vespasian's accession, Paetus' son-in-law Helvidius Priscus tried to lodge an accusation in the senate against a particularly unsavory character who had been a major accuser in the days of Nero and had received a large reward for prosecuting Paetus. This effort was quashed by Vespasian, who apparently felt that an attempt to wreak vengeance for the wrongs of the past would lead to unnecessary complications. Priscus himself continued to be a pest, and was first exiled, then executed in A.D. 75 on an unknown charge. His end shows the basic futility of engaging in opposition simply for its own sake. Thrasea Paetus and Helvidius Priscus were inspired in their principled opposition to injustice by Stoic philosophy, and they and their followers, who were to cause much trouble for Vespasian's son Domitian, are often known as the "Stoic opposition" (see pp. 221–222). In addition, there were a certain number of conspiracies against Vespasian, but details are not known and nothing came of them. Unusually, Vespasian appointed his son Titus to be praetorian praefect, and he exercised his office with notable diligence.

It was one thing to establish Vespasian's personal authority and another to set up a new dynasty on a permanent basis. Upon his return from Judaea in A.D. 71, Titus received both the tribunician power and the *maius imperium*, while his younger brother Domitian was kept in the honorable background.

The pattern of holding the consulship under Vespasian shows a notable change compared to the pattern under the Julio-Claudians, a change that underlines his own insecurity and his determined efforts to insure the succession. After 23 B.C., the Julio-Claudian emperors held the office very infrequently, normally as a mark of distinction for the emperor's colleague. By contrast, Vespasian held the office often, mostly with Titus. Not only did these multiple consulships enhance Vespasian's own prestige, but the joint consulships also served to make perfectly clear the status of Titus as heir apparent.

Thus, when Vespasian died in A.D. 79 after a comparatively unremarkable decade in power, Titus succeeded with no trouble. His short reign is noted for little beyond the sense of loss he left after his death. People had been a bit worried at the time of his accession because of the zealousness with which he had acted as praetorian praefect, but he was benevolent as emperor. Titus had no children, and his natural heir was his younger brother Domitian, who held the consulship with Titus in A.D. 80 but was otherwise not marked out as heir through honors. When Titus died of fever in A.D. 81, he was uniformly mourned. Perhaps Titus did nothing particularly noteworthy, but in retrospect he seemed all the more appealing a personality compared to his unpleasant and unsuccessful successor.

Whereas the friendly and generous Titus had readily won the goodwill of the senators, the new emperor Domitian was cold, humorless, suspicious, and reserved. Instead of enlisting the cooperation of the senate, he apparently felt threatened by it and kept it at a distance, preferring to work through a small coterie of disreputable characters whom he found congenial. Some were of senatorial standing, but others were of much lower status. The senators naturally disliked being at the mercy of the opinion of anyone who could influence the emperor, but it was even worse when their lives could be ruined by "nobodies."

It does seem that Domitian was a competent administrator. In particular, trials of ex-governors for provincial extortion pretty much ceased under him, but reappeared quickly under his successor. This presumably means that either his grim personality and readiness to destroy those whom he found suspect deterred senators from giving him an excuse to do so or (to put a more favorable interpretation on it) that he simply made sure that the governors behaved themselves. Whatever the motive, this and certain other administrative acts have led modern scholars, who are not in a position to be executed by him, to argue that he should not be judged a "bad" emperor simply because of his poor relations with the senate and instead his achievements as an administrator should receive a more balanced and objective assessment. This is the kind of apologetics that is often given for other successors to Augustus and should be rejected on the same grounds. The position of emperor was not simply one of issuing decrees from on high, but of managing the system so that it functioned smoothly. To be sure, maintaining good relations with the senate was not the sole, or perhaps even the most important, element in Imperial administration, but an emperor who had poor relations with the senate was incapable of managing the system in the way that was incumbent upon him. Yet, the ultimate proof that Domitian was intolerable as a person (or at least as one with absolute power) is the fact that he met his death at the hands not of disgruntled senators but of those closest to him, as had been the case with Gaius.

It is a perilous proposition to analyze the character of the dead, but Domitian seems to have lacked confidence in himself and thus was prone to feeling threatened. Perhaps this resulted from his subordinate position in the past. Though at the age of eighteen he was temporarily thrust into importance during the months between the death of Vitellius and his father's arrival in Rome, he was afterwards definitely kept in the background. Titus was clearly the favored son during Vespasian's life, and Domitian was not given much honor under Titus' short reign (supposedly the brothers were not close).

What is beyond doubt is that as emperor Domitian accumulated honors and demanded the formal signs of respect in a way not characteristic of a man at ease with himself. He held the consulship seventeen times, received an unusually large number of military titles, and assumed the unheard-of office of censor for life (Claudius and Vespasian had taken the office for the traditional eighteen-month period). He also wished to be treated with the reverence owed to the gods, something that not only led to much resentment but also illustrates his own image of himself.

Domitian apparently felt the need for personal military glory (perhaps on account of a sense of inferiority compared to his brother, the conqueror of Jerusalem) and in A.D. 83 launched a minor campaign against the Germans across the Rhine. Domitian met little opposition and established a permanent area of occupation on the right bank of the Rhine opposite Mainz. For this, he was awarded a triumph and assumed the title *Germanicus* ("conqueror of the Germans"). The later sources uniformly deride the triumph as a farce, and while Domitian presumably acted as he did in order to increase his own prestige, he simply made himself look foolish.

Domitian's reign was marked by major military troubles along the Danube. There were three groups on the left (north) bank opposed to the Romans: Germans, Sarmatians, and Dacians. The Sarmatians were tribesmen who spoke a language related to Persian and had controlled the Hungarian plains for centuries. The Dacians were another Indo-European population and controlled the lower reaches of the Danube in an area corresponding more or less to modern Romania. They had been unified under one king in the time of Augustus, and the threat they posed had been one reason for the extension of Roman territory up to the Danube in his reign. Since then, they had been riven by dissension, but in Domitian's days they came to be ruled by king Decebalus, who proved to be a very competent opponent.

The sources for Domitian's campaigns along the Danube are poor. The exact chronology often cannot be recovered, and sometimes it is even unclear when Domitian himself was present along the border. Nonetheless, the general picture emerges of a series of clashes along the northern border in which the Romans suffered a number of disasters and found it impossible to impose their will on the unruly tribes across the river. This situation did nothing to improve Domitian's image or his disposition.

In the winter of A.D. 84–85, the Dacians crossed the Danube and inflicted a major defeat on the governor of Moesia, who was actually killed in battle. Domitian had to come to the frontier with his praetorian praefect to restore order, and by the summer or fall of A.D. 85, the situation was restored sufficiently to allow the emperor to return to Rome. Domitian's praetorian praefect, Cornelius Fuscus, continued to operate in the area, despite requests for peace from Decebalus. Fuscus' force suffered another great defeat, and he himself was killed. The chronology of this series of events is particularly hazy, but the defeat fits somewhere in A.D. 86–87. At this time, the large province of Moesia was split into two (Upper and Lower Moesia), which signifies the increased importance attached to the area.

In A.D. 88, after much preparation (including the transfer of troops from Germany and Dalmatia), a new general launched another campaign across the Danube. This time there was a great Roman victory. If Domitian intended to travel to the area and personally oversee the conquest of Dacia, he was prevented by a revolt on the Rhine.

In January of A.D. 89 came news of a revolt in Upper Germany. Unlike Nero under similar circumstances, Domitian reacted vigorously. He promptly set out with the praetorian guard and summoned a legion from Spain. This was not necessary, however: the troops of Lower Germany remained loyal, and the revolt was quickly suppressed. The rebellion had been set in motion by a conspiracy of officers, who enjoyed no particular support among the soldiery. (The troops had little reason to be unhappy with Domitian, who had recently increased their pay for the first time since the days of Augustus, and they would be among the few to lament his death.) The man who was hailed emperor, L. Antonius Saturninus, was an unlikely candidate to replace Domitian. Having received senatorial status from Vespasian and attained the consulship only in A.D. 82, Saturninus was hardly a very prestigious figure. Despite the ease with which the revolt was suppressed, the event doubtless contributed to suspicions harbored by Domitian against the senate.

Meanwhile, Decebalus was still in a perilous position on the Danube, but recklessness on Domitian's part saved him. After the revolt of Saturninus was put down but before the Dacian matter was settled, Domitian provoked a war with German tribes across the Danube from Pannonia, who were (unreliable) Roman allies and were faulted by Domitian for failing to give assistance against the Dacians. Rejecting offers of peace, he crossed the Danube to attack the Germans, and when he suffered a defeat, a Sarmatian tribe allied themselves with the Germans.

Having gotten himself into a bind of his own making, Domitian had to make peace with Decebalus – now on much less favorable terms than could have been gotten before. Though Decebalus agreed to receive his crown from Domitian, the emperor agreed to give him an annual subsidy. In effect, Domitian was bribing Decebalus into behaving. Such a course, while it may have been rational policy, was not likely to win Domitian respect, especially given the disasters along the Danube in recent years. He did not help matters by accepting further inflated honors.

In A.D. 92, there was more trouble along the Danube. A Sarmatian tribe crossed the river and annihilated the legion that opposed them. Domitian returned yet again, and by January of the following year, the situation was again under control. Back in Rome, he celebrated an ovation (a small-scale triumph) despite the senate's willingness to vote him a proper triumph. Perhaps even he realized how ridiculous his false claims to military glory made him look.

While the military failures of his reign were perhaps not entirely his fault, he nonetheless was responsible. He appointed the generals, determined the policy they pursued and was personally culpable for some of the trouble. This loss of face as a result of the troubles along the Danube did nothing to improve the disposition of the insecure emperor.

In the first decade of his reign, Domitian had shown himself to be close to paranoid in protecting himself. He made the disgruntled observation that no one believes in conspiracies against an emperor until he is assassinated. Perhaps there is some truth to this, but it is equally true that Domitian executed many men on the basis of his own paranoia rather than any reasonable threat from the victims, and in so doing he made his claims of conspiracy a self-fulfilling prophesy: those who felt threatened by his paranoia were all the more likely to conspire against him. In A.D. 93 and 94, after his final return from the rather lacklustre series of campaigns along the Danube, Domitian saw to the destruction of a number of senators who were related to each other and to the so-called Stoic opposition from the days of Nero and Vespasian. These and other manifestly unjust executions greatly disturbed the other senators, who had to vote in favor of their condemnations. The outspoken criticism that was leveled against various emperors by members of this Stoic opposition under Nero, Vespasian and Domitian and that inevitably led to the execution of these critics made a great impression on contemporaries, but was of no long-term significance. These men censured immoral Imperial acts on an ad hoc basis, but they had no alternative form of government to offer. As should have been clear since the time of Tiberius, there was no alternative to the Imperial autocracy, and there was no way apart from assassination to deal with an unsuitable autocrat. This "opposition" was merely the last gasp of the senatorial hostility to one-man rule that dated back to the last days of the Republic and was incompatible with the unavoidable realities of the Imperial government. After the reign of Domitian, the senators showed themselves to be reconciled to fawning on the emperors.

Most notable among those impressed by these events was the historian Tacitus, a senator of the time. Tacitus' views not only represent a major strand in the hostile ancient tradition about Domitian, but he interpreted Tiberius on the basis of his understanding of Domitian – a man who concealed his evil thoughts behind an exterior of supposed morality.

As was usually the case with tyrants, Domitian died not at the hands of the senators he persecuted and humiliated but through a plot formed by members of his own household. Supposedly, their assassination of him was motivated by disgust at his murderous treatment of the senate, but it had a more immediate cause. He killed not only one of his freedmen, but also his heir (a cousin). Apparently, Domitian's paranoia was turning on those closest to him, and they decided to act. There is a fair amount of disagreement as to the exact identity of the conspirators. Certainly, the freedmen, including those in charge of his bedchamber (a bad sign since such men had the most intimate acquaintance with the emperor's personality), were involved. Some sources include his wife and his praetorian praefect. With his assassination in A.D. 96, the Flavian dynasty was at an end.

16

PINNACLE OF THE PRINCIPATE,
A.D. 96–A.D. 192

Unlike the case with Gaius, the assassins of Domitian gave some thought to the succession, and a new emperor was immediately proclaimed despite the fact that Domitian had young cousins who might theoretically have succeeded. This indicates that the Flavian dynasty was much less firmly established than the Julio-Claudian had been (one could hardly imagine the foundation of a new dynasty while male descendents of Augustus were still on earth). Nonetheless, the new emperor seems an odd choice. M. Cocceius Nerva belonged to a family that had reached the consulship during the triumviral period. Though the man himself had been chosen by Vespasian as his colleague in the ordinary consulship in the critical year A.D. 71, nothing is known of him after that. It is hard to see what about this not terribly distinguished man of sixty-six years recommended his selection as the new emperor. Without any prestige of his own, he lacked the means with which to impose his authority.

The news of the death of the tyrant brought an immediate reaction against him and everything he stood for. After voting Nerva the Imperial titles, the senate "damned the memory" of Domitian: his official acts were annulled, his statues were to be destroyed, and his name erased from all monuments. Furthermore, those exiled under him were recalled, and the (less important) informers who had been active in his reign were prosecuted. Nerva himself swore an oath not to put a senator to death. This policy was naturally pleasing to those who had been persecuted under Domitian. It was not so pleasing to those who had prospered under the old regime. Some were wicked men who had seized the opportunity for advancement by ingratiating themselves with the suspicious emperor, but others were public men who had had no choice but to comply with the tyrant's wishes if they wanted to pursue an official career. The prosecutions petered out; as had been the case at the end of the Julio-Claudians, too many competent men were implicated in the crimes of the past, and it was easiest to ignore these now that the tyrant himself was gone.

Whatever the opinion of the senate, the troops of the praetorian guard were not at all pleased with the new emperor. Nerva replaced the praefects who had engineered his accession, but in the fall of A.D. 97, the praetorians rebelled with the new praefect at their head and demanded the execution of Domitian's assassins. Nerva at first refused and tried to win them over, but they ignored him, and the conspirators were killed. The praefect even forced Nerva to thank the guardsmen for this act in a public assembly. Nerva's position now ominously resembled that of Galba. He considered abdication, but wiser counsel prevailed. Nerva had apparently grasped the lesson of the Year of the Four Emperors and decided to adopt a provincial governor who commanded a large army. The choice fell on M. Ulpius Traianus (English "Trajan"), the governor of Upper Germany. We do not know why Nerva made this choice, but the legions of Upper Germany were those in the best position to seize Rome, as Vitellius had shown in A.D. 69. Certainly, the selection seems not to have been determined by affection. Trajan never saw his adoptive father and paid him no particular honor when he became emperor upon Nerva's obliging death in early A.D. 98.

From Nerva through Marcus Aurelius, no emperor was succeeded by a natural son, and all procured an heir through adoption. It is sometimes claimed that this behavior was the result of a conscious decision, but the only cause for this was the biological fact that none had a son, and the first emperor to do so (Marcus Aurelius) was succeeded by his son (as it turned out, a poor choice). The dynastic principle was completely unavoidable, and even during the period of "adoptive" succession, the heir was generally in some way related to the old emperor, who was doing the best that he could in dynastic terms in the absence of a son. It is merely fortuitous that for nearly a century, Rome was governed by a series of long-reigning emperors who were forced to seek their heirs through adoption. The succession of emperors from Nerva to Commodus is conveniently called "Antonine," though strictly speaking this term is appropriate only from the time of Antoninus Pius on.

Trajan was born of a prominent family of Italian origin that lived in Spain. His father had been a prominent consular under the Flavians, and Trajan himself was devoted to a military career. Trajan was a forthright, seemingly good-natured individual, who was well suited to the role of emperor; he won the respect of the senators without demanding it and refused the kind of sycophantic adulation that had been so pleasing to Domitian. Though the senators granted as much praise to Trajan as they had to Domitian and addressed him in the same terms, they did so through natural affection rather than fear. Thus, it was not the Imperial powers as such that were the source of discontent under Domitian but the way in which Domitian had exercised them.

Trajan was the most aggressive emperor of the Principate – he took personal command of a number of campaigns, and he achieved the kind of success that had not been seen since the days of Augustus. He was the first emperor to disregard in a thorough-going way Augustus' advice not to expand the empire, and the glory he thereby gained greatly enhanced his prestige and popularity. In the long run, however, Trajan's campaigns proved the wisdom of Augustus' policy.

The sources for Trajan's campaigns are very poor. No cohesive narrative is preserved, and an overall chronology for the fragmentary episodes related in various sources often relies on uncertain evidence of when various titles first appear in inscriptions. Nonetheless, the general course of events is clear enough. For the Dacian campaign, the literary evidence is supplemented by an unusual source. In commemoration of his Dacian victories, Trajan had a new forum constructed with the booty, and in the middle of it was erected a huge column to indicate the height of the nearby hillside that was removed to make way for the forum; the outside of this column was decorated with a continuous spiral containing sculpted vignettes of the campaign. Unfortunately, this visual "narrative" has no verbal description of its own, and the absence of literary evidence makes the exact interpretation of the scenes on the column uncertain.

In his first major campaign, Trajan endeavored to rectify the situation on the Danube. Domitian had eventually been forced to buy peace through subsidies to the Dacian king Decebalus, and in the future the emperors would often find it cheaper to maintain the borders this way. Trajan, however, decided to resolve the situation through warfare. Before coming to Rome in A.D. 99, Trajan spent some time in Germany, presumably making sure that he would not have war there as well as on the Danube, a circumstance that had contributed to Domitian's difficulties. In A.D. 101, Trajan began his attack on Dacia. The Dacians occupied most of the area of modern Romania, but their heartland was in the center of Transylvania, a plain surrounded by the Carpathian mountains. Trajan certainly marched into the westernmost area of Dacia, just as had been done in the successful campaign of A.D. 88–89, and the fact that the column portrays two bridges over the Danube may mean that there was a second line of attack. The Dacians withdrew before him, carrying out a "scorched earth" policy, burning everything in the path of the invading Romans to make it hard for them to find provisions. The purpose of this was presumably to force the Romans to advance rashly into unfavorable territory as Cornelius Fuscus has done with such disastrous consequences under Domitian. After a deliberate advance, Trajan tried to force his way into the central plain through a pass in the mountains toward the west (the Iron Gates) and fought a pitched battle. The Roman victory was not a complete one, and they spent the winter consolidating the area to the west of the Iron Gates. In the winter of A.D. 101–102, Decebalus apparently launched a counter offensive into Lower Moesia. After some initial success on the Dacians' part, Trajan hurried to restore order.

Trajan apparently decided in the spring of A.D. 102 to attack by the longer eastern route. Decebalus attempted to negotiate but no agreement could be reached. Trajan then crossed into the central plain, and when he split his force and was about to encircle Decebalus, the king gave in, agreeing to receive his crown from Trajan and become a client king. The humiliation of Domitian's days had been avenged, but Decebalus' kingdom was intact.

Trajan was apparently not satisfied and in A.D. 105 seized on the lame excuse that Decebalus had harmed his eastern neighbors who happened to be Roman allies to resume the war. Decebalus quickly seized Roman fortifications on the north bank of the Danube, where the Romans were in the process of building a massive stone bridge, and Trajan spent the year A.D. 105 restoring Roman control of the Danube. The next year Trajan took the eastern route to Decebalus' capital, and after once again splitting his forces in two, he took the city by storm. Decebalus escaped but was cut down during flight.

The kingdom was now annexed and a permanent Roman presence established on the north bank of the Danube. This basically consisted of the area of the Carpathian Mountains and the plain to the west (i.e., modern Banat, Transylvania, and Wallachia). The conquest had been a massive affair, involving the participation of contingents from at least eleven legions. The kingdom possessed large gold mines, and Trajan won a very large amount of booty, the proceeds of which paid for the construction of a new forum in Rome, as well as a massive, one-hundred-day celebration in Rome. Three legions were left in Dacia (this was soon reduced to one), and large numbers of Roman settlers were brought in.

However glorious the conquest and however troublesome the Dacians had recently proven to be, the occupation of Dacia made little sense from a strategic point of view. Jutting north of the Danube as it did, the new province was exposed on three sides, which necessitated a disproportionate military presence. Dacia would prove to be the only permanently occupied province that the Romans would abandon before the dissolution of the Empire in the fifth century A.D. Augustus' decision to fix the Rhine and Danube as the northern borders had been a rational recognition of the limits of Roman resources, and while Trajan was doubtless an effective commander, he showed himself lacking in overall strategic vision.

In A.D. 106, Trajan annexed another kingdom, this time on the southeastern border with Arabia. Throughout the later first century A.D., the client kingdoms of the east had been converted into regular Roman provinces, and the only one left was that of the Nabataean Arabs, which controlled the desert to the east and south of Judaea and the wealthy trade routes from India. This peaceful annexation of an area already subject to Roman control did not violate Augustus' counsel against expansion.

The same cannot be said of Trajan's massive war against Parthia, where he won his greatest (though most dubious) victories. Roman relations with the Parthians had been generally peaceful since the war under Nero, but Trajan seized the opportunity offered by Parthian infringement of his rights in Armenia to launch a splendid, though ultimately fruitless, campaign in the east. Again, the detailed chronology is often uncertain, but the general course of events is clear enough.

A dispute over the throne of Armenia led Trajan east in A.D. 113, and without even responding to an embassy from the Parthian king, he invaded Armenia in the following year. The Parthian candidate eventually came to Trajan and set his crown before him, expecting to receive it back, but instead Trajan announced the annexation of Armenia, which became a province with an equestrian governor. The emperor then marched south into northern Mesopotamia, making preparations for the inevitable war with the king of Parthia, who had until now been distracted by rival claimants to his own throne.

Trajan then marched south into Parthian territory. First, he seized territory in northern Mesopotamia, which late sources say was turned into the province of Assyria (there is no numismatic or inscriptional evidence to prove this). Trajan next undertook the conquest of Mesopotamia proper, where the Parthian capital of Ctesiphon lay. Sailing down the Euphrates and then dragging his ships overland to the Tigris, he captured Ctesiphon, and Roman coins celebrated the "capture of Parthia." The prima facie interpretation of such evidence as we have indicates that the title "Parthicus" was received in A.D. 115 for a victory in northern Mesopotamia and that Ctesiphon was not taken until the following year, but many scholars reject this construction and associate the capture of Ctesiphon with the grant of the title in A.D. 115. In any case, at some point after the capture, Trajan sailed down the Tigris to wash his weapons in the Persian Gulf.[1] What exactly he meant to do with southern Mesopotamia is not clear. When all Mesopotamia broke out in revolt in A.D. 117, the south had not yet been formally organized as a province, but at that time Trajan was settling tax matters in Babylon, which suggests that he did have a permanent occupation in mind.

Meanwhile, a somewhat mysterious revolt among the Jews of the diaspora in Roman territory greatly contributed to his problems. The revolt apparently began in Egypt and Cyrene (the area to the west of Egypt) in A.D. 115. In

---

1 This was a not uncommon Near Eastern royal custom to mark the arrival at a new body of water after a campaign of conquest.

Egypt, where there had been serious disagreements between the Jewish and Greek communities since the time of Augustus, the praefect was incapable of restoring order and the Jews forced the Greeks upriver to flee to Alexandria, where the Greeks apparently regained the upper hand. The violence in Cyrene was even more serious, and there was also trouble in Cyprus. Since it is known that a Jew was proclaimed king in Cyrene, it would seem that the revolt had some sort of messianic quality about it. This upheaval forced Trajan to send one of his best generals from the Dacian war to restore order. It took several years to put down these disturbances, an effort that tied up Roman resources at just the time that the new conquests in the east were challenged by the Parthians.

In the spring of A.D. 117, the Parthian king invaded Assyria and the entire area went over to him. Of the two generals that Trajan dispatched there from the south, one was successful, but the other was defeated and killed. The south also went into revolt, but this was put down by the legions there. At this point, another Parthian army invaded northern Mesopotamia, but Trajan took advantage of this by offering the crown of a Babylonian kingdom to one Parthian commander, who proceeded to defeat the other. This allowed Trajan to attempt to restore order in Assyria and Armenia.

What exactly Trajan's long-term intentions were at this point is not clear. His resources were clearly stretched to the limit, with a very uncertain situation in Mesopotamia and revolt at home. In the spring or early summer he is found besieging the city of Hatra in Assyria, where his luck failed along with his health. Abandoning the siege, he eventually decided to return to Italy and died on the journey.

It is ironic that while Trajan's military career is such a prominent aspect of his reign, he also was responsible for one of the few instances of Imperial social legislation. There was apparently concern about the size of the population of Italy in the first century A.D., and Trajan instituted throughout Italy a scheme to help poorer children that had been set up in various cities by wealthy individuals.[2] Since there was no form of financial instruments to guarantee income in antiquity, large sums of money were given to cities for them to loan permanently to local wealthy landowners and use the interest to provide subsidies to poorer children. We are told that the plan had a military purpose in ensuring the availability of new recruits for the army; by this time, few Italians served, so perhaps the effort was meant to reduce the decline in Italian enrollment in the army. If so, this intention failed, as the legions continued to be recruited from the areas where they were stationed.

---

2 Trajan was expanding a program begun by Nerva, and this Imperial program was itself inspired by a number of similar schemes that were set up in various localities by wealthy individuals during the first century after Christ.

Trajan's successor Hadrian was a distant cousin of the emperor but his only male relation. Hadrian had already begun a senatorial career in the mid–A.D. 90s, and in A.D. 100, he married Trajan's closest female relation (his sister's granddaughter). For the rest of his reign, however, Trajan took no further step to mark Hadrian out as his heir, which would prevent an entirely smooth succession. Hadrian's senatorial career continued to advance under Trajan, but without any particular distinction. He is not known to have participated in the Parthian war, but Trajan left him in the crucial position of governor of Syria when he left for Italy in A.D. 117. When news reached Syria of Trajan's death, he was immediately proclaimed emperor, and the story was put out that the emperor had adopted him on his deathbed. There was some doubt about this in antiquity, but it is hard to see what alternative there was.

When he came to the throne, Hadrian was faced with a perilous situation. The Jewish revolt was not yet completely suppressed, and Roman authority had hardly been set on a firm footing in the new conquests. Trajan's generals were keen to resume the war, but Hadrian thought otherwise and abandoned all of Trajan's eastern conquests. It is said that Hadrian wished to abandon Dacia as well but was dissuaded on the grounds that the Roman settlement had progressed too far to be reversed. It would seem that Hadrian decided to adhere to Augustus' advice and renounce Trajan's dangerous policy of expansion.[3]

While dealing with a border difficulty in Dacia in A.D. 118, Hadrian was summoned to Italy, where four ex-consuls had been put to death for allegedly conspiring against him, though many apparently doubted the existence of the conspiracy. Some of these men had been military associates of Trajan, and thus there may have been a plot among those who opposed Hadrian's abandonment of the eastern conquests. In any case, the senate took a dim view of these executions, and Hadrian, whose personality was rather different from Trajan's, was never to enjoy a friendly relationship with the senate. He had a strong affection for Greek culture and seemingly disliked the city of Rome. At any rate, unlike the other emperors of the Principate, he traveled widely throughout the Empire for nonmilitary reasons. He also had an interest in architecture, apparently being directly involved in the design of two important temples in Rome.[4] He provided further evidence of his idiosyncratic personality by instituting a public cult for a boyfriend of his who was accidentally drowned in

3 During this reign, a stone fortification was built all the way across the northern border of Britain ("Hadrian's Wall," parts of which still survive). The exact purpose of the wall is not entirely clear, but it suggests that the abandonment of the new conquests was accompanied by a decision to fortify the traditional frontier.

4 The huge Pantheon, which is an impressive example of the potential for ingenious design provided by the use of cement, was thought until the nineteenth century to be the work of Augustus' general Agrippa, whose inscription is proudly displayed on the architrave. Investigation of manufacturer's stamps on the brickwork, however, demonstrated that

the Nile during an Imperial visit. (The cult became fairly popular in the east.) His fondness for the Greek culture, artistic inclinations, and lack of interest in warfare show some similarity to Nero's interests, but at least building is a royal hobby, and Hadrian could indulge his creative spirit without excessively offending Roman sensibilities in the way that Nero had. At the same time, he made sure to do nothing to offend the sensibilities of the troops. For instance, an inscription in Africa preserves remarks he made assessing the performance of troops who were putting on a display for him during an Imperial visit. While one gets some sense that his heart was not entirely in it, Hadrian nonetheless was dutifully carrying out his role as commander-in-chief.

The philhellenic Hadrian made two decisions that may not have been directly intended as provocations but were nonetheless offensive to the Jews and goaded them into another revolt. First, he banned circumcision. While his immediate motive may have had to do with notions of not mutilating the body (he also tightened the law against castration), this act was a direct affront to the Jews, for whom circumcision was a long-standing tradition that commemorated their special relationship with their god. Second, when he visited the desolate site of Jerusalem, he resolved to rebuild the city as a Roman colony with a temple to Jupiter Capitolinus on the site of the great Temple of the Jewish god that had been destroyed by Titus. The ancient Greeks had a chauvinistic view of themselves and were ill-disposed to the Jews, who were likewise chauvinistic and tended to reject as contrary to their own traditions the Hellenic civilization that was widespread in the Near East. Hence, as a philhellene Hadrian may have been happy enough to act in a way that spited the Jews. Such intolerance for other people's traditions was uncharacteristic of the Romans, and provocation of this sort was incompatible with maintaining peace in a multiethnic empire, as the outbreak of a revolt in Judaea demonstrated. No narrative is preserved, but the war seems to have started in A.D. 131–132 soon after Hadrian left, and the rebels, who were led by a messianic figure named Simon Bar Kokhba, soon had control of Judaea. Several legions were involved in suppressing the revolt, which was put down by A.D. 135. The population of Judaea suffered large losses, and Jews were now forbidden to set foot in Jerusalem. This war represents the last military expression of Jewish messianic expectations in antiquity.

Hadrian fell permanently ill in his final trip to the east and seems to have grown morose in his final years, executing both his brother-in-law and this man's grandson, who was Hadrian's presumed heir. Hadrian became enamored of M. Annius Verus, the young son of a very prominent senator, but since this fifteen-year-old was too young to become emperor, Hadrian selected as

---

the fabric was of Hadrianic date, the emperor having modestly restored the original dedication on his complete rebuilding of the structure.

his interim successor another young senator called L. Ceionius Commodus, who was apparently a fop of no particular talent. In A.D. 137, Commodus was adopted, but in an act of notable ingratitude he soon died, which prompted Hadrian to complain of having wasted so much money on a donative in celebration of the adoption. Hadrian tried again with T. Aurelius Fulvus Boionius Arrius Antoninus, an extremely wealthy senator from southern Gaul, who also happened to be married to the maternal aunt of Hadrian's favorite, M. Annius Verus. Upon receiving the tribunician power, Antoninus adopted not only Verus, who was now known as Marcus Aurelius, but also the son of the recently defunct Commodus; Marcus continued to be the favorite, however, as he alone received the title "Caesar."

Within a few months, Hadrian died, and given how unpleasant he had become, his passing was considered a loss by no one. The senate was even inclined to annul his acts, but the new emperor prevailed upon the senate to deify him, earning for himself the title *Pius* ("the Pius"), so the new emperor is generally known as Antoninus Pius. His reign of twenty-three years is remarkable for nothing apart from the fact that nothing remarkable happened in all those years. This may have something to do with the lack of sources, but the reign was marked by dynastic harmony, good relations with the senate, and the absence of any major military activity. In A.D. 161, Antoninus passed away after a long and dull reign and was succeeded by Marcus Aurelius, as Hadrian had wished.

When Antoninus Pius died, Marcus Aurelius had been acting as a full co-regent for years, but Marcus refused to accept the title "Augustus" unless the full imperial honors were granted to his adoptive brother. The senate acquiesced, and the brother adopted Marcus' birth name, being known as Lucius Verus. This situation of having two full emperors who both bore the title "Augustus" was completely unprecedented, and while there would later be joint emperors, this was normally accompanied by a territorial division of responsibility. In this instance, Marcus, who was the elder by ten years, was the dominant partner despite this ostensible equality.

Marcus comes off extremely well in the sources (and modern works). He was very serious-minded and wrote in Greek a small memorandum of Stoic philosophic ruminations for his own edification. This work has survived to the present day (known in English as the *Meditations*) and appeals to the sententious. Lucius Verus is presented rather differently in the sources, being characterized as indolent and pleasure-loving. This portrait is somewhat belied by the faith Marcus demonstrated in his abilities when he sent Verus to command in the east, though the sources indicate that Verus' exercise of command was not above reproach.

Marcus apparently decided to continue Trajan's policy of aggression in the east. The king of Parthia had taken advantage of the death of Antoninus

Pius to depose the Roman-appointed king of Armenia and replace him with his own candidate. The governor of Cappadocia promptly led a legion into Armenia, but after being surrounded, he committed suicide, and his legion was wiped out. It was decided in A.D. 162 that the situation demanded direct Imperial intervention, so Marcus sent Lucius, who dawdled along the way and did not reach Syria until the following year. In that year, the governor of Cappadocia successfully invaded Armenia and stormed its capital, while the Romans also operated in northern Mesopotamia. The next year was spent in preparation for a major invasion of Parthia, which was launched in A.D. 165. One army occupied northern Mesopotamia, while another, under a Syrian senator named C. Avidius Cassius, marched down the Euphrates. After a major defeat of the Parthians, Avidius' forces captured Ctesiphon, the Parthian capital. In A.D. 166, Avidius marched into territory never reached by Roman arms before, invading Media across the northern Tigris.

Whether this attempt to repeat the deeds of Trajan in violation of Augustus' advice against expansion would have been ultimately successful cannot be known, but there were few concrete gains from these victories. In A.D. 165, the armies in the east had contracted some sort of contagious disease, and it eventually weakened the invasion force to such an extent that the campaign had to be given up – only a few cities in northern Mesopotamia were retained. When the troops returned to their normal bases, they spread the disease throughout the Empire in what was apparently one of the worst outbreaks in antiquity.

It is a great irony that the most philosophical of emperors was forced to spend the last decade of his life along the Danube defending the Empire's borders against a great series of invasions. For the previous two centuries, the Danube border had been relatively quiet.[5] Not since the late second century B.C. had there been any large-scale invasion of Roman territory from the north. From the reign of Marcus on, this situation would change.

For reasons that are not clear, there was great pressure on the tribes (mainly Germanic) along the Danube and Rhine to push across into Roman territory. Some force, whether the arrival of newcomers in Russia or internal overpopulation, was compelling the tribes further away to push west and south, displacing those with whom they came into contact in a sort of chain reaction. Some of these tribes of eastern Europe would push the older border tribes out of the way and cross over into Roman territory themselves. Though there would be periods of respite, these Germanic invasions would increase in intensity well into the third century A.D., at times completely overwhelming the Roman border. The military system set up by Augustus had not been intended to fight prolonged wars, and eventually the resulting pressure would necessitate

---

5 The Dacians had now and again caused trouble, but this was never prolonged, and it was possible to handle their threat without much effort.

a major change in the role of the emperor and in the way in which the military operated.

The sources available for piecing together an account of these wars are similar to those concerning Trajan's wars. Again, no full narrative survives, and while a column is preserved in Rome that is modeled on that of Trajan and clearly refers to some portion of Marcus' Danubian campaigns, it is indicative of how poor the sources are that it is not entirely clear which campaigns it refers to (probably A.D. 172–175).

The troubles began in early A.D. 167 when a comparatively minor invasion was thrown back without too much difficulty, while Marcus was detained in Rome by the troubles resulting from the plague. Soon, disaster ensued on the Danube, when the Marcomanni and Quadi, Germanic tribes along the upper Danube, crossed the river, overwhelmed a Roman army, passed over the Alps, and eventually besieged the town of Aquileia in northern Italy. Marcus felt compelled to move north, accompanied by an unwilling Lucius Verus, who soon died. The exact chronology is uncertain, but by A.D. 169, Marcus was hard pressed by a great invasion. He is recorded in Rome auctioning off valuable possessions from the palace to raise funds for the war, since the plague had made it impossible to raise taxes; he also found the same sort of trouble as Augustus had in trying to raise new troops to replace the large losses in battle. In A.D. 170, Marcus was back in the north, where he suffered a defeat across the Danube. That year, a tribe that held territory along the Black Sea crossed the Danube and advanced as far as the outskirts of Athens. Around this time, the troubles extended to the lower Rhine, where some tribes crossed into Roman territory and were thrown back with some difficulty. In A.D. 171, Marcus managed to make peace with some of the tribes along the Danube, including the Quadi.

In A.D. 172, the emperor began a series of campaigns that beat back the invasions along the Danube (his column in Rome most likely commemorates events from this stage of the war). He first launched a major attack on the territory of the Marcomanni and then turned on the Quadi. With increasing success, the war continued into A.D. 175, when operations were cut short by news of a revolt in the east.

C. Avidius Cassius was a wealthy landowner in Syria, whose father had served Hadrian as the equestrian head of the chancery for dealing with easterners in the Greek language and who had himself provided excellent service as a general in Lucius Verus' Parthian campaign. Avidius was proclaimed emperor in A.D. 175 while governor of his native province of Syria, and soon Palestine, Arabia, and Egypt were in his control. (Sources implausibly claim that he was actually invited to rebel by Marcus' wife, the daughter of Antoninus, who was fearful of her husband's bad health and her son's youth.) The revolt took Marcus by surprise. He responded by hastening the advancement of his fourteen-year-old son Commodus, who immediately adopted the toga of manhood. Word arrived that Cassius had been assassinated by a centurion and that the revolt was over, but Marcus decided to wind down the war on the Danube and visit the apparently disturbed east. Over the next two years, Commodus received the full panoply of Imperial powers: clearly, the ailing emperor considered his own death imminent and wished to ensure the succession for his son.

Troubles continued along the Danube, however, and by A.D. 178 had compelled Marcus to return. Little is known in detail about this final campaign, which lasted until the emperor's death. It seems that military stations were established far across the Danube in Slovakia, and this perhaps lends credence to the claim of an unreliable source that at the time of Avidius' revolt, Marcus had been planning a final campaign to establish new provinces there. If this claim is true, then like Trajan before him, Marcus wished to put an end to troubles across the Danube by annexing the territory of the offenders. If Marcus did have any such plans, they were cut short by his death in early A.D. 180.

Whatever Marcus' intentions had been about annexing territory across the Danube, young Commodus quickly wound up the war and returned to Rome. There he changed his name to make it more like his father's, but the son was nothing like the father. The first emperor since Nero to have been raised in an Imperial household, Commodus once again demonstrated how bad an idea this was. He was completely indolent and given over to debauchery, being manipulated by various freedmen and praetorian praefects. His unsuitability to rule was soon recognized, and an unsuccessful plot against him was undertaken as early as A.D. 182 (his own sister, the widow of Lucius Verus, was involved).

Commodus in the meanwhile went from bad to worse, indulging his urge to perform in the amphitheater, where he engaged in both gladiatorial combat and the killing of animals. In Roman eyes, this was far more degrading than Nero's performance in artistic competitions (only criminals and slaves normally took part in gladiatorial games). As his reign progressed, he also became megalomaniacal, assimilating himself to the god Hercules.

His relations with the senate worsened, and many members of it were executed towards the end. As usual, senatorial conspiracy was futile, and the emperor was assassinated only when those around him judged that he was getting out of control. Apparently at some point in A.D. 192, the praetorian praefect, the emperor's bed chamberlain, and his favorite mistress decided that they had to get rid of him. After the assassination, the story was given out that Commodus had been planning to kill the new consuls on New Year's Day in A.D. 193 and take their place as sole consul in gladiator's attire. This story indicates that the decision to assassinate Commodus was taken at the last minute, but the course of events suggests long planning. In any case, an athlete was brought in to strangle him after an unsuccessful dose of poison. The Antonine dynasty thus came to an ignominious end; though the senate contained a number of Imperial cousins, events prevented them from asserting a claim to the throne. A new emperor was ready to be proclaimed upon Commodus' death, and civil war would again demonstrate the decisive role to be played by the provincial armies at the end of a dynasty.

17

CIVIL WAR AND THE SEVERAN

DYNASTY, A.D. 193–A.D. 235

Commodus' successor, Pertinax, was a remarkable man. Born to an ex-slave, he was given a good education and became a teacher, but finding the pay inadequate (some things never change!), he attempted to become a centurion in the army. His connections proved incapable of finding him such a position, but did get him a command at the rank of junior officer. An appointment as a centurion would have been permanent but offered very little opportunity for advancement, which shows that Pertinax's original ambitions were low. The position that he did receive was temporary but was the first step in the series of equestrian administrative positions available to the competent, which Pertinax apparently was. He showed talent during Lucius Verus' Parthian campaign and went on to hold a number of civilian positions. Finally, the pressures of the Marcommanic Wars led to a shortage of competent commanders, and Marcus Aurelius decided to transfer Pertinax to the senate (he held the consulship in A.D. 175) to allow him to qualify for senior military command. Appointed governor of Britain in the A.D. 180s, Pertinax proved his loyalty to Commodus by revealing treasonous correspondence sent to him, and in A.D. 192 the emperor appointed him to the sensitive position of urban praefect (this post was held by a senior senator, who was responsible for maintaining public order in Rome). This trust proved misplaced, as Pertinax seems to have played a part in the plot against Commodus. Although the conspirators pretended that their actions were taken on the spur of the moment and in the senate Pertinax made a perfunctory show of reluctance to assume the Imperial dignity, the fact that he had already bribed the praetorian guard with the promise of a large donative suggests that the conspirators had previously decided to have him proclaimed emperor.

Pertinax was considered a model emperor – by the senators at any rate. He implemented a policy of fiscal restraint, reining in expenditure and restoring the silver content of the currency to the standard that had prevailed in the time of Vespasian. On the other hand, his frugality and reputation for enforcing discipline made him unpopular with the praetorians, who had no cause for complaint against Commodus. Within a few days of Pertinax's accession, they tried to make a senator emperor against his will (the man ran off and was forgiven by Pertinax). After a second attempt by some guardsmen to replace him fizzled out, a few were executed, which only increased the praetorians' resentment. This situation is reminiscent of the difficulties faced by Nerva, but since he had a son, Pertinax could do nothing to shore up his position through the judicious adoption of a provincial army commander. In late March of A.D. 193, a few hundred rebellious guardsmen marched on the palace, where Pertinax courageously confronted them. At first they were overawed, but one bold spirit stabbed him to death. Merely possessing the Imperial titles and dignities counted for nothing if this was not accompanied by dynastic legitimacy, as the next century would make increasingly clear.

A disgraceful scene followed the assassination. Pertinax's father-in-law, the urban praefect, proclaimed himself emperor and was initially accepted by the praetorians, but it soon dawned on some of them that a relative of the man whom they had just murdered was a poor choice from their point of view, and two officers went to the senate to see if they could find a better candidate. They found just the man: M. Didius Julianus, a very wealthy senior senator. Ignoring Julianus' objection that someone else already was emperor, the officers whisked him off to their camp, where he entered into a bidding war with the urban praefect to see who would give the highest donative. Julianus eventually won with an offer of 25,000 sesterces per head (twice Pertinax's donative) and the promise that he would honor the dead Commodus. This embarrassing manner of accession undermined all legitimacy for the new emperor, who was insulted in public. Already under Pertinax, the bolder spirits among the governors may have considered proclaiming themselves emperor; the tawdry circumstances under which Julianus attained the Imperial dignity now made provincial rebellion a certainty. As in the Year of the Four Emperors, the events of this outbreak of civil war would prove the futility of a coup d'état in Rome, since the real power lay with the provincial armies.

The closest single army to Rome was controlled by the governor of Upper Pannonia, L. Septimius Severus, who had three legions under his command, and within days of receiving news of Pertinax's murder Severus declared himself emperor. He claimed to be the avenger of Pertinax's death and even added the name Pertinax at the end of his own. He first secured the support of the armies of the Danube and Rhine and won over the governor of Britain, D. Clodius Albinus, by offering to adopt him with a grant of the title "Caesar." Since Severus already had two sons of his own, it is hard to imagine him honoring this agreement in the long run, though since the eldest was only five years old, Albinus may have hoped that the goddess Fortune would eventually smile on him. If so, she did not.

Meanwhile, whatever authority Julianus may have had in Rome was quickly ebbing away, with even the praetorians, who were probably embarrassed about their new emperor, exhibiting a distinct lack of enthusiasm. He sent envoys to negotiate with Severus, but they all went over to the man who was apparently destined to win. By now, Severus was already advancing deep into Italy and sent a command to the praetorians instructing them to keep the murderers of Pertinax under arrest. They complied, and the senate followed suit by ordering the execution of Julianus. Severus soon entered Rome, where he dismissed the disgraced old praetorian guard and created a new (and larger) one from the troops of his victorious army. After receiving the Imperial honors, the new emperor had to prepare to meet a challenger from the east.

The governor of Syria, C. Pescennius Niger, had himself proclaimed emperor directly after receiving news of the death of Pertinax. Like Pertinax, Niger had had a successful equestrian military career that resulted in his being enrolled in the senate. Though Vespasian had managed to become emperor from the east, as a general rule it was difficult to repeat his success. The eastern legions did at times have arduous campaigns fighting the Parthians, but such wars were comparatively rare. In between wars, the lifestyle in the urban areas where the eastern legions were stationed tended to weaken their morale and training, and it would often take a few years of training to restore discipline when a new war with Parthia broke out. In any case, it was the Danubian legions that had actually overthrown Vitellius, and this was the very area from which Severus began his attempt in A.D. 193. Niger, on the other hand, gained control only of the legions stationed in Egypt, Syria and Asia Minor, which had not seen service since Verus' abortive Parthian campaign. Niger would thus be at a distinct disadvantage in the impending showdown with Severus.

While Severus was busy occupying Italy, Niger's troops moved forward from Asia Minor to seize the town of Byzantium on the European side of the Bosporus (the channel leading from the Aegean to the Black Sea). While raising three new legions (ostensibly to invade Parthia – they all possessed the title *Parthica*), Severus dispatched forces from the Danube to prevent any further advance on Niger's part. Severus soon arrived in person and offered to allow Niger to go into exile if he abandoned his candidacy, but Niger refused and was besieged in Byzantium.

In the fall, one of Severus' generals led troops across the straits and defeated Niger's forces. Niger himself now crossed back to Asia to take personal command. A battle was fought around New Year's Day in A.D. 194, and Niger's forces were saved from complete defeat only by the fall of night. Niger now abandoned Asia Minor, which went over to Severus, and withdrew to Syria. By now it was evident that Niger's cause was lost, and Egypt and Arabia switched allegiance to Severus. In the spring, Severus' troops managed to cross into Syria and inflicted a final defeat on the forces of Niger, who was cut down in flight.

At this point, Severus was recognized as emperor throughout Roman territory. He showed some restraint in not killing the followers of Niger, but confiscated the property of many (he seems to have been hard pressed for cash, as he issued silver coins with an even lower silver content than those of the last years of Commodus). He gave benefits to the cities that went over to him early and harmed those that had held out. As for Byzantium, when it finally surrendered after two years of siege, its civic status was abolished and its walls torn down.

Now that overt opposition was at an end, Severus undertook to secure his position. He launched a minor campaign in northern Mesopotamia to gain some military prestige at the expense of foreigners. He also took several steps that showed he wished to establish his own dynasty – by adopting himself posthumously into the family of Marcus Aurelius! This peculiar move shows the extent to which Severus felt the need to acquire legitimacy through dynastic continuity, however specious. Severus piously had his "brother" Commodus deified, and gave his wife the title "mother of the camps" that had belonged to Marcus Aurelius' wife. Finally, Severus renamed his own elder son after Marcus Aurelius, which could only mean that this boy and not Clodius Albinus was now Severus' heir. (The boy will be known here as "Antoninus," though he is generally known by the nickname "Caracalla.") Severus apparently argued that the arrangement that he had made with Albinus was meant to be valid only during the civil war, so that Albinus would inherit Severus' claim in the event of his death. Now that Severus had prevailed, he wished to be rid of his relationship with Albinus. Naturally, this was unacceptable to Albinus, who declared himself emperor, and by the end of A.D. 195, civil war was about to resume.

In A.D. 196 Albinus crossed over into Gaul, gaining control of most of it, though some towns as well as the Rhine legions remained loyal to Severus. For his own part, Severus spent many months securing his position in Italy, and it was not till the end of the year that he took to the field. He led his troops across the Alps in order to launch an attack from the north against Albinus, who had taken a position at Lugdunum in southwestern Gaul. This encirclement would cut Albinus off from Britain and trap him against the Alps. In early A.D. 197, the decisive battle was fought near Lugdunum. Initially Severus fell into a trap and was forced to flee, but his cavalry decisively defeated the troops of Albinus, who committed suicide. Severus was now the undisputed ruler of the Roman world.

Severus apparently did not like the city of Rome much, and like Hadrian spent a great deal of time abroad, but whereas Hadrian had no fondness for the military life, Severus' main concern was to maintain his popularity with the army. His dying words to his sons are said to have been, "Do not disagree with each other, give money to the soldiers, and despise everyone else." This indicates that he realized the key to the Principate: so long as there was dynastic harmony and the goodwill of the soldiery, senatorial opinion counted for nothing and the emperor could do what he pleased. In line with this point of view, Severus increased the soldiers' pay for the first time since Domitian, and also ended the long-standing prohibition against soldiers marrying while in service.[1]

Already in A.D. 197, Severus returned to the east to campaign in Mesopotamia. (As a sign of the falling status of Italy, Severus not only left his new praetorian guard in Rome but stationed nearby one of his newly raised legions. Never before had a regular military unit been stationed in Italy as if it were an area in need of a garrison. Clearly, Severus wanted to prevent the possibility of trouble in his absence.) By the fall of A.D. 197, the emperor had journeyed down the Euphrates and captured Ctesiphon, the Parthian capital, but poor logistical planning forced him to withdraw to the north. In A.D. 198, Severus annexed northern Mesopotamia as the province of Mesopotamia. Like Osrhoene, the neighboring area which had been annexed in A.D. 195, this new province was put in the hands of a governor of equestrian rank. This campaign thus marks a major expansion of Roman territory at the expense of the Parthians, and this area would be a source of much strife in the future.

In the same year, a significant event took place when he attempted to take the city of Hatra in northern Mesopotamia. After an initial assault took a section of the city's massive walls, Severus sounded the retreat to allow the inhabitants to surrender (and thereby prevent its being plundered), but they had no intention of doing so and rebuilt the walls during the following night. When faced the next day with the need to take the same walls all over again, the European troops refused the order to attack. Severus then used the Syrian troops, who were rebuffed, and eventually the siege had to be abandoned. It is hard to imagine the troops behaving this way toward an earlier emperor. Apparently, the troops were beginning to feel less constrained by obedience and more "uppity." It would not be long before the armies took it upon themselves to murder emperors.

L. Septimius Severus was the first emperor whose family was of a distinctly non-Roman origin. Certainly, earlier emperors like Trajan had come

---

1 Previously, soldiers entered into permanent relations with women they considered wives, but such "marriages" had no legal validity and any children were not considered legitimate heirs under the law. Such relations would be legalized upon honorable discharge, but many soldiers died before that time, which could lead to legal complications.

from provincial families, but these families had been founded by Italian emigrants. While Severus' family clearly had been Romanized for some time, they belonged to the native aristocracy of the Punic city of Lepcis Magna in Africa. Inscriptional evidence shows that that aristocracy had begun to use Latin only towards the end of the reign of Augustus. The town soon began to adopt Roman forms of local government, eventually attaining the honorable status of a Roman colony under Trajan. By the end of the first century A.D., a wealthy ancestor of Severus had taken up residence in Italy and was so Romanized that a poet commented that there was no sign of his Punic origins. The family entered senatorial politics and by the middle of the second century A.D. had reached consular rank. Thus, Septimius Severus represents the culmination of the process by which foreign communities (and especially their ruling class) assimilated themselves to the Roman political system.

We have contemporary testimony as to Severus' character, but it is hard to gain a clear picture of the man. The Greek historian Dio Cassius was a senator at Rome under Severus (who made him suffect consul in about A.D. 205) and makes it clear that Severus was a very superstitious man with great faith in astrology and dreams.[2] Apparently he justified a number of his actions on the basis of dreams he had had. One prominent trait in his character was vindictiveness. After his victory over Pescennius Niger, Severus was comparatively restrained since Albinus remained as a rival, but once Albinus was defeated, he let loose his vengeance (in a speech to the senate he supposedly poured scorn on the famous clemency of Caesar and praised Sulla, Marius, and Augustus for their severity and cruelty). Twenty-nine senators were then executed along with a larger number of lower-ranking men, and so much property was subject to confiscation that special procurators were appointed to carry out the task – and so much fell into Imperial hands that a new procuratorial position was created to look after it.

While Severus' brutality suggests a domineering man who liked to control the situation around him, at other times he appears as a rather weak individual who could not control his relatives. In the earlier part of his reign, a relative of his mother named Plautianus was appointed praetorian praefect and enjoyed vast influence, never leaving the emperor's side. Anecdotes are preserved in which junior officials refused to carry out orders given personally by Severus without Plautianus' permission. Severus' elder son Antoninus was married to Plautianus' daughter (whom he loathed) and resented Plautianus'

---

2 While such notions were not unknown in the Greco-Roman tradition, the belief in astrology and the expression of divine revelation through dreams was particularly strong in the Near East, and this trait in Severus may reflect the continued influence of his Punic background.

influence. In A.D. 205, Severus' unstable son Antoninus replaced Plautianus as the overbearing influence in the family. While attempting to frame Plautianus for plotting against the emperor, Antoninus got tired of waiting and simply had him murdered by one of his accomplices – in the emperor's presence! How an individual as vigorous as Severus allowed Plautianus to achieve such a dominant position in the first place is hard to fathom, as is his gullibility in believing the accusation (apparently Severus had had a premonition in a dream). In any case, Severus was to prove incapable of restraining his violent elder son.

After spending the next few years in Italy intimidating the senate, Severus decided in A.D. 208 to go to Britain, where the tribes north of Hadrian's Wall were causing trouble: a number of campaigns ensued, but the details are lacking. A prime motive for the Imperial visit to Britain was supposedly to get his sons out of the unhealthy atmosphere in Rome. Back in A.D. 198, Antoninus had been given the rank of Augustus, while his younger brother Geta received the title Caesar. Their fate would prove yet again that it was a bad idea to raise children in the Imperial household. The story has it that Antoninus actually drew a dagger against his father, who for his part threatened Antoninus with removal but could not bring himself to do so. Antoninus not only begrudged his father his life but also could not stand his brother, and Severus tried without success to reconcile the two. Fearing for the life of Geta, Severus proclaimed him Augustus as well in late A.D. 210. It would appear that while Severus was unwilling to remove Antoninus, he wished to prevent Antoninus from murdering him by making them equal in rank. Severus had been in ill health for some time, and in early A.D. 211, he died at Eboracum (modern York). It remained to see if he had saved his younger son's life.

This joint accession of the sons of Severus was a novelty. (Marcus Aurelius had jointly ruled with L. Verus and Commodus, but after he alone had been named heir by Antoninus Pius, he voluntarily shared the title of Augustus with Verus.) The experiment was not a success. Later, it was found to be militarily sensible to divide the empire, but such a step was considered unacceptable at this time. Once they got back to Rome, the new emperors divided the palace, but in early A.D. 212, Antoninus had his brother murdered.

Antoninus disliked the senate even more than his father had and shared his view that only the soldiers' esteem counted; morose and moody, he preferred the life of a common soldier. On campaign he adopted the garb of a soldier and raised the soldiers' pay by a further fifty percent. Like Commodus, he killed beasts in the arena, though he did not go so far as to appear as a gladiator. He developed a delusion that he was a latter-day Alexander the Great – he had a special unit of troops formed in imitation of the Macedonian phalanx, and unofficially adopted the title *Magnus* ("the Great"). Superstitious like his father, he seems to have lapsed at times into a sort of gloomy dementia, and his mother took over the government in his later years (he seems to have had something of a guilty conscience about killing his brother, whose ghost disturbed the Imperial repose).

He seems like his father not to have found Rome congenial. In A.D. 213 and 214, he campaigned along the northern border. Trouble then broke out on the Parthian border, and in A.D. 215, he took up residence in Antioch in Syria. After a disastrous campaign run by a freedman in Syria, Antoninus moved to Alexandria in Egypt, sacking the city because of imagined slights against him. It was clearly a bad sign when the emperor bungled operations against Parthia and instead attacked one of the major cities of the Roman world for no good reason.

By A.D. 216, he was back in Antioch, interfering in the affairs of local allied kings. He then apparently indulged in his imitation of Alexander the Great and resolved to conquer the Parthian empire. He marched beyond the Tigris, but apparently made himself a laughing stock because no enemy troops were met on the journey. His prestige was slipping, and while preparing for a new campaign in early A.D. 217 he was assassinated by a conspiracy of his officers.

Oddly, the unbalanced Antoninus took a step that instituted a definite change in the nature of the Empire. He issued an edict (the *Constitutio Antoniniana*) by which virtually all the free inhabitants of the Empire became Roman citizens. The text is preserved on a papyrus, and the preamble overtly states that it was issued with the intention of giving thanks to the gods of the Roman state for his salvation (presumably from the imagined plotting of Geta) by increasing the number of people who would honor the gods. Looked at more objectively, this act marks the culmination of a process that had been going on since the time of Augustus, by which Roman citizenship was extended to increasing numbers of foreigners, both through individual grants and through the enfranchisement of entire areas. The contemporary historian Dio Cassius actually lists the *Constitutio Antoniniana* among Antoninus' acts to raise money, claiming that its purpose was to increase the number of taxpayers (certain taxes fell only on citizens). While that may have had something to do with the decision, it is hard to believe that that was the main reason, and presumably this assertion is nothing more than an uncharitable guess. This illustrates how hard it was even for a high-placed contemporary to know the reasons behind decisions made by emperors in private.

One of the praetorian praefects towards the end of Antoninus' Principate was a man named M. Opellius Macrinus. Born in Mauretania, he was basically a lawyer.[3] He had come to fear for his life after a prophecy that he would become emperor was brought to Antoninus' attention. In protecting himself, Macrinus fulfilled the prophecy: taking advantage of Antoninus' increasingly obvious incapacity, he persuaded a discontented soldier to stab the emperor. Four days later a council was held in the army, and Macrinus was selected as emperor. As praetorian praefect, he was only of equestrian rank, and never before had a nonsenator become emperor. He immediately assumed all the Imperial titulature without the formality of senatorial consent, though as it turned out he showed himself more respectful of the senate than Severus or Antoninus had been.

As a new emperor and a man of little personal prestige, he was in need of military glory. Antoninus had already committed a large army to campaigning in Mesopotamia, and Macrinus fought an inconclusive battle with the Parthian king. Both sides were apparently happy to come to terms, and after somewhat protracted negotiations Macrinus agreed to buy peace from the Parthians. This was obviously not a very glorious end to the war and did little to improve Macrinus' position. He annoyed the troops further by revoking the increase in pay for new recruits.

It is surprising that Macrinus maintained himself as long as he did. For a whole year, no one rose up in revolt. Just as Severus had adopted himself into the family of Marcus Aurelius, Macrinus added "Severus" to his own name and "Antoninus" to that of his nine-year-old son. He also had Antoninus deified as "Antoninus Magnus." This posthumous adoption into the Severan dynasty did him no good, as trouble soon arose from the family of Severus' wife. In April of A.D. 218, there was an eclipse (a sign of the gods' disfavor) and a comet (a sign of a change in kings), and in May the Syrian Imperial in-laws took advantage of these bad omens by having the great-nephew of Severus' wife proclaimed emperor in Syria. Many troops went over to him, and Macrinus, who was still in Antioch, sent his praetorian praefect at the head of troops to put down the revolt. After a long battle, the rebel troops prevailed; Macrinus fled in disguise towards Rome and got as far as the Bosporus before being discovered and executed.

The new emperor was the chief priest of a Semitic god in Syria. It was common practice in western Asia Minor and Syria for the priest of the chief local god to serve as the secular ruler as well, the god whom he worshipped being the major landowner. These priests generally belonged to a single family that thus became a secular dynasty. The chief god of the Syrian town of Emesa

---

3 The emperors often delegated legal business to their trusted praetorian praefects, and in the early third century A.D. a number of the most important jurists (legal experts) were appointed to the post.

was El Gabal, which means "god of the mountain." This name was made pronounceable for Greeks and Romans under the form Elagabalus. The god himself was represented by a tall, conical-shaped black stone.[4] The chief priests of Elagabalus had acquired Roman citizenship under Caesar or Augustus. Septimius Severus married the daughter of the chief priest. Though she had a Greek education, her relatives at Emesa were closer to their Semitic roots. Severus' widow committed suicide under Macrinus, but her sister Julia Maesa was made of sterner stuff. She had two widowed daughters, Sohaemias and Mamaea, each of whom had married an easterner of equestrian standing and given birth to one son. In A.D. 217, Sohaemias' son was fourteen years old and Mamaea's son only ten, so the former was chosen by his grandmother Maesa to be the new Imperial aspirant. As part of the revolt against Macrinus, the rumor was spread that he was the illegitimate son of Antoninus. As emperor, he adopted the name of his newfound father and became M. Aurelius Antoninus. After defeating Macrinus in the east, the remaining armies acquiesced in this dynastic charade. He was in no hurry to reach Rome, not arriving until the late summer of A.D. 219.

The Romans found that their new emperor was like none other, and certainly bore no resemblance to Marcus Aurelius, whose name he had adopted. He disliked Roman attire and wore the gaudy silken robes of his priestly office. His god's conical stone image was brought from Syria (a special temple was built beside the palace for it), and the only thing that interested the new emperor was the worship of his god, which involved a large amount of public singing and dancing. For this reason, the ancient sources incorrectly name the emperor Elagabalus after his god. The emperor engaged in behavior that made sense in terms of his own religious background but seemed bizarre in Rome. He married his god to the Roman goddess Minerva, but not surprisingly the marriage proved a failure (the goddess was an inveterate virgin) and the emperor secured a divorce. Instead, he had his god marry the more congenial Semitic goddess Unit (known in Latin as Juno Caelestis or "Juno of Heaven"), the patron goddess of Carthage, while the priest-emperor himself married the chief of the Vestal Virgins. Ridiculous though this behavior may seem, it is consonant with the traditions of the Semitic paganism of the Near East, where the symbolic reenactment of a divine marriage by the priest and priestess of the relevant gods is well attested and where it was not unheard of for the devotee of one god to attempt to establish the supremacy of his god

---

4 This stone may be compared to the Black Stone that is housed in the Kaaba in Mecca. Like the stone of El Gabal, the Black Stone had been an object of worship among the pagan Arabs and was rededicated to Allah by Mohammed.

in a town presided over by another god.[5] Not unexpectedly, this behavior was not well received in Rome.

The sources portray the priest emperor in very lurid terms. He was supposedly given over completely to sexual excess, and his administration was dominated by his Syrian friends. While there may well be some exaggeration here, the teenage priest did not cut an impressive figure as emperor. His mother was apparently indifferent to his excesses, but his grandmother realized the dangers and tried unsuccessfully to restrain him.

In A.D. 221, the emperor adopted his cousin as Caesar under the name M. Aurelius Alexander.[6] The emperor soon repented of the adoption, since his heir was looked upon with favor by everyone revolted by his own excesses. In March of the following year, during a visit of the whole Imperial family to the camp of the praetorian guard, a riot broke out: the emperor and his mother were killed and their bodies cast into the Tiber, after which Alexander was immediately hailed as the new emperor. Details are lacking, but it seems that Alexander's mother and grandmother engineered this change of ruler.

The new emperor, known as Severus Alexander, had been raised by his mother in a way that brought him more into line with the norms of Greco-Roman culture, unlike his very eastern cousin. He is very much idealized in the sources, and thus it is at times hard to get a true picture of him. Since he was only fourteen years old when he became emperor, he seems to have been guided both by his grandmother Julia Maesa and his mother Mamaea, who was a much better influence than his predecessor's mother had been on him. Maesa died within a few years, but Mamaea continued to dominate the reign until its (and her) end. Unlike the priest-emperor from Emesa, who had alienated public opinion through his flagrant disregard of Roman sensibilities, Severus Alexander pursued a policy of cooperation with the senate.

In A.D. 225, the seventeen-year-old emperor was married to the daughter of an important senator, and the senator even given the title of Caesar. Presumably the purpose of this arrangement was that in the case of Alexander's early death, there would be an adult who would take over and avoid a usurpation like the one that followed the assassination of Antoninus – as the grandfather of any children from the Imperial marriage, Alexander's father-in-law could

---

5 Babylon provides two precedents for the emperor's behavior. In the famous New Year's Festival, the king represented the city's patron god Marduk in a "Sacred Marriage" with a priestess who played the part of Marduk's consort, and in the mid–sixth century B.C. Nabonidus, the last king of the Neo-Babylonian Empire, came to grief when he attempted to oust Marduk in favor of Sin, the god of his hometown Haran.

6 Alexianus had been part of the heir's original name, but the change to Alexander was presumably connected with Severus' son Antoninus' association with Alexander the Great.

be relied on to ensure the continuity of the dynasty. One can only assume that Julia Mamaea herself concocted this plan, but if so she soon resented the influence of her daughter-in-law: in A.D. 227–228 Mamaea arranged to have the new Caesar executed for treason and her daughter-in-law exiled. Alexander remained childless.

Being under the thumb of his mother did not endear the boy-emperor to the praetorians. They killed one praetorian praefect who displeased them, and when the historian Dio Cassius held the ordinary consulship in A.D. 229, he had to withdraw from the city because of the praetorians' hostility. Clearly, the young emperor's grasp on power was weak if the unruly praetorians could intimidate and murder his associates with impunity. During this period of dynastic instability a new danger arose from the east.

By the later second century A.D., the authority of the Parthian kings was greatly weakened, and the various "princelings" became increasingly powerful. In the early third century, Ardashir, the grandson of Sassan, established himself as king in the territory of the Persians (an Iranian population related to the Parthians). Ardashir led a revolt against the Parthians, and ca. A.D. 224 (the date is disputed) he defeated the last Parthian king and established his control over the whole kingdom, founding a dynasty known as "Sassanid" after his grandfather. This new Persian kingdom would prove much more effective and aggressive than its predecessor, and the eastern border would call for much more attention from the Roman emperors.

In A.D. 230 or 231, news reached Rome that Ardashir had invaded the province of Mesopotamia, and it was decided that this danger necessitated the presence of the now twenty-two-year-old emperor. The accounts of this war are not very satisfactory. After a fair amount of time spent in making preparations, the Romans invaded by three routes: one passed through the north into Media, the emperor himself commanded in northern Mesopotamia, and the third marched south to capture Ctesiphon. This threefold strategy came to naught when Ardashir quickly marched from Media and overwhelmed the southern force. This disaster brought an end to the Roman invasion, and while the force under Alexander himself retreated in good order, the withdrawal from Media turned into a rout. When the troops were settled in Syria, the emperor felt compelled to give them a donative to retain their loyalty: it is a bad sign when the troops need to be bribed to like an emperor. The official interpretation of the campaign claimed a victory, but even if the Persians were forced back, the Roman army gained no proper victories, suffered great losses, and saw its emperor operate ineffectively. Such a lacklustre performance did nothing to enhance Alexander's reputation. Worse was to come.

By A.D. 234, the emperor was back in Rome, where there was news of disturbances from the Germans on the Rhine and Danube. Perhaps the sending of detachments from the northern legions to assist in the Persian campaign had encouraged trouble. In any case, Alexander prepared a campaign against the Alemanni, a newly formed confederation in the angle of the Rhine and Danube. Although a pontoon bridge over the upper Rhine was built, Alexander eventually preferred to buy peace from the Germans. While such a policy may well have made strategic sense, such a seemingly pusillanimous course of action was too much for the troops' patience after the debacle in the east. A general named Maximinus had been entrusted with the task of training new recruits, and after receiving news of the purchased peace, some recruits proclaimed him emperor in the spring of A.D. 235. When Maximinus advanced against him, Alexander was deserted; in March, he and his mother were captured and executed. This assassination marked the end not only of the Severan dynasty but also of the dynastic continuity that had characterized the Principate.

18

INSTITUTIONS OF THE PRINCIPATE

The driving force behind the establishment of the Principate under Augustus was the need to place the military under a permanent and unitary form of command. At the same time, a number of other enduring institutions grew up around the person of the emperor – some were organs of administration, others means of upholding the legitimacy of Imperial power. In effect, a stable form of long-term government was set up to replace the ad hoc institutions of the Republic, and for this reason, it is necessary to examine the structure of the Imperial government in a broader perspective that extends beyond the events of individual reigns.

When the future emperor Augustus took over Antony's forces following his victory at Actium, he substantially reduced the size of the military, disbanding many legions and discharging many troops. He decided that a total of twenty-eight legions was sufficient for the needs of the Empire; with a legion containing 5,000 to 6,000 men, this implies a total of about 150,000 citizen soldiers. Later Imperial practice indicates that there was an approximately equal number of noncitizen troops called auxiliaries. With the addition of unknown numbers enrolled in the navy and 10,000 praetorians, the military establishment was more than 300,000. While Augustus was basically correct in his estimate of future needs, the total number of legions grew over the years (at various times old legions were destroyed or disbanded and new ones created), reaching a total of around thirty by the early second century A.D. and thirty-three in the Severan period.

The legions now had permanent camps, though they would occasionally shift their area of deployment. Augustus had substantial numbers of legions in internal territories like Spain, Dalmatia, and Egypt, but it proved that most of these domestic garrisons could be transferred to the borders. The main areas for the deployment of the legions were the frontier along the Rhine and the

Danube and the province of Syria. Initially, Augustus had stationed a very large force along the Rhine, but the abandonment of the attempt to conquer Germany resulted in a transfer of much of this force to the Danube and the east.

The disposition left behind by Augustus provided for a defensive posture without the undertaking of aggressive wars. This system was basically one of a static defense in which most of the Empire's military strength was committed to guarding the border. Any extensive campaigning in one area would require troops to be stripped from another, and such a posture made it difficult to mount wars of aggression. In effect, this system allowed for the permanent defense of the borders with no military reserve for times of crisis, and the few periods of major activity (e.g., the great Pannonian revolt, Trajan's attempts at conquest in the east, and Marcus Aurelius' wars on the Danube) would show how ill equipped the military was for prolonged periods of warfare. The Augustan system would collapse entirely in the face of major aggression during the third century A.D., but Augustus had clearly planned well in terms of the strategic considerations of his own time, which would continue to hold true for the most part throughout the Principate.

A major factor in the demise of the Republic had been the ability of commanders to exploit the loyalty of their troops for their own purposes, and this problem was solved by subordinating all military activity to the emperor. The troops were professionals who swore an oath of allegiance to the emperor and served for a fixed number of years (twenty years for Roman citizens, twenty-five for auxiliary troops). In return for their loyalty, the emperor rewarded the soldiery with regular pay, periodical donatives, and a plot of land or cash payment upon discharge after a full term of service. An ambitious and talented enlisted man could aspire to rise to the rank of centurion.

The officers were provided by men of the upper classes, who held command for comparatively short periods of time at irregular intervals. Young men at the start of their careers in Imperial service provided the six military tribunes for each legion and the commanders of the auxiliary units. While the emperor was the legal commander of each legion, he exercised this command through legates, who were normally senators of praetorian rank.[1] In a province with one legion, a single legate would be in charge of both the province and the legion, while in provinces in which multiple legions were stationed, a legate of

---

1 The legions of the anomalous province of Egypt were commanded by equestrian prae-fects, and this solution was adopted in the reign of Gaius for the legion in Africa, the only senatorial province with a legion. The three legions raised by Septimius Severus were put under the command of equestrian praefects, a sign of that emperor's distrust of the senate.

consular rank would be in overall charge of the province and its army, while each legion had its own praetorian-rank legate. There was a tendency over the years to break up such large provinces in order to reduce the number of legions under any one legate's command.

Apart from presiding over the military, one of the crucial functions of the emperor was to superintend the system that provided the men to command the armies and govern the provinces. The most prestigious element in this system was the senatorial order. Caesar the dictator died as a result of his inability to fit the traditional Republican ruling class into his personal autocracy, and it took the genius of Augustus to achieve this through the political legerdemain of ostensibly restoring the old institutions of the Republic while retaining military power in his own hands. In fact, the powers of the senate were increased under the Principate. It was now a legally defined order (property worth I million sesterces was necessary for membership), and its decrees were given the force of law. Yet, its independent powers were a sham. The senate did have open deliberations, but only on comparatively trivial matters, and important decisions were made only with the consent of the emperor. It took a great deal of unpleasantness during the first century A.D. for the upper class to become reconciled to the fact that all real power rested with the emperor and that any opposition to him was pointless.

The old magistracies continued to exist, but their importance declined over the years, and only the praetorship and consulship had any real significance. Each year eight praetorians (ex-praetors) and two consulars (ex-consuls) were chosen to govern the traditional senatorial provinces for one year, and there were various posts (e.g., head of the treasury) to be held by praetorians. More important than any of these positions were the military legateships bestowed on praetorians and consulars at the emperor's discretion. In effect, the old magistracies now functioned merely as prestigious prerequisites for high military command. The need for consulars to fill these positions was so great that Augustus instituted the practice of regular suffect (replacement) consulships. The ordinary consuls were the pair who took office on the first day of the new year, and after some months they resigned and were replaced. Over time, the number of suffect consuls appointed each year would increase – one year under Commodus had nineteen consuls – and the prestige of the office was diminished somewhat. Nonetheless, holding the consulship remained the crowning achievement of a senatorial career.

The emperors had effective control over the senatorial order. Imperial permission had to be asked before a man could undertake a senatorial career, and each year the emperor could appoint a certain number of men to each magistracy through a process called commendation. Under the early years of Augustus, the old electoral process continued, but in a process that took place in his later years and the early years of Tiberius and that is not fully understood, the elections for the magistrates not appointed by the emperor were transferred to the senate. In any case, the senatorial positions that held real power were the legateships that the emperor bestowed at his own discretion. Hence, while there was some role for personal influence, the course of an individual's career was highly dependent upon the emperor's goodwill.

Changes in the composition of the senate can be detected over time. When the Principate was established, the most prestigious families were those of the old Republican nobility, but the natural difficulties of reproduction in antiquity and the susceptibility of the nobles to prosecution for treason led to the demise of most old families by the end of the Julio-Claudian period. From the time of Augustus on, the wealthy families of Italy came to prominence in the senate, and the rise of such men, who had no particular attachment to the old Republic, helped reconcile the senate to the Imperial autocracy. There was also a trend towards the admission of provincial families to the senate. Men from Spain and southern Gaul became notable from the mid–first century A.D., while Africa and the Greek east provided important members in the second century. Thus, the senate came to represent the wealthiest landowners throughout the Empire.[2]

Augustus also set up a separate career pattern that was even more directly controlled by the emperor. These positions were created by Augustus to superintend certain governmental functions directly exercised by him, and he filled these positions with men of equestrian rank. While there were certain distinctions within the equestrian order, an equestrian was basically a nonsenator whose property was worth at least 400,000 sesterces. While the equestrian pattern of office holding was theoretically less prestigious than a senatorial career, some men preferred the direct access to the emperor that was offered by these offices. There was less regularity in an equestrian career pattern. An equestrian official began as a junior military commander. After this, there were several rather distinct sets of offices. Some equestrians exercised fiscal functions. In particular, the emperors had large amounts of property, and in each province there was an equestrian procurator to manage these affairs. In addition, equestrians governed minor provinces with small garrisons, and they also commanded the anomalous legions of Egypt and Africa and the fleets. Finally, there were the highest posts, which administered most sensitive Imperial functions: the night watch and grain supply of Rome, the crucial province

2 Though large amounts of money could be made through trade, landowning was the only safe form of long-term investment, and there was something of a social stigma attached to wealth derived from sources other than landholding. Hence, the senate basically consisted of landowners (though individual senators no doubt had some money invested in other activities).

of Egypt, and command of the praetorian guard were the high points of an equestrian career.

A third level of administration consisted of the emperor's slaves and freedmen. Though such a custom may seem odd to modern sensibilities, it was normal practice in the Roman world for wealthy individuals to administer their business affairs through trusted slaves and freedmen, and since the distinction between the private and public functions of the emperor was rather blurry, it was natural for the emperors to follow this procedure in administering their "personal" affairs. Under the Julio-Claudians, certain "public" capacities were treated as such "personal" affairs, and men of servile origin held important posts as procurators and even as fleet commanders. (Particularly remarkable was the great influence that the Greek freedmen in charge of the Imperial chancery exercised over Claudius.) This situation of slaves and ex-slaves exercising important public functions was offensive to upper-class Romans, and in a development that took place under the Flavians and early Antonines, it came to be the accepted practice that the highest offices appointed by the emperors would be filled only by freeborn men of equestrian rank. The emperors continued to hold large numbers of slaves for menial functions, such as running the elaborate aqueduct system of Rome and distributing the grain dole there, and freedmen went on managing this permanent staff of slaves and looking after technical (often financial) functions.

One notable aspect of the Principate is the large extent to which the Imperial legitimacy was demonstrated through spending vast sums of money on the city of Rome. In a memorandum drawn up by Augustus to recount his career he lays great emphasis on his benefactions, which largely consisted of building projects in Rome, games put on there for the entertainment of its inhabitants, and the distribution of money to them. All of these practices had been foreshadowed by Caesar the dictator, and the pattern of largesse established by Augustus would continue throughout the Principate (and even into the Late Empire).

One way in which the emperors exhibited their concern for the city of Rome was to adorn it with new construction. Several emperors provided for the official business that came to the capital by building new forums (administrative centers), and their concern for the gods was demonstrated through the rebuilding and new construction of numerous temples. The emperors also built structures to provide for the daily well-being of the city's inhabitants. The aqueduct system was expanded to provide both water for fountains and sanitation and for the large public baths that were constructed, and both Claudius and Trajan undertook extensive improvements in the facilities of Rome's port at Ostia. The splendor of the city was enhanced with public amenities in the form of porticoes, libraries, theaters, and locales for sporting, the most notable of the latter being the massive Circus Maximus for chariot races and the Coliseum (Flavian Amphitheater) for gladiatorial shows.

The emperors also manifested their concern for the inhabitants of the city in more direct ways. One was the so-called grain dole. Under the Late Republic, the practice had arisen of distributing grain to citizens, first at a reduced price and then for free. This was a large drain on the treasury, and Caesar the dictator and then Augustus reduced the recipients to a fixed number, who were enrolled on a special register (approximately 150,000). Once a person was enrolled, he became the owner of that place on the roll, which he had the right to bequeath or sell, and in this way enrollment became a sort of asset providing a guaranteed income. Hence, the grain distribution had nothing to do with a form of welfare for the poor, but was a formalistic expression of the emperor's beneficence to the Roman People, who were represented by the privileged inhabitants of the city who had acquired a place on the dole registry. A vast system was needed to bring the grain to the city (mainly from Egypt), to store it, and to distribute an allotment every month to each recipient. Those enrolled for the grain dole were also the recipients of Imperial donatives to mark the new emperor's accession or other important dynastic events.

The emperors also showed their concern for the Roman People (in the narrow sense) by providing public entertainment throughout the year. A major element in this public entertainment consisted of the very popular chariot races, which formed the culmination of the traditional religious festivals dating back to the Republic. In addition, there were gladiatorial shows, which included the hunting of wild animals and the public execution of those guilty of heinous crimes. Gladiatorial games put on by the emperor himself were comparatively rare, but the presentation of such games was a regular burden of senatorial office (partially subsidized by the emperor).

The poet Juvenal famously stated that the Roman People had sold their electoral votes for "bread and circus games" (the latter term referring to the chariot races). This was true in a quite literal way. Every year, the men enrolled on the special list for Imperial benefits participated in an electoral assembly that carried on the traditional role of the Roman People by ratifying the real election of the new magistrates that had been carried out in the senate. In this way, the city of Rome functioned as an artificial microcosm of the Roman People of the past. Whereas now the Roman citizenry were scattered throughout the far-flung territories of the Empire, the population of the capital symbolically gave legitimacy to the Imperial government, and for his part the emperor managed the government of the Roman People for them and demonstrated his benevolence to them with his munificent favors to the city. Thus, while the huge sums spent on the residents of Rome may seem pointless in and of themselves, they represent a major element in the self-image of the emperors, whose legitimacy was based on the consent of the Roman People.

It would be useful to know the details of the Imperial budget, but the very limited amount of anecdotal information that survives does not allow the drawing of any detailed conclusions. The emperors themselves probably did not have a well-laid-out budget. In addition to dedicated taxes that had been levies on Roman citizens under Augustus for the provision of discharge rewards for soldiers, the public coffers received all sorts of provincial levies that had been haphazardly imposed on an ad hoc basis during the Republic, while the emperors enjoyed a large private income from the vast amounts of property owned by them throughout the Empire. (The state and Imperial treasuries were theoretically separate, but the latter often subsidized the former, and in any case all expenditure was ultimately dependent upon the emperor.) One might think that certain large expenses such as the military could be calculated since the pay rates were mostly known and a rough estimate of the number of troops could be made, but a few surviving pay receipts show that because of quite variable deductions for pay and equipment, the amounts actually received by the troops were not fixed (and since it seems that the troops did not actually receive their pay as cash but left most of it as a deposit at a legionary bank, even an estimate of the average net pay would not indicate how much money the government actually needed in order to make good on its obligations). Hence, even a rough estimate of the actual expenditure of the government is impossible. What is known is that there must have been some mechanism by which the tax receipts of the wealthy internal provinces were transferred to pay for both the armies on the boundaries and the regular Imperial expenses in maintaining Rome, and that frugal emperors would not only accumulate sufficient sums to pay for periodic donatives but bequeath large surpluses for their profligate successors to squander.

Despite these apparent surpluses, it seems that even under the compara-tively peaceful circumstances of the Principate, the Imperial government could not live within its means. In antiquity, there was no form of paper debt (e.g., paper money or bonds), so the government had no ability to borrow; in times of financial emergency the emperors had to resort to the humiliation of auc-tioning off luxury goods from the palace, but this was no way to deal with a regular shortfall in revenue. The only solution to this was a depreciation of the metal currency. This could take two forms. The first method was to reduce the weight of the coins, and the second was to decrease the bullion in each coin by increasing the amount of copper (a certain amount had to be added to make a more durable alloy). Though the first method was also practiced, the sec-ond had much more dire consequences. (The Roman government issued both gold and silver coins, and while the gold coinage did suffer some reduction in weight, the major devaluation took place in the silver coins.) Over the years, a very noticeable decline in the silver content is detectable, as the government apparently tried to make good its deficit through reducing the silver content of the coinage. Throughout the Principate, the government made good its fiscal shortfall through this procedure, which allowed a coinage of higher face value to be minted from the amount of silver available. In the long run, however, this sort of tampering could provide no permanent solution to the government's fiscal difficulties, since the resulting inflation of prices would simply increase expenses. Though there was a steady and gradual overall decline of the silver content, there are periods when the decline is more noticeable (for instance, under Nero). From the reign of Marcus Aurelius on, however, it seems that the fiscal situation deteriorated: the periodic shortfalls were replaced by a recurrent deficit, with a concomitant increase in the debasement of the currency. Severus' son Antoninus hastened this trend by introducing a new coin called the *antoninianus*, which was apparently worth two *denarii* (the *denarius* being the standard silver coin) but had only about fifty percent more silver than a *denarius*.[3] It would seem, then, that while the Imperial government was hard pressed to make ends meet regularly even in peacetime, the increase in warfare in the late Antonine and Severan periods exacerbated this situation. Imperial finances would collapse during the military crisis of the third century A.D.

Apart from the expenses associated with the city of Rome, the major drain on the Imperial finances would have been the army, since the emperors had little role in local administration. It had been traditional practice under the Republic for the Roman governor simply to maintain order in the provinces and make sure that the taxes owing to the Roman People were paid. Otherwise, local administration was left to the cities, which also exercised jurisdiction over the surrounding countryside. This situation continued under the Empire, and the Romans encouraged the development of cities for administrative purposes in less urbanized areas. The governors played little role in civil administration apart from exercising capital jurisdiction, since they alone had the right to execute. Thus, in terms of daily life, the vast majority of the population had little reason to interact with the Imperial government.

Serving on local city councils was an expensive way to gain prestige, as the offices were unpaid and incumbents were expected to provide services to the city, either through the direct cash payments or by funding public functions like the building of roads or the exhibition of games. (The unpaid exchange of public services for honor is called "eugergetism.") It would seem that eventually the costs of local government would outrun the supply of rich people willing

---

3 Though this denomination was dropped by his immediate successors, it would eventually play a major role in the collapse of the currency during the mid–third century A.D.

to provide for them by holding office. By the second century A.D., a trend was detectable by which this "honor" was converted into an obligation that fell on those who fit the property qualifications for serving. In addition, from the time of Trajan on, the emperors felt compelled to assign important local men to oversee the finances of the communities of Italy. These set the stage for the much more intrusive interference of the Imperial government in local affairs under the Late Empire.

Imperial administrative practices led to a great expansion of Roman citizenship throughout the Empire. Foreigners serving in auxiliary units received citizenship at the time of their discharge, which must have resulted in large numbers of new citizens over the decades. In addition, citizenship was extended through the enfranchisement of non-Roman communities. The first step was the grant of Latin status. The holders of high public office in communities possessing this right were automatically granted Roman citizenship, which led to a gradual Romanization of the local ruling families. Next, a community could be raised to the status of a Roman colony, which resulted in the enfranchisement of the entire population.[4] In effect, the policies of the Imperial government encouraged foreigners to become more integrated into the Roman political system without compelling anyone to do so. In certain areas, Romanization was more thoroughgoing, and the whole populace adopted the Latin language (e.g., in Spain, Gaul, Africa, and the interior of the Balkans). In other regions, particularly in the east, the ruling classes often acquired Roman citizenship, but the local languages and customs were unaffected by Roman traditions.[5]

Over the course of more than two centuries, this policy of gradual, voluntary Romanization was very successful, and by the time of Severus' son Antoninus, it was decided that citizenship should be granted to the entire free population of the Empire. Whatever the exact motives for this step (see p. 243), it marks the culmination in a significant development in nature of Roman citizenship. Under the Republic, all Roman citizens were legally equal (even if some had more status and influence than others), and Romans were distinguished from non-Romans by certain privileges, including the right not to be flogged or executed by a Roman magistrate without the authorization of the Roman People. Under the Empire, in a process that is not well understood, the emperor came to exercise the Roman People's authority and capital cases involving citizens were referred to him. As time went on, this cumbersome process became increasingly hard to justify, especially in light of the

---

4 This status of a Roman colony was considered prestigious and continued to be sought even after it had ceased to confer any material advantage.
5 The Jews represent the only major failure in the Roman policy of accommodating foreigners within the political framework of the Empire (see pp. 205–206).

widespread expansion of citizenship. In particular, all ancient conceptions of society granted special consideration to the wealthy, and as foreign communities came to become part of the Roman world and as Roman citizenship came to be held by many people of lowly status, the distinction of Romans versus foreigners came to be replaced by one of respectable (i.e., wealthy) people versus the poor. By this reckoning, it was unreasonable for a poor person with Roman citizenship to possess privileges that a wealthy non-Roman did not. In effect, ancient sensibilities expected the well-to-do to be treated better than the less affluent, regardless of their citizenship, and the extension of citizenship to the entire Empire simply recognized the fact that everyone was subject to the emperor's power and made it possible to treat people on the basis of their actual social status instead of making unrealistic distinctions based on the historical accident that determined their citizenship.

While the Imperial government of the Principate did not intrude directly into most people's daily lives, the concept of the emperor was nonetheless a widespread symbol of authority. The subjects and citizens of the Empire gave expression to their loyalty through a common institution that makes little sense to those whose religious sensibilities are based on the single god of the Judeo-Christian tradition. Apart from the Jews, the populations of the Mediterranean practiced various forms of polytheism, and in the Greco-Roman conception the "divine" was considered to be anything that had supernatural abilities. This basic premise then gave rise to the habit of granting divine honors to kings. In the Greek world, the roots of this practice can be traced back to the Classical period, when humans who had performed remarkable feats were honored after death as "heroes." Next, Alexander the Great and his successors in the Hellenistic kingdoms were treated as gods during their lifetime. If one imagines the divine to possess powers that surpass those of normal humans, then it is not entirely unreasonable to include kings in such a category, since they have the ability to carry out acts that no mere mortal could conceive.

Once Roman magistrates began to operate in the Greek east during the Middle Republic, and the victories of the Roman People allowed those magistrates to exercise a form of power that surpassed that of the local kings, the Greeks began to bestow on beneficent Romans whom they wished to appease or revere the sorts of honors that had traditionally been given to the Hellenistic kings. Caesar the dictator, then, adopted some of the quasi-divine trappings of Hellenistic kings in his abortive effort to regularize his autocracy. Caesar's fate taught Augustus to avoid any direct claims to the divinity – in the Roman world. In the east, Augustus was worshipped openly as a god, though he generally insisted on being worshipped alongside the goddess Roma, the personification of Rome. In the less Romanized areas of the west, centers for the worship of Rome and Augustus were officially founded to provide a venue where the leading men of the provinces could express their loyalty to the emperor through worship. In Italy, he was already quasi-divine in that he had had his adoptive father enrolled in the state pantheon in 42 B.C., but he refused direct divine honors. Nonetheless, he was given a privileged position in the state religion, and in particular he allowed people to make sacrifice to his *genius* (a sort of guardian spirit). Upon his death, Augustus was himself enrolled among the gods, and it became customary for an emperor who considered himself to be a legitimate heir to the dynasty to have his predecessor deified. Generally speaking, sane emperors did not expect to be treated like gods, but it was regular practice to use adjectives like "sacred" and "divine" to describe the emperor and to make a small offering of wine or incense before an image of the reigning emperor as a sign of loyalty. The refusal of Christians to participate in this civic ceremony became an important element in the conflict that was to arise between the new cult and the Imperial government.

It is a difficult question to determine what exactly the Imperial cult signified to people in antiquity. Certainly, no sane person considered the emperor to be a god in the normal sense of the word, and a fair number of Romans – including certain emperors – made fun of the institution. Nonetheless, the persistence of the cult and the fact that the driving force behind the practice was not governmental coercion but the spontaneous impulse of the "worshippers" show that it fulfilled a deeply felt need. In effect, the emperor was the personification of the state, and the performance of divine ritual in his honor not only provided a vivid means of expressing one's allegiance to the state but also allowed the subject to feel that he had a personal relationship with that state.

Despite his theoretically great powers, for the most part the emperors of the Principate were passive figures, who did not attempt to regulate social behavior. There are only two examples of consistently enforced social policy. Under Augustus, legislation was passed to encourage procreation by penalizing the childless, and these laws were consistently enforced until the fourth century A.D., when the adoption of Christianity brought about a change in attitude regarding celibacy.[6] Second, Trajan instituted a scheme throughout Italy to assist the poor in raising children, but this was perhaps an extension of the traditional Imperial concern for the welfare of the Roman People. As part of their image as beneficent rulers, however, it was expected that the emperors would be willing to listen receptively to petitions from respectable applicants, and a large chancery apparatus grew up in Rome to deal with such petitions.

---

6 These laws affected the wealthy and were motivated by the idea that people in the upper classes were intentionally avoiding having children. While there may have been some truth to this, the perceived phenomenon of important families dying out was more likely the result of the high rates of sterility and infant mortality that prevailed in antiquity.

Famously, when Hadrian told a lowborn female petitioner who confronted him in public that he was too busy and that she should bring the matter to the attention of the praetorian praefect, she replied that in that case he should stop being emperor. Yet, however much the woman felt that the emperor was there to deal with small administrative problems and however much the emperors fostered the view that their affection for the Roman People led them to be interested in such matters, the role of the emperor under the Principate was basically managerial. He was to retain the loyalties of the basically inactive provincial armies, to make sure that competent officials were put in command of those armies, and to see that the Imperial administration functioned smoothly in providing the money to pay for those armies. Thus, the emperor's main duty was to preside over administrative apparatus in Rome, and Trajan fundamentally misunderstood the nature of his office when he engaged in grandiose campaigns of conquest. While his fleeting glory was no doubt sweet, the Empire could not bear the expenses of such campaigns or the risks entailed in defeat. The Principate as established by Augustus was basically a defensive system that had trouble making ends meet in peacetime and was not designed to fight prolonged wars; the half century after the death of Severus Alexander would expose that system to military and political circumstances for which it was not designed.

PART FIVE

THE LATE EMPIRE,
A.D. 235–A.D. 476

As an administrative institution, the Principate established by Augustus was extremely well suited to its circumstances. A basically passive emperor in Rome served as the focus of loyalty for the equally passive armies that stood on the borders. The emperor collected the taxes to pay for the armies and chose the men to command them, dynastic loyalty assured a peaceful succession, and only two civil wars broke out at the end of a dynasty. This blissful situation precipitously changed after the death of Severus Alexander in A.D. 235. The next half century would see an ongoing series of attacks on the Empire's border, both along the Rhine and Danube and in the east. During this period of constant military activity, the structure of Imperial government collapsed, as the soldiery lost all sense of dynastic loyalty, and numerous short-lived emperors were defeated by usurpers or murdered by their troops. The traditional command pattern of drawing officers from the class of rich landowners was replaced by promotion from the ranks, and the position of emperor came to be filled by generals born to peasants rather than by senators. At the same time, the traditional system of tax collection failed, and the currency collapsed. Certain emperors also undertook concerted, though unsuccessful, efforts to suppress Christianity, which they blamed for the clear crisis in the state.

In A.D. 284, the peasant emperor Diocletian undertook to reform the state, instituting a number of reforms intended to restore the success that the Principate had enjoyed. Among his schemes was a novel form of succession. This was a failure, however, and civil war soon broke out after his abdication. The ultimate victor was Constantine, who substantially changed the basis of the Imperial government by adopting Christianity, which soon became the state religion and involved the later emperors in a series of doctrinal disputes. In addition, Constantine's reign saw the culmination of a number of administrative reforms that had been begun by Diocletian and resulted in a basic change in the nature of the Imperial government. Unlike the basically passive Principate, which had little to do with the daily life of the populace as long as the taxes were paid, the government of the Late Empire interfered much more obtrusively in people's lives, both to regulate their religious activities and to make sure that their economic activity benefited the state in its capacity as paymaster of the army. Finally, Constantine would pave the way towards a permanent division of the Empire into two by founding a new capital in the east called Constantinople.

The Christian dynasties of the fourth century attempted with varying success to maintain the system established by Constantine, but in A.D. 395 the Empire was divided for the last time, never to be restored to unity. In the east, the Roman Empire survived with its capital at Constantinople and over time transmogrified into the Greek-speaking Orthodox Byzantine Empire of the medieval period. Meanwhile in the west, Imperial authority quickly collapsed, the power of the ineffective emperors being increasingly restricted to Italy, while Germanic invaders set up kingdoms on the Empire's territory. The Roman army was substantially replaced by Germanic troops, and the men who were capable of controlling those troops held real power and concealed it behind figurehead emperors, until the last such emperor was dispensed with in A.D. 476.

In some ways, there is more attestation for the Late Empire compared to the Principate. Numerous Christian works survive from late antiquity, and they provide much information about the secular world, particularly from fourth century A.D. on. Such works naturally view the world from a religious perspective, and their interpretation of the Imperial government is often colored by doctrinal bias. There is much less traditional historical writing for this period. The major source for the crucial third century A.D. had been a series of Imperial biographies now known as the *Historia Augusta*. This work purports to be the collaboration of six authors writing in the time of Diocletian and Constantine, but from the late nineteenth century on, it has become clear that it is some sort of fraud written (it seems) in the late fourth century A.D. It has been amply demonstrated that while the work does contain some accurate information, much fictitious material was added, though there is no agreement as to the unknown author's motives or how to distinguish fact from fiction. With this work discredited, there is little detailed information about the crisis of the third century A.D. Because of the interest of contemporary writers in the persecutions of the Christians under Diocletian and the triumph of Christianity under Constantine, this important period is much better attested, though the biases of the Christian sources are problematical. The preserved section of the last great pagan historian, Ammianus Marcellinus, gives a much more detailed picture of the years A.D. 354–378. The habit of setting up inscriptions declined (though by no means gave out) after the Severan period, so that epigraphic information is less plentiful for the Late Empire. To some extent, this loss is made up for by the large number of Imperial decrees from the time of Diocletian on that are preserved in two separate law codes (the Code of Theodosius issued in A.D. 438 and the Code of Justinian issued in A.D. 534). Though they by no means record all laws that were issued, these collections provide much information on the administrative policies and practices of the later Imperial government.

19

MILITARY AND DYNASTIC CRISIS,
A.D. 235– A.D. 284

The last dynasty to enjoy long-standing stability ended with the murder of Commodus in A.D. 192; the new dynasty established by Septimius Severus proved a less than resounding success, and its demise with the murder of Severus Alexander in A.D. 235 ushered in a period of dynastic instability that lasted for a half century. This instability was aggravated by the fact that during this time the Empire suffered a number of attacks on the northern and eastern frontiers that were unprecedented in severity. It is not clear why the troops became so lacking in loyalty (we have no evidence with which to gauge their feelings). While the disappearance of military loyalty may simply have been the coincidental result of the succession of feeble emperors, there may have been some more fundamental change in the troops' attitudes. In any case, this disastrous period of fifty years drastically changed the Imperial government, ending the Principate and resulting in a new form of autocracy.

Some scholars deny the traditional designation of this period as a "crisis." On the one hand, attention is drawn to the fact that much of the administrative structure and terminology of the later period can be traced back to the Principate, and hence it is argued that there was no particular crisis in the essential nature of the Imperial autocracy. It is also noted that the term "crisis" is applied to many different phenomena, from military disasters and the frequent overthrow of short-lived dynasties to the breakdown of municipal government and the collapse of the currency. Yet, all of these individual "crises" are simply manifestations of the overall problem, and the superficial continuity in the autocratic nature of the Imperial government should not obscure the fact that institutions of the Principate were found to be insufficient to deal with the many problems that faced the emperors of the third century A.D. and that the form of government that eventually emerged from the reforms of the end of the century was substantially different from the system set up by Augustus more than three hundred years earlier.

C. Julius Maximinus Verus, the man who became emperor upon the assassination of the last Severan emperor in A.D. 235, was apparently born to peasants in Thrace (hence his nickname "the Thracian"). He is thus the first of the so-called soldier emperors of the third century. All emperors down to A.D. 217 had been of senatorial background. The emperors of the mid– and late second century A.D. were from among the wealthiest senatorial families, and Septimius Severus' family had become senatorial in the preceding generation. The only previous nonsenatorial emperor was the praetorian praefect Macrinus, but he at least was a man of education and experience in civil administration. Never had a man risen through the ranks to become emperor. Unfortunately, the exact details of Maximinus' career are not known to us. He was supposedly a shepherd who was drafted into the cavalry and because of his stature rose through the ranks to command armies and provinces, apparently at the equestrian level.

The sources, while not particularly detailed about the events of his short reign, are uniformly unfavorable. They claim that he was hostile to the senate and an old modern conjecture had it that he was eventually overthrown by disgruntled senators who had been passed over by him for their support of Severus Alexander. In fact, investigation of known careers of senatorial governors shows that those who were prominent in Maximinus' reign had also held office under his predecessor. Apparently, Maximinus was at first dutifully accepted by the ruling class as the legitimate emperor. This suggests that to some extent at least his supposed hostility toward the senate may have been concocted after his overthrow. Nonetheless, there were apparently at least two attempts to overthrow him, and it may well be that he persecuted those whom he perceived to be opposed to him. At any rate, he never appeared in Rome as emperor, and instead campaigned in the north.

Trouble arose in the province of Africa, where in late A.D. 237 wealthy youths killed an extortionate procurator. To protect themselves, the murderous crowd went to the home of the governor and proclaimed him emperor. The governorship of Africa was one of the crowning positions of an ex-consul, and since the governor, known as Gordian, was eighty years old, he had his son of the same name proclaimed joint emperor. In March, the governor of Numidia, who had remained loyal to Maximinus, led his legion against the rebels. The younger Gordian resisted with such troops as he could muster, but they were quickly routed, the son falling in battle and the father committing suicide. Crushing the revolt in Africa did not save Maximinus, however.

Maximinus had disregarded the population of Rome, and when news of the revolt reached the city, the general populace eagerly embraced it. Oddly, the senate followed suit, showing initiative that was uncommon for that normally cowed institution. A board of twenty ex-consuls was chosen to oversee the defenses of Italy against the expected attack by Maximinus, which was not long in coming. By the end of February, he reached Aquileia, which blocked the route into northeastern Italy, but the town held out against the siege with unexpected steadfastness.

Meanwhile, when word of the death of the Gordians reached Rome in March, the senate chose two of the board of twenty as new emperors – Pupienus and Balbinus. The whole move was rather peculiar. In the past, there had never been an instance of two fully equal Augusti, but now the two new emperors were completely equal colleagues. Both had enjoyed successful careers, but while Pupienus was of humble beginnings, Balbinus was born of a prominent family. Neither had children, which presumably contributed to their election. They were in effect temporary compromise candidates chosen for the emergency. While Balbinus was to see to the civil administration in Rome, Pupienus was entrusted with the military command against Maximinus.

The election was not unopposed in Rome. Rioting broke out, Pupienus being unpopular because of his strictness as urban praefect (the senior senator who kept order in Rome). To soothe the populace, it was decided that the elder Gordian's thirteen-year-old grandson should be appointed heir apparent with the title of Caesar. The boy adopted the name of his grandfather and is known as Gordian III.

Meanwhile, things were not going well for Maximinus. The siege of Aquileia dragged on, and a failure to provide for supplies put the troops in an ugly mood. By April, the discontented troops had had enough and murdered Maximinus. Pupienus quickly sent the troops back to their camps and returned to Rome. How the system of two Augusti would work out was never put to the test. The praetorian guard was disaffected for trivial reasons, and within days of the arrival of the new emperors, the guardsmen ran amok and murdered the two Augusti, leaving the young boy as emperor.

Occasionally in the past young men had become emperors (Nero, Elagabalus, Severus Alexander), but in such instances some elder (female) member of the dynasty had brought this about and wielded power. In this case, the new emperor's Imperial relations were dead. At first, the board of twenty consulars guided him, but he soon fell under the influence of his praetorian praefect, who married his daughter to the emperor.

The young emperor had the misfortune of facing a new menace in the east, where the ineffectual Parthian kingdom had been replaced ca. A.D. 224 by the more aggressive Persians. Though there is some scholarly disinclination to believe it, Roman sources indicate that the new Sassanid dynasty claimed the territory of the Achaemenid Empire that had been overthrown by Alexander the Great more than five hundred years before. Much of this territory was now in Roman hands, and whatever the exact truth of Persian motives, there would be much conflict in the east. King Ardashir had apparently already begun to capture Roman positions in northern Mesopotamia under Maximinus, and made further gains in A.D. 240. Gordian did not leave for the east until A.D. 242, being distracted by German invasions across the Danube in A.D. 238 and 241 and a revolt in Africa in A.D. 240.

In A.D. 241 or 242, Ardashir died and was succeeded by Shapur, who would cause the Romans much trouble in the next few years. Gordian's campaign against Shapur lasted three years, and because of the poor quality of the sources the course of events is not at all clear. Gordian apparently cleared northern Mesopotamia, but we do not know whether this victory fell in A.D. 242 or 243. In A.D. 243, the emperor's father-in-law, the praetorian praefect, died. At the time there were two praetorian praefects (two were often appointed to lessen the threat posed to the emperor by this important position), and the surviving praefect C. Julius Priscus was given his own brother, M. Julius Philippus, as his new colleague. This was not a very auspicious choice if the purpose of joint tenure was that two praefects could keep an eye on each other! At any rate, Philippus (English "Philip") became the next emperor. While the sources for the mid–third century A.D. are usually inadequate, for the death of Gordian there are several contradictory versions, and the most likely reconstruction is the following. The Romans marched down the Euphrates, but a defeat near Ctesiphon forced a withdrawal, at the end of which Gordian was murdered by the troops in northern Mesopotamia. It seems that their discontent about his conduct of the campaign had been exacerbated by Philip, who intentionally mishandled the commissariat to bring about the emperor's downfall. Philip was then proclaimed emperor in a usurpation that resembles that of Macrinus back in A.D. 217. Once Gordian was disposed of, Philip did have the decency to have him deified.

Philip and his brother came from a village at the edge of the desert in southeastern Syria. Though this area had been inhabited by Arab speakers and late sources call Philip an Arab, it seems that in the second century A.D. Semitic inscriptions cease and only the Greek language was used. Certainly Philip's family must have been Greek-speaking, and given the heavy legal responsibilities of the praetorian praefecture, he and his brother must have been conversant in Latin. They presumably came from a wealthy background, but nothing is known for certain (late sources claim that their father was a brigand leader, but this is probably malicious gossip based on their place of origin).

Philip bought peace from the victorious Shapur at a comparatively cheap price and apparently agreed to provide him with an annual subsidy, though he reneged on the deal once he reached Rome. The new emperor apparently felt it best to preserve his own dignity in the capital, while putting relatives in active command (his father-in-law fought on the Danube and his brother Priscus in charge of the east). By late A.D. 248 or early 249, a revolt had broken out along the Danube, where a governor was proclaimed emperor under unknown circumstances. The urban praefect Decius was dispatched against his will to suppress the revolt, which he quickly accomplished. The victorious Decius was soon proclaimed emperor by his troops in the late spring. He eventually marched on Italy, and Philip set off to face him. In late summer or early fall, the two armies met at Verona, where Philip was defeated and killed.

Decius was an important senator of advanced years when he was sent by Philip to suppress the revolt on the Danube. He had a very distinctive personality and seems to have tried to return Rome to the "good old days." He issued a series of coins commemorating the deified emperors of the past, and the senate bestowed on him the name "Trajan," presumably because of that emperor's associations with military victory. Decius also issued a decree demanding sacrifice to the traditional gods from all the citizens of the empire. Though the decree may not have been specifically directed against the Christians, it must have been foreseen that they would refuse to comply, and presumably its issuance reflects a sense that the difficulties of the state were caused by the gods' unhappiness with the growth of the new cult that rejected them. If Decius hoped that in gratitude the gods would restore the Empire's traditional peace and prosperity, he was to be disappointed.

Decius' march on Italy in A.D. 249 encouraged the Goths to cross the Danube and ravage Moesia. It would seem (to judge by titles in inscriptions) that in A.D. 250, Decius enjoyed some victories over these invaders. If so, his success was short lived. In A.D. 251, the Goths were besieging a city in northern Thrace, and when Decius brought up his army, the Goths fell on him in a surprise attack and defeated him. The governor of Macedonia rose up in revolt, and the Goths ravaged Thrace. As they retreated with their booty, Decius attempted to prevent them from crossing the Danube, but they tricked him into attacking him in a swampy area called Abrittus, where the Roman army was wiped out and the emperor killed.

With Decius' death, two decades of complete dynastic chaos broke out. The list of "legitimate" emperors gives a false sense of tidiness to the situation. Virtually all the emperors during this period seized power through military usurpation, and legitimacy is determined simply by the fact that they had secured the meaningless recognition of the senate in Rome. Thus, the Imperial candidates began as usurpers, and the "emperors" were distinguished from "usurpers" only by the possession of the city of Rome. During this period, there were many temporary military rebellions (some known only through the issuance of coins) that were quickly suppressed and do not warrant mention here. While retrospective narrative can sort out which contenders were "emperors" (however fleeting) and which "usurpers," at the time such a distinction was meaningless; whoever was recognized in a given place was the "emperor," regardless of what was thought in Rome. Thus, the quick succession had made dynastic loyalty impossible even if the troops had been inclined to be faithful.

The troops who survived the disaster at Abrittus proclaimed as emperor Trebonianus Gallus, a senator of whom little is known. Gallus' reign was another disaster. He had to allow the Goths to cross the Danube unhindered with their plunder. Soon major trouble broke out. In A.D. 252, it would seem, several tribes once more broke across the lower Danube and ravaged Moesia and Thrace. The next year, some of them took ship on the Black Sea and crossed into Asia Minor.

In A.D. 253, a governor of Moesia named M. Aemilius Aemilianus scored a major victory over the invaders in the Balkans. His troops naturally proclaimed him emperor. When his and Gallus' armies approached each other in northern Italy, Gallus' troops switched loyalty (they may have been led to believe in greater rewards from the usurper) and killed Gallus. Virtually nothing is known of Aemilianus, whose reign lasted a mere four months. Gallus had sent a senator called Valerian to Germany to bring help against Aemilianus' invasion, and when Valerian learned of the death of Gallus, he was proclaimed emperor in his own right and continued with the campaign. Around September, the armies approached, and this time it was Aemilianus who was murdered by his own troops. Valerian belonged to a distinguished senatorial family, and upon becoming emperor, he immediately made his son Gallienus co-ruler with the title of Augustus. Valerian was to end his life in humiliation, while Gallienus ruled over a truncated domain, with large amounts of Roman territory under the control of others. Valerian also returned to the policy of actively persecuting the Christians.

In the east, meanwhile, more disaster took place. In A.D. 251, Shapur drove out the king of Armenia, and in A.D. 252 or 253 (the dating is disputed), he launched a second major invasion of Roman territory, shattering a Roman army in eastern Syria. After this victory, Shapur split his army in two; the Persian forces seem to have lost cohesion in their pillaging, as one division descended upon Antioch and the other overran southern Syria. At Edessa a local man with a long Roman name rallied troops to fall on the Persians, who apparently were content to return home with their plunder. What exactly this man's intentions were is unknown. Although the coins he minted with Greek legends give him Imperial titulature, those in Latin do not. He seems to have been a local grandee who, in rallying opposition to the Persians, adopted the only garb of power that he knew, that of the Roman emperors. There would soon be a much more extravagant example of an easterner trying to fill the power vacuum left by the breakdown of Imperial authority.

After becoming emperor, Valerian spent most of his time in the east, though his activities are poorly attested. By A.D. 259, there were two major forms of danger in the east. The Goths had again descended upon Asia Minor by ship from the Black Sea, while Shapur was undertaking a third campaign against Roman territory. After an initial effort against the Goths, Valerian moved to counter Shapur. The sources are contradictory about what happened, but it seems that Valerian was disinclined to give battle because he considered the condition of his army unsatisfactory. A battle was fought, and as a result (perhaps through treachery), Valerian was captured by the Persian king. Though hostile Christian sources claim that he was tortured to death, it seems that he died a natural death in captivity.[1] This unparalleled disgrace probably took place in the summer of A.D. 260. Shapur apparently disregarded Syria this time and marched into Asia Minor.

Two separate Roman officials assumed command of local forces and forced the plundering Persians to retreat. They then agreed that Macrianus and Quietus, the children of one of them, should be proclaimed as emperors. Meanwhile, as Shapur passed into Mesopotamia, he was attacked by Septimius Odenathus of Palmyra, a wealthy caravan town that was allied to Rome in the desert between Syria and Mesopotamia. Odenathus was of a locally prominent Semitic family that had gained Roman citizenship from Septimius Severus. Odenathus (the Greco-Roman form of his Semitic name "'Udayntha") bore the unusual title of "exarch" of Palmyra. (Since this title is unique in the Empire, its exact significance is not clear.[2]) Odenathus pursued Shapur as far as Ctesiphon and inflicted a major defeat on him (though as usual the details are not clear). Before examining the result of these events, it is useful to return to Gallienus in the west.

The events in the west after the defeat of Trebonianus Gallus are obscure. From A.D. 253 until about A.D. 256, Gallienus seems to have been detained mainly on the Danube, dealing with the incessant efforts of the Goths to cross into Moesia. By A.D. 256, order was sufficiently restored that Gallienus could begin A.D. 257 in Rome. In the years after A.D. 257, Gallienus was busy dealing with threats from Germans across the Rhine, and in late A.D. 259, he took up residence in Milan in northern Italy, a city whose location was such that forces stationed there could readily move to either the Rhine or the Danube as the situation dictated. This was the first instance of a new strategic importance for Milan, and the city would later regularly be a seat for the emperors guarding the northern boundaries.

The defeat and capture of Valerian in the summer of A.D. 260 had immediate repercussions in the west, though the actual events are dimly understood. The governor of Pannonia went into revolt along the Danube and was quickly suppressed by Gallienus' forces in Pannonia under the command

---

1 After Valerian's death, his hide was preserved and stuffed to be shown to Roman ambassadors as a reminder of past Persian success.
2 "Exarch" is an old Greek title for minor Near Eastern princelings.

of the general Aureolus. Gallienus himself had to move to the Rhine to deal with a major breach of the frontier, and hard on the heels of his departure, a new usurper rose up along the Danube in the form of another Pannonian governor, who quickly disappeared under unknown circumstances.

What forced Gallienus to move to the Rhine was a major invasion by the Franks, a Germanic tribe who now put in their first major appearance and would later play a prominent role in the dissolution of Roman rule in Gaul. After crossing the Lower Rhine in large numbers, they devastated southern Gaul, and some even reached northern Spain and Africa. The depredations of the Franks would continue for a decade. Meanwhile, the Alemanni crossed over the Upper Rhine, not only entering into Gaul but also bursting into northern Italy. Gallienus was forced by this threat to return to Italy from the Danube and defeated the Alemanni near Milan.

The collapse of the Rhine frontier had long-term consequences. When Gallienus moved east in A.D. 259, he left his son Saloninus on the Rhine with the title of Caesar to help maintain the loyalty of the troops. At the time of the great invasion of A.D. 260, the commander in the area was a man of Gallic origin named Postumus, and although he was unable to stop the German marauding, he did manage to defeat some bands as they returned with booty to cross back over the Rhine. Postumus then persuaded the troops to proclaim him emperor, and in response Saloninus was proclaimed Augustus. This was not enough to restore order, and Saloninus was captured and executed. Soon all of the provinces west of the Alps (i.e., those of Gaul, Spain, and Britain) went over to Postumus.

Postumus retained control over this area for years, and after his murder several other men would succeed him as emperors in the west. These "Gallic" emperors made no effort to win over the rest of the empire for themselves, and they set up their own mini-version of the Roman administration, establishing a new senate and appointing their own consuls. This suggests that they wished to maintain a separate, regional empire in northwestern Europe, but it is hard to see how anyone could have imagined that such "regional autonomy" would be tolerated permanently. Perhaps the policy of the Gallic emperors was to husband their resources and wait to repel an invasion from Italy. Certainly the threat from across the Rhine made it inadvisable to remove Rhine legions for an invasion of Italy. In any case, until A.D. 263, Postumus was busy with various campaigns along the border, mostly on the Rhine.

While Gallienus had his hands full dealing with revolts and invasions in the west, the east was taken over by the new emperors Macrianus and Quietus. In A.D. 261, their father (who had engineered their elevation) invaded the west, accompanied by Macrianus (Quietus stayed in the east). Gallienus' general Aureolus again won the day for his emperor, decisively defeating the invading army in Thrace.

Presumably Macrianus and Quietus had had some sort of understanding with Odenathus, who controlled the area around Syria. In the aftermath of the defeat in Thrace, Odenathus decided to throw in his lot with Gallienus and sent troops against Quietus, who was killed after his forces were defeated. Though the evidence is by no means clear, it seems that Odenathus received the unusual title "governor of the whole east" and in some way ruled on Gallienus' behalf throughout much of the A.D. 260s. In A.D. 264–265, he led a major assault on the Persians, recovering the province of Mesopotamia and even attacking Ctesiphon. In A.D. 267, Odenathus attacked the Goths, who had launched another major attack across the Black Sea into Asia Minor. During this campaign (A.D. 267–268) he was assassinated by a relative under unclear circumstances (a Roman governor may have been the instigator). He was succeeded by his young son Vaballathus (the Latinized form of the Semitic name "Wahballath"), but real power was held by Vaballathus' mother Zenobia (the Greco-Roman form of the Semitic "Zainab"). By this time, Gallienus had fallen, and it remained to be seen whether his successors would tolerate the separatist regimes in Gaul and the east.

Meanwhile, Gallienus seems to have been detained for much of the A.D. 260s by troubles on the Danube, but he finally invaded Gaul in A.D. 265. Twice Postumus was nearly defeated, but he managed to survive. Postumus was saved after the second defeat when Gallienus was wounded in a siege and had to return to Italy, calling off the campaign in Gaul. This withdrawal shows the extent to which it was now impossible for the emperor to allow generals to operate independently since the troops would inevitably proclaim any victorious general emperor.

In A.D. 268, there appears to have been yet another massive invasion across the Danube, but Gallienus was called away from dealing with it by the revolt of his old general Aureolus, who had been left behind in Milan in command of the troops guarding the Alps against Postumus. Gallienus marched with troops from the Balkans and besieged Aureolus in Milan. Gallienus' generals seemed to have tired of him and in the late summer or early fall arranged to have him murdered. Claudius, one of their number, was then proclaimed emperor. When news of this reached Rome, Gallienus' relations were executed, which put an end to the house of Valerian.

The Empire reached the apogee of disunity in the A.D. 260s, and for this reason it is hardly surprising that the literary sources are not very sympathetic to Gallienus, whom they portray as lazy and incompetent. The fact that he maintained himself for emperor for fifteen years during this tumultuous period suggests otherwise. He may not have been entirely successful, but it is doubtful that anyone else could have done better. Two trends noticeable in the chaos of the third century A.D. are attributed to him.

A late source claims that Gallienus issued an edict removing senators from military high command. This seems to be false, but it is the case that during the middle third century A.D., a pattern of office holding that had begun earlier became predominant. Now there was a strong tendency for senators to govern the nonmilitary provinces where they owned property and to leave the border provinces with their armies to men of low social standing who had risen through the Imperial administration and the army and did not belong to the major land-owning families. Even if this trend was not caused by Gallienus, perhaps it became particularly noticeable at this time.

Another policy of Gallienus that points the way to the future is his use of mobile formations. Under the Augustan system, the legions and auxiliary units were positioned statically along the borders with no strategic reserves. This meant that aggressive wars necessitated the transfer of troops from peaceful areas, and if the border was breached, troops had to be summoned from elsewhere to help restore order. Such a deployment would cause much trouble if there were wars in numerous areas at once, as was frequently the case in the A.D. 250s and 260s. One solution would be to remove some of the troops (generally the best) from the borders and to station them close to but behind the borders under the command of the emperor, who could move them quickly to threatened areas. This force that was intended to "follow" the emperor was called in Latin the *comitatus* ("retinue"), and the *comitatus* became a regular feature of the military in the fourth century A.D. It would seem that the first steps toward this new military arrangement started under Gallienus, when troops were frequently stationed in Milan, and this policy would be turned into a permanent policy in the early fourth century A.D.

The murder of Gallienus marked a permanent change in the origin of the emperors. Up until then, the third-century emperors had generally been drawn from the Severan aristocracy. Gallienus was murdered by a group of generals who nominated one of themselves to be the new emperor, and among his generals were the future emperors Aurelian and Probus. All these emperors (and a number of other important military figures) came from the Danubian provinces, as would the later emperor Diocletian and his associates. These men would save the Roman state, but in the process bring about radical changes in the nature of the monarchy, the administration, and the military.

After his proclamation as emperor, Claudius had to hurry back to the Danube to repel yet another invasion of Goths. He won a great victory over them at Naissus (in modern Serbia), and for this reason he is known as Claudius Gothicus (to distinguish him from the Julio-Claudian emperor). Claudius also sent a general to occupy southern Gaul, and Spain, too, returned to allegiance to the emperor in Rome. Yet, when the city of Autun in Gaul rebelled in favor of Claudius in A.D. 270, he gave it no assistance. It would seem that he did not yet feel strong enough for a direct assault on the Gallic emperor. Claudius died of plague in August of A.D. 270, and he was later hailed for having begun the process of restoring Imperial authority. Claudius was succeeded by his brother Quintillus, who was in northern Italy at the time of his accession. In the Balkans, however, one of Claudius' generals, Aurelian, was promptly proclaimed emperor, and within a few months Quintillus was murdered in favor of the better-qualified Aurelian (who also had the main army along the Danube on his side).

Another emperor born to peasants, Aurelian played a major role in the restoration of the central authority, reconquering both the east and the west. He first had to fight several campaigns along the Danube and then took a drastic measure. Concluding that the exposed province of Dacia could not be held, he abandoned it and moved the Roman population south of the Danube.[3] This move had two advantages: it greatly reduced the length of the border that had to be defended and at the same time made the frontier more defensible through the advantages offered by using a river as a boundary. Trajan's strategic mistake in occupying the area was now rectified, and Aurelian could undertake the task of reasserting central control over the east.

There, Odenathus' widow Zenobia had been ruling in the name of her young son since her husband's assassination in A.D. 267–268. At first, the Palmyrenes wished to cooperate with the new emperors, the mint in Antioch issuing coins in the name of Gallienus and then Claudius. They tried to reach accommodation with Aurelian, too. Strange coins were issued with Vaballathus portrayed on one side with the Latin legend meaning "ex-consul, king, general of the Romans," and Aurelian on the other with the Imperial titulature. In Semitic inscriptions, Vaballathus takes the eastern title "king of kings" and Zenobia herself is called queen. During this period, the Palmyrenes established control over Egypt and Asia Minor.

By A.D. 272, it was clear that Aurelian was planning to restore order in the east, and Vaballathus finally proclaimed himself emperor. In the summer of that year, Aurelian invaded Asia Minor, and Egypt returned to Roman control. The Palmyrenes withdrew to Antioch, and Aurelian's army defeated them there. Aurelian spared Antioch and advanced up the Orontes river. After defeating the Palmyrenes once more, he moved on to Palmyra itself, which

3 It is sometimes claimed that the modern Romanians, who speak a Romance language, are the descendants of Roman settlers who were left behind, but it seems clear that no Roman population remained after the evacuation and that the area of Romania, which had become depopulated in the early medieval period, was resettled at a much later date by Latin-speaking shepherds similar to the Vlachs of modern Greece (see p. 355).

surrendered after a short siege. Aurelian was again magnanimous, sparing both the city and Zenobia. Late in the year, he had to return to the Danube, and while defeating yet another invasion there, he was informed that Palmyra had risen in revolt. In A.D. 273, this was crushed with such severity that Palmyra never recovered. The attempt to establish a local dynasty in the east was at an end, and direct Roman control was restored.

With his authority established in the east, Aurelian could turn his attention to the so-called Gallic Empire. In A.D. 269, Postumus had quickly suppressed the revolt of a general in Mainz, but when he refused to let the troops sack the city, they murdered him. The troops then chose the closest general at hand as his successor, but the obvious choice was apparently a man called Victorinus, and within a few months the new emperor was murdered and replaced by Victorinus. It was in this period that Claudius regained southern Gaul and Spain, though he declined to support Autun's revolt in A.D. 270. Early in the following year, Victorinus was assassinated as the result of a domestic plot, and a governor named Tetricus became the last independent emperor in Gaul. In early A.D. 274, Aurelian finally invaded Gaul, and at Chalons-sur-Marne in the north, he and Tetricus met in battle. In the middle of it, Tetricus, who was apparently tired of maintaining his authority among his rebellious troops, went over to Aurelian (perhaps according to a prior arrangement), but his troops fought on anyway and were defeated. Aurelian spared Tetricus, even allowing him to retain his senatorial status.

Imperial authority was now reestablished throughout the Empire, and Aurelian took some notable steps in the attempt to maintain order by building a new wall around Rome, whose antiquated and inadequate fortifications dated back nearly seven hundred years to the time of the Gallic sack, and attempting a currency reform. Though this reform was a failure, it shows that there was a sense that there was a need for internal reforms; however, a decade was to pass before the restoration of peace along the frontiers would permit a thoroughgoing attempt to reorganize the civil administration.

After subduing the west, Aurelian marched east again to attack the Persians, but to get out of some trouble, an imperial freedman started a conspiracy against the emperor, who was murdered in Thrace in the fall of A.D. 275. Two literary sources claim that there was actually an interregnum of six months during which the senate was asked by the soldiery to appoint a new emperor but was reluctant to do so. Such a story is hard to believe in its own right, and numismatic and papyrological evidence now proves that the interregnum is unlikely to have been more than two months and may have been considerably less. The literary tradition claims that Tacitus, the emperor who succeeded Aurelian, was a seventy-five-year-old man of senatorial background and that he attempted to restore the senate to its traditional importance in the state. This appears to be a fiction, presumably made up on the coincidence of the emperor's name with that of the great historian of the second century. Fundamentally, nothing is known for sure about the new emperor's real background, and he may well have been another Danubian peasant. Tacitus faced the same sorts of military problems as his predecessors, the Goths having yet again crossed the Black Sea into Asia Minor. When he marched against them, his brother Florian won a victory, but the strain of campaigning was too much for Tacitus, who died a natural death in April of A.D. 276. Florian immediately had himself proclaimed emperor, but a more likely candidate presented himself in the form of Probus, who held command in the southeast. Syria and Egypt immediately went over to him, and in June, Florian's troops murdered him.

Probus was yet another Danubian peasant who rose to become a famous general. Upon his accession, he hurried to the west, where the Rhine frontier had once more collapsed, and by A.D. 277, he had pushed the Germanic Franks and Alemanni back across the river. He may also have had to deal with the Goths (at any rate, he now received the title Gothicus). In A.D. 278, he defeated the Vandals in Illyricum and moved east to put down various revolts there. By A.D. 280, he was back in the west, settling 100,000 Germanic tribesmen in Thrace, which indicates the extent of the desolation in the Balkans.

This seems to have been a time of military discontent. At any rate, a whole series of short-lived usurpers cropped up in the west. While these were suppressed with no difficulty, Probus was murdered in late A.D. 282 in the Balkans by troops who were unhappy about being employed on public works (who did the emperor take them for?). Probus receives high praise in the sources, but since his reign is much less well attested than Aurelian's, it is hard to judge the matter.

It would appear that at the time of Probus' death, his praetorian praefect Carus, another man of Danubian origin, was already in revolt in northern Italy, and once the death of Probus became known, Carus was generally recognized as emperor, giving his two sons, Numerian and Carinus, the rank of Caesar. After dealing with the usual invasions along the Danube, he campaigned against the feeble Persians in A.D. 283 (Shapur's son did not live up to his father's reputation). Carus took Numerian with him, leaving Carinus to mind the store in the west. Carus enjoyed great success, defeating the Persians in Mesopotamia and marching down to their capital at Ctesiphon, which he captured. There, in the midsummer of A.D. 283, he died somewhat mysteriously. The official report had it that Carus was struck by lightning, but later events suggest that the praetorian praefect Aper, Numerian's father-in-law, was a more likely culprit.

Carus' sons automatically became emperors upon his death. While Numerian was returning to Rome in the late fall of A.D. 284 (apparently a peace was patched up with the Persians), a stench emanating from the emperor's litter led to the discovery that he was dead. While Aper may have expected that this would be taken to be a natural death and that he would be able to engineer his own appointment as emperor, the officers decided that the commander of the Imperial bodyguard, a man called Diocles, would make a better choice. Aper was gotten rid of, and Diocles was proclaimed emperor under the more Roman-sounding name Diocletian. In the meanwhile, a general named Julianus had been proclaimed emperor in Pannonia in A.D. 284. In the following year, he invaded Italy but was easily defeated by Carinus at Verona. Later that spring, Diocletian invaded Europe and at a battle in modern Serbia he met Carinus in battle. Carinus was on the point of winning when he was murdered by an officer whose wife he supposedly had seduced. The hapless family of Carus was at an end, and Diocletian was now accepted as emperor throughout the Empire.

Yet another general born to Danubian peasants, Diocletian was at the head of an Empire in deep crisis, and the problems confronting him were perhaps even more daunting than those that had faced Augustus. The main problem of the Late Republic had been the anarchic behavior of the military, and Augustus had solved this problem by binding the troops to himself personally, and throughout the Principate it had been possible to maintain military order through the principle of dynastic loyalty. The accession of peasant generals to the Imperial dignity in the period from the death of Gallienus on reflects the fact that the army had now become an independent and self-sufficient institution. Under the Principate, the army was commanded by men belonging to the wealthiest landowning class and subordinate to Imperial government in Rome. The third century A.D. saw a change in the behavior of the Roman military that presumably derives from developments in the attitude of the soldiery, though our sources give us no direct insight into the soldiers' opinions and the situation can only be inferred from the historical events.

Under the Principate, the soldiers certainly determined the course of events at times of rupture in the dynastic continuity, but when the dynasty was secure and the present incumbent's legitimacy unquestioned, the loyalty of the provincial armies could be counted on. Even the likes of Gaius and Commodus were overthrown through domestic dissension rather than rejection by the armies. Several factors in the third century A.D. changed this situation. One of these may simply be fortuitous. After the death of Severus Alexander, no emperor managed to establish a permanent dynasty. A few emperors left young sons who were kept temporarily by unrelated successors, but Valerian was the only emperor directly succeeded by his son, and even then Gallienus was already acting in his own right as emperor at the time of his father's disaster in the east. Once the principle of clear dynastic succession began to fade in the early third century A.D., it was perhaps a mere accident that this situation became aggravated during the troubled years from A.D. 235 to 285.

A second factor was the apparent need to have the emperor command the armies in person. During the Principate, the comparatively quiet situation along the frontiers allowed the emperors to reside for decades in Rome. This situation began to change with the increasing pressures along the Rhine and Danube and the Persian frontier. Already the Severan emperors had had to attend to military affairs in person, and it was Severus Alexander's inability to gain prestige through military victory that led to his overthrow. Virtually all subsequent emperors of the third century A.D. had to take personal command of the troops. (Philip appears to be the only emperor who attempted to maintain his own prestige by holding aloof from military command, and this policy was not a success.) Until the end of the fourth century A.D., emperors were to take the field on a regular basis. The new necessity of personal command by the emperor had two consequences. First, the emperors were now held directly accountable for military performance, and failure was often attended by murder. Second, generals were generally considered by their troops to be worthy of the Imperial dignity, even if someone else already held this honor. The soldiery thus had a disconcerting tendency to nominate their victorious generals as emperor.

The frequency of warfare probably affected the nature of the officer corps. The somewhat dilettantish method of officer selection employed during the Principate was not well suited for the incessant warfare of the middle third century A.D. Increasingly, it would seem, the junior military commanders were no longer scions of the major landowning families of the Empire; the acclamation of the Danubian peasant generals as emperor suggests that the officers were now selected from the regular soldiers on the basis of talent. In effect, the army was no longer a tool for the Imperial autocracy, which controlled it through the cooperation of the landowning class that provided the officers. Now the soldiery provided the officers of the army, and from them the emperors would be chosen.

The upheavals had led to a complete collapse of Imperial finances, which in turn resulted in a precipitous depreciation of the currency. Even under the Principate, the Imperial government seems always to have a hard time balancing its books. The situation became disastrous under the chaotic circumstances of the third century A.D. In the first place, the main expense of the Imperial government was the army, but the wealthiest provinces like Africa and Asia were not those where the main contingents of the army were stationed. Given the division of the Empire among rival emperors, it must have been impossible to shift resources rationally. In any case, the finances of the Principate involved the completely disorganized collection of a bewildering variety of monetary imposts that had been established in a given province at the time of its establishment. The rates for these taxes were fixed by tradition, and they were progressively reduced to worthlessness by the increasing inflation. The armies resorted to ad hoc exactions in kind as needed, but these could only be collected in the (usually poor) border areas where the armies were stationed. This situation had to be changed, but nothing could be done during the period of chaos.

Since there was no form of state borrowing in antiquity, the only solution to shortfalls in Imperial income was to reduce the weight or metallic content of the coinage, and both processes took place. In the years between the later Severans and Gallienus, the *denarius* lost a third of its weight and the *antoninianus*[4] a half. The loss in silver content was even more striking. For the *denarius*, Septimius Severus' coinage was generally in the range of 54 to 58 percent silver (as opposed to copper alloy). From Severus Alexander to Gordian III, the silver content remained at about 45 percent, but some coins of Gallienus have as little as 8 percent. For the *antoninianus*, which had become the most frequently issued coin, the decline is even more drastic: by the late A.D. 240s, it was often well under 50 percent silver, under Gallienus the amount declined to 10 to 15 percent, and by the time of Claudius the coins were only 2 to 3 percent silver. The result of the debasement was that the normal silver coinage in which prices were determined was reduced to a mere copper coinage.[5] Mysterious numbers on Aurelian's *antoniniani* seem to refer to some sort of attempt to stabilize the currency, but whatever the exact significance of these numbers (perhaps they guaranteed that the coins were 5 percent silver, though other interpretations are possible), this reform was of a limited scope. The problem was a fundamental shortfall in Imperial revenues compared to its (mainly military) expenditures, a problem that Diocletian would later attempt to solve through the introduction of a new tax system that could secure for the Imperial government an income sufficient for its expenses (see p. 297).

This debasement unleashed a great cycle of inflation: being expressed in *denarii* and paid in increasingly common and devalued *antoniniani,* nominal prices skyrocketed. Naturally, this caused many problems with values expressed in monetary terms, and since the ancients had a weak grasp of the economic principles involved, there was a lack of clarity with regard to both the problem

---

4 First coined by Severus' son Antoninus (hence the name), the denomination was halted under his immediate successors, but production resumed during the revolt against Maximinus, and the coin soon became the most common issue.

5 Under Gallienus the practice began of applying a wash of silver to the *antoninianus* to make it look more like a silver coin.

and its solution. Fundamentally, there was no solution, since the Empire did not have the economic resources to support the size of army it now needed because of the endless series of foreign and domestic wars.

By the late third century A.D., the question was whether the Empire would succumb to these dynastic, military, and financial strains or find a way to a solution to the manifold problems that it faced. The emperors Diocletian and Constantine would preserve the Empire, but in the process they would entirely change the principles, operations, and structures of the Imperial government, bringing an end to the Principate.

20

RISE OF CHRISTIANITY

The origins of Christianity are not, strictly speaking, relevant to our theme. Nonetheless, the rise of Christianity during the first three centuries A.D. is necessary for understanding the momentous changes in public life that would take place when a Christian emperor came to power and not only sanctioned the toleration of the hitherto illegal religion but made official policy in support of it.

In the decades leading up to the great revolt of A.D. 66, there arose in Judaea a number of charismatic religious figures who attracted followers (see p. 206). By far the most important of these was a man named Joshua, who is more familiar under the Greek form of his name: Jesus.[1] Early in the A.D. 30s, he was apparently executed by the Roman governor under obscure circumstances.[2] If that were the end of the story, then Jesus would have been nothing more than an obscure footnote in history, but the beliefs of his adherents eventually developed into the most influential religion in the Roman Empire. These followers ("disciples" or "pupils") believed that Jesus rose from the dead and spoke to them before ascending to heaven. While these early followers considered themselves to be Jews and continued to adhere to the Jewish Law, their belief in the resurrection of Jesus was offensive to most Jews. The Jewish cult that worshipped Jesus as the son of God took an entirely different course as a result of decisions taken by a man named Saul.

---

1 The name was quite common at the time. "Christ" is from the Greek for "anointed," the name referring to the Jewish notion of a "messiah," the anointed servant of God who would save the Jewish people from foreign domination.
2 The Gospels provide conflicting and inaccurate information, but the most plausible reconstruction suggests that the priests in charge of the Temple in Jerusalem were mortally offended by his teachings and persuaded the reluctant governor, who alone had the power of life and death, to order his execution (ostensibly for treason, though the priests seem to have been vexed by what they took to be impiety on Jesus' part).

Saul was a Jew who belonged to the hereditary priestly class that presided over the rites in the great Temple in Jerusalem, and while he initially took part in actions that were aimed at suppressing the new cult, he became a convert to the new belief in about A.D. 37. After his conversion, he took a momentous decision: to spread belief in the resurrection of Jesus among the Greek-speaking non-Jewish population of the Roman east. Saul possessed Roman citizenship by birth, and under his Roman name Paul, he traveled far and wide in Syria, Asia Minor, and mainland Greece to spread the new belief, at first among the Jews, but then increasingly among non-Jews as he found the Jews to be for the most part unreceptive. In this effort, he downplayed the significance of the traditional Jewish Law (the complicated system of ritualistic practices that grew up during the last centuries B.C.) by equating it with belief in the resurrection and by rejecting the specific injunctions that constituted the Law. (This led to a certain amount of conflict with the more orthodox followers of Jesus in Judaea.) The followers of the new cult became increasingly estranged from traditional Jews, who rejected the new doctrine, and the term "Christian" came into use to distinguish them from the adherents of old-fashioned Judaic practice. The severance of Christianity from Judaism became complete when the Jewish-style Christians of Judaea were largely wiped out during the First Revolt of A.D. 66.

The development of a separate Christian identity was fostered by a policy of the Roman government. Whereas the Roman government continued to show tolerance towards the Jews (even after their revolts), it treated adherence to Christianity as an illegal practice. The early stages in the formation of Roman policy towards the sect are unknown, but by the end of the first century A.D., it was an established policy to execute those convicted of Christianity. Roman governors took no active steps to look for Christians, however, and merely tried those who were denounced before them. Ironically, this ineffective and haphazard policy had exactly the opposite effect to what was intended. It actually assisted the new religion by making public demonstrations of the fanatical devotion of its adherents in their endurance of painful death on behalf of their God, in that the painful executions of stalwart Christians publicized the new faith and at the same time served to give other believers a strong sense of self-definition, the bravery of the martyrs forming a major element in the identity of Christians.

Thus, the earliest spread of Christianity took place among low-class Greeks in cities, and for two centuries the new religion was a predominantly urban and Greek phenomenon. It did, however, begin to spread among the Greeks who had taken up residence in the Latin-speaking communities of the west.[3] It

---

3 Already in A.D. 64, there were sufficient numbers of Christians in Rome to make it possible to blame a major fire on them (see p. 204).

is clear from an account of an outbreak of mob violence against the Christians of the Gallic city of Lugdunum that as late as A.D. 177, Christianity was still restricted to the Greek-speaking residents of that city and had made little inroad among the Latin-speaking locals. This was already changing by the early third century A.D., when the new religion was beginning to win adherents among the Latin-speakers of the west. From the second century on, it also began to be adopted by more educated men of the upper classes, a process that also became more common during the third century A.D.

From its earliest beginnings, Christianity had a tendency to develop an institutional hierarchy that was focused on urban centers. At first each town with a Christian community had one or more senior priests called "overseers" (Greek *episkopoi*) or "elders" (Greek *presbyteroi*). The practical function of these priests was to oversee the cultic activities, but they also assumed the role of ensuring the "correctness" of the beliefs of the faithful. From the late first to the middle second century, in towns large enough to have multiple priests a distinction came to be made among the priests: the title *episkopos* was specialized to designate the senior priest (and eventually yields the English derivative "bishop"), while the other priests were subordinated to the bishop's authority. It was this public organization of full-time priests that would bear the brunt of periodic attempts to suppress the new religion.

This hierarchy played the dominant role in delineating and refining the doctrines of Christianity. The community of believers in a given town was called a "church" (*ekklesia* in Greek, from the term for a political assembly), and early on, the notion arose that there was a single "Church" that encompassed all the adherents of the new religion. Thus, from the start there was a strong tendency in Christianity to enforce uniformity in doctrine through the suppression of views considered to be wrong. In the earliest church, this problem was not considered a great problem since it was thought that the end of the world was literally at hand. By the middle of the second century A.D., however, it was clear that the Last Days were some days off, and as the new religion assumed a permanent institutional structure, it began to formalize its doctrines in more elaborate ways, particularly with reference to matters not directly addressed in the books of the New Testament. When it was thought that the end of the world was imminent, the core of the new religion was belief in the redemptive power of Christ's death on the cross and in his resurrection. Once the end was postponed, reflective members of the Church hierarchy began to ponder more theoretical issues, including ones that would be extremely divisive in the official Church during the fourth and fifth centuries A.D.: the relationship between God the Father, Christ the Son, and the Holy Spirit. This debate about the nature of god came to be perceived as one of crucial significance in the second century A.D. because of a challenge posed to the church hierarchy by a variant of Christianity known in modern scholarship as

Gnosticism. Gnosticism rejected the connection of Christianity to its Jewish background, and viewed the world as the scene of conflict between the goodness of the "true" god, who is distinct from this world, and the evil associated with a defective divine force that created the world (Christ and God the Father were fit into this conception in various ways). The adherents of Gnosticism held that their conception of God was a secret known only to those to whom this truth had been revealed (hence the name of these variants of Christianity, *gnosis* meaning "knowledge" in Greek). It is against the background of the challenge posed by Gnostic interpretations of Christianity that the Church formalized its tenets about the nature of god in the second century. One of the basic distinguishing characteristics of "orthodox" Christianity is the belief that there is only one God who created the world and that Christ was his "son." Given this, however, there were to be violent debates about the exact nature of the relationship between God and Christ (theorizing about this relationship is called "Christology"). Around A.D. 200, the idea arose that God the Father, Christ, and the Holy Spirit were distinct entities, who in their totality constituted the "One God." This concept of the threefold God is known as the Trinity and would eventually win the theological battle, though the inherently illogical nature of the idea would give rise to much controversy, especially in the east.

Thus, when the Roman government began during the third century A.D. to make concerted efforts to stamp out the new religion, it would find that its spasmodic and at times halfhearted efforts were completely inadequate for the task of overwhelming a well-organized institution with clearly laid out and passionately held beliefs. It remains to be seen why the Imperial government came to be so hostile to Christianity. In the beginning, when the Christians were very few in number and most non-Christians had never seen one, certain aspects of Christianity led to the spread of very negative beliefs about them.

1. It was thought that the exclusivist claims of the Christians signified that they were misanthropic. The Christians' belief that their God was the sole god did not simply lead them to reject the gods of their pagan neighbors. Instead, the Christians asserted that the pagan gods were demons. This attitude was viewed as a rejection of normal society by those who took the traditional gods for granted.
2. It was thought that the Christians had no justification in holding their beliefs on the grounds of tradition. The Romans were not favorably disposed towards similarly exclusivist claims on the part of the Jews, but in their beliefs the Jews were clearly adhering to the traditions of their forebears, an attitude that the Romans could well understand. The early Christians, on the other hand, were almost by definition people who had abandoned their ancestral religious beliefs in order to adopt what the

Romans considered to be at best a groundless superstition and at worst a criminal organization.

3. Two elements of early Christian worship were misconstrued. A reenactment of the Last Supper (the Eucharist) became a central element in divine services. Here, the worshippers symbolically drank Christ's blood and ate his flesh, but this practice was erroneously associated by non-Christians with the cannibalistic activities that were supposedly practiced in certain disreputable magical rites. In addition, the Eucharist formed part of a ceremony called a "love feast" in which they celebrated their love of God in a common feast, referring to their fellow Christians as "brothers and sisters." This practice too was misinterpreted by analogy with disreputable pagan practices, being taken to signify promiscuous sex in general and incest in particular.

However untrue these charges were and however often they were refuted, they recur frequently in pagan invective against the new cult. It seems that there was no single decree to outlaw Christianity in the first century A.D., and the process by which adherence to the new cult was first prohibited is dimly understood. By the early second century, the illegality of Christianity was well established, and the original (and basically misguided) grounds for the ban on the new religion no longer mattered. It was simply accepted policy that the practice of Christianity was illegal and that those who were convicted of adhering to it and refused to renounce their beliefs were subject to execution, often in a rather unpleasant way.

"Persecution" is the term used by the Christians to describe the efforts to stamp out their form of worship. From their point of view, there was no point in distinguishing between different manifestations of hostility towards them, but in fact there are distinct developments in the government's actions against Christianity. For a century and a half, the government's actions against the Christians were mostly passive. If they were accused, they were condemned, but the provincial governors did not go out of their way to harass them. This meant that through the middle of the second century A.D., most executions that we know of concern prominent members of the hierarchy. A change in procedure is first perceptible with the anti-Christian activities in Lugdunum in A.D. 177. There the persecution began with popular rioting against the Christians, but eventually the local authorities became involved and trials and executions ensued. From this point on, it becomes more common to find trials involving comparatively large numbers of regular Christians in addition to accusations against prominent figures.

Christian accounts of martyrs often preserve the "acts" or legal proceedings taken against Christians, and while many are fictional or at least contain fictional elaborations, some are apparently reasonably accurate records of the course of trials and allow us to gauge the attitudes of both the Roman governors and the accused Christians. The main goal of the officials was to compel those who admitted to being Christians to abandon their beliefs. The governors used all sorts of threats and forms of suasion to achieve this end. While some governors were determined in their actions, the records indicate a strong disinclination on the part of many to inflict death. The absolute number of martyrs was always comparatively small, and the percentage of martyrs compared to the total number of Christians must have constantly decreased over time. At Lugdunum it seems that the rioters attempted to find all the Christians they could, but in most martyr acts it is clear that there was no concerted effort on the part of the government to hunt out all Christians. Those in prison were often visited by co-religionists, who were apparently left unmolested. Hence, those on trial had been arrested for some sort of prominence, and in fact among the Christian community a debate arose as to the legitimacy of seeking martyrdom through deliberate provocation of the authorities. Furthermore, while most evidence for the trials of martyrs comes from Christian sources and thus emphasizes the success of the martyrs in maintaining their beliefs as a lesson for the faithful, it is clear that the threat of an unpleasant death was sufficient to induce the less steadfast to recant. Nonetheless, the sight of those who were in fact willing to be burned alive or mangled by wild animals for their beliefs had a powerful impact on both other Christians and on the general population.

The middle of that century saw a change in the methods used to suppress the new religion. Instead of ad hoc prosecutions that were instituted at the discretion of others, certain emperors issued general decrees affecting the entire Empire with the intent to enforce a complete suppression of the religion. We cannot know for certain what motivated the new policy since we have no direct statements from those who introduced the change, but it seems that the military and political turmoil of the mid–third century A.D. was ascribed to the gods' anger at the spread of the new cult. Hence, the traditional prohibition of Christianity took on new significance as a means of restoring the gods' favor and ending the crisis that faced the Imperial government.

Two elements contributed to the new resolve to make a concerted effort to stamp out Christianity. First, there was a traditional (and hazy) belief that the success of the state depended on the favor of the gods. The Romans had always held the belief that they were a pious people, but this idea was never delineated very clearly, being more a vague notion than a clearly spelled out doctrine. Furthermore, since within the context of multifaceted paganism it was not very easy to define which religious practices were the ones that secured the gods' goodwill, it was both impractical and unnecessary to lay out a specific definition of what was religiously acceptable: so long as traditional rites continued to be followed in some form and the military and political integrity of the Empire was successfully maintained, it could be taken for granted that the gods were content. The progressive decline in military success and dynastic stability that characterizes the first half of the third century A.D. called all this into question. Furthermore, the very rise of monotheistic Christianity gave a new coherence to pagan practice, at least by contrast: the Christians' rejection of traditional religious observances and beliefs made it easier to conceive of the worship of the old gods as a unitary practice. In short, the idea seems to have arisen by the mid–third century A.D. that the old beliefs (whatever they were conceived to be) were the basis upon which the favor of the gods was secured and that the spread of Christianity had angered the gods and led to the troubles of the Imperial government. For this reason it was now considered imperative (by some emperors) to stamp out Christianity in order to regain the gods' goodwill. Unfortunately for the old gods, the Imperial government had neither the will nor the means to implement such a policy.

Trajan Decius (see p. 270) was the first emperor to undertake a concerted effort to suppress Christianity. In A.D. 249, at the start of the period when the breakdown of military loyalty reached its low point, he issued a decree mandating universal worship of the traditional gods: all the inhabitants of the Empire had to go before specially appointed boards in whose presence they were to make a sacrifice, pour a libation to some pagan god, and eat the meat of a sacrificial victim, acts that were abhorrent to practicing Christians. In order to secure compliance, the sacrificer was obliged to bring along a certificate that the board members would sign to prove that the sacrifice had taken place. To some extent the edict was not directed against the Christians per se: its main purpose was to compel everyone to sacrifice for the well-being of the Empire, and if in the process the Christians were stamped out, all the better. Nonetheless, no emperor had previously felt the need to enforce sacrifice, and the specific requirement could have no purpose other than to prove that those who were sacrificing were not Christians. In effect, the edict amounted to an effort to suppress Christianity that was couched in positive terms. The penalty for noncompliance was banishment and confiscation of property (some important church figures who refused to obey were executed). Many Christians either complied or acquired false certificates, but the decree soon lapsed when Decius fell in battle. (As would often be the case after intensive Imperial actions against the Christians, the status of those Christians who had given in was to cause some internal strife within the Church.)

Regardless of the consequences in the Church itself, Decius' actions show that the Imperial government did not have the power to stamp out the Christians by edict. Although many people's lives could be disrupted (and some ended), an ancient government simply did not have the power to impose its will on a large number of people against their will, and the effort to compel traditional religious practice was a failure. It is said that this was the first time that the Church was threatened because many people gave in. In fact, this circumstance actually points the way to the ultimate triumph of the Christian movement. In A.D. 250, Christians were not simply deeply convinced "fanatics" ready to die for their beliefs. Instead, large numbers of "regular" people who led otherwise normal lives adhered to the new religion. When their lives and property were threatened, these people, with varying degrees of willingness no doubt, temporarily complied, only to resume their Christianity once the danger was over. Furthermore, numerous local officials who had to impose the dire sanctions for noncompliance were clearly reluctant to inflict severe penalties on otherwise unobjectionable people who happened to adhere to a widespread but disfavored religion. This increasing acceptance of the new religion – manifested both in the large numbers of converts and in its new-found respectability among non-Christians – would thwart all subsequent attempts to suppress it.

Decius' failure did not end attempts on the part of the Imperial government to impose a general suppression of Christianity; the crisis that seemed to necessitate the suppression only worsened during the course of the A.D. 250s, when the emperor Valerian resumed the attempt at suppression, once more demanding general sacrifice, with even more severe penalties for non-compliance. Unlike Decius, Valerian recognized the strength of the Church as an institution and made specific provisions to undermine it. Bishops, priests, and deacons were to be executed on the spot, and Christian assemblies and cemeteries were also prohibited on pain of death. While there is evidence for the execution of certain prominent churchmen, it is not known how rigorously and broadly it could have been implemented in the case of more humble Christians, and the disaster that soon overwhelmed Valerian in the east brought the effort to a halt. Gallienus clearly did not share his father's aversion to the new religion. He not only revoked his father's edicts but ordered the restoration of confiscated Church property.

Though Christianity continued to be illegal throughout the remainder of the third century A.D., there were no more major efforts to stamp it out until the final and most concerted attempt that began towards the end of Diocletian's reign. Since that effort (the so-called Great Persecution) is intimately connected with the accession of the first Christian emperor, it will be treated in the discussion of Diocletian's reign.

21

DIOCLETIAN AND THE RESTORATION

OF IMPERIAL AUTHORITY,

A.D. 284–A.D. 305

D iocletian brought back a certain amount of dynastic stability, temporarily at any rate. During the twenty comparatively peaceful years of his reign, he attempted to correct a number of the problems that arose in the preceding fifty years, some with greater success than others. While by no means all of his policies could be viewed as successful, nonetheless his reign to some extent represents the culmination of the earlier trends, and in any case the Imperial system he left at his abdication was greatly changed when compared to the Augustan system and sets the patterns for the government in the Late Empire.

After establishing himself as sole emperor through the defeat of Carinus, Diocletian was quickly faced with the problem that had dogged so many emperors in preceding decades. Threats to the Rhine frontier demanded the Imperial presence, but there were also problems on the Danube. Diocletian, who was about forty years old, had no sons (though he did have a daughter), and to provide himself with an Imperial assistant, he adopted a fellow general, Maximian, as his heir with the title of Caesar in July of A.D. 285. The new Caesar, who was Diocletian's junior by approximately ten years, would prove to be very loyal to his adoptive father. A decent general, Maximian seems to have had little of Diocletian's political acumen, and readily left the decisions to him. Like so many other generals of this time, Maximian was an uncultured man who had been born to lowly parents in Pannonia.

The first decade of the joint emperors' reign was tumultuous. From the mid–A.D. 280s to the early A.D. 290s, Diocletian shuttled back and forth between the Danube and the east to deal with a variety of external threats. In particular, he forced a weak Persian king to recognize some Roman acquisitions in northern Mesopotamia. In the meanwhile, Maximian was fully occupied with various difficulties in the west. First he had to deal with the so-called Bagaudae (a Celtic word meaning "fighters"). These were organized brigands, a collection of people displaced by the many recent invasions of Gaul by the Germans. By early A.D. 286, Maximian's troops dispersed the brigands, and then he spent the years down to A.D. 288 restoring order on the Rhine. In the meanwhile, it had been necessary to ignore a revolt in Britain.

In A.D. 285, a Gaul named Musaeus Carausius had been given the task of clearing the pirates from the seas. At first he was successful, but then there were rumors that he was cooperating with them for his own profit. When Carausius learned that Maximian had ordered his execution, he proclaimed himself Augustus in Britain and seized the coast of Gaul. In response, Maximian was also proclaimed Augustus, but his campaigns on the Rhine prevented any action against Carausius, who seems to have been content to be left alone, recognizing Maximian and Diocletian as fellow emperors. Maximian and Diocletian, however, did not return the compliment. In the spring of A.D. 289, Maximian was finally able to launch a seaborne assault on Britain, but it failed.

By now it was clear that even two emperors were unable to cope with the many situations that simultaneously demanded an Imperial presence. Diocletian would have faced an impossible situation if the Persians launched an attack on Syria at the same time that the Germans attempted yet again to cross the lower Danube; as for Maximian, he would clearly need to engage in a major campaign to dislodge Carausius, but there was always a very real possibility that troubles would resume on the Rhine. The solution that Diocletian conceived for this situation was a novel model of government called the "tetrarchy."

In the spring of A.D. 293, two men were proclaimed Caesar. In the west Maximian elevated his praetorian praefect, Constantius Chlorus, while in the east a man called Galerius was promoted by Diocletian. The new Caesars were both of lowly origin from the area near the Danube. Constantius had begun his career in the Imperial bodyguard before becoming an officer. Nothing is known of the career of Galerius, but it was presumably similar. These men were approximately the age of Maximian, and each was the son-in-law of the Augustus who had appointed him. Constantius was already married to a daughter of Maximian, having divorced his previous wife, by whom he had had a son called Constantine. Galerius married Diocletian's daughter Galeria Valeria, though it is not known for certain when.

The empire now had four emperors – two Augusti and two Caesars – but there was no firm division of the empire. Maximian generally governed Italy from Milan while Constantius was in charge of Gaul and Britain, but the situation was not so clear in the east. Sometimes Diocletian was in the east and Galerius on the Danube, but they are also attested in the opposite areas. The emperors acted in each other's names, issuing joint decrees. In effect, there was a cooperative board of four men acting jointly as emperors and dividing the responsibilities on an ad hoc basis. Diocletian was clearly the senior member, and the others deferred to his authority.

While the personalities of the emperors allowed them to cooperate, the events of the previous half century demonstrated the need to ensure a peaceful succession, and Diocletian devised a clever solution to this problem. Upon the death of an Augustus, he was to be succeeded by his Caesar, who would in turn appoint a new Caesar. Unfortunately, this theoretically tidy system took no account of dynastic reality. In antiquity, the expectation was that a son would inherit his father's position. While Diocletian had no son, Maximian did, and it would be unnatural for that son to be passed over in the succession. It remained to be seen how this system would work in practice.

In A.D. 293, the new Caesar Constantius attacked Carausius' position on the Gallic coast, taking Boulogne after a monumental siege. The coast of Gaul abandoned Carausius, who was murdered in Britain by Allectus, a financial official. After two full years of preparation, Constantius finally launched an attack across the English Channel in A.D. 296, while Maximian kept things quiet on the Rhine. This is exactly the kind of cooperation that the tetrarchy was designed for, and Allectus was easily defeated.

In the years A.D. 294–295, Diocletian campaigned along the Danube, and won victories that were sufficient to maintain order there for the next few years, while trouble resumed in the east. In A.D. 293, the Persian throne had been seized by a more vigorous king, who wished to repudiate the humiliating agreement made back in A.D. 287. By late A.D. 296, he had driven out the Roman-supported king of Armenia, and in response both Diocletian and Galerius came to the frontier. Galerius led a hasty march into northern Mesopotamia that met with defeat. While he spent the next year gathering a new army along the Danube, Diocletian was occupied with stamping out a major rebellion in Egypt provoked by the introduction of a new system of taxation. In A.D. 298, Galerius resumed the offensive against the Persians; after defeating the Persian army, he marched down the Tigris and captured Ctesiphon, the capital. At this point, Diocletian checked Galerius' advance and negotiated a moderate but notable strengthening of the Roman position on the eastern border: the Persian king was forced to acknowledge Roman control of Armenia, recognize the Roman province of Mesopotamia and surrender five small provinces on the far side of the Tigris. After all the disturbances of the third century A.D., the victorious conclusion of this campaign finally gave the Romans full control of northern Mesopotamia, where they had been spasmodically encroaching since the days of Trajan.

By the late A.D. 290s, peace was mostly restored to the Empire. All areas recognized the central authority, the Rhine and Danube frontiers were relatively peaceful, and the Persians had been soundly defeated. Merely restoring a semblance of calm to the borders was a major accomplishment, but Diocletian also undertook a number of internal reforms designed to stabilize the Imperial government after the turmoil that had beset it during the middle of the third century A.D. These reforms affected not just the government's methods of administration and taxation but also the very nature of the position of emperor. He also endeavored to legislate a new social and religious unity for the Empire. While his efforts did not by any means meet with unqualified success, one must nonetheless admire the breadth of view represented by this attempt to solve so many thorny issues.

Diocletian realized that the breakdown in dynastic loyalty among the soldiery posed a fundamental threat to the long-term stability of the Imperial government. Part of Diocletian's solution was the tetrarchic system of government, which obviated the risk posed by the need to have a general commanding on a front where the emperor was not present. Apparently, feeling that this was not enough, Diocletian decided to reduce the soldiers' inclination to murder the emperor by exalting his person and heightening the godlike awe of the Imperial incumbent. To this end, Diocletian now formalized and elaborated certain tendencies towards enhancing the emperor's mystique that had been going on since the mid–third century A.D.

First, Diocletian established a divine mandate for his rule, abandoning the pretence that an emperor needed senatorial recognition. Diocletian never asked the senate to legitimize his position, and he always counted the start of his reign from the day of his proclamation by the troops. His authority did not, however, derive from the soldiery. Instead, his reign was directly ordained by the gods. Both he and Maximian were associated with specific gods: as the senior member, Diocletian was associated with Jupiter, the chief god of the Roman state, and things connected with Diocletian were termed "Jovian"; Maximian on the other hand was appropriately associated with the deified hero Hercules, who carried out a number of "Herculean" tasks at the instigation of the gods. How this pagan system of legitimacy would have been maintained in later years cannot be known, since the adoption of Christianity by Constantine ended its development, but the Christian emperors did continue to derive their legitimacy from the Christian god.

Diocletian also introduced an elaborate ceremonial that was intended to mark the emperor out as being superior to a normal human being. From now on, the emperors would no longer as a rule mingle with their subjects. Instead, they appeared only on ceremonial occasions, which took on the aspect of a divine epiphany. Commoners who entered the Imperial presence had to prostrate themselves, something inconceivable under the Principate; more exalted personages showed their subordination by kneeling down in front of the emperor and kissing the hem of his purple robe. Elaborate rituals were also created for the now uncommon Imperial appearances, and the Imperial personage was not allowed to act like a normal human being in public (later emperors would take this to ridiculous extremes, refusing to be seen smiling or laughing). This mode of behavior is not congenial to modern tastes, but while usurpation was not brought to an end in the fourth century A.D., dynastic continuity was much greater and this must be attributed at least in part to Diocletian's exaltation of the position of the emperor.

Diocletian also had to make permanent arrangements for the deployment of the army whose loyalty he was attempting to ensure. The hostile Christian writer Lactantius claims that the creation of four emperors meant that soldiery and Imperial employees were quadrupled in number. This is certainly false, but nonetheless there was a major increase in the size of the army. Under Septimius Severus, there were thirty-three legions of approximately 160,000 men and a comparable number of auxiliary troops raised among the non-Roman inhabitants of the Empire. The number of legions became much larger during the disturbances of the mid–third century A.D., but their complements were apparently much reduced. It has been guessed that under Diocletian the army may have numbered between 400,000 and 600,000 troops, though these figures are very conjectural, and some scholars even suggest that the army did not grow in size.

Diocletian apparently attempted to restore the Augustan strategy of stationing the troops along the borders without a permanent strategic reserve. It would seem that Diocletian decided not to pursue the mid-third-century practice (discernible under Gallienus) of creating a permanent strategic reserve stationed at some distance behind the frontier. When the armies of the tetrarchy fought on campaign, they were put together out of detachments from the various local garrisons, as had been earlier practice. It has been suggested that in an attempt to halt the constant breaches of the border by invaders he instituted a policy of creating what can be termed a "defense in depth" by establishing a number of fortified positions at strategic locations for some miles back from the border. These fortifications would have slowed down the invaders until an army could be formed to deal with them and prevented them from using the Roman road system. In the absence of direct statements about Diocletian's intentions, however, conjectures about his policy are perilous, and in any case Constantine was to abandon the attempt to restore the static defense and renew the policy of establishing a strategic reserve.

Diocletian also instituted a radical reform of the structure of provincial government. First, he greatly increased the number of provinces. During the course of the Principate, there had been a trend to subdivide the largest provinces (thereby decreasing the number of legions under any governor's command), but by the late third century A.D., the overall layout of the provinces was still comparable to the arrangement set up at the time of the Augustan settlement. In Diocletian's reform, most provinces were divided into smaller units, which more or less doubled the number of provinces. Now that the provinces were so small, it was felt that a level of administration should intervene between the provincial governors and the central government. Each of the four emperors had a praetorian praefect who oversaw the civil administration as a whole, and the provinces were grouped into twelve units called dioceses (a Greek word meaning "administrative unit"), each diocese being headed by a *vicarius* (literally, a "representative" of the praetorian praefect). (In practice, this hierarchy was not as tidy as it might seem; the governors could ignore the *vicarius* and deal directly with the praetorian praefect or emperor, and vice versa.)

Diocletian instituted a radical change in the powers of governors, who as a result of Republican practice had previously had full control over both civil and military power. Now the governors were stripped of the military authority, and command over the border armies was turned over to generals called *duces* (singular: *dux*), who controlled the military forces stationed in several provinces. There were a number of motives for this. The governors now had more extensive administrative responsibilities, so control of both civil and military affairs would have exceeded the capability of a single man. The separation of military authority would also hinder the ability of military commanders to revolt, since they would need to secure the support of the now separate civil authority. Finally, the separation of civilian responsibilities from military command would ease the promotion of competent officers within the army, since the lack of education would no longer obstruct provincial administration. Previously, either a governor needed to be well educated to handle the legal matters that came before him (which restricted the available pool of candidates to the well born) or those legal matters would suffer (as often happened in the mid–third century A.D.). The new policy would further the autonomy of the military as an institution in general, and in particular it allowed barbarian Germans to attain high command.

In line with his generally antisenatorial stance, Diocletian for the most part excluded senators from most positions as governor, and they provided governors only for the reduced provinces of Asia and Africa and for the administrative subdivisions of Italy. Most other governors were men of so-called equestrian standing, that is, they were wealthy men, who nonetheless owed their prominence in governmental affairs purely to Imperial appointment (rather than great wealth and hereditary membership in the senate). In particular, these officials came from the class of decurions, the wealthiest members of the local city-states (see pp. 298–299).

Diocletian instituted a major reform in the tax system, and an important motive for reducing of the size of provinces was the role that governors would play in supervising this new system. As already noted, the monetary and fiscal crisis of the third century A.D. had seriously undermined the ability of the government to maintain the army, as inflation completely undermined the

Principate's chaotic system of monetary taxes and the incessant civil wars hindered the transfer of tax receipts to the armies on the periphery of the Empire (see p. 255). Instead, ad hoc emergency levies called "indictions" were raised as necessary by the armies wherever they happened to be. Such a system is inherently inefficient and could easily degenerate into extortion.

Diocletian tried to regularize the collection of indictions on a rational basis. He did away with all the traditional Imperial taxes and replaced them with a system based on the varying regional application of a single method of assessing land. Basically there were now two units of measure, the *iugum* (plural: *iuga*) and the *caput* (plural: *capita*). *Iugum* means "yoke" and refers to the productive capacity of land; *caput* ("head") signified the productive capacity of an average man. In a given area, land was divided into different categories on the basis of its productivity and a *iugum* consisted of a certain quantity of land of a given category, so that while the amount of land per *iugum* for each category differed, each *iugum* had (theoretically) an equal productive capacity. For instance, in Syria, one *iugum* consisted of five *iugera* (a land measure) of vineyard, twenty of the best arable land, forty or sixty of lesser quality land, 225 *perticae* (a small land measure) of productive olive trees, or 450 of mountain olive trees. As for "heads," these represented the labor that worked the land. People became liable for taxes based on the "head" registry at the age of twelve or fourteen and were exempted at sixty-five. Men were always counted; women were assessed as a full head in some places, as a fraction in others, and in some were not counted at all. Livestock were also counted as "heads" on the basis of varying prorated standards.

This system was very flexible. On the one hand, it gave a standard measure by which everyone and everything in the rural economy could be assessed. It provided a ready measure to apply to all large landholders, and those whose land constituted less than a whole *iugum* could be added together to form a *iugum* whose tax burden could be distributed equally among the constituent landowners. A vast census system was implemented to draw up a register recording everything and everyone liable to rural taxation. At first, the census was to be taken every five years, but because of the monumental nature of the procedure, the interval between revisions of the census was later increased to fifteen years. Sometimes, the number of *capita* and *iuga* were added together; sometimes charges were distributed on the basis of either *capita* or *iuga* separately. This system could also be used to distribute assessments for taxes in kind and to levy soldiers.

This capitation system of taxation had great advantages for the government. Instead of having an inflexible income that was subject to erosion by inflation and that could not be changed to reflect the government's fiscal needs, the new system allowed the government to determine its projected needs and then impose the necessary taxes equitably amongst the taxpayers. In the long run, the major flaw in the system was its inherent efficiency: there being no practical limit on the government's ability to increase the burden per unit, the government had no particular incentive to save money and could instead simply increase the tax rate, as seems to have been the case in the fourth century A.D. This situation would have unfortunate consequences, in that large landowners could use their influence to shirk their share of the tax burden, which only increased the burden on smaller landowners.

The capitation system had a very important side effect. Since the system was based upon the joint measure of land and its inhabitants, it was inconvenient from the government's point of view if those inhabitants moved elsewhere before the census was revised. This led in the fourth century A.D. to extensive legislation prohibiting peasants from leaving the land under which they had been entered into the census. It is clear that the plan to tie the farmers to the land was motivated by fiscal considerations, but this legislation contributed to the rise of serfdom in the late antiquity.[1]

Tying the peasants to the land was part of a general pattern of regimenting civilian life in the interests of the fiscal needs of the government and army. Like the peasants of the countryside, the rich men of the cities were compelled to act for the benefit of the Imperial government. Local administration under the Principate had been provided by the wealthy members of the city councils, who were called decurions, and an earlier trend towards avoiding office holding became pronounced in the mid–third century A.D., with the wealthy men who had run local government (and who were personally liable for any shortfall in tax collection) often shunning office and withdrawing to their estates. Since these men were indispensable in collecting the taxes needed for the army, Diocletian forced anyone who had the requisite money to belong to the councils and made the position hereditary: one could escape the status only by fulfilling the relevant obligations first. This policy was in inherent conflict with the new trend towards filling the Imperial administration with educated men of equestrian rank, since the decurion class was the natural source of such officials. Furthermore, since Imperial office generally gave exemption from the obligations to which decurions were subject, such men were eager to serve the emperors. This put the Imperial administration in a quandary. The emperors from Diocletian on issued various decrees forbidding decurions from entering Imperial service before they had fulfilled their obligations as decurions, but

---

1 The uncertain evidence does not make it clear whether Imperial legislation was the primary cause in the subordination of free labor to major landowners or merely took advantage of a process that had been going on throughout the Principate; there are some indications that, by the late third century A.D., the free tenants of large landowners had already to some extent fallen under their sway through indebtedness.

it was hard for the emperors either to do without them in their service or to stem the tide of unwarranted acquisition of exemption by men attempting to shirk the burdens of decurions.

Trades that were beneficial to the functioning of the Imperial government also tended to be made hereditary and obligatory. Those who carried out such trades were grouped into guilds (for instance, shipowners, who transported grain to Rome, or the bakers of Rome, who also made the bread for the dole), and the burden of carrying out the state's wishes was distributed among all members. The Roman state was in no position to run the economy itself and did not directly undermine the principle of private landowning or of the market economy. What it could do was pass regulations forcing people to act in ways that the state found beneficial (for itself) and to make sure that the state's needs were fulfilled before those of the individual, in effect destroying the economic life of the individual if he did not fulfill the duty imposed upon him by the state. In effect, the state looked upon its subjects as resources necessary for the upkeep of the army and government.

In addition to reforming the government's fiscal system, Diocletian also endeavored to correct the evils of inflation. Following Aurelian's lead, he attempted to restore a full series of silver and bronze coinage. He also attempted a more direct solution, issuing a decree that established maximum legal prices for a wide variety of goods and imposed death on those who exceeded these prices.[2] This decree is preserved in a number of inscriptions, which shows that a serious attempt was made to implement it. In the elaborate preface in which he castigates the greed that he felt to be responsible for the inflation, Diocletian demonstrates that he (and his advisors) had no understanding of the cause of the problem, confusing the temporary local rise in prices caused by the transit of large armies on campaign with the general trend of increasing prices that was caused by the depreciation of the silver currency and the minting of increasingly debased coins. The draconian sanctions could not change the underlying economic reality that determined prices in a free market, and the law was soon abandoned. As for the currency, governmental shortfalls would soon lead to the return of debasement, and despite dimly understood reforms in the fourth century, the silver currency never achieved stability.

Not content with these major efforts to reform the functioning of the government, Diocletian also attempted to achieve a form of social uniformity in the Empire, something that was alien to the easygoing traditions of the

---

2 About the severity of the penalty, Diocletian makes the charmingly naïve observation that no one can justifiably complain about it, since all they have to do to avoid being executed is not violate the law. By that logic, violation of even the most trivial bylaw should be penalized with death!

Republic and Principate. In the past, there was no thought of imposing unity on the multiethnic territories subject to the Roman People. So long as the taxes were paid and peace maintained, the locals were allowed to follow their own traditions without interference. Following the grant of Roman citizenship to all free inhabitants of the Empire in the early third century A.D., the logical question to ask would have been how this would affect the customs of the numerous populations of non-Roman origin. No one at first seems to have been bothered by these issues, and during the great midcentury crisis, no one had spare time for such considerations. After external peace was reestablished by the mid–A.D. 290s, however, Diocletian seems to have pondered these issues and took steps to bring about the unity of the Empire by imposing upon everyone what he considered to be Roman traditions. The most famous aspect of this effort is the so-called Great Persecution, the last and most prolonged attempt by the Roman state to stamp out Christianity. Yet, this move was by no means isolated, and we can see something of Diocletian's motives and methods in two other edicts that happen to have been preserved, one outlawing marriages with close female relatives that were prohibited by traditional Roman practice (which had not previously been applied to the non-Romanized populations of the Empire) and the other banning the recently introduced Manichaean religion.[3] The prohibited practices are characterized as being contrary to the divine ordinance, and it is assumed that the well-being of the state is directly dependent upon the goodwill of the gods, which is in turn determined by adherence to traditional Roman practices. In the edicts, all customs that conflict with Roman law are disparaged as barbarous or even subhuman, and it is taken for granted that all subjects of the Empire are obligated to adhere to Roman law and practice. By equating the concept of *Romanitas* ("Romanness") with the pagan traditions of the Roman state, Diocletian was obligated to draw the necessary conclusion that the Christians, who rejected those traditions, must be extirpated.

For a good fifteen years, Diocletian appears not to have been too bothered by the Christians. Not only is there clear attestation of Christians serving in the army without trouble, but a church was built within sight of his palace in Nicomedia, and there were Christians serving in the staff of his own household. In A.D. 299, a botched sacrifice led to a command that all the members of his domestic staff should sacrifice under penalty of dismissal and that soldiers

3 Founded in A.D. 240 by Mani, a resident of Persian-controlled Mesopotamia, this religion was introduced into Roman territory ca. A.D. 270 and proved to be quite popular well into the fourth century. Inspired by the Gnostic form of Christianity (see p. 286) and Zoroastrianism's dualist cosmology, the new cult held the view that the present life consisted of a struggle between the equal forces of good and evil that dominated the world and that Mani's revelation of this truth allowed the believer to gain salvation.

should do so under threat of discharge. As persecutions go, this was fairly mild, covering only Imperial employees and leaving the civilian population alone.

In A.D. 303, Diocletian undertook a much more thoroughgoing attempt to suppress Christianity with the so-called Great Persecution. While Christian sources ascribe the driving force behind the new policy to Diocletian's heir Galerius, the action against the Christians fits in exactly with the defense of tradition in the name of the gods that appears in the edicts about incestuous marriages and the Manichaeans. In a series of edicts, increasingly broad measures were promulgated against the Christians. First, Christian religious assemblies were prohibited, all churches were to be demolished, and all liturgical books were to be turned over to the authorities for burning. Obstinate Christians lost all privileges and honors, and the courts were closed to those who would not offer traditional sacrifice. When this proved insufficient, the arrest of the Church hierarchy was decreed. Finally, when an amnesty for those who would sacrifice proved futile, an edict was issued in the east in A.D. 304 decreeing that every single inhabitant had to sacrifice. This order appears to have been an act of desperation. If it had not been possible to overpower the resistance of the Church organization, it is hard to see how it was possible to enforce such a blanket provision.

While the persecution was pursued with determination in the east, efforts to enforce the anti-Christian legislation were rather tepid in the west. The first edict was issued throughout the Empire, though in Gaul Constantius Chlorus refrained from executing anyone and merely demolished some churches. In Africa, hostility to the Christians seems to have been more pronounced than elsewhere in the west, but even here there was much collusion between the officials enforcing the decree and the Christians. Even in the east, it is clear that the anti-Christian legislation by no means met with uniform approval, many pagans apparently being reluctant to take the steps necessary to wipe out otherwise respectable Romans who adhered to the new faith. In any case, the Imperial government lacked the means to overthrow Christianity. It was no doubt still a minority religion in the Empire as a whole, but it was very prominent in urban centers, especially, though by no means exclusively, in the east, and its strong organization and hierarchy easily withstood this final challenge. The Great Persecution lasted ten years, but it never came close to achieving its purpose of suppressing Christianity.

When Diocletian instituted the persecution of Christianity, he had already had a long reign, having not only restored some semblance of stability but attempted a broad array of reforms intended to maintain that stability. The strain of all this activity not surprisingly took a toll on Diocletian, and he decided to abdicate, something virtually unheard of. He persuaded his colleague Maximian to do the same (contrary to his natural inclination, as later events would show); they swore an oath to this effect in Rome, where the two were celebrating the twentieth anniversary of Diocletian's reign in late A.D. 303, and resigned their Imperial office on May 1, A.D. 305. The Caesars succeeded as Augusti and appointed new Caesars. This was the only occasion on which the new tetrarchic system was to function as intended, and it promptly collapsed under the dynastic claims of Imperial sons.

22

___

CIVIL WAR AND THE TRIUMPH OF
CONSTANTINE AND CHRISTIANITY,
A.D. 305–A.D. 337

The tetrarchic system of succession that had an Augustus succeeded by his Caesar regardless of his having a natural son was fundamentally unnatural and had been instituted solely through the personal authority of Diocletian: once he was removed from the scene, the situation promptly degenerated into chaos and civil war. Galerius, the new Augustus of the east, was the major beneficiary of the appointment of the new Caesars. Having only a young son, Galerius appointed his nephew Maximinus as Caesar in the east. Galerius also somehow prevailed upon Constantius, the Augustus of the west, to ignore the claims of Maximian's son Maxentius and Constantius' own son Constantine and to appoint as his Caesar a general named Severus, who is represented in hostile sources as Galerius' associate. The second tetrarchy lasted for little more than a year, falling apart upon Constantius' death in July of A.D. 306.

After his father's death, Constantine assumed the title of Augustus, ignoring the claim of Severus, Constantius Chlorus' Caesar and official heir. Galerius, who was acting as senior Augustus in the way that Diocletian had, attempted to make the best of a situation that he could not substantively change by appointing Constantine as Caesar to the Augustus Severus. Constantine, who was happy enough to gain some official recognition of his claim, acquiesced (for the moment) in his demotion and established his authority over Britain, Gaul, and Spain. In his new capacity, Constantine took a step that pointed the way to his future policy. He not only rescinded the one edict against the Christians that Constantius had issued, but he also ordered the restitution of their property. This act asserted his independence of his colleagues and set himself up as protector of the Christians everywhere.

Meanwhile, Maximian's son Maxentius followed Constantine's lead and took advantage of discontent in Rome with the city's inclusion in the new tax system and fears among the city's garrison that they would be cashiered, securing his proclamation there as emperor in October of A.D. 306. Galerius refused him any recognition (this would have ruined the tetrarchic system since there were already four emperors) and ordered Severus to remove him by force. Maxentius now decided to enlist the help of his father, the ex-emperor Maximian, proclaiming him emperor for a second time. It seems that Maximian had not been happy with Diocletian's decision to abdicate and was delighted to return to power. Severus' invasion of Italy in early A.D. 307 was a debacle – the walls of Rome, Maxentius' bribery and the popularity of Maximian among Severus' troops ensuring his failure. Severus surrendered to Maxentius and abdicated.

Around this time, Maximian and Maxentius tried to get help from Constantine, who married Maxentius' sister. At the wedding, Maximian granted Constantine the title of Augustus, but he gave nothing in return apart from his neutrality. When Galerius finally invaded Italy in about September of A.D. 307, things went no better for him than they had for Severus, though his defeat was not fatal, and he managed to withdraw to the north. Maximian apparently resented sharing power with his son, and in the spring of A.D. 308, he attempted a coup d'état at a military ceremony. The soldiers sided with Maxentius, however, though Maximian managed to flee and escaped to the court of his son-in-law Constantine.

Thus, by A.D. 308, the tetrarchy was in ruins: Constantine had seized western Europe and usurped the title Augustus; Maxentius had done likewise, and in the process of maintaining himself in Italy had killed Severus, the legitimate Augustus of the west, and defeated Galerius; and Diocletian's old colleague Maximian had taken up the title of Augustus again. In an attempt to use Diocletian's prestige to restore order, Galerius convened a conference at Carnuntum on the Danube in the fall, inviting both Diocletian and Maximian. Maximian was compelled to abdicate once more. In place of Severus, Galerius' general Licinius was appointed as Augustus in the west. Constantine was recognized merely as Caesar, but Maxentius was denied any legitimacy. This attempt to restore the tetrarchic system failed. Naturally, Maxentius refused to given up his position. (Licinius took up residence in Pannonia to wait until an opportunity arose to impose his rule in the west.) Constantine never recognized his demotion to Caesar and continued to style himself as Augustus, while in the east, Galerius had to acquiesce when his Caesar Maximinus, who resented the fact that the new appointee Licinius outranked him, started styling himself as Augustus. Thus, by A.D. 310, there were five Augusti. (After the conference at Carnuntum, Maximian had returned to Gaul, but he still yearned for power and was forced to commit suicide after an unsuccessful and ungrateful attempt to overthrow his son-in-law Constantine in A.D. 310.)

During this civil strife, Galerius and Maximinus persisted in the east with Diocletian's vain attempt to suppress Christianity. By April of A.D. 311, Galerius was in the final stages of a fatal illness and issued an edict halting the persecution of Christians. Since in the edict he does not admit to having been wrong in his intentions, the most likely explanation for the revocation is a desire on his part to relieve his successors of the onus of taking such a necessary but difficult step (the persecution was obviously a failure but revoking it would involve a loss of face). Soon thereafter Galerius died, and when news of this reached Maximinus, he moved quickly to add Asia Minor to the areas of the Near East that were already under his control. Revealing himself to be an implacable opponent of the Christians, he suppressed Galerius' revocation of the persecution, and by the late fall of A.D. 311, he was once more openly attacking the Church.

Since it was reasonably clear that Licinius, who controlled the Balkans after the death of Galerius, would be distracted by conflict with Maximinus over control of Asia Minor, Constantine decided to seize the opportunity and go to war with his brother-in-law Maxentius. To secure his flank, Constantine offered Licinius the hand of his sister Constantia. In response, Maximinus decided to seek an ally in Maxentius and agreed to recognize him as emperor. In the spring of A.D. 312, Constantine suddenly invaded Italy. Several victories gave Constantine control of northern Italy, and he advanced slowly to the south, hoping that Maxentius' support would evaporate in the interim. At first Maxentius withdrew behind the walls of Rome, hoping to ride out the storm, as he had done with Severus and Galerius before. When Constantine approached the city, rioting broke out, and Maxentius decided that it was necessary to meet Constantine in battle with such troops as he had. On October 28, A.D. 312, Maxentius crossed the Tiber to attack Constantine in the battle of the Mulvian Bridge. Maxentius' troops were quickly routed, and he drowned in the Tiber during the retreat. This battle was the first occasion on which a Roman army fought in the name of the Christian god: after a dream, Constantine had his soldiers put some sort of Christian symbol on their shields (the sources are confused as to its exact nature). When the Christian victor entered Rome, he did not harm the supporters of Maxentius, but he did finally abolish the praetorian guard. That old symbol of the Principate had lost its function, since emperors no longer normally resided in Rome.

The next year (A.D. 313) saw Licinius take control of the east. With Constantine victorious in the west, Licinius decided to formalize his agreement with him, and in February the two met in Milan, where Licinius finally married Constantine's sister Constantia. At Constantine's request, Licinius agreed to restore Church property as Constantine had done (Galerius' edict had not mandated this). In the late winter or spring, apparently while Licinius was still in Italy, Maximinus marched his army hurriedly across Asia Minor, taking Byzantium and crossing over into Europe. When Licinius brought his army up, Maximinus supposedly vowed to Jupiter that if victorious he would finally exterminate the Christians, while Licinius had his troops invoke (somewhat vaguely) the "Great, Holy God," presumably under the influence of his Christian brother-in-law. Battle was joined on April 30, and after much fighting Maximinus despaired of victory and fled, abandoning his army to Licinius. Licinius pursued Maximinus to the city of Tarsus in Asia Minor, where Maximinus committed suicide after being put under siege. Licinius proceeded to eradicate all relatives of the previous emperors, including children and widows.[1] Licinius also acted harshly against all those who had taken prominent roles in the Great Persecution.

Meanwhile, the new Christian emperor became involved in ecclesiastical affairs, when ecclesiastical figures in Africa urged him to solve a controversy that deeply divided the Christians of that province. Given the circumstances under which Constantine took control of Rome, Christians considered him to be the instrument of God by which the Almighty laid low the persecutors and delivered the faithful from their oppressors, and thus it seemed natural to turn to the emperor to decide the seemingly intractable dispute.[2] In discussing his motives for intervention, Constantine himself commented that if the matter was overlooked, "the highest divinity may perhaps be moved to anger not only against the human race but even against my own self, since by his heavenly will he has entrusted to my care the government of all things on earth" (from a letter preserved as the third document in the appendix to Optatus Milevitanus' untitled work against the Donatists). Here, he clearly equated his own rule and secular prosperity with the favor of God, and indicated his conclusion that it was incumbent upon him to maintain this favor through attending to the preservation of peace in the Church.[3] This attitude is premised on the notion – perceptible in Christianity from the time of Paul and enshrined in official Church doctrine during the second and third centuries A.D. – that there was one correct interpretation of Christianity, while all other views were false lies concocted by the devil; the correct doctrine was termed "orthodox" from the Greek for "correct view," and all opposing views were lumped together under the designation "heterodox" from the Greek for "the other view" (i.e., nonorthodox). Since this view of doctrinal dispute interpreted disagreement as a battle between good and evil, no compromise with opposing doctrine was possible. Hence, once the state authority was in the hands of a Christian emperor, it was natural to use the state's power to suppress heterodox views.

1 Diocletian had apparently died in the meanwhile, though the exact date is open to question.
2 The idea that the Almighty was concerned with the secular success of his people was no doubt reinforced by God's many (albeit erratic) interventions on behalf of the Israelites in the Old Testament; various passages in the New Testament point in the same direction.
3 Ironically, this Christian reasoning is comparable to the logic that compelled various pagan emperors from Decius to Galerius to attempt to regain the gods' goodwill by suppressing Christianity.

Unfortunately, in practice it was not so easy to determine orthodoxy from heterodoxy.

The Donatist controversy concerned institutional issues rather than doctrine (though the issue had serious implications for the Church's legitimacy) and divided the Church between a faction of hard-liners and their opponents, whose views would prevail in the long run and for this reason are traditionally called "orthodox." The dispute originally concerned the status of Church officials who had complied with the order to turn over liturgical texts for burning during the short-lived enforcement of the so-called Great Persecution in Africa (see p. 301). After the persecution ceased, the hard-liners held that anyone who had surrendered such items was no longer capable of acting as a Christian and had to be rebaptized, and that any priests guilty of surrendering could no longer perform their duties. This view was vigorously rejected by the Church hierarchy, which rejected any need for rebaptism and asserted that a priest's legitimacy in no way depended upon his personal behavior. This issue completely divided the African Church, and the specific dispute that was laid before Constantine had to do with the bishop of Carthage, whose legitimacy the hard-liners denied on the grounds that he had been consecrated by invalidated priests. He had been condemned in a local ecclesiastical council, and the hard-liners then chose a replacement. During the course of Constantine's involvement, the hard-line bishop died and was replaced with a man named Donatus, after whom the supporters of the hard-line position were called "Donatists." Constantine was soon recognized in Africa after his victory over Maxentius, and in A.D. 313, the hard-liners sent a petition to the new Christian emperor denouncing the original bishop and asking Constantine to send three bishops from Gaul to adjudicate the dispute. Constantine gave his general assent but changed the details. Instead of going to Africa, the three Gallic bishops were to meet in Rome under the presidency of the bishop of Rome and hear representatives of each side. In effect, Constantine as emperor had called a Church council. Two decisions were given by Church councils against the Donatists, but they refused to concede defeat, and eventually Constantine heard the case himself. He exonerated the original bishop once and for all and now ordered the official closure of churches belonging to the Donatists. To Constantine's exasperation, however, the Donatists were perfectly happy to suffer martyrdom at the hands of the Christian emperor. By A.D. 321, Constantine was tired of the whole affair, and ordered an end to state action against the Donatists, who prospered and became the dominant element among the Christians in Africa.

The Donatist controversy showed that it was easier for the emperor to establish his legitimacy through military victory than to impose unity on the Church through legal coercion, but the affair led to no reconsideration of the underlying premise that it was the emperor's duty to suppress religious practice that was prohibited by the state. In the immediate aftermath of the first Christian emperor's apparently divinely instigated triumph it had not seemed problematical to the Church hierarchy first to involve Constantine in Church affairs and then to allow him to use the state's powers to enforce the decision that he reached. It would soon become clear, however, that invoking the secular power of the state in support of the Church's doctrine meant that the state, that is, the emperor, would have to decide for himself what was orthodox, and not every Church leader would agree with the Imperial definition of orthodoxy. The baneful principle that it was the duty of the secular authorities to suppress religious deviation through coercion was now firmly established and would bedevil Europe for more than a millennium.

Regardless of his ecclesiastical problems, Constantine was determined to seize the whole Empire, which was now divided between him in the west and Licinius in the east. Constantine went to war with Licinius in A.D. 316, a move that may have been prompted by the fact that his half-sister had given Licinius an heir the preceding year. In the fall, Constantine had advanced into the Balkans, and after two victories in the field, he advanced toward Byzantium from the north, presumably expecting that Licinius would retreat toward Asia Minor. Instead, Licinius outmaneuvered Constantine, cutting off his lines of communication with the west. Now in a difficult position, Constantine agreed to favorable terms in early A.D. 317, acquiring control of the Balkans apart from Moesia and Thrace.

It is hard to give a fair assessment to Licinius, whose memory was blackened after his defeat. The most notable difference between the two was in religious policy. At the time of his war with Maximinus, Licinius acted favorably towards the Christians, but after Constantine's attack he reverted to a moderate form of persecution. At first, Licinius merely dismissed Christians from his entourage, doing no active harm to them. Later, he expelled them from administrative office and ordered the troops to sacrifice. Though he obstructed Christian worship, there is little evidence for any martyrdoms at this period, and the effort hardly merits the term "persecution."

Licinius' treatment of his Christian subjects gave Constantine an excuse for resuming hostilities, and relations between the two emperors gradually deteriorated. By the beginning of A.D. 321, each half of the Empire refused to recognize the other's consuls (since Constantine controlled Rome, Licinius appointed his own). In a law issued on December 25, A.D. 323, Constantine threatened to punish any men who forced Christians to sacrifice (as had apparently recently been done at the celebrations of Licinius' twentieth anniversary as emperor). By the spring of A.D. 324, preparations for war were ready: Constantine had gathered a fleet of 2,000 ships at Thessalonica in northern Greece, while Licinius had collected a large army that he stationed in Thrace. Constantine invaded Licinius' territory to the northwest of Thessalonica, and in early July the two armies joined battle across the river Hebrus. That night after a full day's fight, Licinius decided that the situation was hopeless and fled. The next day his troops surrendered to Constantine, who began a pursuit toward Byzantium. Licinius withdrew into the city, which Constantine laid under siege. Then, when Constantine's son Crispus came up with the fleet and destroyed Licinius', Byzantium became untenable, and Licinius withdrew to the Asian shore of the Bosporus. Constantine managed to bring his army over and once more defeated Licinius near Chalcedon. The next day, after Licinius' wife (Constantine's half-sister) and the bishop of Nicomedia interceded with him, Constantine swore on oath to spare Licinius, who then abdicated.[4] The Christian emperor was now the first man to have undisputed control of the Empire in forty years, and would do what he could to establish his religion.

Just at the time that Constantine conquered the east, a major doctrinal issue was being hotly disputed, and given his ready interference in the Donatist dispute, it is hardly surprising that Constantine quickly took part in this new controversy. In the Greek-speaking east, there was much interest in the nature of Christ and his relation to God the Father and the Holy Spirit. The more general notion (the one that eventually came to be Catholic orthodoxy) was that while Christ and the Holy Spirit were distinct from God the Father, they nonetheless partook of his nature, and together the three of them represented different "manifestations" of the one God, the mystical unity of the three being termed the "trinity." Other views took Christ to be either entirely distinct from God the Father or completely equivalent to him. In the early fourth century A.D., a priest in Alexandria named Arius propounded a doctrine that fell into the former category, arguing that Christ was created by God. This doctrine, which eventually was rejected as heretical and is known as Arianism, had become quite popular by A.D. 324, and the east was riven between Arians and their "orthodox" opponents. When Constantine first tried to settle the matter informally by sending a letter to the leaders of the two sides urging them to act like philosophers and agree to disagree, he showed both that the doctrinal dispute had not gripped his imagination and that he entirely misunderstood the passions that the issue aroused in the east (the illogical notion of the trinity was accepted without any dispute in the west). Constantine then decided to summon a universal council.

In the spring of A.D. 325, about 300 bishops convened in Nicaea, mostly from the east. Though the council was a mainly Greek affair, its decisions

---

4 In the spring of A.D. 325, Licinius was put to death, along with his ten-year-old son, on the grounds that Licinius had been caught plotting against Constantine's life. While the truth of the charge cannot be denied absolutely, on several other occasions Constantine concocted false accusations of plotting to give specious justification to convenient actions.

were to be binding in the west. Constantine himself attended, and while he did not preside, his presence was keenly felt. Though other matters were decided, the major issue under dispute was Arianism. The emperor browbeat most of Arius' supporters to accept an orthodox creed (a list of fundamental tenets that all Christians had to adhere to), even though it was not really acceptable to them. At the same time, he thwarted the efforts of the orthodox to humiliate or eradicate the Arians by making the non-Arian elements in the new creed explicit. Instead, Constantine himself proposed an explanation of the sense of the creed that was vague enough to be acceptable to virtually everyone. The council was thus apparently a great triumph for Constantine. The squabble had been quashed through vague language and the force of Constantine's personality. This did not solve the problem, however, and the issue would rage for years (though the Nicene creed turned out in the long run to be the accepted Catholic and Orthodox formulation[5]). Whatever the exact theological results of the Council of Nicaea and its creed, the position of the emperor as the arbiter of Church disputes was universally established and the stage set for the full use of the state's powers to suppress opposition to what it considered to be orthodox doctrine.

Some scholars have cast doubt on either the genuineness of Constantine's conversion or the depth of his understanding of the new cult. His early coinage has the traditional gods on it, and in the years immediately before A.D. 312, prominence was given to the "Unconquerable Sun" (*Sol Invictus*), a comparatively new pagan cult that had monotheistic overtones. In fact, Sol continued to appear on coins until the early A.D. 320s. What exactly this signifies is not clear; Constantine was clearly convinced of the validity of Christianity at least since the battle of the Mulvian Bridge. His devotion after that battle is indisputable, though how exactly he conceived of the new religion in the years before his defeat of Licinius in A.D. 324 is open to question (he constantly mentions the one god in his official correspondence, but there is only one reference to Christ). In any case, once he conquered the east and became involved in doctrinal disputes there, he certainly could have had no doubt about the central importance of the person of Christ in the new religion.

In any case, Constantine in many ways made his sincere devotion to the new religion clear through positive actions on its behalf as well as through negative actions harming its opponents. He realized that he was not in a

---

5 The adjectives "catholic" (from the Greek for "universal") and "orthodox" originally simply served to describe the state-sponsored Church of the Late Roman Empire in terms of its claim that its doctrines and rituals embodied the only legitimate form of religion. In modern usage, the terms have been specialized to distinguish the two divisions into which the official Church was split in the medieval period on account of doctrinal differences: "Catholic" refers to the Latin-speaking Church of western Europe, while "Orthodox" signifies the alternative version in the Greek-speaking east (see p. 356).

position to stamp out polytheistic worship by decree and thus put up with it to some degree, but in his official actions and pronouncements, he made his preference for the new religion and his disgust at the old perfectly clear, feeling no compunction about stripping the statues of the pagan gods of their valuable metals. It would seem that in the A.D. 330s, he went so far as to issue a decree outlawing sacrifice, but if this is so, the decree was a dead letter, and sacrifice would be properly banned only in the A.D. 390s. Given the comparatively small numbers of Christians, he could not dispense with the services of pagans altogether, but he favored Christians, bestowing money and honors on prominent converts. This naturally resulted in a large number of high-class conversions. He introduced Christian ideas into the law by revoking the marriage legislation of Augustus, attempting to ban gladiatorial shows (another move like the ban on sacrifice that would only be enforced much later) and restricting the ease of divorce. He also began the process whereby the Church began to assume the functions of the state by allowing either litigants in a civil suit to remit the case for judgment by the local bishop at any point in the proceedings (one can imagine how a pagan felt about this). He built many new churches, notably in Rome and in Jerusalem, and he also turned over vast amounts of Imperial property as endowments for churches, especially in Italy, where he seems to have despoiled the Imperial patrimony for the benefit of the Church. Since wealthy new converts followed suit, the Church would soon become the single most important landowner. Thus, when he had himself baptized on his deathbed, he no doubt looked back with satisfaction on his efforts on behalf of the One God.[6]

In addition to his importance in establishing Christianity as the religion supported by the state and determining the relationship between the emperor and the Church, Constantine also laid out the basic patterns for the remaining two centuries of Roman government. In this, he largely brought to fruition the reforms begun by Diocletian, though often in a somewhat modified form.

Constantine instituted a number of changes in the formation, disposition, and command of the army. First, he seems to have raised a number of new units. While some of these were composed of Roman subjects, others were recruited among the tribes of eastern Gaul and the Germans across the Rhine. This presumably took place before the defeat of Maxentius, but such recruitment may well have continued later. Constantine's nephew Julian, who was hostile to Constantine's memory, claims that he bestowed the consulship on Germans. If true (and there is no reason to doubt it), then such appointments

---

6 In early Christianity it was a not uncommon practice – frowned on by the Church – for converts to delay baptism till the end to avoid the risks of sinning after baptism. Since Constantine's personal behavior was often characterized by self-serving lies and treachery, he knew what he was doing.

can only have been given to generals of German origin. Thus, Constantine not only continued the earlier practice started in the third century A.D. of directly enrolling Germans in the Roman army, but, as the logical step from Diocletian's separation of civil and military authority, he promoted competent Germans to the highest positions of command. This was not necessarily a good idea.

In another respect, Constantine rejected the military policy of Diocletian, who had tried to restore the old Augustan system of fixed defenses along the borders with no strategic reserves. Constantine reverted to a policy of "elastic" defense with a strong strategic reserve that can be traced back to the days of Gallienus (see p. 257). This change apparently goes back to the time before the conquest of Maxentius. At any rate, some of the units of the *comitatus* (the retinue of the emperor) bear Gallic and Germanic names that suggest they were raised when Constantine's main sphere was in Gaul. He is said to have taken a quarter of his army on the invasion of Italy in A.D. 312, which perhaps indicates the ratio of the *comitatus* to the border troops. Constantine then made the *comitatus* a permanent institution. The troops of the *comitatus* were taken from the best units stationed along the border and were concentrated some distance from the borders in strategically important urban centers. From then on, the troops stationed along the border gradually became inferior in status and quality (though the extent of the difference can be exaggerated). The advantage of this system was that these mobile troops of high quality could be quickly brought in large numbers to deal with invasions. The disadvantage of the policy was that it made the invasions easier to start and guaranteed the long-term depopulation of areas close to the border. There was some criticism of the policy in antiquity, but the fact that it was never changed during the last 150 years of the Empire in the west suggests that there was no alternative.

Two new positions were created to command the troops of the *comitatus*. The "master of foot" was in charge of the infantry, while the "master of horse" commanded the cavalry, and these positions were to become extremely influential during the later fourth century A.D. (Presumably the Germanic consuls mentioned by Julian held such commands.) At the same time, the praetorian praefects were stripped of their military power, becoming purely civilian administrators. This step is not only a logical result of Constantine's abolition of the actual praetorian guard in A.D. 312, but the measure also followed naturally from the separation of civil and military command instituted by Diocletian.

Constantine also formalized the structure of the Imperial government itself.[7] Diocletian had shown himself to be disinclined to use the senators in

7 In some of these reforms, he was formalizing earlier patterns that had arisen during the tetrarchic period and even earlier, but too little is known about the earlier periods to

Imperial administration and restricted them to the governorships of a few areas where they had interests. Constantine changed this, employing a number of senators in provincial command. At the same time, he came to bestow ex officio senatorial status on the higher levels of the Imperial administration, that is, the holding of such positions automatically conferred senatorial status. This change brought an end to the old formal distinction between senatorial and equestrian careers. While traditional senatorial families continued to sit in the senate by right, those who reached sufficiently high level in the Imperial administration automatically became senators. In addition, the decline in status of the old permanent bureaucracy in Rome was now properly recognized. Once the emperors ceased to reside in Rome during the course of the third century A.D., the official business that used to be conducted at Rome began to follow the emperor to his campaigns and his residence in towns away from Rome. The *comitatus* therefore was considered to include not simply the troops in attendance on the emperor in person but also all government officials who followed him. Although at first there was some distinction between members of the *comitatus* who were soldiers and those who were civilian administrators, the staff of the civil administration would over the course of the fourth century A.D. be increasingly assimilated to the soldiery in attire and status.

Apart from his conversion to Christianity, the most important step taken by Constantine was his foundation of a new capital on the site of the ancient Greek city of Byzantium. He ceremonially marked off the site for his new capital in late A.D. 324, very soon after his overthrow of Licinius. There is some evidence that Constantine originally meant to call the city "New Rome," but it quickly came to be known by the Greek phrase for "City of Constantine": Constantinople. His exact motive in founding the new city is open to question. Certainly, there were strategic considerations. By now it was obvious that being so far removed from the actual borders where the military threat was, the old capital in Rome had only a symbolic value, and no emperor with a choice had resided there since the middle of the third century A.D. Both Diocletian and Galerius had as senior emperor under the tetrarchy taken up residence in Nicomedia in northwestern Asia Minor near the Bosporus; presumably, the choice was determined by the fact that the location was in the center of the wealthy eastern half of the empire and allowed easy access to both the often breached lower Danube and the border with Persia. There are two reasons for the move of the capital from Nicomedia to Byzantium. First, in both of his wars with Licinius, Constantine had himself seen the strategic importance of the site on account of its control of the passage between Asia and Europe; second, personal experience in the second war showed that the site was virtually

---

be entirely sure about how much of Constantine's reforms consisted of innovations and how much built on earlier developments.

impregnable so long as control of the sea was retained. Built on a peninsula, the city was surrounded by water on three sides, and Constantine rendered the whole site secure by adding a vast wall to cut off the peninsula in the north, making his new city about five times the size of the old. In addition, the new city was fundamentally a Christian foundation: it was untainted with pagan tradition, and he endowed it with many great churches. It is significant that the date chosen for the city's dedication in the year A.D. 330 was May 11, the feast day of a saint who had suffered martyrdom during the Great Persecution. Constantine was thus making the point that the building of the new city by the emperor favored by God represented the triumph of God over his enemies.

Six years was a rather short period of time to build a vast new city, and a lot of the structures were rather poorly built and would soon have to be reconstructed. Constantine had numerous works of art taken from pagan shrines to adorn the new city; he offered tax incentives and other rewards to induce people to move there, and started a new senate (in the beginning its status was clearly inferior to that of Rome). But soon the strategic importance of the city was undoubted, and it grew appreciably, its central location making it a wealthy trading city.

While Constantine enjoyed success in his public life, his family affairs were less satisfying. In A.D. 326, poorly understood machinations wreaked havoc in the Imperial household. Constantine first had his eldest son Crispus by his first wife executed, and then his second wife died under mysterious circumstances (perhaps she was discovered to have engineered the downfall of Crispus). At this point, Constantine was approaching fifty-five and could expect to die at any time (though in fact he lived another decade). Since none of his sons by the now-dead second wife were older than ten, trouble was likely to result if he died soon. Constantine previously kept his two surviving half-brothers (from his father's marriage to Maximian's daughter) in exile, but now he began to treat them better, appointing them to high positions of responsibility until his sons could reach adulthood. His sons Constantine II and Constantius II already held the rank of Caesar (bestowed back in A.D. 317) and Constans would likewise receive it in A.D. 333, when he reached the age of ten; in A.D. 335, Constantine gave the same rank to Delmatius, the son of one of his half-brothers. As his heirs grew up, he assigned parts of the Empire for them to rule. Since they were all very young, real power was exercised by their praetorian praefects. With the exception of Africa, which for some reason was governed independently by a praetorian praefect of its own, the rest of the Empire was eventually divided up amongst his heirs, with Constantine himself retaining overall command of the whole in his new capital of Constantinople.

There is evidence to suggest that in the late A.D. 330s, Constantine intended to undertake a major war against the Persians, who had been quiescent ever since Galerius' great victory in A.D. 298. Now in addition to the usual territorial conflicts, additional potential grounds for strife arose from Constantine's stance as the defender of Christians in general (there were many in Persian territory) and of the recently converted kingdom of Armenia in particular. He proclaimed his nephew Hannibalianus (brother of the Caesar Dalmatius) "king of kings" and married him to his eldest daughter, but which land was foreseen for Hannibalianus' rule is not clear. Some sources say Armenia, but the title suggests that he was actually meant to become king of Persia. Whatever his intentions, Constantine was prevented from carrying them out by his death in early A.D. 337.

23

HEYDAY OF THE CHRISTIAN EMPIRE,

A.D. 337–A.D. 395

Given that Constantine died after nearly two months of illness, it is rather surprising that he made no provision at all for the succession. Of his sons, Constantine II (now twenty-one years old) ruled in Spain, Gaul, and Britain; Constans (only fourteen) in Italy; and Constantius (now seventeen) in the east, while his nephew Delmatius governed along the Danube in the Balkans. He could hardly have imagined that this arrangement could last after his death. What would become of Africa? Who would take control of Constantinople? Perhaps he realized the impracticality of leaving his power to a single heir but could think of no way to adapt some variant of the tetrarchic system to dynastic succession, and in desperation decided to leave the matter to fate. Clearly, the chaotic set up that he left behind was unsatisfactory, and the natural solution was more or less self-evident: Constantine should be succeeded by his own sons, and his second oldest son, Constantius, proceeded to organize a massacre of all the other adult relations of Constantine apart from his brothers. The details are somewhat unclear, since the sources preserve pathetic official lies: the troops committed the murders of their own accord, or Constantine himself enjoined the murders in a will after being poisoned by his half-brothers. In addition to the Imperial relatives, some of Constantine's leading functionaries (including two of Constantine's brothers-in-law) were killed. Apparently, Constantius wished to be rid not only of all rivals within the Imperial household but also of any senior officials who could thwart the exercise of power by the new young emperors. In the fall, Constantine II, Constantius, and Constans were each proclaimed Augustus, and they divided the Empire among themselves. It appears that some sort of seniority was conceded to Constantine II, but if so this had little practical significance and he gained no addition to his territory in northwestern Europe. Constantius retained the east and was given the diocese of Thrace, which included

Constantinople. Constans in the center gained the most, adding Africa and the Balkans (apart from Thrace) to his possession of Italy.

The frontiers were comparatively quiet in the north during the A.D. 340s, but Constantius was menaced by the threat of war on the Persian border. Constantine had been preparing a war against the Persians when he died in A.D. 337. The Persian king Shapur II was determined to revive the glory of his namesake and to avenge the disgrace inflicted on the Persians by Galerius in A.D. 298. By late A.D. 337, Constantius was already in Antioch, which must mean that he felt the Persian border needed his presence, but it not until A.D. 340 that he actually invaded Persian territory. There is no continuous history of this period, but the disconnected anecdotes that survive show that throughout the A.D. 340s, Constantius was occupied with an ongoing series of campaigns against the Persians, enjoying varied success. Neither side achieved a decisive victory, and the war dragged on until A.D. 350 when both sides became distracted, Constantius having to deal with the overthrow of his brother in the west by a usurper, while Shapur had to campaign against nomadic invaders on his eastern frontier.

Though the brothers had sufficient sense of family loyalty to cooperate in murdering their relatives, they proceeded to act with similar disloyalty towards one another. The first to go was Constantine II. When Constans was on the Danube in the winter of A.D. 339–340, Constantine decided to invade his brother's Italian territory. When Constans learned of his brother's actions in February of A.D. 340, he quickly returned with an army to deal with him, and at Aquileia in northern Italy, Constans managed to ambush his brother's army and kill him.

Constans naturally took over the territory of his dead brother. He is most notable for his staunch support of the orthodox interpretation of the trinity that was codified in the Nicene creed and his hostility towards Arianism, which was becoming increasingly respectable in the east at the time. This situation led to cool relations between Constans and his brother in the east, who for his part favored Arianism. From the secular point of view, Constans' reign was not very remarkable, but he made a poor impression on his contemporaries. The unfavorable way in which he is presented in the orthodox sources despite his defense of the Nicene creed suggests that he was, in fact, an unpleasant man; in any case, a financial official organized a palace plot against him, which led to his murder in Gaul in January of A.D. 350. An officer of elite troops, a man of Germanic origin called Magnentius, was proclaimed Augustus in his place. It is indicative of the prominence that Germanic troops had already acquired in the Roman army that such a man could now be accepted as emperor.

This coup d'état did not go unopposed. In Illyricum, Vetranio, the local military commander, was proclaimed Augustus on March 1, while a nephew of Constantine (one of the children to survive the massacre of A.D. 337) was proclaimed Augustus in Rome, but he was suppressed by Magnentius. Whatever Vetranio's motives had been in allowing himself to be proclaimed Augustus, he apparently had no real desire to maintain his position. At any rate, he seems to have entered into discussion with Constantius to find a peaceful way out of his situation. Toward the end of A.D. 350, Constantius entered Illyricum with an army and was allowed to speak to Vetranio's troops, who were persuaded to return to loyalty to the house of Constantine and swore allegiance to Constantius, while Vetranio publicly abdicated in Constantius' presence.

Constantius was unwilling to enter into a similar agreement with Magnentius, who had, after all, killed his brother Constans. After some initial skirmishing in which Magnentius came off the better, a major battle was fought at Mursa in southern Pannonia. At the end of a long and bloody fight, Magnentius was defeated and withdrew into Gaul. Constantius stayed for some time in the Balkans and did not take over Italy until the early fall of A.D. 352. In the following year, his army invaded Gaul, and Magnentius committed suicide after a defeat. For the first time since the death of Constantine there was now one senior emperor whose authority was recognized throughout the Empire. This would cause difficulties in that the Arian doctrine supported by Constantius was detested in the west.

For the sons of Constantine, there was more to being a Christian emperor than simply murdering relatives. It was necessary to continue their father's heritage of helping the Church eradicate false doctrine. Constantine had forced the Council of Nicaea to accept the doctrine about the trinity that was generally considered orthodox in the Latin west and to reject the more logical Arian view that was popular in the east. During his own lifetime, Constantine had needed to use force against the many Church figures who continued to propound the Arian interpretation, and the dispute continued under his sons. In the west, Constantius and Constans continued to uphold the Nicene formulation, but in the east, Constantius fell under the sway of Arianism and deposed "orthodox" bishops. Once Constantius gained control of the west, he felt duty-bound to force his new subjects to mend their ways, and in A.D. 359, he summoned a council of bishops to Ariminum in Italy, where they were compelled to accept an Arian creed. This noble endeavor proved the undoing of Constantius' reputation among most ancient chroniclers in that he picked the wrong version of Christianity to suppress. A revolt against Constantius halted any long-term efforts to impose Arianism on the west against its will.

Back when the death of Constans had first become known in the east and it was clear that a war with Magnentius was looming, Constantius decided that he needed to have a relative to maintain his authority in the east while he marched west. Unfortunately, Constantius was childless and had to turn to an Imperial relative whose father he had murdered back in A.D. 337. In early A.D. 351, he proclaimed as Caesar his cousin Gallus, the son of one of the elder Constantine's half-brothers (Gallus had been about twelve years old at the time of his father's murder, and was now twenty-six). Gallus did preserve order in the east, but his rule was not considered a success (he was supposedly cruel and tyrannical). In the fall of A.D. 354, Constantius stripped Gallus of his rank and then had him tried and executed.

The only remaining male descendant of Constantine was Gallus' half-brother Julian. Julian had been only five years old at the time of the massacre in A.D. 337, and like his brother Gallus, he was raised in an isolated fortress in Asia Minor. There, Julian was educated as a Christian, but developed a deep love of the pagan literature of Classical Greece and an aversion to the religion of his cousin (though for the moment he kept this to himself). In A.D. 355, Constantius decided to return to the east, and after raising Julian to the rank of Caesar left him behind in Gaul, where he was to be kept in check by senior officials appointed by Constantius. Julian quickly proved himself to be a successful general, and in series of campaigns in the years A.D. 356–359, he crushed the Franks and Alemanni, restoring order along the Rhine. During the winter lull in campaigning, he set about improving administration by halting corruption, and he managed to reduce the capitation assessment from twenty-five to seven gold coins per unit.[1]

Constantius was supposedly fearful of his cousin's success, and Julian in turn feared a fate like his brother's. Accordingly, he found an excuse to become independent. When Constantius demanded that Julian send him some of his best troops on the grounds that the Rhine was now settled and war with Persia was again threatening, Julian worked upon the reluctance of the troops to be transferred so far from home, with the result that they refused to go and proclaimed him Augustus in February of A.D. 360. By the time that Constantius heard of this, the Persian threat was too serious for him to do anything about Julian yet, and he tried to keep him in check through diplomacy until he could disengage in the east. Julian himself wished to avoid a direct confrontation, but finally, in mid–A.D. 361, decided to invade Constantius' territory. While Julian was entering the Balkans, Constantius was marching westwards to oppose him, but died on the journey in November. Julian was quickly recognized as emperor; he was the only pagan emperor after Constantine, and during his short reign he undertook the last attempt to suppress Christianity.

Julian's brand of paganism was very idiosyncratic, its spirit having rather more to do with the Christianity that he rejected than with the paganism

---

1 This huge decrease says something about the extent to which the government took advantage of the capitation system to increase the tax burden inordinately (see p. 298).

of the pre-Christian past. Julian adopted a form of asceticism that was obviously inspired by Christian attitudes. He also adopted the Christian habit of suppressing false doctrine, acting against pagans whose views he considered incorrect. This sort of fanatical exclusivity is very much a characteristic of Christianity and alien to the nondogmatic attitudes of traditional paganism. As emperor, he even wished to set up a sort of pagan hierarchy of priests, clearly in imitation of the Christian church. Julian was very much a pagan fanatic.

Despite the clear influence of Christianity on his religious feelings, two factors in particular seem to have motivated Julian's renunciation of Christianity. He must have associated it strongly with Constantius, whom he not unreasonably detested as the murderer of his family. Julian also came to associate himself strongly with the glories of the Hellenic past as they were reflected in Classical pagan literature, and this association led him to reject the Christianity that seemed opposed to that pagan past.[2]

Two edicts indicate his religious policy. First, he announced the reopening of the pagan temples, and the restoration of the right to perform sacrifices that had been banned under Constantius. At the same time, he openly declared religious toleration, and recalled all Christians who were in exile for religious reasons to weaken the Christians. The recalled exiles were not restored to the earlier positions, and this was intended to cause strife when the "orthodox" exiles returned to find their positions held by Arians. Julian also tolerated anti-Christian violence.

Realizing that a direct assault on the Church would probably benefit it in the long run, Julian attempted to stamp it out through a sort of attrition. In the summer of A.D. 362, he decreed that those who did not believe in the gods could not teach literature. Since the Classical literary texts were all pagan, this would exclude Christians from the literary education that was obligatory in high society and necessary for advancement in the government. Thus, in a generation, the Christians would be compelled to abandon education or convert. It seems that he also prohibited Christians from practicing law.

In addition to the negative step of sapping the vitality of Christianity, he also apparently wished to set up a sort of pagan alternative. He had plans for a formal pagan hierarchy modeled on that of the Christians and wished to set up pagan charitable organizations to rival the alms giving of Christians. Both acts were again inspired by Christianity and had nothing to do with traditional pagan practice.

---

2 A similar attachment to the past caused many members of the hereditary senatorial aristocracy in Rome to cling to the old ways. Though by the late fourth century the majority of the senate consisted of Christians, a certain number of inveterate pagans survived into the first decades of the fifth century A.D.

Whether Julian's artificial version of paganism would have succeeded in the long run is questionable, but his plans were thwarted by a disastrous invasion of Persia. The Persian wars of the A.D. 340s had only been broken off by Constantius' need to deal with Julian's revolt, and by A.D. 363, Julian felt that affairs at home were sufficiently under control to allow him to imitate the exploits of his hero Alexander the Great. After leaving Antioch with 80,000–90,000 men in the spring, Julian split his army, sending 30,000 down the Tigris while he himself proceeded down the traditional route along the Euphrates. The plan was that both armies were to meet at Ctesiphon, but disaster intervened. Julian reached his destination and defeated the Persians, but when he rashly decided to burn his fleet to increase his mobility and the other detachment failed to arrive, he was forced to retreat up the Tigris. The Persians employed a scorched-earth policy in front of the Roman army, which thus suffered from deprivation of supplies in addition to Persian harassment. Finally, Julian received a fatal wound in the midst of a battle that was fought in June. He died of blood loss later that night, leaving his army stranded in a very difficult position. Later it was claimed that a Christian in his own army had done Julian in, but examination of sources written close to the time of his death perhaps shows that the man responsible was an Arab serving in the Persian army. In any case, the last (idiosyncratic) champion of paganism was now dead.

Clearly a new emperor had to be picked promptly, and a council of the leading officers was held. When the first man to be selected (a universally respected pagan) declined, they chose Jovian, a thirty-year-old Christian who was an amiable senior officer of the Imperial bodyguard. The immediate problem facing the new emperor was how to extricate the Roman army from Persian territory, and the dire situation of the army forced him to agree to humiliating terms. He had to cede to the Persians not only the five provinces across the Tigris that had been taken from the Persians after Galerius' victory in A.D. 298 but also two cities that had been lynchpins in the Roman defensive position in northern Mesopotamia since the days of Septimius Severus. One rash campaign thus erased a century and a half of Roman gain. Whether Jovian would have been able to overcome the humiliating start of his reign is not known; he died under mysterious circumstances only eight months later in early A.D. 364 (supposedly smothered while he slept by fumes from a fire).

It is indicative of the extent to which the exalted conception of the monarchy that Diocletian instituted had succeeded in curbing the military that once again the troops did not take advantage of the situation to try to impose their own choice as emperor, as would certainly have been the case a century earlier. Instead, leading Imperial officials met in Nicaea to select the new emperor. After some deliberations, the unanimous choice was a forty-three-year-old officer of the Imperial bodyguard named Valentinian, who was a devout Christian of lowly Pannonian origin who had risen through the ranks. Valentinian was a bad-tempered individual who held the educated in contempt. As emperor he was a competent soldier and took some interest in the administration, but he was overly trusting in his subordinates, whom he often chose injudiciously. It was apparently a general feeling now that the empire could not be ruled by one man, and as soon as he was proclaimed emperor, the army made clear its desire that he should appoint a colleague. Valentinian chose his younger brother Valens, who was given the east to govern, while Valentinian himself retained control over the territory from Illyricum to the west. Soon after Valentinian's accession to power, there was a challenge from the old dynasty. Julian had a relative on his mother's side named Procopius, who had not made much progress in a military career before Julian's reign, but was appointed as a general by Julian. In A.D. 365, he raised a revolt in Thrace and managed to seize Constantinople. His German generals betrayed him, however, and his troops melted away. Valens easily suppressed the revolt and exacted severe vengeance from those alleged to have supported Procopius. In A.D. 367, Valentinian suffered a serious illness, and when he learned after his recovery that people had discussed who might succeed him, he had his eight-year-old son Gratian proclaimed Augustus.

Valentinian and Valens were both insecure and suspicious, and having no liking for the cultured individuals who had gained favor under Julian, they often appointed to Imperial office men of lowly Pannonian origin like themselves who possessed no personal prestige of their own. While Valens seems to have kept his administration under control, Valentinian was apparently a poor judge of character and refused to listen to criticism of his subordinates, who proceeded to abuse their offices. Not surprisingly, Valentinian had bad relations with the senate, and numerous treason trials were conducted under him. He also extended the policy begun under Constantine of equating senatorial status with service in the Imperial administration, and fairly low-level functionaries in the civil service now gained senatorial rank ex officio. In addition, many generals of Germanic origin who had no education at all also received senatorial status. In this way the number of senators in both Rome and Constantinople increased greatly.

Perhaps as a reflection of their lowly origin, the new emperors exhibited a novel interest in defending the lower classes against abuse by their betters. They formalized throughout the empire an official position for which there is scattered evidence from the beginning of the century. This official was called the "defender of the citizenry" (*defensor civitatis*) and before him, lower-class men could lodge minor lawsuits, seek the restoration of runaway slaves, and request the remission of taxes, thereby avoiding the high cost of the regular courts. As a further sign of the emperors' distrust of the traditional ruling classes, they decreed that the members of the decurion class should no longer be appointed as collectors of taxes in kind and that this function should instead be performed by ex-Imperial officials. (Valentinian claimed that such men would be more trustworthy, and that if they did commit fraud, the government could seize their assets more easily.) This plan was not practical, however, since the proposed officials had no desire to assume this new burden, and it was soon abandoned.

Though himself a devout Christian, Valentinian gave up the long-established practice of using state power to impose religious uniformity, proclaiming general religious freedom for pagans and most varieties of Christians, though continuing the traditional ban against the Manichaeans and the Donatists. He allowed most forms of pagan sacrifice to resume, asserting that what was traditional was not in his belief criminal. As for Christianity, Valentinian explicitly refused to become involved in Church affairs, and in refusing a petition to summon a Church council, he told the bishops to hold one on their own if they so chose.

In the west, where the Nicene creed was fairly uniformly supported, this attitude of nonintervention was fairly easy to maintain. Valens had a bit more trouble in the east, where the Arian controversy was dying down. The Nicene creed was becoming more acceptable as its novelty wore off, and some attempt at compromise was being undertaken by its less extreme opponents. Valens would have nothing to do with such tendencies to cave in to the orthodox (whom he of course did not consider to be anything of the kind), and in the A.D. 370s, he began to persecute them. This did nothing to enhance his reputation once the Nicene creed was eventually accepted as orthodox in the east.

For the most part, Valentinian spent the years A.D. 365–375 along the Rhine, where he conducted a number of campaigns against the troublesome Alemanni. In November of A.D. 375, the bad-tempered emperor died of apoplexy when enraged by remarks made by barbarian envoys. Apparently fearing mistreatment at the hands of advisors of Valentinian's young heir Gratian, the disreputable associates of the dead emperor proclaimed as Augustus Valentinian's four-year-old younger son Valentinian, who was in their own hands. (At the same time, the general Theodosius, who in recent years had performed yeoman duty in protecting Britain against all manner of invasion and in suppressing a revolt in Africa, was put to death under mysterious circumstances. This execution was perhaps also part of the effort of these same men to retain power through controlling the young new emperor. In any case, Theodosius' son of the same name would soon be called upon to save Valentinian's dynasty from disaster.) Though Gratian and Valens had had no desire to see Valentinian II made Augustus, they assigned the lad rule over Italy, Africa, and Illyricum.

Meanwhile, Valens had spent most of the A.D. 370s in Syria to keep an eye on the Persians, but in A.D. 376, trouble arose along the Danube.

At this time, the Goths were divided into two groups eventually known as the Ostrogoths and the Visigoths. The Huns, a powerful tribe from central Asia, were pushing into southern Russia, and in the process destroyed the kingdom of the Ostrogoths – from now on the Huns would be an increasingly disturbing presence in eastern Europe. Terrified by the approach of the Huns, the Visigoths petitioned to be allowed to cross the Danube and settle in Roman territory. There was much abandoned land in the region, and Valens consented when the Goths agreed to provide troops for the Roman army. (In this way the Imperial government could make much money by converting the presentation of recruits for the army by taxpayers according to the capitation system into gold payments – the sums raised could purchase an equal number of barbarian troops and leave the government a profit.) The Visigoths were ferried across for settlement in Thrace in late A.D. 376, and while some of these Germanic recruits were immediately dispatched to the east, most stayed in Thrace. Proper provision had not been made for the newcomers, and the local Roman administrators took advantage of the situation for their own profit, which did not improve the disposition of the Goths. Meanwhile, the Ostrogoths also managed to sneak across the river. Finally, a revolt broke out when the Roman commander had the escorts of the Goths' leaders killed. The overall chief of the Goths tried to calm the situation, but after the Romans made an inept attempt to put the revolt down by force, the Goths began to rampage throughout Thrace. Their depredations went unopposed by the Imperial government in A.D. 377, and it was only in the following year that Valens finally returned from Antioch to do something.

Valens had asked for assistance from his nephew Gratian, who dispatched troops to the Balkans. When Valens came upon the Gothic army near Adrianople by the Black Sea, many advised him to wait for these reinforcements, but on August 9 he was persuaded to attack first to reserve the glory for himself alone. The cavalry on the Roman left flank defeated the Goths opposite them and sped off in pursuit. The numerically superior Germans then attacked the Romans from that exposed side. The Romans were surrounded, and after standing their ground for some time, the whole army was overwhelmed, and Valens himself died under unknown circumstances (his body was never found). Since cavalry played a major role in the Goths victory, it used to be claimed that this battle marked the transition from the use of heavy infantry characteristic of Classical antiquity to the dominance of cavalry that is the hallmark of the medieval period, but these days there is a tendency to underplay the tactical significance of the battle. Regardless of any broader significance, the mobile field army of the east was wiped out in a debacle of a magnitude not known for a century (the only previous emperor to die in battle like this was Decius back in A.D. 251). Given his firm support of Arianism and his humiliating defeat, it is hardly surprising that the ancient sources take a dim view of the fallen emperor.

With the death of Valens, there was now no effective Imperial authority: Gratian was an inexperienced nineteen-year-old, and Valentinian II was only seven. Gratian recalled to duty Theodosius, the son of the successful general of the same name who had been executed soon after Valentinian I's death. At that time, the younger Theodosius had returned to his ancestral estates in Spain, but now he was placed in charge of the military situation in Thrace. It was clear that an additional Augustus was necessary, and in January of A.D. 379, Theodosius was raised to that status by Gratian. A devout orthodox Christian (i.e., he subscribed without hesitation to the creed of Nicaea), Theodosius was given rule over Egypt, the east and, most importantly, the Balkans, where he was attempting to overcome the Goths.

The assumption of the Imperial purple by a man such as Theodosius, a born Christian who accepted the Nicene creed without reservation and took the supremacy of Christianity for granted, is indicative of the extent to which Christianity had taken hold in the Empire since the time of Constantine. Now, the cities were to a large extent dominated by Christian populations, who at times (particularly in the East) participated in public doctrinal disputes with violent enthusiasm. (Presumably, adherence to the old rites was stronger in the countryside, but this segment of the population is little noted in the sources.) Large numbers of the wealthy class had also converted. The main holdouts were the senatorial aristocracy of Rome, whose religious sensibilities were definitely close to those of the Christians but who, like the emperor Julian, could not bring themselves to abandon what they considered to be the pagan beliefs of their glorious forebears. Soon, they, too, would go over to the new god.

The secular sources for this period are poor, and the exact details of how Theodosius and Gratian dealt with the Goths are not entirely clear. Soon after their defeat of Valens, the Goths actually attacked Constantinople, but lacking any siege equipment this endeavor was futile. After that, they milled around the Balkans, pillaging as they went. The Ostrogoths moved westwards to Pannonia, and were apparently bought off by Gratian. Meanwhile, Theodosius was occupied with restoring the army of the east after the debacle at Adrianople. In A.D. 379–380, his headquarters were at Thessalonica, but in late A.D. 380, he entered Constantinople. Apparently lacking sufficient confidence in his newly raised forces to risk a major battle, he shadowed the Visigoths to minimize their damage, and attempted to awe their leaders by putting on a show for some who visited Constantinople. The Visigoths themselves apparently got tired of their adventure, and in A.D. 382, a novel sort of treaty was entered into between them and Theodosius.

Under the terms of the peace, the Visigoths were entitled to settle as a corporate body in territory assigned to them by the Imperial government in the (now depopulated) Roman Balkans. In return, they agreed to provide contingents for the Roman army. The Visigoths were to retain their own political structure and to govern themselves; the units that they provided to the emperor would be commanded by Visigoths, though they would obey the orders of the overall Roman general in whose army they served. Because their relations with the Roman state were now established by a treaty (*foedus*, in Latin), the Visigoths are called federates (*foederati*, in Latin). This treaty marked a major change from earlier policy, and this new procedure was followed in the later treatment of Germanic tribes. Previously, Germanic tribal immigrants had been settled on Roman territory, but they were divided into small groups under a Roman overseer (praefect). Such settlers were called *laeti*, and this status was hereditary.[3] They did not maintain their broader tribal allegiance and were obligated to provide recruits for the regular Roman army. These *laeti* became an important source of military recruitment in the fourth century A.D. and contributed to the Germanization of the Roman army. Nonetheless, the *laeti* became regular subjects of the emperor and were controlled within the Roman civilian and military administration. As federates, the Visigoths were being treated as foreign equals of the Roman state on Roman territory, retaining full internal and external autonomy. In terms of the position within the Roman military of the contingents they were obligated to provide, these contingents retained their foreign identity and merely served alongside the regular Roman forces. The time would soon come when large numbers of such Germanic tribes entered Roman territory as federates, providing much of the military force of the western Empire and eventually taking over much of the territory of the west.

In the fall of A.D. 378, when he was sole emperor, Gratian had issued an edict of religious toleration. Two factors soon led to the replacement of this liberal policy, which continued the open-minded ways of Valentinian I, with the sort of religious repression that had characterized the house of Constantine. First, Gratian was influenced by the pushy and fanatical local bishop of Milan (the Imperial seat in the north), "Saint" Ambrose (his sainthood has more to do with his unflinching defense of orthodoxy than any sanctity of deportment). Ambrose was born into the Italian aristocracy and had actually governed a small Italian province before being directly elected to the position of bishop (this career pattern illustrates the great increase in the prestige and power of the Church during the course of the fourth century A.D.). At Ambrose's insistence, Gratian outlawed "heretical" assemblies, abandoned the old religious title

---

3 The etymology of the word *laetus* in this sense is not clear.

pontifex maximus that had exclusively been held by all emperors since Augustus, and abolished the privileges of the pagan priesthoods in Rome.

The second cause of Gratian's less tolerant attitude was the influence of his colleague, the aggressively Catholic Theodosius.[4] In February of A.D. 380, he issued a decree advising everyone to become Catholics (that is, to accept the Nicene creed), calling those who did not "demented and crazed." He not only reminded such people of the impending judgment of God, but also noted that he himself would in due course punish them. One source indicates that he issued this edict after suffering a severe illness from which he recovered and then had himself baptized. It appears from other sources that the illness actually took part later in the year, and hence his actions were not directly motivated by fear of sinning after baptism. Instead, this repression represents the natural sentiment of a loyal son of the Church. Upon entering Constantinople later that year, he deposed the Arian bishop. In January of A.D. 381, he ordered that all churches should be turned over to Catholic bishops and, like Gratian, banned all non-Catholic assemblies (in all, he issued eighteen edicts against various dissenting Christian sects); in May, he called a Church council in Constantinople, which finally reaffirmed faith in the Nicene creed, effectively bringing an end to the Arian controversy.

Theodosius was initially a little more circumspect about pagans. In A.D. 381, blood sacrifice was banned with severe penalties, but other forms of worship were permitted. The temples were not officially closed, but petitions to tear down temples were received favorably, and no action was taken against spontaneous local initiatives (often taking the form of riots) to destroy temples. That Theodosius at first showed much more interest in suppressing deviant forms of Christianity than pagan rites shows how marginalized pagan practice had become since the recognition of Christianity at the beginning of the century.

In the spring of A.D. 383, Magnus Maximus, like Theodosius a military commander from the Spanish aristocracy, was proclaimed emperor in Britain. Gratian rushed with his army to meet Maximus, who had invaded Gaul. Abandoned by his troops, however, he was turned over to Maximus and executed in August. Why Gratian lost control of the situation is not clear. (Some ancient

---

4 The universal Church authorized by Imperial law in the fourth century A.D. is, of course, the ancestor of the modern Catholic Church (as well as the Orthodox Church in the eastern Mediterranean lands; see p. 356), and hence it is reasonable to refer to the Imperial Church with the ancient term "Catholic," but one should beware of equating the modern Catholic Church and the official Church of the Late Roman Empire. While the two institutions do have much in common, the modern Church has developed many doctrines and institutions that make it an entirely different organization from its ancestor.

sources suggest that he had become indolent, though if at this time sloth on the emperor's part was enough to guarantee loss of military support, the situation would soon change.) Valentinian II was in Italy at this time, and Maximus sent envoys to him and Theodosius seeking recognition. While Theodosius played for time, the routes over the Alps were secured, which kept Maximus out of Italy. In A.D. 384, Theodosius feigned a campaign to the west, but never got further than the Balkans, and the situation became a stalemate. While Maximus recognized Valentinian II and Theodosius, they did not return the favor, though they did not attack him either. Maximus was, if anything, a more fervent Catholic than Theodosius, and he had an orthodox Christian dissident in Spain executed. Certain ecclesiastics objected to the execution of one of their number, but such action is the logical culmination of the use of state violence in support of Church dogma that had been going on since the time of Constantine, and one never hears of these ecclesiastics objecting to Imperial laws mandating that Manichaeans should be burned alive.

One reason why Theodosius could not do anything substantive about Maximus was that there was the threat of trouble with the Persians (yet another dispute about the status of Armenia). Only in A.D. 387 was a treaty worked out with the Persians after protracted negotiations. Armenia was to be split, the Romans receiving only one fifth, the Persians the rest. This was a serious Roman loss, but it did allow Theodosius to take action in the west.

Late in A.D. 387, Maximus invaded Italy, forcing Valentinian II to flee to Thessalonica. The next spring, Theodosius invaded, and after a defeat Maximus was handed over to Theodosius for execution. Already in A.D. 383, Theodosius had had his young son Arcadius proclaimed Augustus, and when Theodosius came to Rome after the defeat of Maximus, it was clear that, while he would not get rid of Valentinian II out of loyalty to the old dynasty, he would effectively replace him with his own progeny: his other young son, the five-year-old Honorius, was shown to the senators in Rome as their future ruler, while Valentinian II stayed out of sight in Milan.

Theodosius was not vindictive in his treatment of the senatorial aristocracy that had supported Maximus. Soon, however, he fell under the influence of the intolerant Ambrose. The bishop's ability to control the emperor first became clear in an incident involving the mistreatment of Jews in the east. In A.D. 388, some trouble-making monks in a city on the Euphrates destroyed a synagogue at the instigation of the local bishop, contrary to an Imperial decree protecting such buildings. When Theodosius ordered the bishop to pay for the rebuilding of the synagogue, Ambrose was outraged, arguing that to do so would result in the loss of God's favor. Theodosius first modified his order to have the whole community pay for the repair, but this was not good enough for Ambrose, who demanded that nothing should be done for the repair. The emperor gave in. In A.D. 390, the emperor was subordinated even further to the bishop. In Thessalonica, the local garrison consisted mainly of Goths, who had bad relations with the local inhabitants, and during a riot some Gothic officers were murdered and their corpses abused. In retaliation, Theodosius sent another Gothic garrison to the town, and during some chariot races the gates to the hippodrome were closed and a massacre of the spectators instituted as vengeance. When Ambrose heard of this, he was again outraged, and in effect excommunicated the emperor, denying him access to Church rites. In atonement, Theodosius removed his Imperial attire and moped about in a church as a miserable penitent for some months before Ambrose agreed to give him the sacraments again at Christmas. Such a spectacle of an emperor abasing himself before a religious figure was unprecedented and must have given pagans (and even some Christians) a bad impression. Theodosius was now totally under the thrall of Ambrose and began a full-scale assault on pagan practice. In A.D. 391, all sacrifice, whether public or private, was banned by law, and the temples of the old gods were officially closed. The next year, all forms of pagan religious worship were formally prohibited.

In A.D. 391, Theodosius returned to Constantinople. He left the young Valentinian II under the care of the Germanic general Arbogast, who was the supreme military commander in the west. Arbogast was to control the government, while Valentinian II was reduced in status to a mere figurehead. Arbogast was the first in a long series of Germanic commanders whose control of the military held the real power but who could not assume the title of emperor themselves because of their barbarian origin and ruled in the name of figurehead emperor. Valentinian II not surprisingly resented this situation, and in May of A.D. 392, he was found hanged. Arbogast claimed it was suicide, but he himself was suspected of murder (though it is hard to see how he could have profited from getting rid of Valentinian II). Arbogast sent the body to Milan for burial and protested his innocence. He got no clear response from the east and in August proclaimed a man called Eugenius as Augustus (Arbogast's failure to act swiftly to replace Valentinian II seems to prove his innocence of murder). Eugenius was a middle-ranking civilian administrator and a moderate Christian; Arbogast presumably picked him as someone unobjectionable whom he could manipulate.

Eugenius tried to get recognition from Theodosius, but by the spring of A.D. 393, it was clear that this was not forthcoming, and he invaded Italy. At first Eugenius (i.e., Arbogast) was circumspect in his response to a senatorial petition asking him to restore state support for pagan cults in Rome. After two requests, he merely granted private funding, but once a showdown with Theodosius was inevitable, he sought enthusiastic pagan support by revoking all the antipagan laws of Theodosius, and pagans in Rome enthusiastically restored the old rites. Needless to say, Ambrose did not approve and excommunicated Eugenius.

Now Theodosius prepared for a religious war. In A.D. 394, he marched on Italy from the Balkans. By late August, the two forces met by the river Frigidus near Aquileia, and battle was joined in early September. Eugenius' forces at first fought well, but then a strong wind blew into their faces, which assisted the forces of Theodosius, who thus apparently won through the intervention of God. Once more Theodosius was sparing in his victory. Nonetheless, the antipagan laws were now fully enforced in Rome. Although pagan senators continued to exist for another generation, now that the gods had abandoned their defenders, the adoption of Christianity by the Roman aristocracy began to be completed. Some old curmudgeons would hold out for a few more decades, but the days of the old gods were numbered and their influence was minimal.

Before starting the campaign, Theodosius had supposedly heard the prophecy that he would win the war but die in Italy. So it was: he fell ill and died in January of A.D. 395. The Empire was divided between his two worthless sons, and its unity would never be restored.

24

DEMISE OF THE EMPIRE IN THE WEST,
A.D. 395–A.D. 476

The Christian Empire of the fourth century A.D. had been reasonably successful at maintaining the military situation established by Constantine. Despite
disasters like Adrianople, the frontiers had been held and an effective army
fielded. At the same time, although usurpation was not completely prevented,
the dynastic instabilities of the third century A.D. were not repeated. To
some extent, this comparative stability can be ascribed to the field armies
that Constantine had established. These not only survived as an effective
weapon against external aggression, but also thwarted the ability of regional
commanders to go into revolt.

The new military arrangement was not without its disadvantages, however.
It was apparently difficult to find sufficient troops for the new armies. The
data necessary for determining the true demographic situation is lacking, but
it would seem that the population, in the Western half of the Empire at any
rate, was in actual decline, and in any case there was a strong disinclination
on the part of the landowners to provide recruits for the army.[1] There was
a general tendency to convert the recruits who were to be collected through
the capitation system into cash payments that could then be used to pay for
Germanic recruits. Not only did Germans serve in the army in large numbers
from the time of Constantine, but at the same time German officers became
increasingly influential. After the defeat at Adrianople the custom began of
not simply enrolling Germans into Roman military units but of allowing
contingents of allied Germans to serve under their own leadership alongside

---

1 Through the capitation system, the obligation was placed on landowners to present a
certain number of recruits from among the tenants registered on their land, and since
young adult males were a fixed part of the landowners' capital and in part determined
their tax liability, they were extremely reluctant to part with the sort of tenants most
suited to military service.

the Roman units. This Germanization of the army intensified in the west after the heavy losses suffered at Frigidus that could not be replaced from Roman recruitment. Starting from the end of the fourth century A.D., Hunnish troops also came to be used in large numbers in Roman armies. The result was that in the fifth century, supreme military power came to be held by those who could control these various foreign elements.

This large military establishment cost large amounts of money, and the administrative reforms of Diocletian and Constantine were aimed at providing the necessary funds. This, too, had unintended consequences. The old administrators of the Principate were probably no more honest than those of Late Antiquity, but their lighter duties offered much less scope for corruption. The coercive administrative procedures of the Christian Empire, on the other hand, called for much greater interference in the lives of the civilian population, which provided greater opportunities for the administrators to use their powers to extract money from the populace. Those in the best position to resist the demands of the state were the wealthiest landowners, and the west saw in the fourth century A.D. the steady withdrawal of those hugely wealthy men from the civic life of the Empire. The hereditary members of the senate contributed little to the state apart from some conspicuous and infrequent expenditures in connection with office holding in Rome. The pattern is repeated in the cities, where the less powerful members of the decurion class were saddled with burdens, as the wealthier ones tended to stay on their estates. At the same time, these wealthy landowners would take over increasing amounts of land previously held by smallholders, either through outright sale or by offering to take the smallholders under their patronage, protecting them against the state's demands but at the same time assuming control of their land. This is a process that is characteristic of the west. In the east, where the senatorial aristocracy was of much more recent origin and never attained the dominance in landholding that their western counterparts achieved, it was military officers who took the peasantry under their patronage against the state.

One might wonder how such defiance of public authority could have taken place at the time when the Imperial administration was ostensibly more autocratic than in the past. Fundamentally, the emperor could exercise power only through his subordinates, and the increasingly coercive claims of the state had the ironic effect of lessening Imperial control. Real power was exercised by the civil Imperial officials, who were for the most part drawn from the landowning class and found it more natural and practical to connive with the wealthiest landowners than to carry out their duties in some theoretically even-handed way. The result was that as the wealthy continued to avoid paying taxes, the burdens increased on those who did not have the necessary influence to do so, which, in turn, heightened the pressures on the smallholders to seek the protection of their wealthier neighbors. The perverse result of the fourth-century tax system was to increase the economic dominance of the wealthy and assist them in withstanding the demands of the government. This situation was particularly characteristic of the west and would contribute to the surprisingly swift disappearance of Imperial government within three generations of the permanent division of the Empire upon the death of Theodosius. Circumstances in the eastern half of the Empire would allow it to survive.

The breakdown in Imperial authority that took place in the fifth century A.D. began with the division of the Empire between Theodosius' feckless sons upon his death in A.D. 395. While Theodosius' son Honorius became a boy-emperor in the west, his eighteen-year-old son Arcadius became emperor in the east. Like his brother, Arcadius was rather a nonentity, doing little in his own right and having importance merely through the fact that various factions could acquire or lose power through his support or disapproval. He was generally under the sway of some individual. These men and their equally ineffectual descendants would exercise no leadership while Germanic invasions led to the loss of control over much of the Empire in the first decades of the fifth century A.D.

The man who sets the pattern for warlords who dominate emperors is a half-German named Stilicho. In the late A.D. 380s, Theodosius rewarded him for successful negotiations with the Persians by giving him his niece and adoptive daughter as his wife, and Theodosius took Stilicho with him on the campaign against Eugenius, while leaving a commander named Rufinus in charge as praetorian praefect in Constantinople. Upon the death of Theodosius, Stilicho claimed that Theodosius had enjoined him to act as the guardian of both his sons, and this was resisted in the east by those who controlled Arcadius in Constantinople. Stilicho engineered the assassination of Rufinus, but this did him no good as Arcadius soon fell under the sway of a eunuch called Eutropius. It is indicative of the extent to which the sons of Theodosius failed to exercise real power that such a person could act in an official capacity (eunuchs were considered socially unacceptable). Stilicho's policies are hard to divine. We have much information about him from the poet Claudian, whose sycophantic works are highly biased in his favor, while sources written after Stilicho's downfall are hostile. In the absence of any information from Stilicho himself, it is hard to choose between interpretations that see him as making a legitimate effort to strengthen the Empire to the extent that the military situation allowed on the one hand and those that view him as a man without any long-range plans whose sole aim was to increase his own power on the other. Stilicho constantly claimed to be the guardian of both emperors and seems to have been fixated on establishing his authority in the east, even if this meant poor relations between the two halves of the Empire and the neglect of the defenses of western Europe.

A major problem facing Stilicho was the dissatisfaction of the Visigoths under their king Alaric. These Goths had formed a major element in the force that Theodosius had led against Eugenius, and they felt that at the battle of the Frigidus they had suffered inordinate losses because they had been intentionally exposed to danger in order to save the Roman troops and weaken the Goths. They withdrew to the Balkans while the rest of the field army was still in Italy, and in A.D. 395, they went into open revolt. Stilicho led the field army against them, and was supposedly on the point of defeating them when the eastern government selfishly requested the return of its troops. This is the first of a number of occasions when the contemporary sources present Stilicho as allegedly being thwarted from vanquishing the Goths or intentionally refraining from doing so in order to preserve them as a source of recruits. One might view this interpretation with skepticism and see his actions as reflecting either incompetence as a general or an inability to control his army. The sources do not allow a clear assessment of his goals or methods, but what is clear is that despite numerous campaigns against the Goths, he never did more than contain them.

During A.D. 396, the Visigoths marauded unchecked in Greece. The next year Stilicho returned to the Balkans but again he abandoned the campaign without victory, perhaps because a revolt broke out in Africa (it was suppressed within a year). Meanwhile, in A.D. 397, Alaric was apparently given a position as a Roman general after Stilicho's withdrawal from the Balkans. In A.D. 398, Stilicho further strengthened his position by marrying his daughter to Honorius.

Meanwhile, in A.D. 398, the Roman east was invaded by Huns from the Caucasus, and the eunuch Eutropius led a successful campaign against them. There is no evidence as to his official capacity, but it is indicative of the impotence of Arcadius and the now isolated position of the emperor that a eunuch should exercise authority so openly, receiving the consulship of A.D. 399 as a reward. That year saw a resolution in the east of the threat to the Imperial government by the dominance of Germans in the army. In an attempt to seize control of the government, Gainas, the German general who had effected the assassination of Rufinus for Stilicho, gained control of Constantinople temporarily, and Eutropius fell from power. As the events in Thessalonica under Theodosius had shown, the population of the east was hostile to the Germans, and when for unknown reasons the Germans decided to quit the capital, a riot broke out and a large number were killed. The survivors were wiped out by a loyal Gothic commander when they tried to cross over to Asia Minor. While the Germanic troops continued to be important in the east, they were replaced in positions of importance in the administration, and it would be a long time before they threatened the east again.

For some reason, in the aftermath of Gainas' downfall, Alaric, who had been quiescent since A.D. 397 and used his official position to equip his Goths with weaponry, decided to seek territory in the west. In the fall of A.D. 401, Alaric seized the opportunity to invade northern Italy while Stilicho was distracted with an invasion of Raetia and Noricum by Vandals. Honorius was in Milan, which Alaric put under siege. Stilicho in the meanwhile not only threw back the Vandals but received troops from them for his campaign against Alaric. In the winter of A.D. 402, he forced Alaric to lift the siege of Milan and withdraw to Pollentia to the west. There, a hotly contested battle was fought on Easter. No one achieved victory but the Goths abandoned their camp and Stilicho captured Alaric's family. The Goths now agreed to retire to the northeastern border of Italy, but invaded again in A.D. 403. Stilicho defeated them again at Verona, and they agreed to withdraw to the territory between Dalmatia and Pannonia, where they would be ready to aid him in any attempt to establish control over the eastern government. If Stilicho was intentionally refraining from finishing off the Goths in order to preserve them as a military resource, his reasoning was purely selfish.

During this period, the Roman civil administration upon the mid Danube continued to exist, but large amounts of land were held by Ostrogoths, Huns and other tribes. In late A.D. 405, a horde mainly consisting of Ostrogoths fell upon Italy. Stilicho's field army was sufficiently small that, in order to deal with this invasion, he had to summon Roman troops from the Rhine frontier and hire Hunnish troops from across the Danube. By late summer of A.D. 406, Stilicho finally managed to wipe out their scattered bands.

A side effect of this victory was disaster in northwestern Europe. On the last day of A.D. 406, vast numbers of invaders poured across the river into Gaul, where Roman control was never to be fully restored. Instead of dealing with this situation, Stilicho apparently decided to abandon Gaul to its fate while he continued his vendetta against the east. In A.D. 407, he was preparing to seize control of Illyricum, hoping to take advantage of an ecclesiastical dispute to further his ends. In A.D. 398, John Chrysostom, an eloquent preacher, had become bishop (patriarch) of Constantinople, but being a tactless man, he had on several occasions upbraided the eastern emperor Arcadius' wife in public. The upshot was that, in A.D. 404, he was deposed and exiled, and Stilicho seized upon this as grounds for interference in the affairs of Constantinople. When demands for his restoration were ignored, Stilicho actually cut off trade with the east. Although Chrysostom died in A.D. 407, Stilicho decided to champion his cause as an excuse to establish control over the east. Stilicho's campaign was cut short, however, both by erroneous news that Alaric had died and correct news that a usurper had arisen in the west in the aftermath of the collapse of the Rhine frontier. While Stilicho was apparently prepared to abandon the west to the barbarians, he could not tolerate a threat to his emperor's authority.

In A.D. 408, Alaric decided to invade Italy once more. Apparently he felt threatened by the eastern government and concluded that the west was not in a position to resist. After advancing into northern Italy, he demanded 4,000 pounds of gold as recompense for his efforts on behalf of Honorius, and Stilicho induced a reluctant senate to agree. In the meanwhile, however, Arcadius died in the east and was succeeded by his seven-year-old son Theodosius II, and Stilicho was once more distracted by his obsession with establishing his authority in Constantinople. (Since the east was comparatively peaceful under Theodosius II while the corresponding period in the west is tumultuous, it would be best to concentrate on the dissolution of the authority of the western emperors under the western branch of the dynasty established by the elder Theodosius, and then return to the affairs of the east.) While he would himself go to Constantinople, Alaric was to be given authority to restore Honorius' power in Gaul. There was much discontent with the situation, and when Stilicho set off in August, a coup d'état was engineered by certain members of Honorius' retinue. When his supporters were murdered, Stilicho returned to investigate the situation (apparently confident of Honorius' goodwill) and submitted meekly to his own arrest. He was promptly executed, his motives in this incident being as unclear as his overall policy. The anti-German policy of the conspirators was implemented, large numbers of German troops being killed in Italy (the remnants fled to Alaric). As in the east, Germanic domination of the government was checked, but the western government's reliance on Germanic troops continued.

In the fall after Stilicho's death, Alaric resumed his invasion of Italy and actually besieged Rome. Supposedly the pagans suggested that sacrifice to the gods was called for and gained the approval of the bishop of Rome for secret sacrifice, but no one was willing to do so openly. In any case, Alaric agreed to withdraw after receiving a vast ransom that necessitated stripping the gods of their dedications and retired northwards into Etruria. Honorius agreed to the terms and was to negotiate a permanent settlement. Alaric demanded all the western Balkans, but the emperor proved recalcitrant in his stronghold at Ravenna and refused to grant either Alaric an Imperial office or the Goths land. Though Alaric moderated his demands, Honorius again refused, and Alaric returned to the offensive in late A.D. 409. Capturing the port of Rome, he proclaimed the praefect of the city Attalus as emperor and was in turn appointed praetorian praefect by him. Things seemed hopeless for Honorius, but at this point he received reinforcements from his nephew the new eastern emperor and decided to hold out in Ravenna. Meanwhile, Attalus and Alaric sent a force under Roman command to seize Africa, which was essential to Rome's grain supply, but this effort failed. With the grain cut off, Rome became desperate, and the senate was willing to authorize Alaric to seize Africa himself, something that Attalus had opposed. Now, in the summer of A.D. 410, Attalus abdicated and was pardoned by Honorius but remained with Alaric in his camp to the north of Rome. At this point, a rival Visigoth attacked Alaric, who assumed Honorius' complicity and again marched on Rome. The weary city was captured on August 24 and sacked for two or three days. Although Rome was of little military significance, the event shocked the Roman world. The pagans took the sack of the old Imperial capital as a sign that the gods were displeased with the prohibition against sacrifice. When Rome was sacked again forty-five years later, the stature of the Imperial government had sunk so low that no one would pay much attention. Within days, Alaric marched south with the intention of invading Africa, but a storm destroyed the ships that had been gathered for this purpose. Late in the year, Alaric died and was succeeded as king by his brother-in-law Athaulf, who led the Visigoths to Gaul.

In the meanwhile, as Stilicho remained fixated on the goal of taking over the east, he allowed western Europe to slip out of control. At the end of A.D. 406, the Vandals, Suebi, and Alans crossed the Rhine in force, after the Franks, who served as Roman federates, had unsuccessfully attempted to block them; the Burgundians and Alemanni then followed in their wake. The details are not preserved, but the bands of invaders spread all over Gaul, plundering at will since Stilicho had removed the Roman field troops for his own purposes. During A.D. 407, two usurpers were quickly raised up and done away with in Britain, but then a soldier named Constantine gained permanent control of the military there as emperor and crossed over to the mainland, where the remaining Roman forces went over to him. While Constantine engaged in poorly attested campaigns against the barbarians, an attack from Italy to restore Honorius' authority failed, and Constantine took over Spain. In A.D. 409, Honorius was in such dire straits that he actually recognized Constantine as Augustus, but soon he not only repudiated this recognition but also rejected Constantine's offer of assistance against Alaric. In late A.D. 409, the invaders crossed over into Spain, and when Constantine tried to sack Gerontius, his commander there, Gerontius proclaimed a certain Maximus as emperor. By A.D. 411, Gerontius had invaded Gaul, besieging Constantine in Arles.

At this point, Honorius dispatched to Gaul a man who would dominate events for a decade. Constantius was a Roman from the Balkans and he was the first man to assume control of the western military with the title "patrician," which would mark out the supreme military commander for the rest of the century. Upon Constantius' arrival in Gaul, Gerontius withdrew back to Spain, where mutinous troops murdered him. Meanwhile, Constantius continued the siege of Arles, and Constantine surrendered after the defeat of a relief army that he had summoned from the Alemanni and Franks. Honorius violated his guarantee of Constantine's life and had him executed in retaliation for his own killing of certain relatives of Honorius.

Constantius returned to Italy, but the Burgundians and Alans raised up a new puppet emperor (Jovinus) on the Rhine. Under rather mysterious circumstances, Athaulf led the Visigoths out of Italy and marched toward Jovinus in A.D. 412, taking with him the ex-emperor Attalus and Galla Placidia, Honorius' half-sister who was being held as a hostage. If Athaulf meant to offer his services to Jovinus, the latter was unreceptive, and Athaulf moved against him in the name of Honorius. By late A.D. 413, Jovinus was crushed, but the Burgundians, who had supported him, were confirmed in their possession of Upper Germany as federates. This recognition of a Germanic kingdom on Roman territory was the first step in the permanent alienation of Gaul from Imperial control. The subsequent fate of Britain is completely unknown. Presumably, Imperial government was to some extent restored there, but by later in the century it disappeared.[2]

The year A.D. 413 saw Constantius distracted with a revolt in Africa. There, Heraclian, the man who had repelled Attalus' invasion in A.D. 410, went into revolt and invaded Italy by fleet. Soon defeated, he fled back to Africa, where he was abandoned and executed. Constantius' supremacy in Italy was now secure. As part of his agreement to crush Jovinus, Athaulf was to be provided with grain by the Imperial government, but the revolt in Africa prevented this. As a result, he went into revolt and seized southern Gaul. Both Honorius and Constantius were anxious to get Galla Placidia back (Constantius was apparently in love with her), but Athaulf prevailed upon her to marry him in January of A.D. 414. It is reported that at the wedding Athaulf stated that whereas previously he had intended to destroy Roman power, he was now minded to restore it through the infusion of Germanic vigor. Whether or not he really said these words, they do reflect the fact that the Germanic forces invading the populous sections of the Empire would reach accommodations with the Roman inhabitants; this process would eventually lead to the end of Imperial rule in the territories occupied by the Germans and the increasing restriction of the authority of the western emperors to Italy. In any case, Honorius was not receptive to his new brother-in-law, who restored Attalus to Imperial power – it was still not considered conceivable for a Germanic king to rule in his own name without a Roman acting as a figurehead with the title of "emperor." This attitude would also eventually change.

---

2 In the A.D. 440s, the local inhabitants petitioned the Imperial government for help against Germanic invasion, but by then the emperors were in no position to render assistance to a distant place like Britain. The island was left to its own fate, and the part that is now England was soon overrun by the Germanic Angles and Saxons from northwestern Germany.

Constantius cut off supplies to southern Gaul, which forced Athaulf to cross the Pyrenees into northwestern Spain. (Attalus was abandoned and, after being captured, was mutilated at Constantius' order to make him unacceptable as an emperor.[3]) Athaulf was assassinated in A.D. 415 in connection with a feud and after some disturbances was succeeded by Wallia. The Romans continued to withhold supplies by sea, and Wallia decided to move south and cross over into Africa. When his fleet was destroyed by storm at the Straits of Gibraltar in early A.D. 416, he decided to enter Roman service in return for supplies and returned Galla Placidia. Wallia spent two years subduing the Vandals, Suebi, and Alans in Spain, a task aided by Imperial diplomacy whose goal was to prevent their mutual cooperation. The Imperial government decided that after the Visigoths' victory, they should receive a kingdom in southwestern Gaul. The Roman landowners retained one-third of their property, while the rest was given over to the Germans (later settlements saw the proportions reversed). Here was a second step in the alienation of Gaul. The invaders in Spain had been defeated but not overwhelmed or removed, however, and after the Visigoths' departure, they continued causing trouble. In early A.D. 422, the Vandals moved to the south of the province, in the process inflicting a major defeat on a Roman general who had been sent from Italy to restore order.

As part of his agreement with Honorius in A.D. 416, Wallia returned Galla Placidia, who was prevailed upon to marry the patrician Constantius the following year. Galla Placidia promptly bore him a daughter, and in A.D. 419 gave birth to a son named Valentinian, who was the natural choice as heir to the childless Honorius. In A.D. 421, Honorius finally gave his reluctant approval to the appointment of Constantius as Augustus, a step that was not recognized in Constantinople. Constantius soon fell ill, however, and died before the end of the year. A rift then arose between Honorius and Galla Placidia, who fled with her children to her nephew Theodosius II in the east in A.D. 423. Within a few months Honorius, whose long reign had seen virtually no positive action on his part and a monumental collapse of Roman authority in the west, ceased to exist.

Upon the death of Honorius, a middle-level civilian administrator named John was proclaimed Augustus at Ravenna, presumably by those opposed to Galla Placidia. John at first tried to secure recognition from Theodosius II in Constantinople, but this failed. In A.D. 424, Valentinian was proclaimed Caesar in Thessalonica, while an army was being collected from the east to install him in the west. In the following year, an invasion fleet was wrecked

---

3 The notion had arisen that the emperor had to be physically fit; in the medieval Byzantine period, deposed emperors were routinely blinded rather than murdered, since such mutilation was thought to render them unfit for restoration.

by a storm, but John hesitated to attack the land force while he awaited the arrival of a force of Huns. Quick action against John resulted in his capture and execution. Thousands of Huns showed up too late but were given money and sent back home. Valentinian, now six years old, was proclaimed Augustus in October.

Valentinian III was raised as emperor by his indulgent mother and became just as useless as his uncles Honorius and Arcadius, though much less is known about him as a personality (he does not seem to have been as religiously minded as his cousin Theodosius II). His thirty-year reign would see steady progress in the dissolution of the western half of the Empire. For the first twelve years of his reign, he was dominated by his mother Galla Placidia. Though she could control the person of the emperor, she could not command armies, and those that she appointed as patrician (commander-in-chief) held an extremely important position. The two military officials who dominated the scene were Boniface and Aëtius. While Boniface had supported Valentinian III during the usurpation of John, it was Aëtius whom John had sent to fetch assistance from the Huns. Aëtius' father had been a general of Theodosius I, and he himself had become a familiar of Rugila the king of the Huns while a Roman hostage at the Hunnish court. Aëtius received a pardon after the defeat of John, but it is not surprising that for all his military talents, Aëtius was not much liked at the court of Valentinian III. Nonetheless, Aëtius was a competent military figure and to the extent that the Imperial government maintained itself in Gaul and Italy during the reign of Valentinian III, this must be attributed to Aëtius.

Aëtius first demonstrated his competence against the Visigoths in southwestern Gaul. They had never really abided by their agreement with the Romans and whenever possible sought to expand the territory under their control. In the late A.D. 420s under king Theoderic (who had succeeded Wallia in A.D. 418), they tried to take over the Mediterranean shore, and Aëtius won a reputation for himself by raising the siege of Arles in A.D. 427. After more hostilities, peace was concluded in A.D. 430, the Goths being confined to the territory originally granted to Wallia.

Meanwhile, trouble was being caused by the Salian Franks, who had been settled in on the Roman side of the lower Rhine since the days of Julian. They, too, attempted to expand their territory in the A.D. 420s, and Aëtius defeated them in A.D. 428. Though pacified, they do seem to have been allowed to expand their territory and continued to serve as federate allies of the Imperial government. In A.D. 429, Aëtius used his prestige as victor in Gaul (and probably his control of the loyalty of Hunnish troops) to secure an appointment as patrician (murdering his predecessor the following year). Galla Placidia also needed the services of Aëtius against her erstwhile supporter Boniface, who was now in revolt in Africa.

Boniface had been appointed as the local military commander in Africa once Valentinian III's rule was established in Italy, but the court at Ravenna grew suspicious of his intentions. When he refused a summons to return to Italy, an army was sent against him in A.D. 427, but he defeated it. In the following year, another army was sent under a Goth, who did better, capturing the important towns of Carthage and Hippo Regius. At this point, Boniface decided to seek help from the Vandals, who had been in southern Spain since A.D. 423. The king of the Vandals was a man named Gaiseric, who proved to be not only an able military commander but also a capable politician and intriguer. Boniface proposed to split North Africa with Gaiseric if he would bring his people across the Straits of Gibraltar. Gaiseric agreed and in May of A.D. 429 brought over all 80,000 of his people. The Vandals immediately began to plunder Mauretania (more or less modern Algeria) in brutal fashion, proving to be much more unpleasant than the Goths had been. Many people, including bishops, fled before them. In particular, like many other Germanic tribes, the Vandals had converted to the Arian form of Christianity under Constantius II and thus they were bitterly hostile to the Catholic locals.

Realizing that any hope of retaining Africa, which supplied the grain for Rome, depended on Boniface, Galla Placidia quickly came to terms with him. Gaiseric decided to capture the rich province of proconsular Africa[4] and besieged Boniface in Hippo for more than a year (mid–A.D. 430 to mid–A.D. 431). The siege was ended by the arrival of a new army from Italy, but after this army had joined forces with Boniface, they suffered a disastrous defeat at the hands of the Vandals. The next year Boniface returned to Italy, and in the meanwhile the Vandals secured their territory in Numidia, to the immediate west of the proconsular province. Aëtius was now in control in Italy, and being occupied with new troubles in Gaul decided to negotiate with Gaiseric. In A.D. 435, an agreement was made on the basis of the territorial division at the time: while the Imperial government kept proconsular Africa, Gaiseric retained Numidia and Mauretania.

Gaiseric had no intention of honoring his agreement and continued with his attempts to conquer proconsular Africa. Finally, in A.D. 439, he took Carthage, and while he gathered a fleet, Italy prepared for invasion. Aware of this, Gaiseric decided to invade Sicily instead in A.D. 440. The next year the government in Constantinople, which feared Gaiseric's piratical policy, sent an invasion fleet to Africa. Gaiseric decided to negotiate, and while he dragged things out, an invasion by the Huns forced the eastern government to abandon its planned attack. Both emperors now had to submit to Gaiseric's terms, and the territorial division was reversed. The Empire retained Mauretania and

---

4 That is, the original province of Africa that had been established in 146 B.C. and that under the Empire was one of the two senatorial provinces governed by an ex-consul.

western Numidia, while Gaiseric received the rest of Numidia and procon-sular Africa, one of the wealthiest provinces. In addition, Gaiseric's son was betrothed to a daughter of Valentinian III.

The Vandals, unlike other Germanic tribes, came to no accommodations with the local Romans. Gaiseric decided to maintain his power by having noth-ing to do with the native aristocracy, and all Roman ways were rejected. The landowners were expelled and the Catholic Church persecuted. The Vandals would maintain themselves in Africa until Justinian reconquered the area more than a century later.

Back in Italy, when Galla Placidia recalled Boniface from Africa in A.D. 432, she transferred the title of patrician from Aëtius to him, but Aëtius refused to comply, and a civil war between their forces broke out. At a battle fought near Ariminum in northern Italy, Boniface emerged victorious but soon died. His son took over his position but was promptly dislodged by Aëtius, who had previously sought refuge with his friend Rugila, the king of the Huns, and with his help was restored to power in A.D. 434. In A.D. 437, Valentinian III went to marry Theodosius II's daughter and presumably was now considered an adult, but Aëtius' position was so strong that his son was betrothed to the daughter of Valentinian III's new marriage.

The loss of Imperial control in the northwest continued unabated. In A.D. 435, Aëtius was called back to Gaul, where the Burgundians invaded across the lower Rhine (this is what caused him to come to terms with the Vandals). Not having enough troops to spare any for Gaul, Aëtius asked for assistance from his friends the Huns. They obliged and overwhelmed the Burgundian kingdom (the remaining Burgundians were later settled near Savoy in northern Italy in A.D. 443). Meanwhile, the Visigoths under Theoderic were up to their old knavish tricks. In A.D. 436–437, a drawn-out campaign was fought with them, though eventually peace was restored. At the same time, the natives in central Gaul, who had gotten little enough out of the Imperial government, revolted and had to be suppressed.

In the early decades of the century, the Huns had established control over the tribes of eastern Europe, and the policy of Theodosius II to provide them with an annual subsidy had kept them quiet in the A.D. 430s and 440s (see pp. 345–346). The subsidies ended with the death of Theodosius II in A.D. 450, and instead of attacking Theodosius' less accommodating successor, king Attila of the Huns decided to turn his attention to the west, aided by astonishing circumstances. Valentinian III had an older sister called Honoria, who, unlike her indolent brother, was intelligent, forceful, and energetic. After a botched plan to get rid of her brother, she was to be forced into a marriage she did not want. She sent a eunuch with her ring (as a sign of reliability) and money to Attila to request his aid. Attila decided to consider this a marriage proposal, and sent word to Valentinian III that he should turn over Honoria to Attila with half of the territory of the western empire as her dowry! Galla Placidia barely managed to get Valentinian III to agree grudgingly to spare his sister. Meanwhile, when consulted for advice, the craven Theodosius II suggested that Valentinian III should comply, which he refused to do.

In early A.D. 451, Attila invaded Gaul with a huge army, apparently in cooperation with Gaiseric. Aëtius took such troops as he could muster, and enlisted the help of the Franks and Burgundians, as well as the Celtics of central Gaul. The attitude of the Visigoths was uncertain at first, but Theoderic eventually brought troops as well. When this "Roman" army approached, the Huns decided to withdraw from central Gaul, and the Romans caught up with them at a battle generally known as "Chalons-sur-Marne." After much hard fighting, in which Theoderic died, the Huns were pushed back to their camp. The next day, they were allowed to depart, and Aëtius broke up his army by persuading the Germans to return home. He had no desire to destroy the Huns, since part of his influence rested on his ability to manage them. This battle is often considered a great victory in the defense of western Europe against the nomads from Asia, but it is unlikely that a victory by Attila would have had any more lasting consequence than his earlier defeats of the eastern half of the Empire had.

In A.D. 452, the Huns returned, this time to invade Italy. After destroying Aquileia (which never recovered), they moved towards Rome, but an outbreak of plague and shortage of food caused them to retire. The next year Attila died while consummating a wedding, and none of his sons proved capable of replacing him. His Germanic allies revolted and defeated the Huns in A.D. 454.

By now Aëtius' control of Valentinian III was total, and the emperor resented it. This was played upon by a wealthy and prominent senator called Petronius Maximus, who also resented Aëtius' influence and persuaded Valentinian III that Aëtius was a threat to the throne. During an interview about a financial matter, Valentinian III accused the unarmed Aëtius of treason, and the emperor and another conspirator murdered him there and then (September of A.D. 454). It was snidely remarked at the time that Valentinian III had cut off his right hand with his left. Maximus got no benefit from this plot, as others convinced Valentinian that it was no use to replace one Aëtius with another. Maximus sought vengeance against Valentinian by conspiring with two Germanic retainers of Aëtius who also enjoyed the confidence of Valentinian. On March 16, 455, they killed him and the eunuch opposed to Petronius, bringing him the Imperial diadem. In the male line, the house of Theodosius was now dead in the west.

This is a convenient place to return to the eastern branch of the Theodosian dynasty. When Arcadius died in A.D. 408, he was succeeded by his seven-year-old son Theodosius II. All the children of Arcadius had been raised as very devout Christians: Theodosius' four sisters resolved to remain virgins, and the emperor himself was more interested in piety and theology than in government. He was soon content to let his older sister Pulcheria have her way (later others would dominate him). It was lucky for the eastern empire that his reign did not experience the same sort of crises as were going on at that time in the west. At first the government was controlled by Anthemius, the praetorian praefect. He seems to have been an able character, who reached an agreement with the Persians, repelled an invasion of the Huns on the Danube, attempted to restore order in the Balkans, instituted a major remission of tax arrears, and built a great wall that included the northern suburbs of Constantinople and made the city virtually invulnerable for a millennium. He also restored good relations with the west after the downfall of Stilicho.

A notable event in Theodosius II's comparatively peaceful reign is the publication of a collection of Imperial decisions. In the time of Diocletian, two collections of Imperial decisions had been made, and in A.D. 429 Theodosius II resolved that a new collection of the constitutions issued by Constantine and later emperors be made. The task took nine years, and the resulting Theodosian Code, issued in A.D. 438, is preserved today. While the code is by no means a full compilation, the laws contained in it are an important historical source for administrative policy of the fourth and early fifth centuries A.D.

Under Theodosius II, new religious controversies showed once again how much trouble could be caused by the principle that the state was to suppress doctrinal deviation if there was considerable disagreement about which doctrines were orthodox. In the years after the rejection of Arianism at the Council of Constantinople in A.D. 381, the Nicene Creed had gained general acceptance as the orthodox formulation, while support for Arianism faded away, but two new doctrines arose in the early fifth century A.D. to challenge the orthodox position about the trinity. The problem now was the relationship not of Christ and God the Father but of the human and divine elements in Christ. In the west (once again), there was not much dispute. The idea that there were two natures ("substances") in Christ, one human, one divine, was accepted without much difficulty. The logical problems of this proposition led to controversy in the east.

On the one hand, there arose in Antioch the doctrine that the person of Christ was fully human and that this humanity remained distinct even as Christ was "conjoined" with divinity. This doctrine came to be particularly associated with Nestorius the patriarch of Antioch and is known as "Nestorianism."[5] At the same time a rather different conception arose in

---

5 The bishops of five cities – Alexandria, Antioch, Jerusalem, Rome, and Constantinople – came to be recognized as having a preeminent position in the Church hierarchy for various historical reasons and were termed "patriarchs." The Arab conquests

Alexandria as part of the attack on Arianism. This view started with the premise that it was impossible for the perfect human and perfect god to exist at the same time in one body and argued that in the person of Christ the divine element completely supplanted the human. This doctrine is called monophysitism ("one-nature-ism") and came to be widely held in Alexandria. The patriarchs of Antioch and Alexandria supported the views associated with their cities, and the doctrinal dispute was combined with rival claims to authority within the Church. Patriarch Cyril of Alexandria was by far the better schemer, and at the Council of Ephesus in A.D. 431 Nestorius was outmaneuvered and exiled. Though Nestorianism was for the most part stamped out in the Empire, it was the only form of Christianity tolerated in the Persian empire, and from there spread into central Asia as far as China.

With the downfall of Nestorius, the dominance of the Alexandrian Church in the eastern half of the Empire was assured, and this was fully realized in A.D. 449 when another council was held in Ephesus. Its decisions were determined by Dioscorus the patriarch of Alexandria, who brought about the deposition of some bishops who adhered to the western notion of the coexistence of two natures (divine and human) in Christ. This result was considered outrageous in the west, but when the western Imperial family complained to Theodosius II, he took no notice. He was under the influence of a eunuch who supported Dioscorus, and his sister Pulcheria, who opposed the Alexandrian position, could do nothing. Following the death of Theodosius II, however, she would overthrow the victory of the monophysite doctrine.

Although the devout Theodosius II was willing to assert his will in theological matters, he showed rather less determination in military affairs. The major source of trouble during his reign was the Huns. The Huns were a nomadic Mongol people from the steppes of central Asia, and included within their group others that they had subordinated to themselves, including both Turkic and Germanic tribes. Like many others from this region, the Huns were naturally prone to falling into separate groups that would be united temporarily by a charismatic leader. Since the late fourth century A.D., the Huns had been an important power in southern Russia and the area north of the lower Danube. Their arrival forced the Germanic tribes westwards towards Roman territory, and they often provided troops for the Imperial government. An invasion by the Huns had been repelled at the start of his reign, but they were to be the major source of trouble for Theodosius II's government, which preferred to keep the peace with money.

of the seventh century marginalized the first three, while the bishops of Rome came to be designated by the distinctive title "pope" in recognition of their domination of the Church in medieval western Europe.

Around A.D. 425, the eastern government agreed to pay 350 pounds of gold per year to king Rugila, who to some degree united the Huns, and somewhat later the western government allowed them to reside in Pannonia. About ten years later, Rugila died and was succeeded by two nephews, one of whom was named Attila. At this point the eastern government came to a new agreement with the Huns, doubling their annual subsidy and agreeing not to assist those with whom the Huns were at war. For the next few years the Huns were kept busy attacking tribes to their east, but in A.D. 441 they took advantage of the fact that Imperial governments were engaged in conflict with both the Persians and the Vandals to attack the Balkans, seizing many cities and causing much destruction. Peace was again bought, through a humiliating agreement made in A.D. 443: the annual tribute was tripled, and a further 6,000 pounds of gold were to be paid immediately. The Romans were graciously allowed to ransom back Roman captives. (Such was the result of having an emperor who was more interested in theology than in ruling.) Soon after this peace, Attila found an excuse to have his brother executed, and with sole control of all the Huns and their allies, he was the most important man in Europe until his death in A.D. 453. In A.D. 447, he again invaded the Balkans, ranging as far as central Greece and Constantinople, and the following year Theodosius II agreed to grant the Huns a huge area in Roman territory along the middle Danube. The government continued to pay vast sums to him until the death of Theodosius II. The new emperor refused to pay the subsidy, but surprisingly enough, nothing much came of this. Presumably concluding that the easy pickings were over in the east, Attila decided to turn his attention to the western half of the Empire (see pp. 342–343).

When Theodosius II died in A.D. 450, there was no male heir. Theoretically his cousin Valentinian III could have claimed the east, but by now the eastern half of the empire was beginning to develop notions, especially religious ones, that were rather distinct from those of the west. It had been arranged before his death that Theodosius II was to be succeeded by a general named Marcian. This was apparently done with the cooperation of the emperor's aged (and virgin) sister Pulcheria, who agreed to marry Marcian, whose reign was a basically peaceful one. Rid of the vast expense of the subsidy to the Huns, he set about reducing taxes and repairing the Huns' depredations in the Balkans. His reign was later viewed as a sort of golden age. He died in A.D. 457 (Pulcheria having already died three years before), and with him the dynasty of Theodosius ceased to rule in the east.

The most notable act in Marcian's reign was the rejection of the monophysite views as the officially recognized doctrine in the east. Marcian and Pulcheria summoned a new council to Chalcedon in A.D. 451. Under heavy Imperial pressure, this council came up with a sort of compromise position that was fundamentally equivalent to the western doctrine and was considered obnoxious in Alexandria, where monophysitism lost none of its appeal. From then on, the Imperial government made strenuous but futile efforts to suppress monophysitism in Egypt, often resorting to military force in trying to impose Orthodox clergy. The Christians in Egypt were so alienated by the time of the Arab invasion in A.D. 640 that they preferred to be ruled by Moslems rather than by officials imposed by the Orthodox government in Constantinople.

When Marcian died in A.D. 457, there was no available male heir in either his own or the old Theodosian line, and the new emperor was determined by Aspar, the senior Germanic general, who was barred from assuming the position himself both by his ethnic origin and by his Arian faith. Aspar chose a middle level officer named Leo, who ruled until A.D. 474. Leo realized the difficulties inherent in such reliance on Germanic troops and set the stage for their removal by attempting to find a domestic source of hearty warriors, which he found in the Isaurians, a troublesome mountain-dwelling people in southwestern Asia Minor. Marrying his daughter to an Isaurian chieftain, who assumed the name Zeno, Leo used Zeno to counterbalance Aspar's desires to have his family wedded into the Imperial family. Finally, in A.D. 471, Aspar and his family were murdered. When Leo died in A.D. 474, Zeno's infant son succeeded to the throne. Zeno was then proclaimed Augustus, and though the infant emperor died a few months later, he ruled in his own right until A.D. 491. By that date, there was no longer an emperor in Rome.

It is now time to return to the situation in the west, where chaos ensued in the aftermath of the assassination of Valentinian III. Petronius Maximus got no benefit from his plot to overthrow Aëtius, as others convinced Valentinian III that it was no use to replace one Aëtius with another. Maximus sought vengeance against Valentinian III by inducing two Germanic retainers of Aëtius who also enjoyed the confidence of Valentinian III to assassinate the emperor in A.D. 455.[6] Petronius Maximus bribed his way to being accepted as emperor the day after the assassination, forcing Valentinian III's widow to marry him and betrothing the dead emperor's daughter to his own son. This churlish attempt to gain legitimacy from the family of the man he had just murdered did Maximus no good, as king Gaiseric of the Vandals seized the

---

6 This sort of feud arising from loyalty to a fallen leader is very characteristic of primitive Germanic custom (note the assassination of Athaulf: p. 339), and the fact that such attitudes could be manipulated to overthrow an emperor shows the dominant position held in the Imperial court by military men of Germanic origin. The main factor that gave warlords like Aëtius such prominence in the western half of the Empire in the fifth century A.D. was their ability to gain and retain the loyalty of such warriors (whether of Germanic or Hunnish origin).

opportunity to go on the offensive. In addition to occupying the part of Africa still in Imperial possession and Sardinia, he dispatched a fleet to Italy. When it landed near Rome in late May, everyone deserted Maximus, who was killed by a stone during a riot while fleeing Rome.

Three days later, the Vandals arrived in Rome, many people having already fled. The bishop of Rome met the invaders and persuaded them to refrain from murder. For the next fourteen days, they methodically ransacked the city (hence the modern term "vandalism" with its meaning of "pointless ruining of property" is not entirely correct). Along with their loot, they carted off Valentinian III's widow and her two daughters, one of whom married Gaiseric's son (her mother and sister were eventually sent to Constantinople).

When the death of Petronius Maximus became known in Gaul, the Visigothic king decided to proclaim as emperor a Gallic nobleman named Avitus, whom Maximus had appointed senior general in Gaul. (In this period, the Gauls seem to have become rather independent-minded towards the Imperial government in Italy – no Italian was appointed as senior military commander there). Avitus was recognized by Marcian, the eastern emperor, and in late A.D. 455 he crossed into Italy, where he received a tepid welcome. The only success of his short reign was the defeat of a Vandal invasion of Sicily by a force sent there under the command of a Germanic officer named Ricimer. The populace of Rome blamed Avitus for the famine caused by the Vandal seizure of Africa, and a riot ensued when he tried to take bronze tiles from public buildings to pay his Gothic troops. This forced Avitus to retreat toward Gaul, and the generals Ricimer and Majorian revolted. When Avitus was captured at Placentia, he was forced to abdicate and become bishop of the town (October of A.D. 456).

The man who decided the fate of the Imperial government in the west during its last days was Ricimer, who held supreme military command as had Stilicho and Aëtius. Related to the Visigothic royal family, he entered Roman service in his youth and rose in rank. As a man of Germanic origin, he was barred from becoming emperor himself, and unlike those other, earlier military figures, he had no weak member of the Theodosian dynasty in whose name he could rule. Hence, two options were open to him if he wished to maintain his control. He could rule in the name of the eastern emperor or set up figureheads. He chose the latter route, with middling success.

After the removal of Avitus there was an interregnum lasting some months. (This situation would recur in the next few years, and the fact that everyone could do without an emperor for months or even years shows how little the position now meant.) To gain legitimacy any new emperor had to be recognized by the emperor in the east. The death of Marcian delayed this, and in April of A.D. 457, the new eastern emperor Leo recognized Majorian, one of the generals who had revolted against Avitus.[7] At the same time Leo recognized Ricimer as patrician.

After Majorian managed to restore order in Gaul, where the Visigoths were expanding from out of their territory in the southwest, while the Burgundians were moving into the southeast, the next task was to attempt to do something about the Vandals, whose piratical activities affected all the islands of the western Mediterranean. Majorian gathered a large fleet on the Spanish coast, but Gaiseric managed to surprise and destroy it. Majorian returned to Italy via Gaul, and in late A.D. 461, Ricimer had him murdered. Majorian had shown himself to be independent but not terribly competent; Ricimer now preferred a more compliant emperor of his own choosing.

In late A.D. 461, Ricimer proclaimed as emperor a complete nonentity in the form of an Italian called Livius Severus. Severus was not recognized in the east, but this hardly mattered, as Ricimer was the real ruler of Italy. Meanwhile, Roman authority was ebbing elsewhere in the west. The Imperial commander in Gaul whom Majorian had appointed was called Aegidius. Perhaps he could have proclaimed himself emperor like Avitus, but he did not bother. While not recognizing Severus, he simply led the defense of Gaul against the Visigoths, dying in A.D. 464. There was also trouble in Sicily. In A.D. 461, a local commander named Marcellinus was defending the island against the Vandals with a force of Huns, but Ricimer decided to undermine his authority among his troops, and Marcellinus fled to Illyricum, where he set up an independent command under the eastern emperor and harassed Italy. At this time Gaiseric decided to take advantage of the fact that Eudoxia, the daughter of Valentinian III whom he had captured in A.D. 455, was the bride of his son; Gaiseric claimed the property of Valentinian III as the dowry for Eudoxia and wished to install Olybrius, the husband of Eudoxia's sister, as the western emperor. (By marriage Olybrius could be claimed as a representative of the old dynasty.) Gaiseric used the failure to fulfill these claims as an excuse for raiding.

In mid–A.D. 465, Livius Severus died, and another interregnum ensued. Throughout A.D. 466, there was no western emperor, but an act of Gaiseric led to the appointment of one. He raided the Peloponnesus, and Leo decided to set matters in the west in order. He appointed as western Augustus the patrician Anthemius. This man was the son-in-law of the dead emperor Marcian and could thus be viewed as representative of the old Theodosian dynasty (and something of a counterbalance to the similar claims of Gaiseric's candidate, Olybrius). Ricimer was persuaded to accept Anthemius through marriage to his daughter.

---

7 Majorian had been an associate of Aëtius, and after the assassination of Valentinian III in A.D. 455, the emperor's widow had favored the acclamation of Majorian as the new emperor, but Petronius Maximus' bribery had prevailed.

At this point, the fact that Anthemius had been appointed emperor in the west by the eastern emperor facilitated military cooperation, and a huge, three-fold campaign against the Vandals that involved forces from both halves of the empire was to be set in motion in A.D. 468. All went well at first and Gaiseric was in despair, but he managed to destroy the eastern fleet, which caused the whole operation to collapse. The debacle of this extremely expensive campaign ate up all the reserves of the eastern emperor and must have been a huge Roman humiliation in the eyes of the Germanic tribes of the west. It marked the last serious attempt to maintain the power of the western emperor outside of Italy.

Meanwhile, the Visigoths continued their depredations in Gaul, and despite the requests of the local Romans Anthemius could do little beyond inciting the Burgundians against the Visigoths. Relations between Anthemius and his son-in-law, the patrician Ricimer, deteriorated. Unpopular for being a Greek inclined to theology (and accused of pagan leanings), Anthemius resided in Rome, while Ricimer ruled from Milan. In A.D. 472, Leo sent Olybrius, Gaiseric's Imperial candidate, to Rome. He also sent a message advising the execution of Olybrius, but Ricimer intercepted it and instead had Olybrius proclaimed Augustus in place of Anthemius. Ricimer then besieged Rome, and after Ricimer's defeat of a relief force from Gaul, Anthemius' supporters abandoned him. (He tried to disguise himself as a beggar but was found and executed.) Ricimer did not enjoy his success, dying within weeks; his creation Olybrius followed suit within a fortnight.

By this point, the collapse of Imperial authority in the northwest was complete. The Visigoths greatly expanded their power, taking over all of Gaul and expanding their control over Spain. With the Vandals in control in Africa, and rebellious generals controlling Illyricum, the last vestiges of Imperial government in the west were restricted to Italy, where Germanic generals squabbled among themselves, appointing figurehead emperors to give legitimacy to their power.

Following the death of Ricimer, the Burgundian Gundobad assumed control of the troops, and after another interregnum (nine months), he proclaimed Glycerius, a middle-ranking officer, as Augustus in early A.D. 473. The eastern emperor Leo did not recognize Glycerius and instead nominated Julius Nepos, who was the husband of a niece of the empress and had replaced Marcellinus as military commander in Illyricum. In A.D. 474, Nepos entered Italy, where Gundobad and Glycerius offered little resistance. Glycerius became the bishop of a town in Illyricum and Gundobad returned to the Burgundians, where he succeeded his father as king. For his part, Nepos could not exercise real control over the Germanic troops in Italy and appointed to the post of patrician a man named Orestes, who had served as secretary to Attila; when Orestes raised a revolt in his son's name in A.D. 475, Nepos fled to Illyricum. The child emperor is derisively known as Romulus Augustulus ("little Augustus"). Orestes ruled on behalf of his child for only one year. The Germanic soldiers were being quartered on the land of Italians, and they wanted land to be granted to them according to the usual formula used in Roman territory outside of Italy whereby a third of local land was given to federates and the original owners retained the rest; apparently Orestes thought such a division unacceptable on Italian soil and rejected their request. A Germanic officer named Odoacer turned this discontent into revolt, and after he fled, Orestes was captured and executed. The child emperor was then turned over to his relatives.

Odoacer now had to decide how to rule in Italy. Instead of setting up yet another puppet emperor, he decided instead to regularize his position under the aegis of the eastern emperor. He sent the Imperial insignia to Zeno in Constantinople and asked to be entrusted with the rule of Italy as patrician. Zeno was a bit embarrassed, since the emperor recognized by him was Julius Nepos in Illyricum. Zeno replied by appointing Odoacer as patrician but indicated to the senate that Nepos should be restored to power. He must have known that this would not be done and made no effort on behalf of Nepos, who removed the problem when he was assassinated by retainers in A.D. 480. Never again would a Roman emperor rule in the west. Zeno caused trouble for Odoacer by sending Germanic tribes in his direction, and in A.D. 489 the Ostrogoths under their king Theoderic destroyed his power and established a kingdom of their own in Italy.

The deposition of Romulus Augustulus in A.D. 476 is generally accepted to be the demise of the empire in the west, though strictly speaking one continued to exist in Nepos until A.D. 480. In a remarkably short period of time, the territory of the Empire in the west was replaced by a series of Germanic kingdoms. The end of Imperial rule in Rome is a convenient place to end the story of the community that had begun as a collection of mud huts on the Tiber in the early Iron Age. It is hardly a tidy ending, though, as the Roman Empire in the east went on unaffected, and in the form of the Greek Byzantine Empire into which it developed, the eastern Empire would continue for nearly a millennium.

The question of why the Roman Empire fell is one of perennial interest. In terms of the fifth century A.D., it is clear that the Empire as a whole did not fall, and the question then becomes an explanation of why the western government succumbed to Germanic conquest while the eastern half of the Empire survived with comparatively little difficulty. There is no single answer to this question or even a single set of possible explanations, but a few interrelated factors can be suggested.

First, simple geography had an important influence on the course of events. The major incursions came from central and eastern Europe, which lessened the exposure of the eastern half of the Empire. Of the territory controlled from Constantinople, only the Balkans was directly exposed to depredation in conquest, while the Bosporus protected the wealthy provinces in Asia Minor, Syria, and Egypt. Thus, the eastern emperors had large amounts of unharmed territory under their control, and from this territory they could both recruit native troops and raise substantial tax revenues to pay for the military. In the west, much more territory was directly exposed to invasion, and even distant Africa was eventually lost to the Vandals after the Imperial government failed to contain the Germans in western Europe. As more and more territory was lost to Germanic control in the early part of the century, the Imperial government in Italy increasingly lost the resources necessary to exercise its authority elsewhere, which only hastened the loss of territory.

To some extent, historical accident led to a military imbalance at the time of the great invasions that started soon after the death of Theodosius I. While the mobile army in the east had suffered great losses at Adrianople in A.D. 378, the intervening two decades had allowed this army to be restored in part at least before the invasions began. Though the eastern government would rely on Germanic recruits as the west did, these Germans never came to play a significant role in the eastern army, and there were self-conscious efforts in the east to minimize the dependence on Germans and to recruit native troops. In the west, however, the battle of Frigidus in A.D. 394 had seriously damaged the mobile army at exactly the moment when the military pressure from the Germanic tribes began in earnest. Hence, the Germanic (and at times Hunnish) troops became an indispensable element in the army of the western half of the Empire, and real power soon rested in the hands of those generals who could command the loyalty of these troops. After several generations of needing a Roman emperor to provide legitimacy to their authority, these generals eventually found that they could dispense with the pretense.

From an internal point of view, the ease with which the Empire was replaced by Germanic kingdoms has to do with the changed nature of the Imperial government as it was reconstructed by Diocletian and Constantine. Whereas the Principate of Augustus had been a vehicle by which a single man controlled the army with the cooperation of the wealthiest landowners, the army had become an independent institution during the crisis of the third century and chose its own officers. Beginning with Claudius Gothicus, the emperors were chosen from such peasant officers and the old connection between the landowners and the Imperial government was broken. While the landowners did continue to provide governors for some militarily unimportant provinces, they no longer provided the leading officials for the central administration and the army, and hence they became disaffected from the Imperial government. These landowners increasingly directed their attention to looking after their vast holdings, and their money and social influence enabled them to avoid paying taxes. This only increased the burdens on the smaller landowners, who in turn fell under the sway of their wealthier neighbors.

Thus, it made little difference to the landowners whether the government to which they paid taxes was headed by a Germanic king or a Roman figurehead, and it turned out that giving up one-third of their land for distribution to Germanic tribesmen guaranteed their possession of the remainder.

The adoption of Christianity has often been blamed for the demise of the Imperial government, though this is obviously an unsatisfactory explanation since the eastern government was no less Christian than the western. It is true that the religious propensities of Theodosius I's male descendants detracted from their leadership, but there is no reason why effective rule could not have been exercised in their name by other, less exclusively devout Romans. The conversion to Christianity that had taken place among the majority of upper-class Romans by the early fifth century A.D. led to an equation of "Romanness" with adherence to the officially recognized version of Christianity. Thus, the Roman self-identity of the landowners was divorced from being under the direct rule of the Imperial government. While many Germanic tribes retained their "deviant" Arian views for some time, none but the Vandals persecuted Catholic inhabitants of the land they occupied.

Furthermore, for the most part the German kings were happy enough to enlist their wealthy Roman subjects to run the civil administration. Eventually, the Germanic settlers would adopt the Romance speech of their subjects, and the successor kingdoms of the early Middle Ages would maintain in a somewhat attenuated way the traditional forms of Roman administration. Though the trappings of the Imperial government ended in the A.D. 470s, it was not so much the case that the Empire came to a clear and precipitous halt as that it was supplanted by localized kingdoms based on Germanic military forces. This "sub-Roman" period of the early medieval period would last until the Arab and Viking invasions of the eighth and ninth centuries A.D. did away with the last vestiges of Roman-style government.

EPILOGUE: SURVIVAL AND TRANSFORMATION OF THE EMPIRE IN THE EAST AFTER A.D. 476

The demise of the last western emperor in A.D. 476 (or 480) had no significance for the east, where the Late Imperial form of government established by Diocletian and Constantine went on intact. The eastern government following the permanent division of the Empire at the death of Theodosius I is often described as the Eastern Roman Empire. This is not a particularly tidy term, since for a good eighty years after that division, the east still operated to some extent in tandem with the west and there was no legal division of the Empire. Even in the A.D. 470s, the theoretical right of the emperor in Constantinople to appoint a western emperor was still recognized, and the eastern emperor retained a legal claim to all the territory that had come under the sway of Germanic kingdoms. Nonetheless, the term "Eastern Roman Empire" is a convenient term for designating the Imperial government in the east until it lost its Latin character in the seventh century A.D., at which point it is best described as the Byzantine Empire.

In A.D. 518, the old pattern repeated itself when Justin, a general of lowly origins from the Latin-speaking Balkans, became emperor. Justin was succeeded by his nephew Justinian (A.D. 518–565), who in many ways marks the pinnacle of the Late Empire. Apart from marking the final triumph of Christianity by suppressing the pagan schools of Athens and adorning Constantinople with the largest church of antiquity, he embarked on an astonishing number of campaigns to reconquer the west, overthrowing the Vandal kingdom in Africa, subduing most of Italy, and establishing an enclave in Spain. In doing so, he was merely attempting to restore the Empire to its previous glory, but in hindsight it can be seen that the effort was counterproductive in the long run. Apart from the huge expense that it took to make the initial conquests, the western territories felt no particular affection for the emperor resident in the Greek-speaking capital of the east and the maintenance of these new acquisitions was more trouble than they were worth. Military disasters that then befell the east in the late sixth and early seventh centuries A.D. made it impossible to keep the new conquests and led to fundamental changes in the so-called Eastern Roman Empire.

In the late sixth century A.D., the Indo-European Slavs became the latest population group to invade the Balkan peninsula from the north. Like the Germans and Celts before them, the Slavs emerged from western expanses of modern-day Russia and Ukraine, first pushing to the south and west the pre-vious occupants of eastern Europe and then crossing the Danube into the now Latinized provinces of the interior of the Balkans that had provided so many recruits (and emperors) for the later Empire. In the seventh century A.D., the Slavic incursions became a deluge, and they were able to establish permanent control of the countryside, driving the Latin speakers into the mountains, where they became a migratory population devoted to shepherding.[1] This Slav occupation of the Balkans greatly reduced the Latin-speaking element in the Eastern Empire.

In the late sixth century A.D., the Eastern Empire and the Persians engaged in a monumental struggle that merely paved the way for the Arab conquest of the near east. First, in the disastrous first decades of the seventh century A.D., the Persians launched a great offensive that eventually captured not simply the Roman Syria and Palestine but also Egypt. It took the emperor Heraclius (A.D. 610–641) nearly two decades of extremely strenuous campaigning to throw the invaders back. Then, as the two sides lay exhausted from the years of conflict, an entirely new force arose that permanently changed the near east. United and inspired by the new Moslem faith that had been propagated by the prophet Mohammed, the Arabs rapidly conquered Roman Syria and Palestine in a series of campaigns in the A.D. 630s, while they completely overwhelmed the Persian empire in A.D. 637; in A.D. 641, Egypt, too, fell to the Arabs, who added Roman Africa by the end of the century. The Christian population of the Roman territories preferred Moslem rule to the persecution of the Orthodox government in Constantinople and were permanently lost to the rest of the Christian world.[2]

---

1 These Latin-speaking herders are the ancestors of the Vlachs of modern Greece, and it was from such herders that the plains of present-day Romania were reoccupied centuries later (see p. 276 n. 3).
2 In the initial centuries after the conquest, the Christians were reduced to minority status through conversion to Islam and Arabic immigration. While small Christian minorities continue to exist in Syria and Egypt, the Arabic language came to supplant the native idioms in the conquered Roman territories. The fact that, apart from a feeble attack on Egypt in the mid–A.D. 640s, the Imperial government in Constantinople made little effort to reclaim its losses in the near east may reflect a realization that it was not worth the trouble to regain these disaffected areas.

While some outposts were retained in Italy (the Spanish enclave had been lost by the early seventh century A.D.), the heartland of the Eastern Empire was now Asia Minor, and its most important city by far was the capital of Constantinople. This restricted Empire underwent a number of changes that distinguish it from the previous "Eastern Roman Empire" stage that directly follows from the unified Roman Empire. First, Heraclius instituted a number of administrative reforms that reflected changed circumstances and marked a substantial break with earlier practice. Second, the loss of the Balkans and the near east meant that the reduced Empire exhibited much less ethnic and linguistic diversity and could reasonably be conceived of as a Greek-speaking territory. Finally, the loss of the heterodox areas to the south secured the permanent victory of the Orthodox form of Christianity officially recognized by the Late Empire. Over the years, the Orthodox Church of the Empire in the east and the variant form of the old state-supported religion that survived in the west as the Catholic Church began to diverge in doctrine and practice, a distinction that is reflected in the modern use of the term "Catholic" for the Latin Church and "Orthodox" for the Greek one (the division between the two branches of late antique state religion would be officially recognized only in A.D. 1054, though their mutual animosity became evident much earlier). Thus, while the process of transition was to some extent a gradual one and there is no single point where the Eastern Roman Empire with its Latin traditions ceased to exist and was replaced by the Greek-speaking Orthodox Empire of the medieval period, there is a clear difference between the two, and the later manifestation of the Eastern Empire is known in modern terminology as the Byzantine Empire (after the original Greek name of the city of Constantinople). For their part, the Byzantine emperors, who continued to rule in Constantinople until the city's capture by the Ottoman Turks in A.D. 1453, always styled themselves as the "Kings of the Romans" in Greek, but they shared little in common with emperors of the Principate (though somewhat more with those of the Late Empire).

CHRONOLOGY

ca. 1800–1200 B.C. Apennine Culture (Bronze Age)

ca. 1200–900 B.C. Proto-Villanovan Culture

ca. 900 B.C. Start of Villanovan Period/beginning of Iron Age; introduction of cremation

ca. 1000–875 B.C. Latial I

ca. 875–750 B.C. Latial II

814 B.C. Traditional Greek date for the foundation of Carthage

753 B.C. Varronian date for the foundation of Rome

ca. 750–700 B.C. Latial III

ca. 700–580 B.C. Latial IV

509 or 507 B.C. Varro's and Polybius' dates, respectively, for the expulsion of Tarquinius Priscus and the foundation of the Republic

494 B.C. Varronian date for the first secession of the plebs and the establishment of the tribunate of the plebs

493 B.C. Varronian date for the Foedus Cassianum

479 B.C. Varronian date for the defeat of the Fabii in their assault on Veii

451–450 B.C. Varronian dating for the *decemviri legibus scribundis* (board of ten that drew up the Twelve Tables)

447 B.C. Varronian date for the first elections of quaestors

443 or 435 B.C. Varronian date for the first election of censors

444–367 B.C. Varronian dates for the period when military tribunes with consular power were elected

431 B.C. Varronian date for the defeat of the Volsci at the Algidus Pass

406–396 B.C. Varronian date for the siege of Veii

390 or 386 B.C. Respectively, Varro's and Polybius' dates for the Gallic sack of Rome

380 B.C. Varronian date for the annexation of Tusculum

376–367 B.C. Varronian dates for the disputes that culminated in passage of the Sextian-Licinian rogations, including five years of anarchy

367 B.C. Varronian date for the establishment of the praetorship and the curule aedileship and for the grant to plebeians of the right to hold offices with *imperium*

341–338 B.C. Varronian date for the revolt of the Latin League, which ends with its dissolution

333, 324, 309, 301 B.C. Varronian "dictator years"

326–304 B.C. Varronian dates for the Great (Second) Samnite War

321 B.C. Varronian date for the defeat at the Caudine Fork
298–290 B.C. Third Samnite War
295 B.C. Roman victory at Sentinum
ca. 287 B.C. *Lex Hortensia* grants plebiscites the full force of laws
280 B.C. Pyrrhus' arrival in Italy
275 B.C. Final departure of Pyrrhus
264–242 B.C. First Punic War
241 B.C. Creation of the last two tribes
238 B.C. Roman seizure of Sardinia
227 B.C. Creation of two more praetorships for Sicily and Sardinia
218–202 B.C. Second Punic War
216 B.C. Battle of Cannae
211 B.C. Capture of Capua, Syracuse
209 B.C. Capture of New Carthage
207 B.C. Battle of Metaurus
211–205 B.C. First Macedonian War
202 B.C. Battle of Zama
200–197 B.C. Second Macedonian War
197 B.C. Battle of Cynoscephalae; two new praetorships created for Spain
196 B.C. Proclamation of the "Freedom of Greece"
195–194 B.C. M. Porcius Cato campaigns in Spain
192–188 B.C. Syrian War
189 B.C. Battle of Magnesia
188 B.C. Arpinum granted full citizenship
181–178 B.C. First Celtiberian War in Spain
178 B.C. Senate's decision against the Rhodians in their war with the Lycians; Ti.
    Sempronius Gracchus the elder works out permanent settlement in Celtiberia
171–168 B.C. Third Macedonian War
170 B.C. Ex-praetor C. Lucretius Gallus condemned by the Roman People for
    misconduct in Greece
168 B.C. Battle of Pydna, abolition of Macedonian kingdom; the Roman People barely
    dissuaded from declaring war on Rhodes
167 B.C. L. Aemilius Paullus enslaves 150,000 Epirotes
154–149 B.C. War with the Lusitani in Spain
154–151 B.C. Second Celtiberian War
149 B.C. Passage of *lex Calpurnia*, which established a permanent court for provincial
    extortion
149–148 B.C. Macedonian Revolt
149–146 B.C. Third Punic War
147 B.C. Popular agitation leads to illegal election of P. Cornelius Scipio Aemilianus as
    consul
146 B.C. Achaean War, sack of Corinth; sack of Carthage; creation of provinces of
    Macedonia and Africa
144/143–134 B.C. Numantine War
139 B.C. Secret ballot introduced for elections
137 B.C. C. Hostilius Mancinus surrenders to Numantines; secret ballot introduced for
    most trials before the Roman People
135 B.C. Popular agitation leads to second illegal consulship for P. Cornelius Scipio
    Aemilianus
134 B.C. Capture of Numantia

133 B.C. Tribunate and death of Ti. Gracchus; Asia becomes province

131 B.C. Secret ballot introduced for legislative elections

130–129 B.C. Suppression of revolt in Asia

129 B.C. End of land distribution under Gracchan law when allies complain

125 B.C. M. Fulvius Flaccus unsuccessfully tries to grant citizenship to allies

125–120 B.C. Conquest of southern Gaul; Narbonensis becomes province

123–122 B.C. Tribunates of C. Gracchus

121 B.C. Death of C. Gracchus after passage of "Final Decree" of the Senate

113 B.C. Consul Cn. Papirius Carbo defeated by the Cimbri in Balkans

112 B.C. Jugurtha's capture of Cirta

111–105 B.C. War against Jugurtha

109 B.C. M. Junius Silanus defeated by the Cimbri in Gaul

107 B.C. Law passed granting the consul C. Marius command against Jugurtha, and he raises troops without regard for census status. Consul L. Cassius Longinus defeated by allies of the Cimbri

106 B.C. Consul Q. Servilius Caepio passes law adding senators to jury panels

105 B.C. Jugurtha handed over to Sulla in Mauretania. Proconsul Q. Servilius Caepio and consul Cn. Mallius Maximus suffer overwhelming defeat at Arausio

104–100 B.C. Marius consul

103 B.C. First tribunate of L. Appuleius Saturninus

102–100 B.C. Praetor M. Antonius' campaign against Cilician pirates

102 B.C. C. Marius' defeat of Teutoni

101 B.C. C. Marius' defeat of Cimbri; Saturninus elected tribune through murder of a candidate; C. Servilius Glaucia as praetor passes law restoring jury panels to equestrians and reforming the extortion court (?)

100 B.C. Second tribunate of L. Appuleius Saturninus. C. Memmius killed during consular elections. Saturninus and C. Glaucia are suppressed under "Final Decree" of the Senate, then murdered

95 B.C. Consuls establish *quaestio* to investigate fraudulent claims to Roman citizenship

92 B.C. Conviction of P. Rutilius Rufus for extortion

91 B.C. Tribunate of M. Livius Drusus the younger

90–89 B.C. Social War

90 B.C. Citizenship granted to allies

89–86 B.C. First Mithridatic War

88 B.C. Command against Mithridates voted to C. Marius; consul L. Sulla's march on Rome

87 B.C. *Bellum Octavianum.* L. Sulla crosses over to Balkans

86 B.C. Death of C. Marius; L. Sulla defeats Mithridates' forces at Chaeronea, Orchomenus; L. Valerius Flaccus brings an army to Balkans and is killed in a mutiny instigated by C. Fimbria

85 B.C. L. Sulla refuses to cooperate with Fimbria in Asia and makes peace with Mithridates

84 B.C. L. Cornelius Cinna killed in a mutiny

83–82 B.C. L. Sulla conquers Italy

81 B.C. Proscriptions

80 B.C. Q. Sertorius seizes Spain

78 B.C. Consul M. Aemilius Lepidus opposes Sullan settlement, goes into open revolt

77 B.C. Collapse of M. Lepidus' revolt; Cn. Pompeius ("Pompey") extorts command against Q. Sertorius

74–72 B.C. Praetor M. Antonius' campaign against pirates

73–71 B.C. Slave revolt of Spartacus

73–63 B.C. Third Mithridatic War

73 B.C. Assassination of Sertorius

70 B.C. Joint consulship of Crassus and Pompey, in which the tribunate is restored to traditional powers; jury panels shared by senators, *equites*, and *tribuni aerarii*

69 B.C. L. Licinius Lucullus invades Armenia

67 B.C. Roman campaign in east halted by Mithridates' victory at Zela; Pompey granted *imperium* against the pirates under *lex Gabinia*

66 B.C. Pompey granted command of war against Mithrates under *lex Manilia*

64 B.C. Organization of province of Bithynia and Pontus, annexation of province of Syria

63 B.C. Consulship of Cicero, suppression of Catilinarian conspiracy

59 B.C. First consulship of C. Julius Caesar

59–49 B.C. C. Julius Caesar governor in Gaul

58–57 B.C. Exile of Cicero

55 B.C. Second joint consulship of Pompey and M. Licinius Crassus; Pompey given command over Spain; C. Caesar's command in Gaul extended

54–53 B.C. M. Crassus' defeat at Carrhae

52 B.C. Sole consulship of Pompey

49–45 B.C. Civil war

48 B.C. Battle of Pharsalus; Pompey assassinated

46 B.C. Battle of Thapsus in Africa

45 B.C. Battle of Munda in Spain

44 B.C. C. Caesar appointed dictator for life, is assassinated; conflict between consul M. Antonius ("Antony") and Caesar's heir (Young Caesar or "Octavian"); M. Junius Brutus and C. Cassius Longinus seize Macedonia and Syria

43 B.C. Proconsul Dolabella fails to take Syria from Cassius; Young Caesar cooperates with consuls in attacking Antony, who is pushed into Gaul; Young Caesar seizes consulship and reconciles with Antony; triumvirate established by law, proscriptions enacted, Cicero killed; Sex. Pompey seizes major islands

42 B.C. Battle of Philippi

41 B.C. Perusine War

40–38 B.C. Parthian invasion of east defeated

36 B.C. Imp. Caesar (new name for "Young Caesar") seizes Sicily from Sex. Pompey; Lepidus removed from position as triumvir

32–31 B.C. War of Imp. Caesar against Antony and Cleopatra, culminating in the defeat of the latter at Actium

30 B.C. Suicide of Antony and Cleopatra, annexation of Egypt

27 B.C. Imp. Caesar "restores" Republic and is granted title "Augustus"

27 B.C.–A.D. 14 "Reign" of Augustus

23 B.C. Augustus receives tribunician power, ceases to hold consulship regularly

15–9 B.C. Conquest of the Balkans up to the Danube

13 B.C.–A.D. 6 Wars of conquest in Germany

12 B.C. Augustus elected *pontifex maximus*

2 B.C. Augustus acclaimed as *pater patriae*

A.D. 6–9 Pannonian revolt

A.D. 9 Defeat at Teutoburg Forest, loss of conquests in Germany

A.D. 14 Succession of Tiberius; revolts along the Rhine and the Danube

A.D. 14–37 Reign of Tiberius

A.D. 31 Downfall of Sejanus

A.D. 37–41 Reign of Gaius ("Caligula")

A.D. 41–54 Reign of Claudius

A.D. 42 Revolt of L. Arruntius Camillus

A.D. 43 Invasion of Britain

A.D. 54–68 Reign of Nero

A.D. 66–70 Great Revolt in Judaea

A.D. 68 Revolt of Vindex; accession of P. Sulpicius Galba upon suicide of Nero

A.D. 69 Year of Four Emperors: M. Salvius Otho replaces Galba; A. Vitellius replaces Otho; T. Flavius Vespasianus replaces Otho, founds new dynasty

A.D. 70 Titus captures Jerusalem, Great Temple destroyed

A.D. 79–81 Reign of Titus

A.D. 81–96 Reign of Domitian

A.D. 84/85–93 Campaigns along Danube

A.D. 89 Revolt of L. Antonius Saturninus

A.D. 96–98 Reign of Nero

A.D. 98–117 Reign of Trajan

A.D. 101–102 First campaign against Dacia

A.D. 105–106 Annexation of Dacia

A.D. 106 Annexation of Nabataean kingdom

A.D. 114–117 Invasion of Parthia

A.D. 115–117 Jewish revolt in Egypt, Cyrene, and Cyprus

A.D. 117–138 Reign of Hadrian

A.D. 132–153 Jewish revolt in Judaea

A.D. 138–160 Reign of Antoninus Pius

A.D. 160–180 Reign of Marcus Aurelius (with L. Verus, A.D. 160–169)

A.D. 165–166 Verus' campaign against Parthia

A.D. 167–180 Campaigns along Danube

A.D. 175 Revolt of C. Avidius Cassius

A.D. 180–192 Reign of Commodus

A.D. 193 Acclamation of M. Helvius Pertinax as emperor after assassination of Commodus; Julius Didianus acclaimed by praetorians after murder of Pertinax; Revolts of L. Septimius Severus, C. Pescennius Niger

A.D. 193–194 Severus' suppression of Niger

A.D. 196–197 Severus' previous heir, D. Clodius Albinus, is proclaimed emperor, seizes Gaul, and is then suppressed by Severus

A.D. 197–198 Severus campaigns against Parthia, annexes province of Mesopotamia

A.D. 211–217 Reign of Antoninus ("Caracalla"), who murdered his brother and co-emperor Geta (211–212)

A.D. 212 *Constitutio Antoniniana* grants Roman citizenship to all free subjects of the Empire

A.D. 217 Praetorian praefect M. Opellius Macrinus proclaimed emperor after assassination of Antoninus, becoming first emperor of nonsenatorial rank

A.D. 218 Revolt engineered by in-laws of Septimius Severus; Macrinus is defeated and killed, replaced by grandson of wife of Severus

A.D. 218–222 Reign of younger Antoninus ("Elagabalus")

A.D. 222 Younger Antoninus murdered in riot of praetorians, replaced by his cousin Severus Alexander

A.D. 222–235 Reign of Severus Alexander

ca. A.D. 224 Persian Ardashir founds new, Sassanid dynasty that replaces Parthians

ca. A.D. 232–233 Unsuccessful campaign against Persians

A.D. 235–238 Reign of Maximinus

A.D. 238 Revolt of Gordians in Africa suppressed; Pupienus, Balbinus and Gordian III proclaimed emperors in Rome; Maximinus murdered by troops during siege of Aquileia; Pupienus and Balbinus murdered by praetorians

A.D. 238–244 Reign of Gordian III

A.D. 244–249 Reign of Philip

A.D. 249–251 Reign of Trajan Decius, who is killed when he suffers a severe defeat at the hands of the Goths; Imperial persecution of the Christians

A.D. 251–253 Reign of Trebonianus Gallus

A.D. 253 Reign of Aemilian

A.D. 253–260 Reign of Valerian; Resumption of Imperial persecution of the Christians

A.D. 253–268 Reign of Gallienus

A.D. 260 Defeat and capture of Valerian by Shapur

A.D. 260–261 Reign of Macrianus and Quietus

A.D. 260–273 "Gallic Empire"

A.D. 261–267/268 Odenathus governs east

A.D. 260–269 Reign of Postumus in Gaul

A.D. 267/268–272 Palmyrene "empire"

A.D. 268–270 Reign of Claudius "Gothicus"

A.D. 269–271 Victorinus emperor in Gaul

A.D. 270 Reign of Quintillus

A.D. 270–275 Reign of Aurelian

ca. A.D. 271 Abandonment of Dacia

A.D. 271–274 Tetricus emperor in Gaul

A.D. 272 Overthrow of Palmyrenes by Aurelian

A.D. 273 Destruction of Palmyra

A.D. 274 Aurelian's conquest of "Gallic Empire"

A.D. 275–276 Reign of Tacitus

A.D. 276 Reign of Florus

A.D. 276–282 Reign of Probus

A.D. 282–283 Reign of Carus

A.D. 283–284/285 Reigns, respectively, of Numerian and Carinus

A.D. 284–305 Reign of Diocletian

A.D. 285–305 Reign of Maximian

A.D. 285–293 Reign of Carausius in Britain

A.D. 293 Establishment of tetrarchy with appointment of Galerius as Caesar in the east and Constantius Chlorus in the west

A.D. 293–296 Reign of Allectus in Britain

A.D. 296 Suppression of Allectus

A.D. 298 Galerius defeats Persians and extends Roman territory in northern Mesopotamia

A.D. 303–313 "Great Persecution" (in the east)

A.D. 305 Diocletian and Maximian abdicate; Galerius and Constantius Chlorus become Augusti, appointing Maximinus and Severus, respectively, as Caesars

A.D. 306 Upon death of Constantius Chlorus, Severus assumes title of Augustus in west, as do Constantine and Maxentius; defeat of Severus

A.D. 306–308 Second reign of Maximian

A.D. 308 Council at Carnuntum: second abdication of Maximian, appointment of Licinius as Augustus for the west

A.D. 311 Galerius halts Great Persecution, then dies; Maximinus becomes Augustus in east

A.D. 312 Constantine defeats Maxentius at Mulvian Bridge

A.D. 313 Licinius defeats Maximinus

A.D. 316–317 First war between Constantine and Licinius

A.D. 324 Constantine overthrows Licinius

A.D. 325 Council of Nicaea

A.D. 330 Dedication of Constantinople

A.D. 337 Death of Constantine; murder of his adult male relatives apart from his sons

A.D. 337–340/350/361 Reigns, respectively, of Constantine II, Constans, and Constantius II

A.D. 350–353 Reign of Magnentius Magnus

A.D. 355–361 Julian acts as Caesar in Gaul

A.D. 361–363 Reign of Julian

A.D. 363 Disastrous Persian campaign

A.D. 363–364 Reign of Jovian

A.D. 364–375 Reign of Valentinian I

A.D. 364–378 Reign of Valens

A.D. 367–383 Reign of Gratian

A.D. 375–392 Reign of Valentinian II

A.D. 378 Battle of Adrianople

A.D. 379–395 Reign of Theodosius I

A.D. 381 Council of Constantinople restores the Nicene creed, prohibits Arianism in the east

A.D. 383 Revolt of Magnus Maximus; death of Gratian

A.D. 387 Suppression of Magnus Maximus

A.D. 392 Death of Valentinian II; revolt of Eugenius; Theodosius prohibits all pagan worship

A.D. 394 Battle of Frigidus; suppression of Eugenius

A.D. 395 Final division of Empire upon death of Theodosius

A.D. 395–408/423 Respective reigns of Arcadius and Honorius

A.D. 395–408 Dominance of Stilicho in the west

A.D. 398 Coup of Germanic troops is thwarted in the east

A.D. 406 Collapse of the Rhine frontier

A.D. 408–450 Reign of Theodosius II in the east

A.D. 410 Visigothic sack of Rome

A.D. 421 Reign of Constantius III

A.D. 423–425 Usurpation of John in west after death of Honorius

A.D. 425–455 Reign of Valentinian III in the west

A.D. 429–432, 434–454 Dominance of Aëtius in the west

A.D. 429 Vandals cross from Spain to northern Africa

A.D. 431 First Council of Ephesus prohibits Nestorianism in the east

A.D. 432–434 Civil war in Italy between Aëtius and Boniface (and his son)

A.D. 439 Vandals' capture of Carthage

A.D. 441–453 Sole reign of Attila as king of the Huns

A.D. 449 Second Council of Ephesus makes monophysitism official doctrine in the east

A.D. 450–457 Reign of Marcian in the east

A.D. 451 Council of Chalcedon overrules second Council of Ephesus, restores the Nicene creed as official doctrine in the east; Huns' invasion of west repelled

A.D. 455 Murder of Valentinian III; short reign of Petronius Maximus; Vandals' sack of Rome

A.D. 455–456 Reign of Avitus

A.D. 456–472 Dominance of Ricimer in the west

A.D. 457–474 Reign of Leo in the east

A.D. 457–461 Reign of Majorian in the west

A.D. 461–465 Reign of Livius Severus in the west

A.D. 466–472 Reign of Anthemius in the west

A.D. 468 Defeat of joint invasion of Vandal kingdom by forces of both the east and the west

A.D. 472 Reign of Olybrius

A.D. 472–474 Reign of Glycerius

A.D. 473–480 Reign of Julius Nepos

A.D. 475–476 Reign of Romulus Augustulus

A.D. 476 Odoacer deposes Romulus Augustulus, the last western emperor

A.D. 527–565 Reign of Justinian, who undertakes reconquest of the west

A.D. 610–641 Reign of Heraclius in the east; "Eastern Roman Empire" now is referred to as the "Byzantine Empire" after the loss of Latin-speaking Balkans to the Slavs and of Syria and Egypt to the Arabs leaves a Greek-speaking Orthodox heartland centered on Asia Minor and Constantinople

APPENDIX: ROMAN PERSONAL NAMES

The Romans had a system of nomenclature that diverges in significant ways from contemporary name giving, and because Roman names turn up not infrequently in the present work, it is sensible to begin with a short introduction to the Roman system. This system changed notably over the centuries. In the earliest known stages, every Roman male had a threefold name. First, there was a personal name (*praenomen*). The number of these was limited, and in the historical period, fewer than ten were at all common; all these had a uniformly used abbreviation: A. = Aulus, C. = Gaius, Cn. = Gnaeus, D. = Decimus, L. = Lucius, M. = Marcus, P. = Publius, Q. = Quintus, T. = Titus, Ti. = Tiberius.[1] Next came the *nomen*, which indicated the clan (*gens*) to which the man belonged. The name was then closed with the patronymic ("filiation"), which indicated the man's paternity, representing it with the abbreviated form of the *praenomen* (e.g., *T. fil.* = "the son of Titus"). This original nomenclature followed principles that were shared with most other populations in the Italian peninsula, and two further elements came to be added during the Roman Republic. First, after the filiation came an abbreviation for the "tribe" (a voting district) to which the man belonged. After this came the last element of the official name, the *cognomen*. The *cognomen* began as a personal nickname but eventually came to be hereditary.[2] Though there is some indication of a corporate identity for the members of the *gens*, this was supplanted at an early stage by a unit that more or less corresponded to the nuclear family of two parents and their children and that was indicated by the husband's *cognomen*. The late development of the *cognomen* is reflected by its placement at the end of the name. It was only commonly used in official documents by the last century of the Republic. To give an example of a full Roman name, the dictator commonly known as Julius Caesar was officially styled C. Julius C. fil. Fab. Caesar, or "Gaius Julius Caesar, son

---

1 In the abbreviations "C." and "Cn." the use of the letter "C" to indicate the sound "g" reflects an archaic spelling. The Romans adapted their alphabet from the Etruscans, who did not distinguish the sounds "k" and "g," and hence the Romans used the letter "C" for both sounds; the form "G" was a later development, with the bar added to "C" to differentiate the two usages. The abbreviations thus go back to the initial period, when the two sounds were not distinguished in the Roman script.
2 Because of its origin as a nickname, the *cognomen* is commonly an (often uncharitable) description of a mental or physical trait: Brutus = "stupid," Cato = "clever man," Paetus = "squint-eyed."

of Gaius, of the Fabian tribe." Even the Romans found this something of a mouthful, so not only was the tribal affiliation and patronymic dropped in informal contexts, but it was common practice to omit the *nomen* of a high-ranking individual if it was a widespread one; hence, this same Caesar could be referred to simply as "C. Caesar."

A small number of families still had no *cognomen* at the time of the foundation of the Empire, but under the Empire virtually all men had one. Hence, possession of the *tria nomina* or "three names," consisting of the *praenomen*, *nomen*, and *cognomen*, became the distinctive mark of Roman citizens under the Empire. Even under the Republic, this complicated set of names could be manipulated in various ways, and under the Empire, it became common to dispense with the rather indistinctive *praenomen* in nonofficial contexts; in connection with this change, the habit arose of giving all the sons the same *praenomen* as the father but various *cognomina*. From this habit has arisen the practice of referring to the men of the Republic by their *nomen* and *cognomen*, like Julius Caesar.[3] Under the Empire, the *tria nomina* (with *praenomen* often ignored) long remained the common method of naming males among the general populace, but among the higher classes it became common practice to include famous names from maternal sides of the family. Eventually, the name of a senator with a particularly choice lineage could contain several entire names (include *praenomen*).

Under the Republic, the nomenclature for women was simple. There is early evidence for the use of female versions of *praenomina*, but this practice soon died out, and a woman was known only by the female version of her father's name (e.g., Caesar's daughter was simply called Julia). To avoid confusion with multiple daughters, they were distinguished with "elder" and "younger" in the case of two and with ordinal numbers ("the first," "second," "third" . . .) in the case of more than two. By the late Republic, the use of the female version of the father's *cognomen*, often in the form of a diminutive, arose (e.g., the daughter of M. Livius Drusus was Livia Drusilla). In a practice parallel to the development of male names, multiple daughters under the Empire received individual *cognomen*.

3 This practice is further exemplified by the fact that the procurator of Judaea under whom Jesus was crucified is identified in the New Testament only as Pontius Pilatus (this last anglicized as "Pilate"). An inscription discovered in the early 1960s at one time gave the man's praenomen, but an annoying break at the beginning cheated us of this information.

SUGGESTIONS FOR FURTHER READING

This section includes both ancient and modern sources. These are usually referred to as "primary" and "secondary" sources, respectively, but this terminology is not without ambiguity. In modern historiography, "primary" sources are those written by contemporaries of the events to which the compositions relate, and works written by later historians are termed "secondary" sources. By this definition, most of the works from antiquity are simply very old secondary sources. Nonetheless, the distinction is worth keeping in that there are fundamental differences in methods that distinguish the literary historians of antiquity from modern writers. Hence, while it is always worthwhile to consult the ancient sources first, they cannot always be taken at face value. A convenient collection of many excerpts of ancient texts is provided by N. Lewis and M. Reinhold, *Roman Civilization: Selected Readings. The Republic and the Augustan Age* (vol. 1) and *The Empire* (vol. 2), 3d ed. (New York: Columbia University Press, 1990). Before the citations, I give a short summary of the authors (if known) and the works as an aid for finding the texts or translations. In a few instances, I have included collections of translations of ancient documents.

Since this work is intended as an introduction for an English-speaking audience, I have decided to include only English books rather than loading it down with obscure articles and works in foreign languages that are more likely to confuse than assist the foreseen reader. Those who wish for information on a specific name or concept should consult Simon Hornblower and A. Spawforth (eds.), *The Oxford Classical Dictionary*, 3d ed. (Oxford and New York: Oxford University Press, 1996) and G. W. Bowersock, P. Brown, and O. Grabar (eds.), *Late Antiquity: A Guide to the Postclassical World* (Cambridge, MA: Belknap Press of Harvard University Press, 1999).

It has not been an easy task to decide how to present modern works. A mere alphabetical listing would make it difficult to find relevant works, yet a division according to the parts and chapters of this book was in some ways impractical because some general books and ones on broad themes did not correspond to the divisions of the book. I have therefore placed general and thematic works separately at the front of the section on secondary sources, the thematic section being further subdivided into books about domestic and foreign affairs. All these works are arranged in roughly chronological order, and after those thematic books whose titles do not make the content self-evident, I have included a short description in square brackets. Part One is not divided into individual chapters, because works tend to treat many aspects of this period as a result of the uncertainties of the sources. For the other parts, there is an introductory section on books that treat themes that span chapters, and then there follows a listing of books that are specific to the individual chapters.

ANCIENT SOURCES

Alphabetical List of Authors

Ammianus Marcellinus (ca. A.D. 310–395). A Greek-speaking Syrian, Ammianus became a military officer, serving Constantius II and Julian. He became so fluent in Latin that by the early 390s, he composed the last great history in the pagan Latin tradition, a thirty-one-book history down to the battle of Adrianople. The early section is lost, and the preserved material picks up in the year A.D. 353. The work is very detailed, and the earlier preserved sections are colored by his personal participation in events.

Appian (late first century A.D.–A.D. 160s). A Greek born in Alexandria, he served as an equestrian procurator under Antoninus Pius. He wrote a history of Rome that was organized partly geographically and partly chronologically. The earlier sections treat the various areas that the Romans conquered, arranging them on the basis of when the Romans first became involved there. The culmination of his Republican narrative is Augustus' conquest of Egypt and the establishment of the Empire, and this period he narrated in five books, which in modern times are generally considered a separate unit called the *Civil War*. The rest of the work is lost. His account of the Mithridatic War is the most extensive one preserved. Book One of the *Civil War* is particularly important because it is based on a knowledgeable and accurate source (the other books of the *Civil War* are less accurate). Appian is prone to distortion through excessive abbreviation of his sources, and his focus is on political conflict and violence.

Augustus (63 B.C.–A.D. 14). The emperor Augustus wrote a short summary of his achievements (*res gestae*), which were set up on bronze tablets in front of his mausoleum after his death. The text is preserved in both the Latin original and in a Greek translation in several places in Asia Minor, most completely on the Temple of Rome and Augustus in Ancyra (modern Ankara). This work gives his own (rather misleading) account of his public career.

Aurelius Victor (Sex. Aurelius Victor, mid–fourth century A.D.). A high-ranking Imperial official, he wrote a collection of Imperial biographies from Augustus down to Constantius II in Latin.

Caesar (C. Julius Caesar, ca. 100–44 B.C.). The great dictator worked up his dispatches to Rome concerning his Gallic conquests into a seven-book masterpiece of self-justification known as the *Gallic War*. To justify his actions during the subsequent civil war, Caesar began a work (*Civil War*) that he brought down to his arrival in Egypt in Book Three and left incomplete upon his death. An eighth book was added to the *Gallic War* by his adherent A. Hirtius (consul of 43 B.C.) to fill in the small gap before the start of the *Civil War*.

Cicero (M. Tullius Cicero, 106–43 B.C.). As the most respected orator of Roman antiquity, large numbers of his works are preserved. His speeches give his public interpretation of events; all have some relevance to the political scene, but the ones mentioned here directly address political events. His letters, which were not written for publication and were published posthumously, reveal his private thoughts. The largest collection is *Letters to Atticus,* in which he writes to his boyhood friend, a very wealthy equestrian. The *Letters to Friends* also preserves much correspondence to Cicero from others. The *Letters to Quintus* (his brother) give a lively account of the political scene in the 50s B.C. The *Letters to M. Brutus* are particularly useful for the events following the assassination of Caesar the dictator. (I give the chronological numbering of the editions of Shackleton Bailey, which supersede the traditional numbers.)

Claudian (Claudius Claudianus, ca. A.D. 370–ca. 404). A prolific poet attached to the western court, Claudian wrote several panegyrical works in honor of both Honorius and Stilicho. These poems provide much historical detail about Stilicho's actions and the response in the east, but their bias makes them unreliable.

Dio Cassius (L. [uncertain praenomen] Cassius Dio, ca. A.D. 164–after 229). A wealthy Greek senator of Bithynia, he had a prestigious public career that culminated in the ordinary consulship of A.D. 229 with Severus Alexander. He first wrote a pamphlet about the portents foretelling the accession of Septimius Severus, and this impelled him to write a massive history of Rome in Greek, of which only Books 36 to 60 are preserved reasonably intact, though there are extensive excerpts for the rest. His narrative is a major source for the Late Republic and Early Empire, though he has little understanding of the Republican form of government. His treatment of the Severan period is particularly important, since he was a high-placed contemporary.

Dionysius of Halicarnassus. Prolific Greek author of the time of Augustus. Relevant here is his *Roman Antiquities*, a historical work on the origins of Rome down to the First Punic War. Originally in twenty books, of which the first eleven are preserved intact and the remainder in fragments, the work is highly rhetorical, but being based on earlier annalistic sources, it often preserves traditions at variance with Livy's account.

Eusebius (ca. A.D. 260–339). Elected bishop of Caesarea in Judaea in ca. A.D. 313, he played an important role in the politics of the Church in the east during the period of the Arian controversy. His *Ecclesiastical History*, a narrative of the development of Christianity down to his own time, is marred by some bias but preserves many official documents. In addition, he wrote an unfinished *Life of Constantine*, and his speech for Constantine on his thirtieth anniversary is also informative.

Eutropius (mid–fourth century A.D.). A high-ranking Imperial official who served Julian and Valens, he may have been the consul in A.D. 387. He dedicated to Valens a ten-book compendium of Roman history in Latin (*Breviarium*). The earlier sections are of no value, but the work provides useful information about the third and fourth centuries A.D.

Herodian (early third century A.D.). A minor Imperial official (perhaps a freedman), Herodian composed a history from the reign of Marcus Aurelius down to Gordian III. The work is given to rhetorical elaboration and is often unreliable.

Josephus (Flavius Josephus, born A.D. 37/38). A high-born Jewish priest, Josephus served as a general in the Great Revolt, and after being captured he received pardon from Vespasian. In the A.D. 70s, he published a seven-book account of the revolt (*Jewish War*), which provides the most elaborate account of the Imperial military in action. He went on to write an extensive history of the Jews.

Julian (A.D. 331–363). The last pagan emperor considered himself a Greek man of letters, and his many surviving works present a vivid picture of the man.

Lactantius (L. Cae[ci?]lius Firmianus Lactantius, ca. A.D. 240–ca. 320). A prolific Christian writer, Lactantius was an African rhetorician who lived in Diocletian's capital of Nicomedia at the outbreak of the "Great Persecution" but soon returned to the west. In his work *On the Deaths of the Persecutors*, he celebrated the triumph of Constantine and the eventual downfall of the Imperial opponents of Christianity in the aftermath of Diocletian's abdication. The work provides the main narrative for the civil war of the early fourth century A.D. and is often relied on despite its obvious (and self-proclaimed) bias.

Latin panegyrics. A collection of speeches of praise spoken by various orators before assorted emperors. The numeration here follows the chronological arrangement of C. E. V. Nixon and B. S. Rodgers, *In Praise of Later Roman Emperors: The Panegyrici Latini* (Berkeley: University of California Press, 1994).

Livy (T. Livius, 59 B.C.–A.D. 17). A 167-book history of Rome from the foundation of the city to his own time in an annalistic format. His style so surpassed his annalist predecessors that their works fell into oblivion and virtually nothing of them survives. Books 1–10 and 21–45 survive. (Some sense of the content of the lost books can be gotten from the summaries made in Late Antiquity.) Since Livy had no experience in public life, he often misunderstands constitutional procedure. His main interest is in improving on the style of his sources and in giving an edifying interpretation on the material.

Origin of Constantine (*Origo Constantini*)/*Anonymus Valesianus*. Biography of Constantine by an unknown author (hence the alternative name, which refers to the manuscript in which the work was preserved).

Orosius (Paulus Orosius, late fourth to early fifth century A.D.). A young Spanish priest who moved to Africa, Orosius was inspired by Augustine in the aftermath of the sack of Rome in A.D. 410 to write a seven-book history of Rome (down to A.D. 417). The purpose of the work was to refute pagan claims that the sack was the result of Theodosius I's abolition of pagan sacrifice by showing that Roman history had always been characterized by disaster. The early sections are of little value, but the work is more useful for contemporary affairs (though he naturally emphasizes the troubles in the pagan past and plays down contemporary disasters).

Pliny the Younger (C. Plinius Caecilius Secundus, ca. A.D. 61–ca. 112). A senator of moderate wealth from northern Italy, Pliny specialized in accounting and held high office under Domitian, Nerva, and Trajan. He prepared his correspondence for publication, and in addition to revealing much of his literary and social interests, the first nine books of his letters provide valuable information about affairs in the senate. Pliny was also renowned as an orator, and after being suffect consul in A.D. 100, he elaborated for publication the speech of thanks (*Panegyricus*) that he gave to Trajan. This tedious work gives much useful information about the senatorial conception of an ideal emperor. Book Ten of Pliny's letters consists of letters addressed to Trajan; most concern his special appointment as governor of Bithynia for the purpose of settling affairs in the financially troubled province and are often accompanied by Trajan's response. This correspondence provides the most vivid picture of the activities of an Imperial governor.

Plutarch (L. Mestrius Plutarchus, before A.D. 50–after 120). A prolific Greek author. Relevant here are his parallel lives, a series of biographies in which the life of a Greek statesman is paired with that of a Roman one. As a biographer, he is not too concerned about absolute historical truth, and sometimes rearranges and adapts his material to suit his biographical purposes. Nonetheless, he preserves much valuable information.

Polybius (ca. 200 B.C.–ca. 118 B.C.). His father was an important leader of the Achaean League, and in the aftermath of the Third Macedonian War, Polybius was taken as a captive to Rome, where he made many acquaintances among the nobility and became something of a mentor to Scipio Aemilianus. He wrote a major history of Rome's rise to power in forty books. Originally, his aim was to explain for a Greek-speaking audience Rome's conquest of the Mediterranean during the half century from the Second Punic War to the Third Macedonian War, but he later expanded the material to include the First Punic War as an introduction and then to examine the effects of the conquest. Polybius was very self-conscious about his methodology and his work represents the culmination of the Greek historiographical tradition going back to Thucydides. While he was very concerned about historical accuracy and the explanation of historical processes, he had little interest in rhetoric, and hence, because his style was not esteemed in antiquity, only Books One to Five are preserved intact, though many of the later books were extensively excerpted in medieval works. His (rather theoretical) analysis of the Republican constitution in Book 6 has been influential.

Pseudo-Caesar. Three works were written by contemporary and unknown partisans of Caesar's to continue the narrative of his campaigns at the point where he himself stopped in his *Civil War*. These three works, which clumsily attempted to copy Caesar's style, were later attributed to him.

Quintus Cicero (Q. Tullius Cicero, ca. 102–43 B.C.). A work (generally known as the *Commentariolum petitionis*) is preserved that purports to be a memorandum of advice written for the orator Cicero by his brother Quintus in preparation for the former's run for the consulship. While many scholars still consider the work to be genuine, verbal similarities to Cicero's speeches and inaccuracies concerning the state of Cicero's career at the time when the work was supposedly written strongly suggest that the work was a later literary fiction. The work is the only extensive discussion of electoral politics from antiquity, but the value of this information is uncertain because of the dubious nature of its authorship.

Rufinus of Aquileia (ca. A.D. 345–411). An Italian churchman who translated a number of Greek works into Latin, including Eusebius' *Ecclesiastical History*, to which he added two books on subsequent events.

Sallust (C. Sallustius Crispus, ca. 85–35 B.C.). Sallust was a Roman politician towards the end of the Republic; an adherent of Caesar, he withdrew from public life in the mid-40s. He wrote two historical monographs, one on the war with Jugurtha and the rise of Marius and the other on the so-called Catilinarian conspiracy. His highly rhetorical works are characterized by much vague moralizing, along with inaccuracy of detail and chronology.

Scriptores Historiae Augustae. The somewhat unsatisfactory names for the putative authors of the collection of Imperial biographies supposedly written in the early fourth century A.D. It is generally held that these lives were written, presumably by one person, in the late fourth century A.D. The author's identity and purposes are unknown, but it is clear that the work commingles fact and fiction in ways that are difficult to unravel.

Sidonius Apollinaris (C. Sollius Modestus Apollinaris Sidonius, ca. A.D. 430–ca. 484). A high-born Gallic nobleman, he was deeply involved in Imperial politics in the A.D. 450s and 460s. In the 470s, he served as a bishop in Gaul. In addition to the information provided about Imperial affairs by his panegyrics of emperors, his numerous letters also shed light on Roman accommodation with the Germanic invaders during the dissolution of the Western Empire.

Socrates Scholasticus (ca. A.D. 379–ca. 440). A lawyer, he continued Eusebius' *Ecclesiastical History* from A.D. 305 down to A.D. 439. He was not particularly interested in theological disputes and drew attention to the interrelationship between ecclesiastical and secular affairs.

Sozomen (first half of fifth century A.D.). A lawyer, he continued Eusebius' *Ecclesiastical History* down to A.D. 439 and included secular affairs. His main source was Socrates Scholasticus.

Suetonius (C. Suetonius Tranquillus, ca. A.D. 70–ca. 130). A high-ranking official in the Imperial chancery, Suetonius undertook to write a series of biographies of the Caesars, starting with the dictator and continuing down to Domitian (the last emperor who did not belong to the dynasty under which he was writing). Suetonius mostly organized his lives by first giving a narrative of the man's life and then presenting information about personality and physical characteristics in a relatively fixed format. Suetonius had little sense of historical judgment, often giving a mix of contradictory information and being prone to overgeneralization. For the early lives, Suetonius had access to the Imperial archives and quotes letters written by various emperors. He lost access to this confidential source of information once he lost favor with Hadrian and was dismissed from office, and the later lives are comparatively cursory.

Symmachus (Q. Aurelius Symmachus, ca. A.D. 340–402). A member of the highest senatorial aristocracy, he was esteemed in antiquity as a great orator (an opinion undermined by the discovery of fragments of various panegyrics by him). His extensive correspondence fails to provide much historical information, but his *Relationes* ("reports" to the Valentinian II from his tenure as praefect of Rome in A.D. 383–384) provide a wealth of information about the administration of the capital. The *Third Relatio* is particularly famous for its defense of the traditional pagan cults of the city.

Tacitus (P. [praenomen uncertain] Cornelius Tacitus, ca. A.D. 56–ca. 120s). A senator of moderate standing from Cisalpine Gaul or Narbonensis, he held the suffect consulship of A.D. 97. Tacitus was the greatest historian of ancient Rome. All his works dealt with the Empire, and his historical perspective was heavily influenced by his perceptions of Domitian's tyranny. The *Agricola* was ostensibly a biography of his father-in-law but had the additional purpose of justifying those senators (like Tacitus himself?) who had not actively opposed Domitian. The *Dialogus* was a dialogue that discussed similar themes, specifically dealing with the role of oratory under the Imperial government. His first work of narrative is known as the *Histories*, which begins with the start of A.D. 69. It narrates the subsequent civil war, but breaks off at the start of Book Five, which deals with A.D. 70. The lost remainder treated the Flavian dynasty. His greatest work was the *Annals*, which treated the Julio-Claudian dynasty after the death of Augustus. Tacitus' very pessimistic views about the exercise of Imperial power at times distorts his account.

Theodoret (ca. A.D. 393–466). First a monk and then a bishop in the east, Theodoret was deeply opposed to monophysitism. His *Ecclesiastical History* in Greek covers the years from Constantine down to A.D. 428. Including many documents, the work coincidentally sheds light on secular matters. His main source was Socrates Scholasticus.

Velleius Paterculus (ca. 20/19 B.C.–after A.D. 31). Velleius was created a senator under Augustus and dedicated a potted history to Sejanus in A.D. 31. The work concentrates on the actions of individuals and is of little value for earlier history, but it provides useful information about the reigns of Augustus and Tiberius. Velleius was a loyal adherent of the dynasty, a stance that sometimes leads to excessive adulation.

Zosimus (early sixth century A.D.?). A middle-ranking Imperial official, he wrote a history of the Empire that breaks off just before the sack of Rome of A.D. 410. A committed pagan, he attributes the problems of the fourth century to the adoption of Christianity.

CHAPTER 1 (KINGDOM)

Dionysius of Halicarnassus 1–4
Livy 1
Plutarch, *Romulus, Numa*

CHAPTERS 2 AND 3 (EARLY REPUBLIC)

Plutarch, *Publicola, Camillus*
Livy 2–10
Dionysius of Halicarnassus 5–20

CHAPTER 4 (STRUGGLE WITH CARTHAGE)

Appian, *Roman History* 8 ("Punic Wars")
Livy 21–30
Plutarch, *Fabius Maximus, Marcellus*
Polybius 1–5, 7–15

CHAPTER 5 (CONQUEST OF THE EAST)

Appian 11 ("Syrian War")
Livy 23–45 (passim)
Plutarch, *Aemilius Paullus, Flamininus*

CHAPTER 6 (CONQUEST OF SPAIN)

Appian, *Roman History* 6 ("Wars in Spain")
Livy 21–43 (passim)

CHAPTER 7 (EFFECTS OF CONQUESTS)

Appian, *Civil War* 1.7–8
Polybius 6

CHAPTER 8 (ASSAULT ON THE OLIGARCHY)

Appian, *Civil War* 1.1–102, *Roman History* 12 ("Mithridatic War")
Cicero, *In Defense of Sex. Roscius of Ameria (Pro Sex. Roscio Amerino)*
Dio Cassius 24
Plutarch, *Tiberius and Gaius Gracchus, Gaius Marius, Sulla, Sertorius*
Sallust, *Jugurthine War*

CHAPTER 9 (RESTORED OLIGARCHY)

Appian, *Civil War* 1.103–2.8
Cicero, *Verrine Orations, In Favor of the Manilian Law (Pro Lege
    Manilia), In Opposition to Rullus (Contra Rullum), Attack on Catiline
    (In Catilinam), Letters to Atticus (Ad Atticum)* 1–22

Dio 36–37
Plutarch, *Crassus, Lucullus, Pompey, Cicero, Caesar, Sertorius, Cato the
    Younger*
Sallust, *Conspiracy of Catiline*

CHAPTER 10 (CAESAR)

Appian, *Civil War* 2.9–117
Caesar, *Gallic War, Civil War*
Cicero, *Attack on Piso (In Pisonem), On the Consular Provinces (De
    Provinciis Consularibus), In Defense of Sestius (Pro Sestio),
    Philippic Orations; Letters to Atticus (Ad Atticum)* 23–354, *Letters to
    His Friends (Ad Familiares)* 12–20, 77–98, 146–57, *Letters to His
    Brother Quintus (Ad Quintum Fratrem)* 2–27
Dio Cassius 38–44
Plutarch, *Crassus, Pompey, Brutus, Caesar, Cicero*
Pseudo-Caesar, *Alexandrine War, African War, Spanish War*
Suetonius, *Caesar*

CHAPTER 11 (CONFLICT OF WARLORDS)

Appian, *Civil War* 2.118–5
Cicero, *Letters to Atticus* 354–426, *Letters to His Friends* 325–435, *Letters
    to Marcus Brutus (Ad M. Brutum)*
Dio Cassius 45–50
Plutarch, *Brutus, Cicero, Antony*
Suetonius, *Augustus*
Velleius Paterculus 2.59–87

CHAPTER 12 (POLITICS OF LATE REPUBLIC)

Cicero, *In Defense of Flaccus (Pro Flacco), In Defense of Plancius (Pro
    Plancio); Letters to His Brother Quintus* 1
Quintus Cicero, *Pamphlet on Running for Office (Commentariolum
    Petitionis)*

CHAPTER 13 (AUGUSTUS)

Augustus, *Res Gestae*
Dio Cassius 51–57
Suetonius, *Augustus*
Velleius Paterculus 2.88–123

CHAPTER 14 (JULIO-CLAUDIANS)

Dio Cassius 57–63
Josephus, *Jewish War* 2–4.439
Suetonius, *Tiberius, Caligula, Claudius, Nero*
Tacitus, *Annals* 1–6, 11–16
Velleius Paterculus 2.124–131

CHAPTER 15 (YEAR OF FOUR EMPERORS, FLAVIANS)

Dio Cassius 64–67
Josephus, *Jewish War* 4.440–7
Plutarch, *Galba, Otho*
Suetonius, *Galba, Otho, Vitellius, Vespasian, Titus, Domitian*
Tacitus, *Histories* 1–5, *Agricola, Dialogus*

CHAPTER 16 (PINNACLE OF PRINCIPATE)

Dio 68–73
Herodian 1
Pliny the Younger, *Letters, Panegyricus*
Scriptores Historiae Augustae, *Hadrian, Antoninus Pius, M. Aurelius
  Antoninus, L. Verus, Commodus*

CHAPTER 17 (SEVERANS)

Dio Cassius 74–80
Herodian 2–6
Scriptores Historiae Augustae, *Pertinax, Septimius Severus, Caracalla,
  Macrinus, Elagabalus, Severus Alexander*

CHAPTER 18 (INSTITUTIONS OF PRINCIPATE)

Levick, Barbara, *Government of the Roman Empire: A Sourcebook*, 2d ed.
  (London and New York: Routledge, 2000)

CHAPTER 19 (THIRD CENTURY CRISIS)

Aurelius Victor 25–38.14
Scriptores Historiae Augustae, *Two Maximians, Three Gordians,
  Maximinus and Balbinus, Two Valerians, Two Gallieni, Claudius,
  Aurelian, Tacitus, Probus*, and *Carus, Carinus and Numerian*
Eutropius 9.1–19
Herodian 6–8
Zosimus 1.13–73

CHAPTER 20 (EARLY CHRISTIANITY)

Eusebius, *Ecclesiastical History*
Pliny, *Letters* 10.96–97
Musurillo, H., *Acts of the Christian Martyrs* (Oxford: Clarendon Press, 1972)

CHAPTER 21 (DIOCLETIAN)

Aurelius Victor 38.14–39
Eusebius, *Ecclesiastical History* 8
Eutropius 9.19–28

Lactantius, *On the Deaths of the Persecutors* (*De Mortibus Persecutorum*)
   1–19
Latin Panegyrics (*Panegyrici Latini*) 1–4
Zosimus 2.1–7

CHAPTER 22 (CONSTANTINE)

Origin of Constantine (*Origo Constantini*)/*Anonymus Valesianus*
Aurelius Victor 40–41.21
Lactantius, *On the Deaths of the Persecutors* (*De Mortibus Persecutorum*)
   20–52
Socrates 1
Theodoret 1
Zosimus 2.9–39
Sozomen 1–2
Eutropius 10.1–8
Latin Panegyrics (*Panegyrici Latini*) 6–10
Eusebius, *Ecclesiastical History* 9–10, *Tricennalian Oration,*
   Life of Constantine

CHAPTER 23 (CHRISTIAN EMPIRE)

Ammianus Marcellinus 14–31
Aurelius Victor 41.22–42
Eutropius 10.9–18
Julian, *Misopogon* (*The Beard Hater*), *Against the Galileans,*
   Caesars, Letters
Latin Panegyrics (*Panegyrici Latini*) 10–11
Orosius 7.29–35
Rufinus, *Ecclesiastical History* 10–11
Socrates 2–5
Sozomen 3–7
Symmachus, *Relations*
Theodoret 2–5.25
Zosimus 2.39–4

CHAPTER 24 (DEMISE OF THE WEST)

Claudian *Against Rufinus* (*In Rufinum*), *Against Eutropius* (*In Eutropium*),
   On the War against Gildo (*De Bello Gildonico*), *On Stilicho's
   Consulship* (*De Consulatu Stilichonis*)
Orosius 7.36–43
Sidonius Apollinaris, *Panegyrics on Avitus, Majorian,* and *Anthemius*;
   Letters
Socrates 6–7
Sozomen 8–9
Theodoret 5.26–39
Zosimus 5–6

MODERN SOURCES

(Subsections A and B are arranged chronologically by period covered; Subsection C is alphabetical.)

GENERAL

Cambridge Ancient History, vol. 7, pt. 2, 2d ed., *The Rise of Rome to 220 B.C.*, eds. F. W. Walbank, A. E. Astin, and M. W. Frederiksen (Cambridge and New York: Cambridge University Press, 1989).

Cambridge Ancient History, vol. 8, 2d ed., *Rome and the Mediterranean to 133 B.C.*, eds. A. E. Astin, F. W. Walbank, and M. W. Frederiksen (Cambridge and New York: Cambridge University Press, 1989).

Scullard, H. H., *A History of the Roman World, 753–146 B.C.*, 4th ed. (London and New York: Methuen, 1980).

Cambridge Ancient History, vol. 9., 3d ed., *The Last Age of the Roman Republic, 146–43 B.C.*, eds. J. A. Crook, A. Lintott, and E. Rawson (Cambridge and New York: Cambridge University Press, 1994).

Scullard, H. H., *From the Gracchi to Nero: A History of Rome from 133 B.C. to A.D. 68*, 5th ed. (London and New York: Methuen, 1982).

Cambridge Ancient History, vol. 10, 2d ed., *The Augustan Empire, 43 B.C.–A.D. 69*, eds. A. K. Bowman, E. Champlin, and A. Lintott (Cambridge and New York: Cambridge University Press, 1996).

Garzetti, A., *From Tiberius to the Antonines: A History of the Roman Empire, A.D. 14–192* (London: Methuen, 1974).

Cambridge Ancient History, vol. 11, 2d ed., *The High Empire, A.D. 70–A.D. 192*, eds. A. K. Bowman, P. Garnsey, and D. Rathbone (Cambridge and New York: Cambridge University Press, 2000).

Southern, P., *The Roman Empire from Severus to Constantine* (London and New York: Routledge, 2001).

Jones, A. H. M., *The Later Roman Empire, A.D. 285–602: A Social, Economic and Administrative History* (Oxford: Blackwell, 1964).

Jones, A. H. M., *The Decline of the Ancient World* (London and New York: Longman, 1966).

Cameron, A., *The Later Roman Empire, A.D. 284–430* (Cambridge: Harvard University Press, 1993).

Cambridge Ancient History, vol. 13, 2d ed., *The Late Empire, A.D. 337–A.D. 425*, eds. A. Cameron and P. Garnsey (Cambridge and New York: Cambridge University Press, 1998).

Cameron, A., *The Mediterranean World in Late Antiquity, A.D. 395–600* (London and New York: Routledge, 1993).

Cambridge Ancient History, vol. 14, 2d ed., *The Late Empire, A.D. 425–600*, eds. A. Cameron, B. Ward-Perkins, and M. Whitby (Cambridge and New York: Cambridge University Press, 2000).

THEMATIC

DOMESTIC

Lintott, A. W., *The Constitution of the Roman Republic* (London and New York: Clarendon Press, 1997).

Sherwin-White, A. N., *The Roman Citizenship* (Oxford: Clarendon Press, 1939) [from the foundation to the third century A.D.].

Brunt, P. A., *Social Conflicts in the Roman Republic* (New York: W. W. Norton, 1971).

Münzer, F., *Roman Aristocratic Parties and Families*, trans. T. Ridley (Baltimore: Johns Hopkins University Press, 1999).

Develin, R., *The Practice of Politics at Rome, 366–167 B.C.* (Brussels: Latomus, 1985).

Scullard, H. H., *Roman Politics, 220–150 B.C.* (Oxford: Clarendon Press, 1951).

Gelzer, M., *The Roman Nobility*, trans. with intro. by R. Seager (Oxford: Blackwell, 1969).

Badian, E., *Publicans and Sinners: Private Enterprise in the Service of the Roman Republic*, rev. ed. (Ithaca: Cornell University Press, 1982).

Badian, E., *Foreign Clientelae* (Oxford: Clarendon Press, 1958) [examines the role of foreign clients in Republican politics].

Crawford, M. H., *Coinage and Money under the Republic: Italy and the Mediterranean Economy* (Berkeley: University of California Press, 1985).

Syme, R., *Roman Revolution* (Oxford: Oxford University Press, 1939) [prosopographical treatment of the period from Caesar the dictator through Augustus].

Harl, K. W., *Coinage in the Roman Economy, 300 B.C. to A.D. 700* (Baltimore and London: Johns Hopkins University Press, 1996).

Bauman, R. A., *The Crimen Maiestatis in the Roman Republic and Augustan Principate* (Johannesburg: Witwatersrand University Press, 1967).

FOREIGN

David, J.-M., *The Roman Conquest of Italy*, trans. A. Nevill (Oxford: Blackwell, 1996).

Harris, W. V., *War and Imperialism in Republican Rome, 327–70 B.C.* (Oxford: Clarendon Press, 1979).

Kallett-Marx, R. M., *Hegemony to Empire: The Development of the Roman Imperium in the East from 148 to 62 B.C.* (Berkeley: University of California Press, 1995).

Lintott, A., *Imperium Romanum: Politics and Administration* (London and New York: Routledge, 1993) [treats both the Republic and Empire].

Sherwin-White, A. N., *Roman Policy in the East, 168 B.C.–A.D. 1* (London: Duckworth, 1984).

Badian, E., *Roman Imperialism*, 2d ed. (Ithaca: Cornell University Press, 1968) [treats the Republic].

Millar, F., *Roman Near East, 31 B.C.–A.D. 337* (Cambridge: Harvard University Press, 1993).

Dudgeon, M. D., and S. N. C. Lieu, *The Roman Eastern Frontier and the Persian Wars, A.D. 226–363: A Documentary History* (London and New York: Routledge, 1991).

Greatrex, G., and S. N. C. Lieu, *The Roman Eastern Frontier and the Persian Wars, Part II. A.D. 363–630: A Narrative Sourcebook* (London and New York: Routledge, 2002).

SPECIFIC TO INDIVIDUAL PARTS AND CHAPTERS

PART ONE

Alföldi, A., *Early Rome and the Latins* (Ann Arbor: University of Michigan Press, 1963).

Bietti-Sestieri, A. M., *The Iron Age Community of Osteria dell'Osa: A Study of Socio-political Development in Central Tyrrhenian Italy* (Cambridge and New York: Cambridge University Press, 1992).

Cornell, T. J., *The Beginnings of Rome. Italy and Rome from the Bronze Age to the Punic Wars (c. 1000–264 BC)* (London: Routledge, 1995).

Frier, B. W., *Libri Annales Ponticum Maximorum: The Origins of the Annalistic Tradition* (Rome: American Academy in Rome, 1979).

Halloway, R. R., *The Archaeology of Early Rome and Latium* (London and New York: Routledge, 1994).

Harris, W. V., *Rome in Etruria and Umbria* (Oxford: Clarendon Press, 1971).

Ogilvie, R. M., *Early Rome and the Etruscans* (Atlantic Highlands: Humanities Press, 1976).

Pallottino, M., *A History of Earliest Italy* (Ann Arbor: University of Michigan Press, 1991).

Pallottino, M., *The Etruscans*, trans. J. Cremona, ed., David Ridgway 2d ed. (London: Allen Lane, 1974).

Palmer, R. E. A., *The Archaic Community of the Romans* (Cambridge: Cambridge University Press, 1970).

Salmon, E. T., *Roman Colonisation under the Republic* (London: Thames and Hudson, 1969).

Scullard, H. H., *The Etruscan Cities and Rome* (Ithaca: Cornell University Press, 1967).

Smith, C. J., *Early Rome and Latium: Economy and Society c. 1000 to 500 B.C.* (Oxford: Clarendon Press, 1996).

PART TWO

General

Astin, A. E., *Scipio Aemilianus* (Oxford: Oxford University Press, 1967).

Chapter 4 (Struggle with Carthage)

Lancel, S., *Carthage: A History*, trans. A. Nevill (Oxford: Blackwell, 1995).

Lazenby, J. F., *The First Punic War: A Military History* (London: UCL Press, 1996).

Lazenby, J. F., *Hannibal's War: A Military History of the Second Punic War* (Warminster: Aris & Phillips, 1978).

Chapter 5 (Conquest of the East)

Gruen, E., *The Hellenistic World and the Coming of Rome* (Berkeley: University of California Press, 1984).

Chapter 6 (Conquest of Spain)

Richardson, J. S., *Hispaniae: Spain and the Development of Roman Imperialism, 218–82 B.C.* (Cambridge: Cambridge University Press, 1986).

PART THREE

General

Gruen, E., *The Last Generation of the Roman Republic* (Berkeley: University of California Press, 1974).

Chapter 8 (Assault on the Oligarchy)

Badian, E., *Sulla: The Deadly Reformer* (Sydney: Sydney University Press, 1970).

Boren, H. C., *The Gracchi* (New York: Twayne, 1969).

Carney, T. F., *A Biography of C. Marius*, 2d ed. (Chicago: Argonaut, 1970).

Evans, R. J., *Gaius Marius: A Political Biography* (Pretoria: University of South Africa, 1994).

Keaveney, A., *Sulla: The Last Republican* (London: Croom Helm, 1982).

Kildahl, P. H., *Caius Marius* (New York: Twayne, 1968).

Lovano, M., *The Age of Cinna: Crucible of Late Republican Rome* (Stuttgart: Franz Steiner Verlag, 2002).
Stockton, D. L., *The Gracchi* (Oxford: Clarendon Press, 1979).

Chapter 9 (Restored Oligarchy)
Fuhrmann, M., *Cicero and the Roman Republic*, trans. W. E. Yuill (Oxford and Cambridge, Blackwell, 1992).
Greenhalgh, P. A. L., *Pompey: The Republican Prince* (London: Weidenfeld and Nicolson, 1981).
Greenhalgh, P. A. L., *Pompey: The Roman Alexander* (London: Weidenfeld and Nicolson, 1980).
Rawson, E., *Cicero: A Portrait* (London: Allen Lane, 1975).
Seager, R., *Pompey: A Political Biography*, 2d ed. (Oxford: Blackwell, 2002).
Stockton, D. L., *Cicero: A Political Biography* (London: Oxford University Press, 1971).

Chapter 10 (Caesar)
Gelzer, M., *Caesar*, trans. P. Needham (Cambridge: Harvard University Press, 1968).
Meier, C., *Caesar*, trans. D. McLintock (New York: BasicBooks/HarperCollins, 1995).
Tatum, W. J., *The Patrician Tribune: Publius Clodius Pulcher* (Chapel Hill: University of North Carolina Press, 1999).

Chapter 11 (Conflict of Warlords)
Clarke, M. L., *The Noblest Roman: Marcus Brutus and His Reputation* (Ithaca: Cornell University Press, 1981).
Lacey, W. K., *Cicero and the End of the Roman Republic* (London and Toronto: Hodder and Stoughton, 1978).
Powell, A. and K. Welch (eds.), *Sextus Pompeius* (London: Duckworth, 1992).
Weigel, R. D., *Lepidus: The Tarnished Triumvir* (London and New York: Routlege, 1992).

Chapter 12 (Politics of Late Republic)
Brunt, P. A., *The Fall of the Roman Republic and Related Essays* (Oxford: Clarendon Press, 1988).
Gruen, E., *Roman Politics and the Criminal Courts, 149–78 B.C.* (Berkeley: University of California Press, 1968).
Lintott, A. W., *Violence in Republican Rome*, 2d ed. (Oxford and New York: Oxford University Press, 1999).
Millar, F., *The Crowd in Rome in the Late Republic* (Ann Arbor: University of Michigan Press, 1998).
Morstein-Marx, R., *Mass Oratory and Political Power in the Late Roman Republic* (Cambridge and New York: Cambridge University Press, 2004).
Mouritsen, H., *Plebs and Politics in the Late Roman Republic* (Cambridge and New York: Cambridge University Press, 2001).
Nicolet, C., *The World of the Citizen in Republican Rome*, trans. P. S. Falla (Berkeley: University of California Press, 1980).
Taylor, L. R., *Party Politics in the Age of Caesar* (Berkeley: University of California Press, 1949).
Wiseman, T. P., *New Men in the Roman Senate, 139 B.C.–A.D. 14* (Oxford: Clarendon Press, 1969).

Yakobson, A., *Elections and Electioneering in Rome: A Study in the Political System of the Late Republic* (Stuttgart: Franz Steiner Verlag: 1999).

PART FOUR

General

Alston, R., *Aspects of Roman History*, A.D. *14–117* (London and New York: Routledge, 1998).

Bauman, R. A., *Impietas in principem: A Study of Treason against the Roman Emperor with Special Reference to the First Century* (Munich: Beck, 1974).

Brunt, P. A., *Roman Imperial Themes* (Oxford: Clarendon Press, 1990).

Wells, C., *The Roman Empire*, 2d ed. (Cambridge: Harvard University Press, 1992).

Chapter 13 (Augustus)

Holmes, T. R., *The Architect of the Roman Empire* (Oxford: Clarendon Press, 1928–31).

Jones, A. H. M., *Augustus* (New York: Norton, 1970).

Lacey, W. K., *Augustus and the Principate: The Evolution of the System* (Leeds: Francis Cairns, 1996).

Southern, P., *Augustus* (London and New York: Routledge, 1998).

Syme, R., *Roman Revolution* (Oxford: Clarendon Press, 1939).

Zanker, P., *The Power of Images in the Age of Augustus* (Ann Arbor: University of Michigan Press, 1988).

Chapter 14 (Julio-Claudians)

Barrett, A., *Caligula: the Corruption of Power* (London: B. T. Batsford, 1989).

Ferrill, A., *Caligula: Emperor of Rome* (London: Thames and Hudson, 1991).

Griffin, M. T., *Nero: The End of a Dynasty* (London: B. T. Batsford, 1984).

Hammond, M., *The Augustan Principate in Theory and Practice during the Julio-Claudian Period* (Cambridge: Harvard University Press, 1933).

Levick, B., *Claudius* (New Haven: Yale University Press, 1990).

Levick, B., *Tiberius the Politician*, rev. ed. (London and New York: Routledge, 1999).

Momigliano, A., *Claudius: The Emperor and His Achievement; with a New Bibliography (1942–59)* (Westport: Greenwood Press, 1981).

Seager, R., *Tiberius*, 2d ed. (Oxford: Blackwell, 2002).

Sørensen, V., *Seneca: The Humanist at the Court of Nero* (Chicago: University of Chicago Press, 1984).

Chapter 15 (Year of Four Emperors, Flavians)

Greenhalgh, P. A. L., *The Year of the Four Emperors* (New York: Barnes & Noble Books, 1975).

Jones, B. W., *Domitian and the Senatorial Order: A Prosopographical Study of Domitian's Relationship with the Senate* (Philadelphia: American Philosophical Society, 1979).

Jones, B. W., *The Emperor Titus* (New York: St. Martin's Press, 1984).

Jones, B. W., *The Emperor Domitian* (London and New York: Routledge, 1992).

Levick, B., *Vespasian* (London and New York: Routledge, 1999).

Nicols, J., *Vespasian and the* Partes Flavianae (Stuttgart: F. Steiner, 1978).

Southern, P., *Domitian: Tragic Tyrant* (London and New York: Routledge, 1997).

Wellesley, K., *The Long Year* A.D. *69* (London: Elek, 1969).

Chapter 16 (Pinnacle of Principate)
Bennett, J., *Trajan, Optimus Princeps: A Life and Times* (Bloomington: Indiana University Press, 1997).
Birley, A. R., *Hadrian: The Restless Emperor* (London and New York: Routledge, 1997).
Birley, A. R., *Marcus Aurelius: A Biography*, rev. ed. (New Haven: Yale University Press, 1987).
Champlin, E., *Fronto and Antonine Rome* (Cambridge: Harvard University Press, 1980).
Hammond, M., *The Antonine Monarchy* (Rome: American Academy in Rome, 1959).
Hekster, A., *Commodus: Emperor at the Crossroads* (Amsterdam: J. C. Gieben, 2002).
Lepper, F. A., *Trajan's Parthian War* (London: Oxford University Press, 1948).

Chapter 17 (Severans)
Birley, A. R., *The African Emperor: Septimius Severus*, rev. ed. (London: B. T. Batsford, 1988).
Campbell, J. B., *The Emperor and the Roman Army 31 B.C.–A.D. 235* (Oxford: Clarendon Press, 1984).

Chapter 18 (Institutions of Principate)
Crook, J. A., *Consilium Principis* (Cambridge: Cambridge University Press, 1955).
Duncan-Jones, R., *Money and Government in the Roman Empire* (Cambridge and New York: Cambridge University Press, 1994).
Elton, H., *Frontiers of the Roman Empire* (London: B. T. Batsford, 1996).
Fishwick, D., *The Imperial Cult in the Latin West* (Leiden: Brill, 1987–2003).
Gradel, I., *Emperor Worship and Roman Religion* (Oxford: Clarendon Press, 2002).
Isaac, B., *The Limits of Empire: The Roman Army in the East* (Oxford: Clarendon Press, 1990).
Millar, F., *A Study of Dio Cassius* (Oxford: Clarendon Press, 1964).
Millar, F., *The Emperor in the Roman World: 31 B.C.–A.D. 337* (London: Duckworth, 1977).
Price, S. F. R., *Rituals and Power: The Roman Imperial Cult in Asia Minor* (Cambridge and New York: Cambridge University Press, 1984).
Talbert, R. J. A., *The Senate of Imperial Rome* (Princeton: Princeton University Press, 1984).
Taylor, L. R., *The Divinity of the Roman Emperor* (Middleton: American Philological Association, 1931).
Webster, G., *The Roman Imperial Army of the First and Second Centuries A.D.* (New York: Funk and Wagnalls, 1969).
Yavetz, Z., *Plebs and Princeps* (Oxford: Clarendon Press, 1969).

PART FIVE
General
Arnheim, M. T. W., *The Senatorial Aristocracy in the Later Roman Empire* (Oxford: Clarendon Press, 1975).
Barnes, T. D., *The New Empire of Diocletian and Constantine* (Cambridge: Harvard University Press, 1982).
Burns, T. S., *Barbarians within the Gates of Rome: A Study of Roman Military Policy and the Barbarians, ca. 375–425 A.D.* (Bloomington: University of Indiana Press, 1994).
Burns, T. S., *History of the Ostrogoths* (Bloomington: University of Indiana Press, 1984).
MacMullen, R., *Corruption and the Decline of Rome* (New Haven: Yale University Press, 1988).

Matthews, J. F., *Western Aristocracies and Imperial Court, A.D. 364–425* (Oxford: Clarendon Press, 1975).

Nicasie, M. J., *Twilight of Empire: The Roman Army from the Reign of Diocletian until the Battle of Adrianople* (Amsterdam: J. C. Gieben, 1998).

Southern, P., and K. R. Dixon, *The Late Roman Army* (New Haven: Yale University Press, 1996).

Wolfram, H., *History of the Goths* (Berkeley: University of California Press, 1988).

Wolfram, H., *The Roman Empire and its Germanic Peoples*, trans. T. Dunlap (Berkeley: University of California Press, 1997).

Chapter 19 (Third-Century Crisis)

Drinkwater, J. F., *The Gallic Empire: Separatism and Continuity in the North-western Provinces of the Roman Empire, A.D. 268–274* (Stuttgart: Franz Steiner Verlag, 1987).

Potter, D. S., *Prophecy and History in the Crisis of the Roman Empire: A Historical Commentary on the Sibylline Oracles* (New York: Oxford University Press, 1990).

Stoneman, R., *Palmyra and its Empire: Zenobia's Revolt against Rome* (Ann Arbor: University of Michigan Press, 1992).

Watson, A., *Aurelian and the Third Century* (London and New York: Routledge, 1999).

Chapter 20 (Early Christianity)

Fox, R. L., *Pagans and Christians in the Mediterranean World from the Second Century A.D. to the Conversion of Constantine* (London: Penguin Books, 1986).

Frend, W. H. C., *The Rise of Christianity* (Philadelphia: Fortress Press, 1984).

MacMullen, R., *Christianizing the Roman Empire, A.D. 100–400* (New Haven: Yale University Press, 1984).

Wilken, R. L., *The Christians as the Romans Saw Them* (New Haven: Yale University Press, 1984).

Chapter 21 (Diocletian)

Williams, S., *Diocletian and the Roman Recovery* (London: B. T. Batsford, 1985).

Chapter 22 (Constantine)

Barnes, T. D., *Constantine and Eusebius* (Cambridge: Harvard University Press, 1981).

Jones, A. H. M., *Constantine and the Conversion of Europe*, rev. ed. (New York: Collier Books, 1962).

MacMullen, R., *Constantine* (London: Weidenfeld and Nicolson, 1969).

Chapter 23 (Christian Empire)

Athanassiadi, P., *Julian: An Intellectual Biography* (London and New York: Routledge, 1992).

Barnes, T. D., *Athanasius and Constantius: Theology and Politics in the Constantinian Empire* (Cambridge: Harvard University Press, 1993).

Bowersock, G. W., *Julian the Apostate* (Cambridge: Harvard University Press, 1978).

Browning, R., *The Emperor Julian* (London: Weidenfeld and Nicolson, 1975).

Matthews, J., *The Roman Empire of Ammianus* (London: Duckworth, 1989).

McLynn, N. B., *Ambrose of Milan: Church and Court in a Christian Capital* (Berkeley: University of California Press, 1994).

Williams, S. *Theodosius: Emperor at Bay* (New Haven: Yale University Press, 1995).

Chapter 24 (Demise of the West)

Cameron, A., *Claudian: Poetry and Propaganda at the Court of Honorius* (Oxford: Clarendon Press, 1970).

Harries, J., *Sidonius Apollinaris and the Fall of Rome, A.D. 407–485* (Oxford: Clarendon Press, 1994).

Holum, K. G., *Theodosian Empresses: Women and Dominion in Late Antiquity* (Berkeley: University of California Press, 1982).

Maenchen-Helfen, O. J., *The World of the Huns: Studies in their History and Culture* (Berkeley: University of California Press, 1973).

MacGeorge, P., *Late Roman Warlords* (Oxford: Clarendon Press, 2002).

O'Flynn, J. M., *Generalissimos of the Western Roman Empire* (Edmonton: University of Alberta Press, 1983).

Oost, S. I., *Galla Placidia: A Biographical Essay* (Chicago: University of Chicago Press, 1968).

INDEX

Romans are listed by the cognomen if they possessed one. (Academic works list them by nomen, but since most Romans are known by the cognomen, it seemed pedantic to follow this practice here.) Those without cognomina are listed under the nomen. Roman kings are listed under the first element of their name. Consuls of the Republic are given the date of their first consulship (indicated by the Roman abbreviation cos.).